First Impressions

© AlanMaltz.com

This book belongs to:

_____

Date

_____

D0869582

Monarch

Refuge Crocodile
© Blake Sobczak

Snowy Plover chick
© Rob Pailes, Santiva Images

Living Sanibel

A Nature Guide to
Sanibel & Captiva Islands

by Charles Sobczak

Living Sanibel
A Nature Guide to Sanibel & Captiva Islands

Cover design by Maggie May Designs and Bob Radigan. **Book design** and layout by Maggie May Designs. **Cover photo** by Hung V. Do taken in Everglades National Park and used with the permission of the photographer.

Although the author and publisher have exhaustively researched all sources to ensure accuracy of the information contained in this book, they assume no responsibility for errors, inaccuracies, omissions, or any other inconsistency herein. Any slights against people or organizations are completely unintentional.

ISBN: 978-0-9676199-8-9
This book is nonfiction.

Living Sanibel, along with all of the titles published by Indigo Press LLC, may be purchased for educational, business, or sales promotional use. For additional information and a discount schedule please write to: Indigo Press, 2560 Sanibel Blvd., Sanibel, FL, 33957 / E-mail at: livingsanibel@ earthlink.net / Phone: 239-472-0491 / Fax: 239-472-1426.

This is a second edition printing, February 2014
Printed in the United States by United Graphics Inc., Mattoon, Illinois.

Table of Contents

Living Sanibel

"When we try to pick out anything by itself, we find it hitched to everything else in the universe."

~ Naturalist John Muir

Heraclitus, the Greek philosopher, is quoted as saying, "The only thing that is constant is change." He was right. Since the publication of the first edition of Living Sanibel in 2010, the island's only crocodile died of exposure (January 2010), two large predators arrived on the island (both in 2011), flocks of razorbill auks were spotted offshore (2012), and cane toads, a new invasive species, arrived (2013). During that same time period a second crocodile was brought to Sanibel and quickly set up residence in the freshwater lakes of The Dunes subdivision, Sanibel's only black bear was darted and relocated to northern Florida, and the cane toads and coyotes keep spreading like wildfire. Sadly, the razorbills have vanished.

Sanibel continues to thrive. In 2012, travel writer Arthur Frommer named Sanibel Island the #1 destination in the world, winning out over places such as Bali and Paris. He did so because of the island's intrinsic beauty and the abundance of preserves that give wildlife the space it needs to flourish. This boost in stature was soon followed by an unwelcome boost in traffic. Wisely, the City of Sanibel added several miles of new bike paths and widened some of the older trails, helping ease the congestion at least a little.

The first edition of this book sold out in just over three years. At the height of its sales it reached #32 on Amazon's list of best-selling nature guides. With the printing of this second edition, a few corrections have been made, some species added, and one species—the panther—removed. The kind e-mails, comments, and recommendations I've received have all been appreciated, and when pertinent, have been incorporated into this second edition.

Over these past three years, I have renewed my appreciation of Sanibel and Captiva, not just as spits of sandy beaches and swaying palms, but as two tiny arks filled to overflowing with life. They are microcosms of all life on earth, a complex matrix of plants, insects, birds, fish, crabs, mollusks, mammals, reptiles, amphibians, and people interacting and intertwined. Like all natural treasures, however, Sanibel and Captiva face a host of challenges. In the 2009 November/December issue of National Geographic Traveler, these two islands finished ninth on the list of 133 of the most endangered natural environments in North America, just after the Colorado Rockies and before Everglades National Park. The article warned of continued water-quality degradation, overdevelopment issues, and excessive tourism—or what I like to call "being loved to death." We must all work diligently to keep these living beacons of coexistence shining brightly for generations to come.

In writing this book, because of time and space restraints, I was unable to include many important plants and animals. Because of this I feel the need to apologize, not to my readers but to the unbelievable creatures that have been left out: those whose stories will remain untold for the moment—such as the errant American flamingo that passed through "Ding" Darling National Wildlife Refuge a few winters back, or the tiny crayfish I sometimes find crossing Island Inn Road in the rain.

Now, as this edition draws to a close and I write this introduction, I realize that Living Sanibel has been one of the greatest journeys of my life. This book has taught me that all living things—from the lowly, multilegged Florida ivory millipede to the resplendent swallow-tailed kite—are absolutely perfect in their own design. The journey has taught me that all living things have their stories to tell: how they germinate, seed, and spread; how they mate, raise their young, and flourish; and how they grow old and perish.

For everything in nature is ruin and renewal. There is not a plant or animal in existence that does not have the task of feeding itself today and the day after that. Minnows feed on algae and zooplankton, sea trout on minnows, and cobia on sea trout—just as a lucky angler in the back bay ultimately feeds on the cobia. The circle of life and death never sleeps and never changes. Life is, as John Muir expressed it more than 100 years ago, intimately interconnected and intertwined. When we carelessly flood the estuary with excess fertilizers and urban runoff, the minnows perish. When the minnows die, the pelicans and terns that rely on them for nourishment follow suit.

I have also learned that we still have much to learn. We all know our human life expectancy (78 years in the U.S.), but it amazed me to find out that we don't seem to care very much about how long a cardinal (15 years) or a box turtle (100 years) lives. We still don't know how monarch butterflies, over five generations, pass on their migration routes or how sea turtles can navigate the open ocean for 1,000 miles to return to within yards of where they were born years later. We cannot translate the language of dolphins or comprehend the complex nuances of the superorganisms that are termite colonies, anthills, and beehives. We still have no idea how many plants and animals share this planet, though I suspect that number may well exceed a billion living organisms.

Finally, this book is a checklist. The box in front of every bird, mammal, reptile, fish, shell, insect, and plant is there so you can make this book your personal Sanibel and Captiva life list. In doing so, some species will be easy to find, while others may take a lifetime. The house sparrow, grackle, and mourning dove are as simple as a bike ride to Bailey's General Store, while the mangrove cuckoo and two-striped walking stick might prove a lot more challenging.

When you do discover your first snowy plover, check it off, then make sure to read through the information section at the top of each new species carefully. The various nicknames speak volumes about the animal or plant described. You will also find the current stable, endangered, or threatened status of the plant or animal, both in Florida and in the world; its age (when available); its height and weight (when available); where it nests and reproduces; and most importantly, where you are most likely to find it on the islands.

This book has been my joy to write and I hope that you will share in that joy while reading it. From here, I will let the animals and plants speak for themselves.

Charles Sobczak
January 2014

Acknowledgments

Writing this book would have been impossible without the help of many others—historians, biologists, entomologists, ichthyologists, malacologists, herpetologists, and naturalists. There is not a chapter in this book that has not been studied and reviewed by a specialist or scientist trained in his or her respective field to make certain that I got it right. We have made hundreds of revisions and re-revisions in the process.

Science is not an exact science. Recent advances, such as the study of mitochondrial DNA, rewrite old lineages and former relationships. Myths are dispelled while new questions arise about the behavior of various plants and animals. In writing this book, I always deferred to the experts whose daily life revolves around this constant flow of new and often exciting information. I cannot ever thank all of them enough for the work they have done.

While there are many to mention herein, I want to place a special emphasis on the staff members of SCCF (Sanibel-Captiva Conservation Foundation). These hard-working individuals would time and again take my early morning calls, with the author in a panic, wondering if this or that insect really belonged in the book, or what were the best plant species to include in that section. Because of that, my heartfelt thanks goes out to Amanda Bryant, Chris Lechowicz, Dee Serage, Sabrina Lartz, and Jenny Evans of the SCCF staff. Without their help, Living Sanibel could not have been written.

I would like to thank Sanibel historians Betty Anholt and Alex Werner for their extensive help in reviewing and correcting the chapter on the Environmental History of Sanibel and Captiva. They were both gracious in giving their time and expertise to this vital part of the book, and I deeply appreciate their efforts.

For the bird section, which I entered into as a complete amateur, I have to thank first and foremost two island expatriates who, much to our loss, have moved to Arizona: Bev and Clair Postmus. They guided me though the process of choosing which birds to include, and Clair generously sent me his entire 35mm slide collection to pick and choose any of the glorious birds he has photographed over the years on Sanibel and Captiva. They are both angels.

I also have to thank Vince McGrath, an avid birder and master naturalist at South Seas Island Resort, and Jim Griffith of the Sanibel-Captiva Audubon Society for their help, corrections, and input. Jim insisted on more birds of prey, while Vince fought equally hard for seabirds and shorebirds.

The Island Mammals chapter, as well as the section on sea turtles, belong in large part to Amanda Bryant of SCCF. She was especially helpful with the bobcat, which is her current field of study. I would also like to thank God for the first appearance in recorded history of a leatherback turtle in Southwest Florida just as I was completing the sea turtle section.

The reptile and amphibian section belongs to another invaluable member of the SCCF staff, Chris Lechowicz. He provided me with the extensive list of "herps" as he loves to call them, and corrected many an error or oversight. Eric Holt, whom I discovered via his Website, empireoftheturtle.com, was a fabulous second pair of eyes in this segment; he also contributed some wonderful photos. Both Chris and Eric were indispensable.

The chapter on fish would have been impossible without the help of Chris Koenig, PhD, a professor and marine biologist at Florida State University. His years of experience in the Gulf of Mexico working with Goliath, red, and gag grouper helped tremendously.

Dr. José Leal and Kathleen Hoover of the Bailey-Matthews Shell Museum are the true talents behind the shell sections of this book. They not only helped with the photographs, but also guided me through which "live" shells to include, as well as the list of the best choices of different shells. Almost every shell photograph in this book is from the museum's extensive collection. They both deserve my highest praises.

Finding an entomologist to review the arthropod section was not easy. In the end it was serendipity that led me to Elinor "EJ" Blitzer, who at the time of publication was completing her doctorate work in entomology at the University of California at Berkeley. Her read-through and suggestions were invaluable. Once again, I also turned to the staff at SCCF, specifically Chris Lechowicz, and to the Lee County Mosquito Control Board's staff entomologist, Jonathan Hornby, PhD, for their help with spiders and mosquitoes, respectively.

Then there was Jenny Evans, manager of SCCF's native plant nursery, who guided me though the plant selection, walking me down the nature trails behind the SCCF Nature Center, pointing out wax myrtle and white indigo berry long before I knew one from the other. She is the plant section of this book, and for her I will always remember what should be her motto, "Plant native and plant often."

A special thanks goes to city manager Judie Zimomra and her executive assistant, Crystal Mansell, for their help with the City of Sanibel maps and permissions needed to include the Sanibel Recreation Center in the book.

There are so many more people to thank, but I have to put Maggie May Rogers at the top of the list. The entire layout of this book rested on her shoulders, and she has put her heart and soul into making the book look as good as it possibly can. I have to thank all of the photographers and artists who captured these images, especially Dick Fortune and Sara Lopez of Miami. I also have to thank Bob Radigan for his input and help in the cover design. The copy editing of this book is the handiwork of editor Susie Holly, owner of MacIntosh Books on Sanibel. As she so aptly put it, I can't really write but I've got good ideas. I also have to mention Mary Harper, my Oregonian indexer, who once again came through with shining colors.

Last, I have to sincerely thank my lovely wife, Molly Heuer, who has my deepest thanks, appreciation, and at times, sympathy. She and I biked and hiked every trail in the map section of this book, and she put up with my constant rambling on during our nature walks and bike rides as I pointed out tree snails and walking sticks, kestrels and loggerhead shrikes, all the while driving her half-crazy with "too much information." I love you all the more for it, Molly K.

I did not really write Living Sanibel. All of the above mentioned people did. Without each and every one of you this never could have happened. How can I possibly thank you enough.

Charles Sobczak
Sanibel Author

The Chaos of Nature

This book is dedicated to the legacy of
J.N. "Ding" Darling
and his incredible vision
and
to the artists and photographers who helped
make this book come alive,
especially
Dick Fortune and Sara Lopez,
who allow all of us to see the true beauty of nature.

Sanibel Lighthouse

An Environmental History of Sanibel and Captiva Islands

Born of sea and sand, Sanibel and Captiva remain some of the most pristine stretches of shoreline and underdeveloped real estate in the continental United States. From early on, the citizens of these islands have shown a rare preference for conservation over the unbridled growth that has unremittingly altered Florida's coastlines. From J.N. "Ding" Darling's first visit to Captiva in 1935 to that emotionally charged afternoon in 1956 when environmental activists Willis and Opal Combs stood down a bulldozer with a crossbow in hand in front of their Woodmere Preserve at the end of West Gulf Drive, effectively stopping that rumbling machine from plowing through their preserve and connecting West Gulf Drive to the Gulf Pines subdivision, Sanibel's dream of living with wildlife has prevailed. Even today, with the continued refinement and ongoing defense of *The Sanibel Plan* and the hardships that defense entails, the residents and visitors of Sanibel and Captiva have time and again stood up against the powerful and well-moneyed forces of development.

The oftentimes hard-fought battles of the past have, for the most part, been won. Because of that, more than two-thirds of Sanibel, the vast majority of Buck Key, as well as both Patterson and Albright Islands off Captiva remain preserves.

Although this brief history recalls many of those former victories, the future of these islands is not a foregone conclusion. We must remain vigilant. There will always be another battle, another line to be drawn in the sand between the short-term, selfish nature of mankind and the long-term, silent needs of the flora and fauna that share these islands and their fragile ecosystem with us. This is a brief environmental history of the two dominant forces that have sculpted these slender spits of shell and sand over the past 5,000 years—hurricanes and humans.

The Pre-Columbian Islands

It has been estimated that between 160,000 and 320,000 major hurricanes have hit Florida over the past 2 million years. The number and intensity of these storms have varied over time as a result of climactic oscillations, and it is highly probable that the first Paleo-Indians in Florida did not experience many hurricanes. The earth's temperature was colder 15,000 years ago as the thick Laurentide Ice Sheet pushed as far south as the Ohio River Valley during the last ice age. Winters on Sanibel were cold, summers brief, and the climate closer to the deserts of present-day Arizona than to the subtropical temperatures we enjoy today. The water's edge lay nearly 100 miles to the west of today's shorelines.

Paleo-Indians killing a mastodon with spears.
Courtesy Demeter Museum

At the peak of the Pleistocene glaciations, about 30 percent of the world's land mass was covered in ice. These enormous ice sheets and glaciers, at one point covering 90 percent of Canada, tied up so much fresh water that sea levels were 100 meters below what they are now. With this falling sea level came the emergence of land bridges, which connected the Yucatan to Cuba, as well as Cuba to Florida. The Isthmus of Panama was much wider at that time than it is today.

It was just such a conduit, forming between Siberia and western Alaska, that allowed the first human beings to cross over into North America. It is known today as the Bering land bridge, though it now lies beneath the Bering Sea.

The impact of the first Paleo-Indians on the Americas was significant. Massive creatures roamed the landscape back then, including immense land tortoises similar to those found on the Galapagos Islands today, woolly rhinoceros, cave bears, sabertooth tigers, giant ground sloths, and several species of mastodons. They had never encountered such accomplished and skilled predators as the Paleo-Indians. Using weapons, fire, and the sophisticated skills that they had perfected over the previous 50,000 years of human culture, the first human immigrants to the New World systematically hunted the megafauna of both North and South America. Some believe these megafauna were hunted to extinction.

This theoretical mass extinction, labeled the *Pleistocene Overkill*, speculates that during the first 5,000 years after the Paleo-Indians arrived in the Americas, dozens of large herbivores and carnivores were annihilated. Some scientists believe the megafauna of the Pleistocene were also impacted by climactic oscillations, while others argue that a meteor or asteroid collision 12,500 years ago in the high arctic contributed to the demise of so many massive creatures in such a short time. In the end, however, there is little doubt that the Paleo-Indians had a hand in the megafauna's rapid demise.

It was a familiar pattern. In Australia, some 30,000 years earlier, the same process had occurred. There, the Aborigines navigated across the Timor Trough and entered an unspoiled Australia. They were soon dining on giant kangaroos, birds similar to but larger than the ostrich, and the now extinct two-ton Diprotodon, a rhino-sized wombat. Tens of thousands of years later a similar extinction occurred in New Zealand, where the seafaring Maoris exterminated an entire genus of giant, flightless birds known today as the moas. The largest moa stood 14 feet tall, and its single egg was the size of a basketball.

This pattern of extinctions should be familiar to everyone, for in large part it is what we humans do. Our impact on indigenous species over time can be compared with that of natural disasters such as a category 5 hurricane—the difference being that they are brief cataclysms that heal over time, while the damage that humans cause does not.

The nomadic tribes that first came to the Americas were the first "hominoid hurricanes" to impact Florida. It is important to understand that the Paleo-Indians who slowly worked their way up and down peninsular Florida millennia ago had no concept of their environmental damage or the mass extinctions they left behind. For them, killing a mastodon or a woolly rhinoceros was all about surviving in a harsh and unforgiving landscape. With no writing, no intertribal communications, and no concept of conservation, it was impossible for these scattered and diverse tribes to understand that they were eradicating an entire order of megafauna.

The atlatl made hunting larger animals possible.

Conversely, the indigenous animals had no natural defenses against sophisticated killing devices such as Clovis spear points and the deadly atlatls used by these wandering tribes. Atlatls are sophisticated throwing devices that extend the human arm an additional three to four feet, allowing a spear to be thrown with amazing force. Centuries later, when the Spanish encountered the fierce Calusa Indians in Southwest

Florida, they aptly called the atlatls *shooting sticks*. The Spanish soon discovered that these primitive but ingenious devices allowed the Calusa to hurl a flint-tipped dart more than 100 yards at speeds in excess of 100 miles per hour. It was more than likely just such a dart that killed the explorer Ponce de Leon near present-day Punta Rassa, across the bay from Sanibel. Atlatl-propelled darts are capable of piercing two layers of Spanish armor, or, in the case of the Pleistocene extinctions, the one-inch-thick skull of the mastodon.

Evidence of the existence of such animals on Sanibel was verified by longtime islander Wil Compton, who discovered a petrified humerus bone of a mastodon in 1978 while digging footings for a building off of Dunlop Street. The ground he was digging into was dredged up from the lagoon behind the nearby Sanibel Library. The mastodon bone is on display today at the Sanibel Historical Museum. While no one can know for certain, that mastodon may have been felled by an atlatl-hurled dart, marking the first of many future effects *Homo sapiens* would have on the indigenous wildlife of the region.

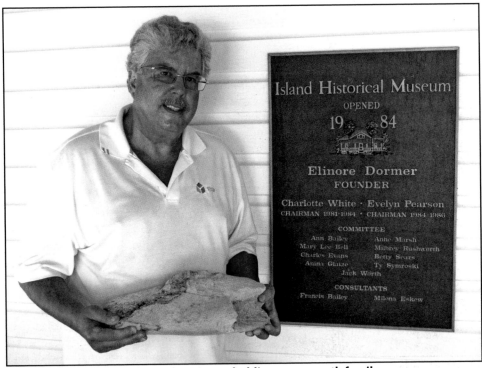

Historical Museum President Alex Werner holding a mammoth fossil.

© Blake Sobczak

The migration of the first Native Americans across a vast continent took centuries, but it is believed they reached a much wider Florida peninsula roughly 12,000-13,000 years ago. Over the next 7,000 years the earth's atmosphere warmed and the ice sheets receded. Florida became a much wetter environment, and the landmass that is now Sanibel and Captiva may have appeared and vanished beneath the changing sea levels several times.

Beginning around 5,000 years ago, Captiva started to form in a process typical of all barrier islands. The prevailing littoral drift from north to south slowly pushed up sand, forming a permanent sandbar. Eventually trees and mangroves took hold and a series of beach ridges was formed, creating Captiva Island, which up until the 1921 hurricane, extended an additional four miles to the north (now called North Captiva Island) and a mile or more to the west.

Most geologists believe that Sanibel began as a formation of beach ridges shooting south and east from Captiva. The unusual east-to-west orientation of Sanibel is believed to be caused by a deep, underlying fault line. Sanibel has more than 300 beach ridges. The shifting nature of sand and sea is still evident today. Within the past 100 years Captiva has lost more than a mile of shoreline on the Gulf side, while sections of Sanibel's beaches have both widened and narrowed over time. As a beach gains width, it is called accretion. When a beach loses sand, it is known as erosion.

The Calusa

Alligator hunting   – Engraving by Theodore De Bry, 1590

Evidence of Native Americans living on Sanibel dates to about 400 B.C., some 2,400 years ago, which is when most archaeologists agree that the pre-Calusans arrived. These first tribes are known as the Shell-Age people, and the few scattered artifacts they left behind were unearthed in the early 1900s in an archaeological dig in the Wulfert area of Sanibel.

Over time these roaming tribes began to coalesce into a more defined regional tribe known as the Calusa. Archaeologists believe that by the first century A.D. the area began to see the formation of what would become the dominant tribe throughout

Floridians fishing and netting
- Engraving by Theodore De Bry, 1590

Southwest Florida. The origins of the Calusa are still a matter of some debate. They were described by the first explorers as tall, handsome, and having reddish-colored hair. The Spanish found them quite unlike the other tribes living in Florida. Some have speculated that the Calusa originally came from Central America and were not closely related to the other native tribes inhabiting Florida at that time.

They had other names. Ponce de Leon called them Carlos or Calos, and the English referred to them as Caloosa, Kasala, and Calusi. Frank Cushing, one of the first archaeologists to study the Calusa in great detail, named them the Pile Dwellers and the Mound People.

The Calusa did not practice any significant form of agriculture. Early Spanish explorers reported seeing small garden plots near the settlements where the Calusa planted gourds, peppers, and papaya, but these gardens were nothing compared with the corn, beans, squash, pumpkins, and tobacco grown by the much larger Timuca and Apalachee tribes living in northern Florida. The Calusa traded for some of these items, but for the most part they took their sustenance from the abundance surrounding them. They harvested shellfish, fish, and marine mammals from the surrounding estuaries and the Gulf of Mexico. They killed deer, tortoise, and small game from the uplands. The Calusa were traditional hunter/gatherers, not farmers.

Perhaps because of their reliance on these wild foods, the Calusa never became a large tribe. Estimates put the number of Calusa living in Southwest Florida prior to European contact at 4,000 to 5,000. The total number of their settlements and temporary encampments, running from Charlotte Harbor to Cape Sable, was around 400, with approximately 50 larger, more permanent settlements. The powerful Calusa also dominated several tribes to the east, including the Mayaimi, Tequesta, Jaega, and to a lesser extent, the Ais.

Sanibel was home to several Calusa encampments. The best known of these is the Wightman site, located in the Wulfert area where the Sanctuary Golf Club is today. Another confirmed site is a burial ground, known as the "mortuary of the dead," located along the shores of Tarpon Bay. Some Calusa shell middens can still be seen on the Shell Mound Trail located at the very end of Wildlife Drive in the J.N. "Ding" Darling National Wildlife Refuge. Estimates put the total number of Calusa living on Sanibel at any given time to be fewer than 200. Although they frequented all of the barrier islands, it is interesting to note that the Calusa never built any major settlements on any of them. All of their major shell mounds and villages were located on interior islands, locations that lay well behind the protection of the barrier islands facing the gulf.

The reason for this strategy was simple: hurricanes. Their capital was located on Mound Key, located in Estero Bay near the base of the Estero River. The highest point in Lee County and a state archaeological site, Mound Key is 32 feet above sea level. Early Spanish explorers recorded that Mound Key was almost 60 feet tall. Either height would have been sufficient to ensure surviving the highest recorded storm surges in modern history, which have been verified at 14 feet above mean high tide.

The Calusa knew far more than the early Spanish explorers did about hurricanes. The word *hurricane* is derived from the Arawak Indian word *yuracan,* meaning evil spirit. The Carib and other Caribbean tribes called the storms *hyrorokan, yurakon,* and *yuruk.* As the Calusa were familiar with these tropical cyclones, the first indication of an approaching storm sent them inland to find higher, safer ground. They gathered on shell-mound islands such as Cabbage Key, Mound Key, and Useppa to weather out the storms. Many of these safe havens have long since been removed by developers in search of inexpensive fill for railroad grades and roadbeds, but there were once large shell mounds at Shell Point, up the Caloosahatchee River, on Marco Island, and elsewhere across Southwest Florida.

The Calusa worshiped several gods, the most powerful having complete control over the planets, the weather, and, naturally, hurricanes. They were not cannibals, but they did engage in ritualistic human sacrifices similar to but not as gruesome as the practices of the Aztecs of Central America. They were excellent wood-carvers and fishermen, and were formidable warriors. Although they lost several early skirmishes with the Spanish, the Calusa, known for their fierce resistance, were for the most part left alone by the early Spanish explorers.

The European Arrival

First reported contact with the Europeans is believed to have occurred in 1513. There were earlier contacts, but these were unofficial visits by explorers not sanctioned by the Spanish Crown and therefore went unrecorded. The exact location and date of Ponce de Leon's arrival is still in question, but the landfall is believed to be in the area between Charlotte Harbor and Cape Romano. The Calusa, already aware that the conquistadors wanted them as slaves, were extremely wary of their presence within their territories. Within days several skirmishes broke out as the Calusa resisted further intrusion into Southwest Florida. In the end Ponce de Leon and his men managed to capture only eight Calusa Indians.

The exact location of the capture is also unknown, but shortly thereafter the name *Passeo Cautivo* or "pass of the captive," was applied to the area between what is now North Captiva and Cayo Costa. The name later came to include all of Captiva Island, which in 1513 extended north to Captiva Pass.

Some people contend that Captiva was named after the maidens held captive for ransom on the island by José Gaspar, the Spanish pirate also known as Gasparilla. He died in 1821, a few years after Spain sold Florida to the United States. The trouble with the Gasparilla version of Captiva's namesake is that it was in all likelihood a legend propagated by Juan Gómez, a Cuban fisherman who lived in Southwest Florida around the turn of the 20th century, renowned for telling tall tales and drinking rum.

The naming of Sanibel is also in question. Some believe Ponce de Leon christened the island in 1513 in honor of Queen Isabella, who died in 1505. A more telling argument comes from old nautical charts with the term, *Puerto de S. Nivel*, or port of the south flat or level plain. This referred to an island that was more of a treeless, grassy plain than Sanibel is today. Over the years various maps and references have referred to the island as Y Bel, Ybel, Isabella, San Y bel, San Ybel, Sanybel, Senybel, Sanabal, and Sannybal.

Regardless of how either island was named, the environment Ponce de Leon encountered was vastly different from the Florida we know today. Christopher Columbus, who was familiar with the Florida Gulf coast, once said, *"The mangroves grew so thick a cat couldn't get ashore."* The waters teemed with fish, including massive manta rays, sawfish, and king mackerel in such numbers that they turned the water dark as mile-long schools swam by.

Caribbean monk seal Courtesy Florida Archives

Also living in the region at the time were Caribbean monk seals (officially declared extinct on June 6, 2008), manatees in numbers now unimaginable, pilot whales, and several species of porpoises. On the islands were bears, panthers, wild turkeys, deer, the Carolina parakeet (officially declared extinct in 1939), king vultures (presently extirpated from the area—i.e., localized extinction), flamingos, and hundreds of sea turtles, including loggerheads and the once plentiful green sea turtles. Although we can never know for certain, there may well have been seal rookeries on the beaches of Sanibel and Captiva.

With a population of 5,000 Calusa covering an area larger than the state of Delaware, the tribe had established a sustainable equilibrium with the surrounding environment. With the arrival of the Europeans, along with their pigs, rats, and diseases, this situation would soon change.

A few years after his first visit Ponce de Leon returned to the west coast of Florida in 1521, this time with 200 men, including priests, farmers, and artisans, and

50 horses, pigs, chickens, and farming implements. Within weeks the Calusa attacked the colonists, and Ponce de Leon was injured by a poisoned arrow, possibly dipped in the sap of the manchineel tree, still found in the Everglades today. Called "the little apple of death" in Spanish, the manchineel is one of the most poisonous trees in the world. Ponce de Leon died 10 days later in Havana, Cuba.

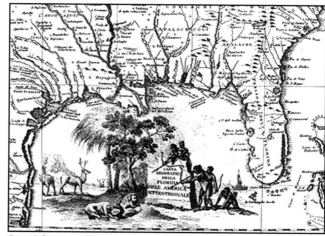

Spanish map of Florida, circa 1650.

After the death of Ponce de Leon, the Spanish left the territories of the Calusa alone. There were several subsequent encounters, including an event that occurred sometime between 1566 and 1569 when the independent Calusa, rather than submit to the Spanish priests, burned down their own village at Mound Key and disappeared into the interior of Florida for several years.

Over time, the Calusa did begin to barter fish, hides, and fruit with the Cuban fishermen who came north along the *Costa de Caracol* (the Spanish name for the land between Cayo Costa and Estero Island, sometimes referred to as the *coast of shells*). Unfortunately, these bartering encounters ultimately killed the fearless Calusa. By the end of the 1700s, most of the tribe had succumbed to tuberculosis, yellow fever, chicken pox, and measles. By 1800, except for a handful of mixed-blood refugees living in Cuba, the Calusa Indians, through diseases and intermarriage, were eradicated.

In the early 1800s Sanibel and Captiva were all but deserted. There were some Seminoles who practiced subsistence living along the coast, as well as several Cuban fishing camps, where the fishermen used the native buttonwood to smoke, dry, and salt their catch, after which it was shipped back to markets in Havana. These were profitable times for commercial fishermen, with bountiful catches of drum, pompano, flounder, mullet, sheepshead, and sea trout.

The peninsula changed political hands several times over the next two centuries. The Spanish held it until 1763, when it was ceded to England through the Treaty of Paris at the end of the Seven Years' War, also called the French and Indian War. England's hold on Florida was tenuous, and shortly after its defeat in the American Revolution, England handed the peninsula back to Spain at the Treaty of Versailles in 1783. Over the next several decades Spain encouraged Americans, especially runaway slaves from the Carolinas, to settle in Florida where they were converted to Catholicism and set free.

Holding on to Florida became more and more difficult for Spain. The first Seminole War (1817-1819) created untold problems for the Spanish monarchy. In 1821, shortly after the end of the first Seminole War, Andrew Jackson became the military governor of Florida and was determined to stamp out the Indian rebellion.

Later, when Jackson became president in 1824, he sent U.S. soldiers deep into the Everglades in pursuit of the renegade Indians, slaves, and outlaws who had joined forces with Florida's Native Americans to create the makeshift tribe known as the Seminoles. The Seminoles retreated deep into the Everglades and to this day remain the only Native American tribe that was never defeated by the military.

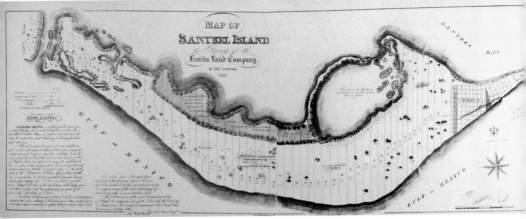

1833 map of Sanybel by the Florida Land Company   Courtesy Sanibel Historical Museum

$5 Million for all of Florida

In 1821, Sanibel and Captiva officially became a territory of the United States through the ratification of the Adams-Onis Treaty. Spain was paid $5 million for all of Florida, along with a promise that America would never lay claim to Texas. The entire state was purchased for less than a penthouse condominium would sell for today, and in the end, America broke its promise and took Texas from Spain as well.

Soon thousands of Americans began pouring into Florida. In 1831 a New York investment group called the Florida Peninsula Land Company put together a scheme to subdivide and sell off Sanibel. The group had purchased the island, then known as Sanybel, from an American bureaucrat and former ambassador to Spain, Richard S. Hackley, whose title to the island was questionable.

The first group of investors and mercenaries arrived on the island in the summer of 1833. They were expecting a second group of colonists to arrive sometime in the fall, but there is scant evidence the second group ever made it. A total of 50 shares were sold at a cost of $500 each. Each share granted the buyer a slice of land running north/south across Sanybel.

By 1835 the Florida Land Company went bust. Over the next few years the colonists managed to plant and harvest a decent sugar crop, along with a number of fruit and vegetable crops, but they discovered that they had nowhere to sell or barter their harvest. Ft. Myers didn't exist at the time. The nearest towns were Trabue (later to become Punta Gorda) to the north and Key West to the south, hardly easy commutes circa 1834.

The settlers requested a lighthouse from the federal government several times, but their requests were denied and they were told to leave the island.

Two other factors leading to the demise of this first settlement were the mosquitoes and the unbearable summer heat. Entomologists have estimated that there were 2 billion salt marsh mosquito eggs per acre before the first mosquito control efforts were made. With no chemical repellents aside from bear grease, the first unlucky owners of Sanibel property must have been driven mad by the constant buzz and biting of millions upon millions of bloodthirsty mosquitoes. The summer thunderstorms, tropical storms, and relentless heat and humidity must also have taken a heavy toll on these northern transplants.

Within four years of their arrival, Sanibel's first investors had deserted the island. In 1903 the Supreme Court adjudicated all the Florida Land Company claims to be invalid. All that remains of the whole venture are several fascinating maps discovered at a garage sale in upstate New York in 1977.

Seminole Chief Billy Bowlegs
Courtesy Florida Archives

The Second Seminole War (1835-1842) kept anyone from venturing into South Florida for the next decade. Soon thereafter, on March 3, 1845, Florida became the 27th state of the United States of America. No one was living on Sanibel or Captiva on that date. For the next decade and a half very little changed along the gulf coast. By 1860 the population of the entire state of Florida was 140,424, less than the current population of Cape Coral.

The Civil War was about to bring change to the area. Siding with the south, Florida seceded from the Union on January 10, 1861. Punta Rassa played an important part in the war, serving as a shipping station for selling cattle to Cuba, as well as to the Confederate Army. As the great War between the States raged on, however, Sanibel and Captiva remained isolated and devoid of settlers.

The Agricultural Years

Several years after the Union's victory in the Civil War, Florida's representation to the United State Congress was restored on June 25, 1868. That same year, an ex-Union soldier named William Smith Allen showed up on Sanibel to try his hand at growing castor beans. The plants were to be used in the production of castor oil, which in turn was used to treat yellow fever, a disease that was ravaging the prisoners at Ft. Jefferson in the Dry Tortugas.

Castor bean plants are still found on Sanibel.
© Charles Sobczak

Sanibel when it was an agricultural center.   Courtesy Sanibel Historical Museum

Castor beans weren't the first plants introduced to the islands. The U.S. Agriculture Department reported that some years earlier, Dr. Henry Perrine and his family had introduced *Agave sisalana Perrine* (a type of century plant) from the Yucatan into South Florida in an attempt to establish commercial sisal production on some of the remote barrier islands, including Sanibel and Captiva. Dr. Perrine was massacred by the Seminoles in 1840 before his plans made any headway.

Just prior to the Civil War a handful of other hardy farmers introduced bowstring hemp (a.k.a. mother-in-law's tongue) for twine production. They also brought in wild pineapple, common pineapple, and ramie. The bowstring hemp, century plants, and castor bean plants can still be found on Sanibel and Captiva, the first in a long list of exotic and invasive vegetation that would be brought to the islands.

Remarkably, the castor bean crop of 1868 flourished and Allen prospered for the next several years. Because of Allen's unexpected success, he was soon joined by a Mr. Harris from Key West, and the two of them planted a huge crop of castor beans in the spring of 1873.

Their plans were ruined on October 6 that same year when a massive category 5 hurricane storm surge put Sanibel and Captiva completely under water. The height of that storm surge is marked today on the south side of the balcony of the "Ding" Darling Wildlife Interpretative Center on Sanibel-Captiva Road. That mark represents the highest storm surge ever recorded in Sanibel's history—a frightening 14 feet above mean high tide.

The two farmers miraculously survived the storm, salvaged what they could of their operation, and returned to Key West a few weeks later. They never set a foot on Sanibel again. Allen moved to a small Seminole village known today as Immokalee and helped start the farming industry that still thrives there today. Meanwhile, the saltwater that had washed over the islands made the soil useless for growing crops for decades to come. Only the hardy native plants and trees survived, having adapted over the millennia to tolerate such catastrophic events.

Aside from an occasional Indian or a Cuban fisherman coming ashore to stock up on fresh water, Sanibel and Captiva remained uninhabited. In 1877 the General Land Office of the United States declared all of Sanibel a lighthouse reserve (though the lighthouse itself was not erected for another seven years), and the island was closed to all private ownership. Captiva was not included in the reserve, but no one attempted to settle that remote island either.

The great hurricane of 1878 swept unnoticed across both barrier islands on September 7. Only the mangroves, wildlife, and Spartina grass took any note of what others called the worst storm to come up from the Caribbean in 40 years.

On August 20, 1884, after taking years of getting approved, funded, and shipped to the island, the Sanibel lighthouse—the same structure we see today on the eastern tip of the island—was officially lit. Aside from an occasional mishap during fierce storms or a rare malfunction, it has remained lit ever since.

Homesteaders

In 1888, under the Homestead Act, Sanibel and Captiva were opened to settlers. That same year, Reverend George Barnes ran his boat aground where Casa Ybel resort is today and became the first official homesteader on Sanibel. The General Land Office retained the eastern tip of the island for the lighthouse reserve but elected to open up the rest of the island for adventurous settlers willing to try their hand at farming or fishing.

The first white child born on the island was Flora Sanibel Woodring, daughter of homesteaders Sam and Anna Woodring. She was born in January 1889. A year before her birth, in the fall of 1888, yet another hurricane had swept across the island, but the hearty settlers

Commodore Edwin Reed's homestead, circa 1894.
Courtesy Sanibel Historical Museum

stuck it out, and Sanibel and Captiva were never without inhabitants again.

By the turn of the century a few dozen families were living, fishing, and farming on the islands. The entire population of Sanibel and Captiva hovered around 150. They had all survived a second major hurricane, on September 24, 1894. Fortunately, it had no major storm surge, and its heavy rains helped to leach out what little saltwater washed over the beaches. The wind and rain ruined crops across the entire state, however. The storm exited Florida just north of Cape Canaveral on September 26.

The family names of these first settlers should be familiar to anyone looking at a Sanibel map today: Bowen (Bowen's Bayou), Woodring (Woodring Point), Dinkins (Dinkins Bayou), and Brainard (Brainard Bayou). Though few in number, these early settlers had a substantial impact on the native wildlife. They dined on wild turkey, ibis (still known today as Chokoloskee chicken), manatee, loggerhead and green turtles and their eggs, smoked mullet, white-tailed deer, quail, and roseate spoonbills.

At about the same time these families were settling in on the islands, a far greater threat to the birds of Florida appeared in the form of the plume hunters. Driven by the growing market demand for the long, elegant plume feathers worn on ladies' hats in New York, London, and Boston, the value of certain types of feathers (i.e., the *aigrette*—a feather found in the snowy and great egrets' breeding plumage) surpassed that of gold. Armed with 10-gauge shotguns and punt guns, these notorious bird hunters killed millions of egrets, herons, and spoonbills in their rookeries, often leaving their eggs abandoned and the fledglings to starve.

Shooting a white pelican for fun.
Courtesy Sanibel Historical Museum

In a single auction conducted in London in 1902, 1,608 packages of herons' plumes were sold. The average weight of each package was 30 ounces. That adds up to a total of 48,240 ounces of feathers. Because it takes four birds to produce an ounce of suitable hat feathers, this meant that 192,960 birds were killed for one auction. Auctions in London were held weekly.

In 1886, in response to the carnage taking place because of the plume trade, George Bird Grinnell formed the first Audubon Society in New York. Although that initial organization failed, the Massachusetts Audubon Society was formed in 1896, followed by the Florida Audubon Society in 1900. Guy Bradley was hired in 1902 by the Florida chapter to protect the remaining rookeries against further decimation. In 1905 he was gunned down near Flamingo, and his assassination created a national scandal that ultimately resulted in the collapse of the plume industry. In 1908, a second Audubon warden, Columbus G. MacLeod, was killed in the line of duty in nearby Charlotte Harbor.

There can be no question that the egret, heron, ibis, and other rookeries on Sanibel and Captiva were affected by the plume trade. Many contend that the slaughter of these birds was so monumental that they have, more than a century later, yet to fully recover. One of the hardest hit birds of the trade was the roseate spoonbill, a favorite of birdwatchers on Sanibel.

Ironically, it was another assassination, this time of President William McKinley in 1901, that allowed the vice president, Theodore Roosevelt, to become the first conservation-minded president in American history. On March 14, 1903, by executive order, Roosevelt created the first National Bird Preserve—Pelican Island, Florida. It later became a part of the National Wildlife Refuge system that today encompasses more than 150 million acres and 550 national wildlife refuges.

**Pioneering conservationists President
Theodore Roosevelt and John Muir**
Courtesy National Archives

The residents of Sanibel and Captiva were passionately involved with this initial conservation movement. In 1913, the Sanibel Association declared Sanibel a state bird reservation, with no shooting or bird hunting allowed. The conservation efforts on the island attracted the attention of Teddy Roosevelt who came to visit in 1914, a few years after his presidency ended in 1909.

In the fall of 1910 the islands suffered a major setback to farming. On October 17 the worst storm since the 1873 hurricane came ashore just north of Cape Romano. Known as the "loop" hurricane, it was the first such storm the U.S. Weather Bureau had ever observed to make a stalled-out loop off of western Cuba before picking up momentum and heading north-northeast toward Florida.

Because of its slow forward motion, the loop storm built up a tremendous storm surge. In Key West the storm tide measured 15 feet, with pounding waves running another five to seven feet on top of the surge. The French steamship *Louisiane* was driven aground on Sombrero Light with 600 passengers on board. All survived the harrowing event and were ultimately rescued. The devastation throughout the Keys was monstrous. The barometer dropped to 28.40 inches in Ft. Myers, and seven men drowned in the wreckage of four Cuban fishing schooners anchored near Punta Gorda. The total death count from the "loop 'cane" was estimated at more than 100.

The soil and the wildlife of Sanibel and Captiva suffered major damage. After the bumper tomato crop of 1909, the soil of both islands was affected by the salts left behind. As bad as the storm surge was, the wind damage was worse. The winds destroyed the entire citrus and tomato crop of that year, as well as seriously impacting the white-tail deer and wild turkey population. It wiped out a sizable

Large Cuban fishing smack
Old Florida postcard

herd of deer living on Buck Key, so named because of the large whitetail bucks that were once hunted there.

Natural catastrophes such as this can cause more environmental damage in a few minutes than mankind can wreak on any given environment in a decade. The 1910 loop hurricane was the first of three successive hurricanes over the next 16 years that severly impacted Sanibel's era as a farming community.

Another factor that contributed to the demise of Sanibel's farming industry was the arrival of the trains into Ft. Myers. This meant less expensive shipping costs from places such as Immokalee and Alva than from remote barrier islands such as Sanibel or Captiva.

Old Florida fish house   © Throughthelensgallery.com

After the 1910 storm a number of island farmers looked for other ways to make a living. A new industry was born on March 12, 1885, when a New York tourist, W.H. Wood, caught a tarpon in Southwest Florida. Game fishing soon grew into a viable business for the area. Several floating lodges were built, and fishing guides slowly began to replace truck farmers. The tourist business got under way in the 1890s when the former Matthews home on Sanibel became a fishing and tourist lodge. In 1937 its name was changed to the Island Inn. The Casa Ybel resort also started to add cottages around the turn of the 20th century. The island's first scheduled ferry service began operating in 1928.

Ferry service routes and schedules, circa 1935   Courtesy Sanibel Historical Museum

Fertilizer was shipped in to restore the island's soil, and by 1921 Sanibel's farmers were once again harvesting respectable crops of tomatoes, string beans, coconuts, oranges, and grapefruit—but it didn't last. That same fall another storm hit both islands wiping out thousands of the newly planted fruit trees.

A few years earlier, looking to create quick-growing wind breaks, local farmers imported the first truly invasive plant to the islands. The tall, feathery-looking tree is known in its native Australia as the Botany Bay oak. Today it is commonly called the Australian pine. These hardwoods (they are not a true pine) thrive along our coast because their hard, marble-size seeds can survive in saltwater. Over the decades since they were introduced, hurricane surges have spread the seeds over a wide area. Australian pines eventually lined almost every stretch of beach from Tampa to the Keys. The irony is that their pancake-like, shallow root systems cannot withstand

A day of tarpon fishing, circa 1929   Courtesy Sanibel Historical Museum

the intensity of the very storms responsible for their spread. They topple easily after being undermined by the storm surge or are simply blown down by hurricane-force winds. Only the very northern tip of Australia is ever hit by storms with the intensity of hurricanes (known as cyclones in the Southern Hemisphere). Australian pines grow primarily south of that region of Australia and thus have never adapted to the extreme conditions of a hurricane or tropical cyclone.

On October 25, 1921, after a sweltering summer, a fairly small hurricane swept up from the Keys and headed toward Tampa Bay. Although the wind speeds were clocked at a mere 68 miles per hour in Tampa, the real trouble with this storm lay in the accompanying surge.

In St. Petersburg the rising tide crested at 10.5 feet above mean high tide. At Punta Gorda the tide was seven feet above normal, and at Punta Rassa, the tide rose more than six feet. With the tremendous volume of water pushed into San Carlos Bay and Charlotte Harbor by the storm, a small section of Captiva, called the narrows, was carved open by the out flowing tide. The narrows never filled in again, and after the huge Miami hurricane of 1926, the pass became a permanent part of Southwest Florida's coastline.

That pass was named in 1923 when a group of islanders observed it teeming with a school of redfish. Redfish Pass separates Captiva from North Captiva. The 1926 hurricane, a classic Cape Verde hurricane similar in size and power to Hurricane Andrew in 1991, devastated the burgeoning town of Miami and was instrumental in the collapse of the first Florida land boom. It created a storm surge reported to be 15 feet high that swept over Coconut Grove. One anemometer on Miami Beach recorded a wind velocity of 128 mph for five consecutive minutes. Gusts along the beachfront exceeded 140 miles per hour from the storm.

The storm crossed over the state and exited just north of Sanibel. Its storm surge put both Sanibel and Captiva almost completely under water. The few farms that were operating before the storm were abandoned. Aside from a key-lime plantation on Captiva that would later become the South Seas Plantation resort, commercial agriculture never fully returned to the islands.

The Modern Era

In 1931, with the country in the throes of the Great Depression, about 100 people were living on Sanibel and Captiva. Tourism was minimal, the mosquito population was thriving, and many long-time islanders were struggling to make a living. Several cottage industries were started but met with no long-term success.

The Ocean Leather Company, originally from New Jersey and with another small facility in the Keys, started up near the lighthouse reserve property in an attempt to turn shark, porpoise, sawfish, and devil-fish hides into fish-leather products. They also harvested shark oil, shark teeth, and shark and manta-ray skins. The business began on January 8, 1919, but closed down several years later because of slumping economic conditions and the over harvesting of local sharks and manta rays.

A small clam-dredging company operated for a time in the early 1930s but it too fell on hard times. It worked the near-shore waters just south of Sanibel, and cooked and canned the clams on the island. The small cannery was located a few blocks up the bay from the lighthouse.

The single most important event during these lean years occurred in the winter of

Sawfish caught by the students of the Synder School
Courtesy Sanibel Historical Museum

1935. An Iowa man and his wife came to vacation on Captiva, where they stayed in a cottage at 'Tween Waters Inn. His name has become synonymous with the islands: Jay Norwood "Ding" Darling ("Ding" is a contraction of his last name, Darling).

Born on October 21, 1876, J.N. "Ding" Darling was a renowned political cartoonist with a reputation as a staunch conservationist when he and his wife, Penny, first arrived on Captiva in March 1935 for a two-week vacation. The year before, President Franklin D. Roosevelt had appointed Darling head of the U.S. Biological Survey, the forerunner of the U.S. Fish and Wildlife Service. In February 1936 Darling became the first president of what

J. N. "Ding" Darling
Courtesy Sanibel Historical Museum

is known today as the National Wildlife Federation. Alarmed by the loss of habitat caused by the draining and filling of wetlands by agricultural and development interests, Darling, along with several other leading conservationists, created the revenue-generating program that is still a major force in wetlands acquisition and preservation today: the Federal Duck Stamp Program. Darling was known in many circles as "the best friend a duck ever had."

The first 1935 Duck Stamp by "Ding" Darling
Courtesy U.S. Fish and Wildlife

Having been impressed with the islands, Darling and his wife returned the following winter and purchased property on Captiva. With one Pulitzer Prize for his political cartooning already to his credit in 1924 (another would come in 1943) and his stature as a leader in the budding conservation movement, Darling was just what the islanders needed as a catalyst for turning the direction of the islands toward the conservation ethic.

On February 17, 1937, Darling gave a presentation to an overflow audience at the Fisherman's Lodge on Captiva. He rallied the troops behind this growing green movement, and shortly after his presentation the Inter-island Association for Conservation (IIAC) was formed. The association's logo was a sketch of two candles—the two islands burning together as a fire for conservation.

As a result of the IIAC's persistence, all of Sanibel and Captiva were declared a wildlife refuge by the Florida legislature in 1939, though there was little enforcement to protect the wildlife until after the end of World War II. Founding members of the IIAC included Hallie Matthews, Dr. Louise Perry, Webb Shanahan, and Ernest Bailey. The IIAC looked into the causes and effects of red tide, promoted catch-and-release tarpon fishing, studied the bays and estuaries, and with Darling's help, pushed hard for the establishment of a wildlife preserve in the 1,900-acre mangrove forest located along the northern edge of Sanibel.

Times were changing on the islands. In 1941 electricity was run out to Sanibel by the Lee County Electric Co-op under the auspices of the Rural Electrification Act of 1936. One of the island's ferries had been commandeered by the military as a troop transport, but the remaining ferry kept shuttling more and more tourists and shell seekers across the three-mile mouth of the Caloosahatchee. Another major storm hit the islands in 1944, and the resulting storm surge killed

Darling during a visit to Captiva.
Courtesy Sanibel Historical Museum

Refuge manager's quarters.   Courtesy Sanibel Historical Museum

most of the burrowing owls, as well as the quail that were once commonly found here. The burrowing owls recovered only to be extirpated not by a storm surge, but by the construction of the Dunes golf course in 1963. The owls and quail, now gone from Sanibel, are just two more examples of the impact hurricanes and humans have had on native wildlife.

The Sanibel National Wildlife Refuge, it's original name, was officially established in 1945. The first resident manager, Tommy Wood, was sent by the U.S. Fish and Wildlife Service in 1949. He remained the manager for 20 years, overseeing the construction of the cross dike (today's 4.5-mile Wildlife Drive) and the renaming of the refuge in honor of J.N. "Ding" Darling.

The dike was originally built not as an access road for visitors and birdwatchers but as part of an overall plan to control the salt-marsh mosquito population on the islands. The Lee County Mosquito Control Board, founded in the early 1950s to keep the rampant mosquito population in check, had also dredged and straightened out much of the Sanibel freshwater river to provide additional habitat to the native gambusia, or mosquitofish. Gambusia feed on mosquito larvae. They, along with the spraying of DDT and other pesticides throughout the 1950s, helped control mosquitoes.

In the mid-1950s, despite several victories, "Ding" Darling had become disenchanted with the snail-like pace of the conservation movement in Florida and across the entire United States. These were the post-World War II boom years in America. Suburbs such as Levittown, New York, were springing up everywhere just as pesticides and commercial fertilizers were transforming the breadbasket of the Midwest. Conservation became a dirty word. Progress was the only language spoken.

Darling eventually sold his Captiva holdings but continued to visit the islands until his death on February 12, 1962. Sadly, he died disheartened with Florida and the lack of foresight people had toward conservation. His death shocked the islanders, and less than one month later, on March 6, 1962, the Jay N. "Ding" Darling Memorial Committee was formed. Its purpose was to work toward the renaming of the refuge in honor of the man who had labored so tirelessly on behalf of ducks, birds, and wildlife across America. Prior to this renaming, no wildlife refuge in the United States had ever been named after an individual. It was a worthy honor for a man who was decades ahead of his time.

In the years that followed the U.S. Fish and Wildlife continued purchasing land and expanding its holdings to the approximately 6,000 acres it encompasses today. During the same time period huge changes were happening on Sanibel and Captiva. Hurricane Donna hit the islands on September 10, 1960. Only one person, a truck driver in Ft. Myers, was killed, but hundreds of Floridians were injured. The official damage report concluded that 1,844 homes were destroyed, 3,253 suffered extensive damage, and another 31,000 had minor damage. Until Hurricane Andrew in August 1992, Donna was considered to be the most devastating storm to hit Florida in modern times. Because Sanibel was still so sparsely populated in 1960, the damage to the island was nowhere near what it would be if a storm of this magnitude were to hit the islands today.

The Causeway

Even as islanders were recovering from Donna, there was a persistent rumor of a forthcoming bridge to Sanibel and Captiva. Most of the old-timers living on these two sister islands were united in opposing the construction of a causeway to Sanibel. On the other side of the fence sat the developers and the Lee County Commissioners. They understood that there was money to be made on Sanibel if two things could be accomplished: (1) a bridge that would connect the island to the mainland; and (2) securing a reliable potable water source. A third important factor, the rise of modern air conditioning, had already taken place during the 1950s. This invention forever changed the way people viewed Florida's hot and humid summers.

Building of the first causeway, circa 1962
Courtesy Sanibel Historical Museum

The driving force behind the construction of the original causeway was a developer named Hugo Lindgren. He had purchased hundreds of acres on the east end of Sanibel in the 1950s and was determined to develop the property (known today as the Shell Harbor and the Sanibel Estates subdivisions). Sanibel was not a city at the time, though its residents were represented at the county level by an inter-island organization called the Planning and Zoning Authority.

That organization, headed by long-time islanders John Kontinos, Priscilla Murphy, Alan Nave, William MacIntosh, Mary Gault, Francis Bailey, and Mr. and Mrs. Floyd Snook among many others, took up the anti-causeway drive, going so far as filing suit and challenging the Lee County Commissions' legal right to impose its authority over the islands. What followed was a complicated series of votes, court rulings, and appeals that ultimately left the Planning and Zoning Authority powerless. Using what many islanders perceived was a pro-development environmental study conducted by the U.S. Army Corps of Engineers, the permits to build the new bridge were eventually granted.

It was only a matter of years after the bridge was constructed that residents noticed that the scallops that once thrived between the tip of Sanibel and Punta Rassa were gone. The two spoil islands connecting the bridge had dramatically altered the bay's salinity, and the scallop population collapsed. Exacerbating the problem was the dredging of more than 100 miles of saltwater canals in Cape Coral by the Rosen brothers a few years earlier (1957-58). Acres upon acres of sea-grass beds and scallop grounds were permanently ruined.

Lindgren, meanwhile, was thrilled that the causeway he wanted so badly was built. He donated a strip of land to the county, allowing the causeway to connect to the island and head straight down Lindgren Blvd.—unsurprisingly, directly into his newly dredged, seawall-lined subdivision. The land where the Sanibel-Captiva Chamber of Commerce is located was donated by Lindgren, though he reserved a sales office along the side to help sell off his substantial holdings.

The causeway officially opened for traffic on May 26, 1963. On that day 1,120 vehicles came onto Sanibel, bringing more people to the island in a single day than any other day in the past 15,000 years. Humans were not the only animals to make use of the new causeway. Within a few years of its opening, the causeway provided passageway to the islands for opossum, armadillos, West Indian anoles, and Norwegian rats. All of these creatures were more than likely stowaways on trucks carrying exotic landscaping onto the island. They were all small enough to hide in the root balls or canopies of the various palms and ornamentals brought across the three spans during the early boom years. Prior to the construction of the causeway and the great land rush that followed, very little landscaping had been ferried over to the islands.

To the old-time islanders, the causeway forever changed Sanibel and Captiva. Since that day in the spring of 1963, the traffic counts across the bridge have increased exponentially. To put it into perspective, in 1958 the average winter car traffic via the ferry boats was approximately 257 automobiles a day. In 1975, 12 years after the causeway was completed, the average daily traffic count in March was 2,991 cars per day. In 1985, that number had increased to 8,417 cars per day. Six years later, in the winter of 2001, the peak-season March traffic set an all-time high with 373,881 cars coming through the toll booth in 31 days, an amount equal to more than 12,000 automobiles a day. Since then, the average daily traffic count has remained between 10,000 and 11,000 automobiles per day during the height of the tourist season.

The last thing that needed to be put in place for Hugo Lindgren's plans for Sanibel was a reliable source of public water. Sanibel and Captiva were riddled with shallow

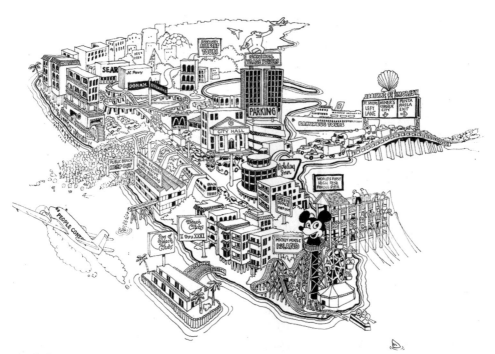

Sanibel as it might have been   © Pete Smith

wells and cisterns in the early '60s, and much of the water was generally brackish and undrinkable. With Lindgren's help, the Island Water Association was formed in 1965, and by November 1966 potable water was flowing through the faucets of most of the islands' homes and businesses.

The number of real estate agents quadrupled overnight. New canals were dredged, entire sections of the island were bulldozed flat, and the sound of the surf was soon replaced by the sound of hammering construction crews and the ringing of cash registers. There was money to be made developing Sanibel and Captiva, and the Lee County Commissioners had big plans for these two sleepy islands on the gulf. The "construction crane" was jokingly proposed to be the new state bird.

In 1967 the Lee County Commission hired an Atlanta-based firm to help determine the best course of action for the future of Sanibel and Captiva. Under its guidelines, high-rises and high-density subdivisions with 50- by 75-foot lots would allow Sanibel to support a population of 95,000 people. With the addition of the winter tourists, Sanibel and Captiva island, on any given day during the tourist season, might hold as many as 125,000 people.

Once the study became public, islanders were outraged. They felt that their destiny was no longer in their hands. The quiet, laid-back lifestyle of Sanibel and Captiva was going to be destroyed forever at the hands of money-grubbing developers. The Sanibel-Captiva Conservation Foundation (SCCF), the Audubon Society, and the newly formed Sanibel and Captiva Planning Board all worked together to determine if Sanibel and Captiva could incorporate and put a stop to Lee County's grandiose plans.

Dredging the Panama Canal, the long, deep freshwater canal that runs between Middle Gulf Drive and Beachview
Courtesy of Sanibel Historical Museum

Meanwhile, more and more environmental damage was happening. Lindgren, with some of the money he had acquired selling off his Shell Harbor parcels, turned around and purchased what is now known as the Beachview subdivision. Lindgren's plans called for extending the Shell Harbor concept west to Casa Ybel. While dredging the Panama Canal, the long, deep freshwater canal that runs between Middle Gulf Drive and Beachview, his crew went so deep (25 to 30 feet) that it broke through the clay seal that separates the salt from the freshwater. Within days the saltwater held in check below the clay intruded into the freshwater slough, destroying plant and animal life miles away from the actual dredging site.

It's important to point out that no fines or actions were levied against Lindgren for ruining the freshwater ecosystem of the island. There was no Clean Water or Endangered Species Act in place in 1970. Permits for dredging were issued for a few hundred dollars. Owing to the extent of the damage, however, concerned residents filed a court action against Lindgren, and he was ordered to stop the dredging, effectively putting an end to his extensive canal plans.

The Fight for Incorporation

The islands were being bulldozed, dredged, subdivided, and sold off at an alarming rate. In the fall of 1973, after a frenetic building spree in which 1,300 new dwelling units had been started since the first of the year, members of the Sanibel and Captiva Planning Board went to the Lee County Commission to request a building moratorium. The answer from the commissioners was a resounding NO!

For a while in the early 1970s it looked as if Lee County's projected population of 95,000 for Sanibel was inevitable. Islanders quickly rallied behind individuals such as Roy Bazire, a real estate broker with Priscilla Murphy Realty, who became the chair of SCCF in 1968. He, along with many others, pushed toward incorporation.

Membership in SCCF soared and by May 1972, the foundation had more than 1,500 individual and 1,000 family memberships. Using various grants, working with The Nature Conservancy and other state and federal programs, SCCF continued to increase its holdings in the interior wetlands' regions of Sanibel, but the struggle against the onslaught of dredge-and-fill development was interminable.

More and more islanders felt the only real, long-term solution to overdevelopment was to secede from Lee County. The movement to incorporate into the city of Sanibel and the conservation movement became one and the same. Many islanders, especially those whose real estate holdings put them in a position to make a fortune on the ongoing land rush, vehemently opposed incorporation. In November 1973 the Sanibel Home Rule Study Group was formed to raise money to hire an expert and explore the options for incorporation.

The fight between these two camps quickly divided islanders. The Chamber of Commerce, who by and large opposed incorporation, formed an ad hoc action committee to look into various methods of derailing incorporation. An informal group of supporters calling themselves SOS (Save Our Sanibel), organized and, together with SCCF and the Audubon Society, spearheaded the movement toward incorporation. Some of the town meetings in the early '70s got so intense that Lee County sheriffs had to escort angry residents out of the heated debates.

Despite several lawsuits filed by both individuals and organizations to stop the incorporation referendum, it made its way onto the ballot, and on November 5, 1974, 84 percent of all registered voters on Sanibel went to the polls to cast their vote. In the end, 63.6 percent voted to incorporate and the referendum passed. Because of concerns over the funding of their beach renourishment programs, Captiva opted out of the referendum and remains under county control to this day.

Soon after the incorporation vote, Walter Condon, an attorney and head of a group of investors in the Island Beach Club condominium development, filed suit in March 1975, claiming that Sanibel was not legally incorporated because of certain technicalities. For reasons still unclear to this day, the attorney general of the state of Florida enjoined Condon in the suit. It was rumored that this move came at the request of then-Governor Reubin Askew, who had invested in a high-rise condominium project on Sanibel called The Sundial. Under Sanibel's newly drafted land-use plan all condominiums would have to stay below 45 feet above mean high tide, so if the City became official, investors stood to loose a considerable amount of money. As long as its legitimacy was being contested, Sanibel didn't have the authority to tax its citizens, and the newly formed city of Sanibel would go broke. In April, 124 individuals donated more that $300,000 to keep the island out of bankruptcy, an unprecedented show of support for the fledgling city.

The newly elected mayor, Porter Goss, and the city's attorney, Frank Watson, flew to Tallahassee where Representatives Frank Mann and Paul Nuckolls offered their support. Shortly thereafter, the Condon lawsuit was dropped, and the city of Sanibel as we know it today started to coalesce.

The first five city council members, elected in December 1974, were Porter Goss, Vernon MacKenzie, Zelda Butler, Charles LeBuff, and Francis Bailey. Their first order of business was a building moratorium, which passed unanimously. Although it would be a mere 90-day "respite" from the building boom that had been ravaging the island since the late 1960s, it helped to give the newly formed city a chance to catch its breath and get a handle on the unbridled growth that was threatening the heart and soul of the island.

In February 1975 the council established a planning commission to oversee building permits. A firm was hired to help come up with a viable plan that would allow for more controlled growth, and SCCF hired a well-respected naturalist from The Conservation Foundation in Washington, D.C., to conduct a complete and comprehensive study of the natural ecosystem of the island. Written by John Clark, this document, called *The Sanibel Report,* has become a classic in environmental planning circles worldwide and can still be found online today (http://www.worldpolicy.org/projects/globalrights/environment/report/index.html).

The report begins in an unusually poetic style, *"Islands always seem special. But Sanibel Island is absolutely unique. North America has no shore, no island, no other place equal to it. Nature will not again create such a place."*

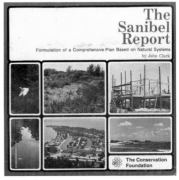

Courtesy the City of Sanibel

The first few years of incorporation were tenuous and stressful to everyone involved. More than 30 individual lawsuits were filed by people and corporations impacted by the building moratorium and the reduction in density brought about by the Comprehensive Land Use Plan (CLUP) passed on July 19, 1975. The changes brought about by the CLUP were dramatic.

An excellent example can be found in the Sanctuary Golf Club development. That 465-acre parcel had a density of 3,400 dwelling units under Lee County's regulations at the time of Sanibel's incorporation. After the new density rules were established by the passage of the CLUP, the number of dwelling units fell to 56, a net loss of 3,344 marketable properties to the owners of the land. The investment group was outraged.

It filed suit against the city of Sanibel and after a legal battle that dragged on for more than a decade, the court ordered a final density settlement of 470 dwelling units. In the end a second development company purchased the property, and the total number of units actually built at the Sanctuary, along with a clubhouse and a championship 18-hole golf course, was 280. The result was a net loss of 3,120 homes and condominium units but a tremendous gain for the flora and fauna of Sanibel.

Over the next three decades battles were constantly waged between those who would pave over paradise and those who, like "Ding" Darling, wanted to save and protect it. Some lawsuits were won, a few were lost, and most were negotiated into settlements acceptable to both parties. Controversial ordinances such as ROGO (Rate of Growth Ordinance) were instigated and securing a building permit became a tedious and frustrating process. Growth was curtailed dramatically.

At the same time that the city was fighting the powers of unchecked development, two more battles were drawn—this time not against developers but against invasive plants. The worst of these was the Brazilian pepper, and the other was melaleuca, or "paperbark tree" as it is sometimes called.

Sanibel's battle against the melaleuca began in earnest in 1982 after wildlife management experts realized that its unique ability to thrive in wetlands would, if left unchecked, eventually dry up the interior of Sanibel. The city hired Charles Pounds as their Noxious Plant Control Officer and he quickly went to work, sometimes cutting trees down by hand and at other times resorting to poison. On September 18, 1989, the last known melaleuca tree was cut down on Sanibel, though some biologists believe there may be a few residual specimens along the Sanibel River.

A far larger battle still rages to this day against Brazilian pepper, an exotic originally brought to Florida by a well-meaning but misguided botanist from Punta Gorda in the 1920s. Perhaps more than any other plant, Brazilian pepper has laid waste to tens of millions of acres of Florida's landscape. Spread by songbirds and winter migrants such as the robin and cedar waxwings, these pepper plants form a tangled monoculture that smothers out native vegetation. The Brazilian pepper battle was joined by SCCF's famous "Pepper Busters," and it is a battle that will undoubtedly continue for years to come. Hopefully, someday we will see a complete eradication of this invasive plant from the islands.

From 1976 to 1989 the city of Sanibel, along with SCCF and others, went on an extraordinary shopping spree in an attempt to accumulate environmentally sensitive interior wetlands. They purchased, sometimes parcel by parcel, large tracts of vulnerable subdivisions such as the Sanibel Highlands, Sanibel Gardens, and Tarpon Bay subdivisions. Lawsuit after lawsuit was filed, and time and again the CLUP was rigorously defended.

In 1997, knowing that these lawsuits had increased the projected dwelling-unit cap outlined in the CLUP from 7,800 homes and condominiums to around 9,000, the city reworked the original plan into a new document, *The Sanibel Plan*, designed to govern future development and changes for decades to come. (To view *The Sanibel Plan*, go to http://www.mysanibel.com/Departments/Planning-and-Code-Enforcement/The-Sanibel-Plan-Volumes-1-and-2).

Hurricane Charley

For 44 years no significant hurricanes since Hurricane Donna in 1960 hit Sanibel or Captiva. That all changed on Friday, August 13, 2004, when Hurricane Charley roared up from the Caribbean. Charley became a tropical storm on August 9, forming just east of the Lesser Antilles. Its track took it just south of Jamaica where it became a category 1 hurricane. As it moved across the warm waters of the Caribbean Sea, it picked up momentum, becoming a category 3 storm (sustained winds of 111-130 mph) just before making landfall in western Cuba, where four deaths and considerable damage were reported.

The storm swept over the Dry Tortugas and continued to strengthen as it approached the western edge of Florida. Originally forecasters had predicted that Charley would remain offshore until it neared Tampa. But soon after passing close to Ft. Jefferson, Charley took a turn to the east and within five hours grew from a dangerous category 2 storm with winds of 115 mph to a devastating category 4 storm with winds in excess of 145 mph. Both the new direction and the rapid increase in intensity took forecasters by surprise.

For a while, at around 2:00 p.m. August 13, it looked as if Hurricane Charley was

Devastation caused by Hurricane Charley
© James Anderson Photography

going to make a direct hit on Sanibel, but the storm veered west just 10 miles from the island. It made landfall at approximately 3:45 p.m., coming straight through Captiva Pass between Cayo Costa and the northern tip of North Captiva. Damage to the homes located on the edge of the pass was extensive, with dozens of homes suffering a complete loss.

At this writing, Hurricane Charley is the fifth costliest storm to hit the continental United States, with an estimated toll of $18.6 billion in direct losses. Before the 2005 hurricane season, which produced hurricanes Katrina and Wilma, Charley was the second most expensive storm in history. Hurricane Katrina, far and away the costliest storm to make landfall in the United States, caused damages estimated to be in excess of $89 billion.

In Florida Charley caused eight direct fatalities, 16 indirect, and 792 reported injuries. At 6.5 feet the storm surge was minimal. This was owing to two factors: the small size of the storm and eyewall; and the rapid forward motion of the storm. Had the storm slowed down or stalled, both Sanibel and Captiva would likely have been covered in yet another massive storm surge.

While the damage to human enterprises was considerable, the damage to the natural environmental systems was worse. Throughout Southwest Florida, the storm severely damaged 4,651 acres of forest, 63 percent of these being red and black mangroves. Another 6,720 acres were moderately damaged, and 15,172 acres were impacted.

Years later, you can still see evidence of this destruction, especially along the Shell Mound Trail in the J.N. "Ding" Darling National Wildlife Refuge. Along with the destruction of the canopy came the loss of waterbird rookeries, mangrove crabs, fiddler crabs, golden orb-weaver spiders, mangrove cuckoos, black-whiskered vireos, and butterflies. The sea-grass beds, upon which the endangered West Indian manatee depends, were devastated. It has been estimated that 48 percent of all sea turtle nests located between Marco Island and Sarasota were destroyed by Hurricane Charley. Beaches were heavily eroded, and countless shorebird nests were lost.

On Sanibel, Captiva, North Captiva, and Cayo Costa the most dramatic impact was the toppling of tens of thousands of Australian pines. The city of Sanibel, working with the Federal Emergency Management Agency (FEMA), hauled thousands of tons of vegetation debris to several emergency burn sites on the island where fires burned nonstop for months afterward. One report stated that there was enough debris to fill 100 dump trucks a day for three straight months, and the majority

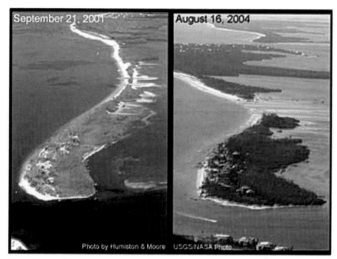

September 21, 2001   August 16, 2004

Photo by Humiston & Moore   USGS/NASA Photo

North Captiva before and after Hurricane Charley struck the islands in 2004.   Courtesy NOAA

of that debris was Australian pine.

Another dramatic remnant of Charley was a huge swath of land, some 1,600 feet across on North Captiva, that was swept away by the winds and storm surge, splitting the island in two. Known as Charley's Cut, the opening has since sanded over, but it reminded everyone living in Southwest Florida of the shifting nature of these fragile barrier islands.

Over the next few years the islands were narrowly missed by hurricanes and tropical storms. The 2005 hurricane season was the most active storm season in recorded history. It spawned 28 storms that raced across the western Atlantic, 15 of which became hurricanes, seven major storms, and four category 5 hurricanes: Katrina, Wilma, Dennis and Emily. Although Sanibel and Captiva managed to avoid a direct hit, the rain produced by storm after storm created a series of events that proved to be equally, and some would argue, even more damaging.

Over the entire summer of 2005, storms dumped record rainfalls on the interior of Florida. After every storm the Kissimmee River basin brought millions of gallons of rainwater into the dike-impounded Lake Okeechobee in the center of the state. By September the Herbert Hoover Dike surrounding the lake, originally built in the 1930s as a flood-control device, was dangerously close to collapsing. The Army Corps of Engineers had little choice but to open the floodgate down the Caloosahatchee River to the west and the Port St. Lucie gate to the east to relieve the tremendous pressure on the earthen structure. This was not a typical freshwater release.

At the peak of the outflow, millions upon

Fish kill from the freshwater releases of 2005 © Charles Sobczak

millions of gallons of freshwater a minute were pouring down the Caloosahatchee into the bays and estuaries along the coastline of Lee County. Because of the stirring-up of the lake bottom and the unprecedented urban runoff from cities such as Orlando and Kissimmee, the water was far from clean. It carried tons of suspended nutrients, including nitrogen, phosphorus, and other pollutants.

Within weeks Sanibel, Captiva, Ft. Myers Beach, and Bonita Springs were seeing the harmful effects of this unwanted fertilizer. Harmful algae blooms including red drift algae, green filamentous algae, cyanobacteria, and a harmful single-celled organism called *Pfiesteria piscicida* were inundating the coastline. Red drift algae piled up on Sanibel and Captiva's beaches two feet deep and ten feet wide, choking to death everything beneath it. Fish kills were everywhere.

Hurricanes and humans had inadvertently combined forces to create what many islanders now refer to as the "Big Kill of 2005." Organizations such as PURRE (People United to Restore our Rivers and Estuaries) were formed, and political pressure was put on the Army Corps of Engineers to stop the dumping of this toxic water into the Caloosahatchee. Eventually drought put an end to the water releases. Recently the state of Florida has made arrangements to purchase some of U.S. Sugar's agricultural holdings in an attempt to develop a south flow-way should such an event ever happen again.

In 2007, in an attempt to curtail future harmful algae blooms, the City of Sanibel enacted a fertilizer ordinance that is being adopted by counties and cities across Florida and beyond to help reduce the impact of nutrient loading to our rivers, bays, and estuaries. The future of water quality across all of North America hangs in the balance of this and similar legislation.

In the end, the industries of mankind are more destructive than hurricanes on the environment. Whereas hurricanes may destroy 10,000 acres of mangroves, drown out entire populations of burrowing owls, and cut football field-size passes through barrier islands, over time the decaying vegetation will nurture new growth, the owls will return, and the passes only confirm the shifting nature of barrier islands. On the other hand, no mangroves can flourish along a seawalled stretch of estuary, and burrowing owls cannot find their way through asphalt and urbanization. Man has altered the atmosphere, polluted the environment with chemicals and fertilizers, and overwhelmed entire ecosystems with development, agriculture, and highways.

The native flora and fauna have, over the millennia, learned to adapt to the ravages of hurricanes. The live oak wisely releases its leafy canopy in the rushing wind, and the tree is spared. Sensing an approaching storm, birds, fish, and animals seek shelter and await its passing. Where do these same animals go to seek shelter from us? Sadly, many find their only shelter on the endangered species list.

Also damaging are the exotic plants and animals we accidentally or intentionally introduce into our environment. Water hyacinth and Hydrilla choke out waterways, while Australian pine, Brazillian pepper and melaleuca outcompete natives and drain wetlands. Red drift algae, over-nutrified by agricultural, urban, and suburban runoff, piles up along our beaches, killing the shellfish and diatoms beneath it and starving out the shorebirds that feed on them.

There will be more introduced species in the future. Our present invasives will be followed by damaging plants, disease carrying insects, and exotic creatures yet unimaginable. Biological pollution is yet another by-product of this human hurricane.

The fight to keep Sanibel and Captiva safe from the powerful forces of development is never over. Today, most of the important lands, especially along the Sanibel River corridor, have been purchased and are secure for the near term.

There are still a handful of parcels that remain to be purchased by SCCF, the city of Sanibel, or other conservation organizations, but the lion's share of wetlands acquisition is complete on Sanibel. Combined, SCCF and the city of Sanibel now manage 1,828 acres (some of which are islands and off-island properties) of land while the J.N. "Ding" Darling National Wildlife Refuge oversees an additional 6,390 acres. As the island itself is approximately 11,000 acres in size, more than two-thirds of Sanibel is officially held as wildlife preserve. Most of the land on Captiva has been developed just as most of Buck Key has been preserved.

In 1990, Sanibel Councilman Mark "Bird" Westall summed up the unprecedented conservation achievements of the island and its residents when he said, *"If you compare the Sanibel of today with the Sanibel of 20 years ago, it's been destroyed. If you compare Sanibel to the rest of Florida, it's a paradise."*

The laws, regulations, and ordinances that protect these sanctuary islands were written by humans and can be undermined and unwritten by humans. Unforeseen special interest groups and political agendas will challenge the validity of *The Sanibel Plan* and work greedily to unravel the nature and beauty of these islands. The citizens of Sanibel and Captiva must remain ever vigilant in preserving wildlife habitats. People such as "Ding" Darling, Willis and Opal Combs, and Roy Bazire must be followed by dedicated environmentalists who will continue to stand up for those whose voices cannot be heard in the hallways of power—the birds, the insects, the animals, and the plants with which we share this stretch of sand. *LIVING SANIBEL* is a moment in time, a snapshot of what we now have, a reminder of what we have already lost, and a prayer for everything we must preserve for generations to come.

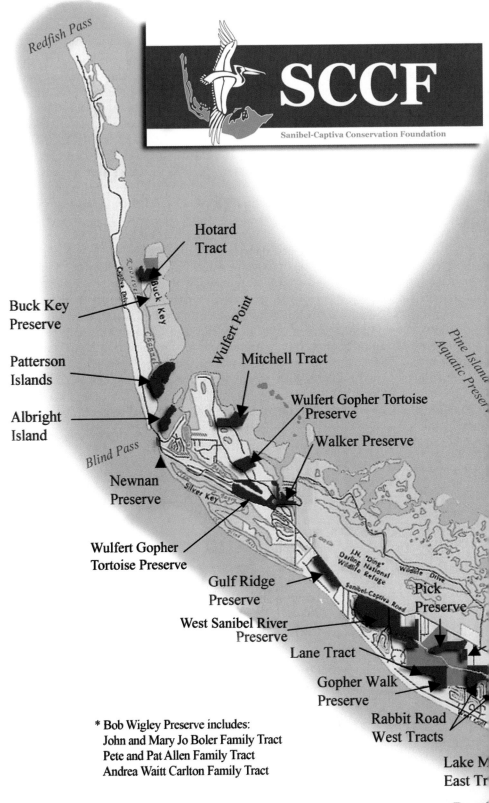

Redfish Pass

SCCF
Sanibel-Captiva Conservation Foundation

Hotard Tract

Buck Key Preserve

Patterson Islands

Albright Island

Blind Pass

Newnan Preserve

Wulfert Point

Mitchell Tract

Wulfert Gopher Tortoise Preserve

Walker Preserve

Pine Island Aquatic Preserve

Wulfert Gopher Tortoise Preserve

Gulf Ridge Preserve

West Sanibel River Preserve

Lane Tract

Gopher Walk Preserve

J.N. "Ding" Darling National Wildlife Refuge

Pick Preserve

Rabbit Road West Tracts

* Bob Wigley Preserve includes:
  John and Mary Jo Boler Family Tract
  Pete and Pat Allen Family Tract
  Andrea Waitt Carlton Family Tract

Lake M
East Tr

Beatti

Preserved Lands, Major Tracts

Sanibel-Captiva Conservation Foundation ■

City of Sanibel □

* State of Florida ■

J.N." Ding" Darling NWR □

* Managed by JNDDNWR

Pine Island

Matlacha Pass

Long Cut Preserve

rk Island   Coconut Island

Sanibel-Captiva Conservation Foundation

Nature Center and Preserve

Dixie Beach Preserve

Woodring Point

Mazur Preserve

Bay Drive Tracts

San Carlos Bay

Sanibel Causeway

Sanibel Light

Tarpon Bay

Dunes Tracts

Sanibel Gardens Preserve

Island Woods Preserve

Craig Tract

Vinca Way Tract

Periwinkle Way

East Gulf Drive

Whisperwood Preserve

Bob Wigley Preserve

Periwinkle Preserve

Blue Skies Preserve

Sanibel Highlands Tract

Algiers Tract

Middle Gulf Drive

Dayton Preserve

Frannie's Preserve

Johnston Preserve

© Sanibel-Captiva Conservation Foundation

Important Abbreviations and the IUCN

In an effort to save space I have created a set of abbreviations for the ecological zones where different species can most readily be found on Sanibel and Captiva. I've not shared this information with the birds and animals, which don't always conform to our categories, so don't be surprised if you discover a mangrove cuckoo flitting around the interior wetlands of the Bailey Tract. These are only guidelines, not definitive.

For convenience I've placed multiple ecological zones into a single category. For example, within the broader zone of interior wetlands (IW) are the sub-categories of upland communities, swales and hammocks, and freshwater wetlands. Attempting to isolate each sub-category to the behavior of wrens, warblers, and other animals covered herein would be overwhelming. As a result, these categories are more inclusive than some readers might want but they are easier to follow.

Here are the definitions for the different abbreviations used throughout the book. There are a few more, similar abbreviations, that will be presented in the fish and shellfish sections.

IW—Interior Wetlands: These are essentially wild, open upland or lowland areas generally held in a preserve or a part of the J.N. "Ding" Darling National Wildlife Refuge. These areas include the Bailey Tract, Sanibel Gardens Preserve, Blue Skies Preserve, SCCF Center Tract, Lighthouse Beach Park, Bowman's Beach Park, Pick Preserve, Buck Key Preserve, and Pond Apple Park, to name a few.

UA—Urban Areas: These include the commercial development along Periwinkle Way, subdivisions such as the Dunes, Beachview, East and West Rocks, Little Lake Murex, and Sanibel Bayous, as well as interior condominium complexes such as Captain's Walk and Blind Pass. This zone also includes all other residential or light commercial locations. For the most part, all of Captiva should be considered **UA**, with the exception of certain parts of South Seas Resort, Buck Key, and Patterson Island.

GB—Gulf Beach: This includes the surf zone, beach dunes, and beach ridges, which are often considered distinct ecological zones. In *Living Sanibel* this definition includes the entire length of the beach, from the tip of Captiva abutting Redfish Pass to the Sanibel Lighthouse. Because of coastal development it includes the gulf-front residential properties, as well as the hotels/motels and condominiums that line a large portion of the beachfront.

MZ—Mangrove Zone: Once again, this broader category consists of several ecological zones, including the mangrove fringe and the intertidal zone. In this book the mangrove zone includes most of Wildlife Drive (there is some IW located near the end of the drive), the backside of Captiva, Buck Key, Patterson Island, Tarpon Bay, the Mazur Preserve, Peace Park, and the Causeway Beach Park.

CW—Causeway: This includes the two spoil islands and the three bridges that link Sanibel and Captiva to the mainland. It does not extend into Fort Myers, nor does it include the large tidal flats found on the south side of McGregor Blvd., just north of the toll plaza.

The IUCN

Finally, it is important to mention the status of each species presented here, when available. The primary reference point for establishing how a bird, mammal, or other living thing is doing in the wild for this entire work has been the IUCN Red List of Threatened Species (www.iucnredlist.org) maintained by the International Union for the Conservation of Nature and Natural Resources, established in 1948. The IUCN (www/iucn.org) has more than 60 offices worldwide, with some 1,000 members in 140 countries and 11,000 volunteer scientists and experts contributing to its database, which is updated annually. This is its mission statement:

> *"Our vision is a just world that values and conserves nature. Our mission is to influence, encourage and assist societies throughout the world to conserve the integrity and diversity of nature and to ensure that any use of natural resources is equitable and ecologically sustainable."*

Each animal or plant on the IUCN Red List is placed into one of the following nine categories:

NE=Not Evaluated / Generally, little cause for concern about the status of the species, as in the case of the black rat or the brown anole.

DD=Data Deficient / Not enough data available to assess of the risk of extinction.

LC=Least Concern / Lowest risk. Includes widespread and abundant species.

NT=Near Threatened / Likely to become endangered in the near future, meaning the species is in trouble.

VU=Vulnerable / High risk of endangerment in the wild.

EN=Endangered / High risk of extinction in the wild.

CR=Critically Endangered / Extremely high risk of extinction in the wild.

EW=Extinct in the Wild / Known only to survive in captivity or as a naturalized population outside of its historic range.

EX=Extinct / No individuals remaining in the wild or in captivity.

Understand that while a species such as is the black skimmer may be in trouble in Florida, the IUCN looks at the skimmer's worldwide populations. With ample populations of this species thriving in South America, the IUCN lists it as LC (Least Concern). On the other hand, Florida is about to delist the goliath grouper, while the IUCN, looking at its entire former range, has it listed as CR (Critically Endangered). Whenever possible I have provided both Florida's and the IUCN's status for each and every species in this book.

Enjoy.

The Birds of Sanibel and Captiva

Approximately 10,000 species of birds exist in the world today. There is little disagreement that the number of species has decreased in the past 2,000 years. The moa of New Zealand, the dodo, and the passenger pigeon all provide evidence of this. The most important thing we can do today, and into tomorrow, is to ensure that not another single species is lost to extinction.

North America, excluding Mexico and Central America, has 925 species of birds, according to the American Ornithologists' Union. Florida ranks in the top five for bird diversity, with 497 verified species, of which about 150 are permanent residents, nesting and raising their chicks in the Sunshine State. The remainder of these species are either migratory—staying in Florida for the winter or passing through as they travel between the north and the Caribbean or Central and South America—or introduced, such as the various parrot species commonly found in Miami.

Sanibel and Captiva, ideally located for north/south migrations and offering thousands of acres of rich and varied habitat, are considered among the best birding locations in North America. There have been 291 confirmed species observed on these two small islands. This is an astonishing statistic: just under 30 percent of all the birds found in North America, which has 9,358,340 square miles of habitat, have been observed on two small islands with a combined size of 19 square miles. When

Roseate Spoonbills   © ThroughTheLensGallery.com

you arrive on Sanibel and Captiva, you might as well be entering an aviary, lacking only the double set of doors on the causeway and the immense net it would take to cover both of the islands.

The islands' early settlers understood the importance of this long ago. They declared Sanibel and Captiva a Wildlife Preserve in 1913, when making such declarations was unheard of. J.N. "Ding" Darling fought his entire life to establish national wildlife preserves, funded by the Duck Stamp Program he created. Land purchases are still being added to the holdings of the Sanibel-Captiva Conservation Foundation, "Ding" Darling, and city-held preserves today in a continuing effort to maintain a bird-friendly island.

The following section is divided into resident (50) and migratory birds (55). The trouble with such lists is that the birds don't always stay in their categories. If you happen to see a migratory shorebird in the dead of summer, please don't write me an e-mail about it. Immature shorebirds, still too young to breed, will sometimes forgo migration, as will older birds. On the other hand, it is sometimes impossible to find certain resident species living here. Bear in mind that all the birds on the islands have wings and none of them read books, so these categories should be viewed with some degree of flexibility. A complete list of the 291 species verified on the island can be found at the end of the migratory chapter.

Resident Birds
Every Season

Brown Pelican   © ThroughTheLensGallery.com

☐ _____ **Brown Pelican** (*Pelecannus occidentalis*) Nicknames: none / Status: FL=species of special concern, ICUN=LC / Life span: to 27 years / Length: 40-50 in. (100-127 cm) / Wingspan: 78-84 in. (187-213 cm) / Weight: 8.2 lb (3.7 kg) / Nests on islands / Found: GB, MZ, CW.

As you bike across the Sanibel causeway, it is impossible not to spot this large, easily recognized bird feeding on the threadfin herring and minnows that gather along the flats and in the shadows cast by the bridge. What is harder to grasp is that the ubiquitous brown pelican was fast approaching extinction in the 1960s and '70s.

Widespread use of DDT to control the Florida mosquito population altered the calcium metabolism in pelicans and other birds, causing them to produce eggs with shells too thin to support the embryo to maturity. In nearby Louisiana (where, ironically, the pelican is the state bird) the population completely collapsed because of the overuse of these pesticides. Louisiana had to import Florida pelicans through the 1980s to help rebuild its decimated flocks.

The brown pelican is the smallest of the seven species of pelicans found in the world. The only other indigenous North American species is the American white pelican, a common winter resident on Sanibel and Captiva. The largest pelican in the world is the Australian pelican, which can weigh more than 22 pounds (10 kilograms).

Unique among the species in that it is the only one that dives for its prey, the brown pelican hovers from heights of 20 to 60 feet, then collapses its wings and plunges headfirst into the water, filling its pouch with a combination of minnows and saltwater. A fully extended pouch can hold almost three gallons of water. As the bird strains out the excess water, terns and gulls flock around hoping to pick off some of the outflow.

The brown pelican is especially vulnerable to water quality. Excessive nutrient run-off and the resulting harmful algae blooms can cause severe declines in minnow populations, and with each chick requiring 150 pounds (67 kilograms) of fish over the eight-month nesting period, an entire breeding season can be lost to environmental degradation.

Predation occurs mostly to the eggs and nestlings from raccoons, opossums, bobcats, snakes, fish crows, and exotics such as Nile monitor lizards. Adults may be taken by sharks and alligators, though rarely. Coastal development, pollution, and pesticides are the pelican's primary threats. The pelican roosts and nests in colonies.

Diving pelican © Hung V. Do

Brown Pelican stretching his pouch.
© ThroughTheLensGallery.com

White Ibis feeding on the flats ©ThroughTheLensGallery.com

☐ _____ **White Ibis** (*Eudocimus albus*) Nicknames: Chokoloskee chicken, Spanish curlew / Status: FL= species of special concern, ICUN=LC / Life span: to 16 years / Length: 21-27 in. (53-68 cm) / Wingspan: 38 in. (96 cm) / Weight: 2.3 lb (1 kg) / Nests on islands in large colonies / Found: UA, GB, IW, MZ.

Although statewide the population of the white ibis is in decline, these unmistakable birds are found abundantly throughout our islands. The ibis feeds on fish, frogs, crabs, insects, and small reptiles. Its long decurved beak, as well as its legs, turns bright red when in breeding plumage. The distinctive black tips at the end of each wing when in flight make it an easy bird to identify. The juvenile is a mottled brown color. In Lee County you can sometimes find a similar species, the glossy ibis, which is the same size and shape but a dark, blue-brown color similar to an oil slick.

Black wing tips visible on bird in flight
©ThroughTheLensGallery.com

The ibis was a particular favorite with early Sanibel homesteaders, producing an edible breast slightly larger than that of a popular game bird, the ruffed grouse—hence the nickname Chokoloskee chicken. Ibis were hunted throughout Florida well into the 1950s. Even today it is an easy bird to approach and still is hunted illegally in certain areas.

The white ibis mates for life and generally nests in large colonies with other wading birds. Its predominant threat statewide is habitat destruction. It is preyed upon by alligators and eagles, and its nesting sites are raided by raccoons and bobcats.

Immature Ibis ©ThroughTheLensGallery.com

☐ _____ **Great Egret** (*Ardea alba*) Nicknames: American egret, white crane, plume bird / Status: FL=stable, IUCN=LC / Life span: to 22 years / Length: 46-52 in. (116-132 cm) / Wingspan: 77-82 in. (195-208 cm) / Weight: 5.7 lb (2.5 kg) / Nests on islands / Found: UA, GB, IW, MZ.

This species, along with the smaller snowy egret, was decimated by the plume hunters in the late 1800s. During breeding season the great egret displays a long, elegant train of lacy plumes (aigrette) that made them a constant target of the hat industry. Although it has recovered statewide, the population is still impacted by this slaughter more than 100 years ago.

The great egret flies with a slow, steady beat and with its long neck tucked back. It feeds on fish, snakes, and insects and can often be seen strolling along Periwinkle Way in search of brown anoles.

Spearing a seatrout   ©ThroughTheLensGallery.com

The winter population on the islands is greatly increased by migratory birds, which are easily distinguishable from the resident birds by their innate fear of man.

The great egret is monogamous and nests in large colonies with other wading birds. Predominant threats include water quality and habitat loss. Alligators and bobcats prey on the great egret, and its rookeries are sometimes attacked by various tree-climbing predators.

©ThroughTheLensGallery.com

Great Egret in breeding plumage and fine aigrettes. ©ThroughTheLensGallery.com

☐ _____ **Snowy Egret** (*Egretta thula*) Nicknames: snowy heron, short white, little plume bird / Status: FL=species of special concern, IUCN=LC / Life span: to 17 years / Length: 22-27 in. (56-68 cm) / Wingspan: 38-45 in. (96-114 cm) / Weight: 13 oz (.36 kg) / Nests on islands / Found: GB, IW, MZ.

Yellow slippers   © ThroughTheLensGallery.com

The nickname, "little plume bird," best identifies this delicate bird. The snowy egret, along with its taller cousin, the great egret, was the principal target of the late 19th- and early 20th-century plume hunters. This was the most persecuted of all the Florida birds because of its soft, lacy, breeding finery. It was killed in such tremendous numbers that it was nearly driven to extinction.

Provided you can see its feet, with its bright yellow "slippers," the snowy is simple to identify. Other identifying characteristics are the long slender black bill, yellow lores (area between eye and beak), and equally yellow eyes. The snowy and the three herons and egrets that follow in this section, however, make up a quartet of similarly sized birds that are at certain times pure white, making it a challenge for the amateur birder to tell one from the other.

The snowy egret feeds on crustaceans, large insects, and fish. It has a peculiar feeding habit that is very entertaining to observe. It puts one of its bright yellow

feet forward in the water and vibrates it rapidly in the soft bottom, scaring up fish and small crustaceans. Then it quickly runs them down and feeds on them.

The snowy egret nests in mixed colonies with other herons. This smaller egret is preyed upon by alligators, eagles, hawks, and bobcats. Its primary threat is habitat destruction.

☐ _____ **Little Blue Heron** (*Egretta caerulea*) Nicknames: calico crane, blue crane / Status: FL=population declining, IUCN=LC / Life span: to 13-14 years / Length: 24-29 in. (61-73 cm) / Wingspan: 40-41 in. (101-104 cm) / Weight: 12.9 oz (.35 kg) / Nests on islands / Found: IW, MZ.

Although the little blue heron was not as much a target of the millinery trade as other local species at the turn of the last century, it is suffering now from drained wetlands and habitat loss. Unlike some other herons and egrets, it is seldom seen along the beaches, preferring fresh or

©ThroughTheLensGallery.com

brackish waters where it feeds upon small vertebrates, crustaceans, and large insects.

It is almost the same size as the snowy egret, and although it doesn't remain white, the immature bird, both female and male, is pure white for the first year, after which it molts into its adult purplish-maroon plumage. One theory for the similar coloration is that the snowy egret tolerates the white adolescent bird over the blue-colored adult, thereby allowing it to feed in larger and, therefore, safer colonies of egrets.

The easiest way to distinguish an immature little blue heron from a snowy egret is the absence of the bright yellow

Breeding plumage   © Hung V. Do

"slippers." Another method is the beak, which, for the little blue, is grayish with a dark black tip. The little blue heron is monogamous and nests with other egrets and herons for protection both during the nesting season and the rest of the year. It is preyed upon by bobcats, eagles, and alligators.

❏ _____ **Reddish Egret** (*Egretta rufescens*) Nicknames: none / Status: FL=species of special concern, IUCN=LC / Life span: to 12 years / Length: 27-32 in. (68-81 cm) / Wingspan: 46 in. (117 cm) / Weight: 15.9 oz. (.44 kg) / Nests on islands / Found: predominantly in MZ.

Reddish Egret white phase   ©ThroughTheLensGallery.com

This is one of only a handful of herons that has more than one color morph, another being the great blue heron (which comes in blue, white, or a mixture known as Würdemann's heron). Although slightly larger than either the snowy egret or the little blue heron, the reddish egret from a distance is very difficult to distinguish from the other two birds.

When trying to identify a white-morph reddish egret, look for a pink bill with a black tip and dark blue legs and feet. Perhaps one of the best ways to identify the reddish egret is by observing its feeding behavior. It performs a "canopy dance," spreading its wings open to form a shaded area over the water, then chasing down the minnows that come to find shelter in the shade. It is far and away the most

Reddish Egret red phase   ©ThroughTheLensGallery.com

animated feeding behavior of all the wading birds—making the reddish egret a very entertaining bird to watch.

The reddish egret suffered dramatic losses from plume hunters and is now considered fairly rare in the United States, but fortunately is often seen in the J.N. "Ding" Darling National Wildlife Refuge on Sanibel. Like most herons, the reddish egret is monogamous and nests with other wading birds. Since it feeds almost exclusively in saltwater, it is vulnerable to water-quality issues, as well as habitat destruction.

❏ _____ **Cattle Egret** (*Bubulcus ibis*) Nicknames: buff-backed heron, cowbird / Status: FL=population dramatically increasing, IUCN=LC / Life span: to 17 years / Length: 19-21 in. (48-53 cm) / Wingspan: 36-38 in. (91-97 cm) / Weight: 11.9 oz (.33 kg) / Nests on islands / Found: UA, IW.

Although this is the fourth white bird that is roughly the same size as the previous three in this section, it is the easiest to distinguish from the others. It has yellow legs and feet and a solid yellow beak. It is also quite a bit stockier, with a larger head, a thicker neck, and shorter legs, than the snowy egret. It feeds almost exclusively inland and is rarely seen along the beaches or mangroves. It's not uncommon to see a cattle egret saunter across Periwinkle Way midday, stopping traffic and creating a commotion. During breeding season it displays patches of buff orange on its crown, nape, and lower neck.

The cattle egret has one of the most fascinating stories of any bird living in Florida. Originally a native of Africa, then spreading to Europe and Asia, the cattle egret first appeared in the New World in 1877 on the northeastern tip of South

Cattle egret during mating season   © Hung V. Do

America in Venezuela. There was some speculation that a flock actually rode across the Atlantic in the eye of a major hurricane and broke away from the storm near the Lesser Antilles. Seeing this bird on Sanibel or Captiva today represents the only "natural" migration of a major animal most of us will ever witness.

After stabilizing its small immigrant population in South America, the cattle egret began expanding its range. It reached Florida in 1941, long after the devastating plume hunts, and began nesting here in 1953. Over the past 50-plus years the cattle egret has steadily increased its range throughout the United States and is now pressing into southern Canada. It nests in all the lower 48 states. It nests and roosts with other herons and egrets.

The cattle egret is an opportunistic feeder. In Africa it is often found on the backs of large ungulates such as water buffalo and rhinoceros where it forages behind them, but in the Americas it has adapted to cattle, horses, deer, and sometimes follows behind tractors or along the edge of grass fires where it feeds on fleeing insects. It also eats mice, warblers, lizards, grubs, frogs, and snakes. Because it prefers open pasture, the cattle egret is readily preyed upon by red-tailed hawks, crested caracaras, bald eagles, and red foxes and may be inadvertently aiding in raptor recovery. Because of its tendency to forage in urban settings, the cattle egret is vulnerable to automobile fatalities.

In the past five decades the cattle egret has become the most common heron in the Sunshine State, and unlike so many of its foreign counterparts, it is not an introduced species. It has adapted well to both agricultural and urban settings and is currently thriving.

☐ _____ **Tricolored Heron** (*Egretta tricolor*) Nicknames: Louisiana heron, blue crane / Status: FL= species of special concern, IUCN=LC / Life span: to 17 years / Length: 24-26 in. (61-69 cm) / Wingspan: 36 in. (91 cm) / Weight: 14-16 oz (.45 kg) / Nests on islands / Found: IW, MZ.

This medium-size egret is aptly named. The adult tricolored heron has a bluish head, neck, and wings, with maroon coloring at the base of the neck, and a white belly. In breeding plumage it adds a beautiful white plume trailing off the crown of its head. The tricolored suffered extensive losses during the plume-hunting era. Although the species is recovering, Florida Fish and Wildlife has kept it listed as a species of special concern.

Formerly called the Louisiana heron, the tricolored heron is known to be among the deepest waders of all the herons, sometimes going into the water all the way to its belly. Similar to the reddish egret, the tricolored is also a "canopy" feeder, making it fascinating to observe. It feeds almost exclusively on minnows.

Shying away from the beaches and only seldom seen inland, this attractive bird can be seen near the culverts of the "Ding" Darling refuge and along mangrove tidal flats. For the most part, the tricolored heron is monogamous and like all the egrets and herons, tends to nest in large colonies with other wading birds. Its primary threat is habitat loss and poor water quality.

Tricolored Heron in breeding plumage　　© Hung V. Do

Green Heron (*Butorides virescens*) Nicknames: little green heron / shietpoke / skeow / Status: FL=stable, IUCN=LC / Life span: to 7 years / Length: 18-22 in. (46-56 cm) / Wingspan: 26 in. (66 cm) / Weight: 7-8 oz (.20 kg) / Nests on islands / Found: IW, MZ.

Fond of dense mangrove roosts and reclusive in nature, this small, solitary heron may be difficult to spot on Sanibel and Captiva. One amazing characteristic of this bird is its ability to use tools. It commonly uses crusts of bread, insects, earthworms, twigs, and

Green Heron in Flight   ©ThroughTheLensGallery.com

even feathers (think artificial flies) as bait to lure small fish to within reach.

The green heron is actually not very green; only a hint of that color can be seen on the crown and back under good lighting conditions. It has yellow legs and a chestnut neck with patches of white. It tends to remain in a crouched position when feeding. It resembles the crow when flying and lets go with a loud *skeow* when disturbed. It is monogamous, but unlike most other herons and egrets, the green heron tends to make solitary nests and does not roost in colonies.

Green Heron feeding   ©ThroughTheLensGallery.com

Black-crowned Night Heron (*Nycticorax nycticorax*)

Nicknames: quock, Indian pullet / Status: FL= increasing. IUCN=LC / Life span: to 21 years / Length: 22-28 in. (56-71 cm) / Wingspan: 42-44 in. (106-112 cm) / Weight: 1.6 lb (.62 kg) / Nests on islands / Found: IW, MZ.

Black-crowned Night Heron

©ThroughTheLensGallery.com

With a range that spans five continents, the black-crowned night heron is one of the most widespread herons in the world. A beautifully fashioned bird, the night heron is a favorite of many photographers. Similar to the yellow-crowned night heron, which is far more common on the islands, this attractive bird can be seen along the riprap in the "Ding" Darling refuge, as well as in the Bailey Tract. It is seldom seen along the beaches.

Although it generally hunts at night, during the nesting season it may also be observed feeding during the day. Like the equally successful cattle egret, the night heron feeds on a wide assortment of creatures including frogs, rodents, snakes, crabs, plant material, eggs, and young birds. The adult black-crowned night heron does not distinguish between its own young and those from other nests and will occasionally brood chicks not its own.

©ThroughTheLensGallery.com

Yellow-crowned Night Heron (*Nyctanassa violacea*)

Nicknames: crab-eater, crabier, gauldin / Status: FL=stable, IUCN=LC / Life span: to 6 years / Length: 22-28 in. (56-71 cm) / Wingspan: 42-44 in. (107-112 cm) / Weight: 1.6 lb (.72 kg) / Nests on islands / Found: MZ.

Found only in North and South America, the yellow-crowned night heron is virtually identical in size to its close relative, the black-crowned night heron, but has less than one-third the life span. The easiest way to tell the two birds apart is by the large, yellowish tuft of feathers on the yellow-crowned heron, making it appear to have a punk-style haircut. Its wings are also much more variegated than the solid gray of the black-crowned heron.

The yellow-crowned heron tends to feed more often during daylight hours and does not have as diverse a diet as their cousins. As its nicknames imply, the yellow-crowned night heron specializes in eating crabs. A curious habit of this bird is carefully to remove all the legs on a captured crab before eating.

It is monogamous and tends to nest in small colonies of fellow yellow-crowned night herons. Its eggs are preyed upon by snakes and other birds, and alligators and bobcats will take the adult bird. Its population is stable, but it suffers from habitat loss resulting from the drainage of wetlands and coastal development.

Yellow-crowned Night Heron
© Hung V. Do

Roseate Spoonbill (*Platalea ajaja*) Nicknames: pink curlew, pink / Status: FL=species of special concern, IUCN=LC / Life span: to 15 years / Length: 30-40 in. (76-101 cm) / Wingspan: 50-53 in. (127-135 cm) / Weight: 2.54 lb (1.13-1.81 kg) / Does not nest on islands / Found: IW, MZ.

Without question, the roseate spoonbill is the poster child of Sanibel bird lovers. A difficult bird to add to anyone's life list, the roseate is commonly found in the "Ding" Darling refuge year round and thus attracts thousands of avid birders annually to the islands. It is probably the most photographed bird on Sanibel. Because of its pink coloration, the roseate is sometimes confused with the flamingo.

©ThroughTheLensGallery.com

Unmistakable for its spatulate bill, baldhead, and flamboyant pink coloration, the roseate was nearly extirpated from Florida during the 1800s. Not only was it taken by the plume hunters, it was also killed for its meat, and its rookeries were repeatedly raided for eggs. Now recovering, the numbers of these lovely birds are still only a fraction of what they were when Ponce de Leon first landed in Florida.

The roseate's feeding style is unique, similar to wood storks. It swishes its spatulate-shaped bill back and forth through the soft, exposed muck in any tidal flat. When it comes across a shrimp or crustacean, it claps its bill together, eating the prey, then quickly resumes feeding. It also has a unique behavior called "skypointing" where it tends to extend its bill and neck upward toward other spoonbills flying overhead.

The roseate is monogamous and tends to nest with other wading birds. Its nests are sometimes raided by raccoons and other predators. It needs extensive tidal flats to survive, and it suffers from polluted waters, as well as long-term habitat loss.

☐ _____ **Wood Stork** (*Mycteria americana*) Nicknames: flinthead, Spanish buzzard, wood ibis / Status: FL=Endangered species, IUCN=LC / Life span: to 18 years / Length: 33-45 in. (85-115 cm) / Wingspan: 59-69 in. (150-175 cm) / Weight: 6 lb (2.72 kg) / Does not nest on islands / Found: UA, IW, MZ.

©ThroughTheLensGallery.com

With its distinctive black-tipped wing feathers and extended neck and legs, the wood stork is easy to recognize in flight. It can often be spotted soaring and circling high above the islands. Because the wood stork uses thermals to travel as far as 80 miles from its roosting site to arrive on the islands, you are unlikely to spot any of these birds early in the day before the land heats up sufficiently to create these rising air currents. Good places to search for the wood stork are along Wildlife Drive and in the Bailey Tract in the afternoon, especially during times of drought.

The wood stork has a unique way of feeding, which makes it amusing to observe. It captures its prey using a specialized technique known as grope feeding or tactolocation. It prefers to feed in water 6 to 10 inches deep, with its long black bills partly open. When the fish touches the bird's bill, it snaps shut with an average response time of 25 milliseconds, one of the fastest reflexes found in all vertebrates. To put this number into perspective, humans blink at 330 milliseconds, so a stork snaps its bill shut on an unsuspecting minnow 13 times faster than the blink of a human eye.

From a high of 20,000 nesting pairs in the 1930s, the wood stork population in the southeastern United States. declined to a low of approximately 5,000 pairs by the late 1970s, mostly because of habitat and nesting-site loss. Two wood stork chicks require up to 400 pounds of fish from the time they hatch until they reach the fledgling stage, in addition to the nutritional needs of both rearing parents.

©ThroughTheLensGallery.com

Woodstork
© Joseph Blanda, M.D.

The wood stork requires almost ideal conditions to nest: summers with high rainfall (producing ample breeding ponds for small fish) followed by winters with little to no rainfall (concentrating the minnows into shallow, crowded ponds). Lacking these conditions in any given season, the wood stork does not nest.

One of the best places in Southwest Florida to observe wood storks is the Audubon Corkscrew Swamp Sanctuary, where they roost every evening in the ancient bald cypress trees. (Corkscrew Swamp is located just south of Immokalee approximately 55 miles from Sanibel. After the J.N. "Ding" Darling National Wildlife Refuge, it offers the region's best up-close wildlife viewing, including very large alligators. Go to http://www.corkscrew.audubon.org/Visit/Visit_Us.html for hours, directions, and additional information.)

Although slowly rebounding from its record low numbers, the wood stork is struggling to adapt to Florida's rampant growth. Urban sprawl, coupled with the paving over of feeding ponds and wetlands, is especially hard on this large bird. It has a distinct population in Central and South America that is not endangered, but preserving the North American species may yet prove to be a challenge. Wood stork rookeries are sometimes preyed upon by snakes and owls, and the adult birds are occasionally taken by alligators. Sadly, its primary threats are humans.

❑ _____ **Great Blue Heron** (*Ardea herodias*) Nicknames: blue crane, pond scoggin / Status: FL=stable, IUCN=LC / Life span: to 24 years / Length: 38-54 in. (97-137 cm) / Wingspan: 66-79 in. (167-201 cm) / Weight: 5.7 lb (2.59 kg) / Nests on islands / Found: GB, IW, MZ.

The great blue heron is the largest and most widespread heron in North America. A magnificent bird to watch, this skilled hunter can be found throughout Sanibel and Captiva. It has adapted well to human environments and can often be found leaning over open bait wells at marinas or begging for hand-outs at the fishing pier. Migratory herons, which frequent the islands during winter, tend to be far more skittish than the resident herons.

Although there is a white morph called the great white heron, its range does not extend as far as Sanibel, though it can be readily found in the Florida Keys and may be seen rarely on Captiva. There is also a mixed breed, known as Würdemann's heron, that is a meld of the blue and white morphs.

Fledgling Great Blue Herons   ©ThroughTheLensGallery.com

Catching a Florida Garter Snake   © Hung V. Do

Dieting mostly on fish, which it spears with amazing precision, the great blue heron also eats mice, lizards, and snakes and has even been observed feeding on hatchling alligators. On rare occasions a great blue will choke to death when attempting to eat a fish or animal too large to swallow.

An injured or captured great blue heron must be handled with extreme caution. It has been known to drive its long, powerful beak into a person's eye, sometime resulting in death. Covering its head with a towel or t-shirt is always advised.

When disturbed, the great blue heron lets loose with a very loud squawk that can be quite alarming. It is monogamous, nesting in large single-species colonies. When discovered these colonies should not be disturbed, as any intrusion could result in the agitated chicks falling from their nests where they will be readily preyed upon by raccoons, otters, and bobcats. The adult bird is sometimes taken by alligators, but overall, the great blue heron is thriving.

☐ _____ **Osprey** (*Pandion haliaetus*) Nicknames: fish hawk / Status: FL=species of special concern, IUCN=LC / Life span: to 26 years / Length: 21-23 in. (54-58 cm) / Wingspan: 59-71 in. (150-180 cm) / Weight: 3.1 lb (1.41 kg) / Nests on islands / Found: UA, GB, IW, MZ, CW.

Feeding her chicks   ©ThroughTheLensGallery.com

In the classic work, *The Nature of Things on Sanibel*, Sanibel author and naturalist George Campbell noted that during the 1974-75 nesting season, 24 osprey nests produced 10 offspring island wide. Two years later, during the 1976-77 nesting season, 37 nests produced 12 young. In the 2007-08 nesting season, the International Osprey Foundation recorded 109 nests producing 79 healthy chicks. Most of this impressive rebound is a result of the elimination of DDT and related chlorinated hydrocarbon pesticides, which caused the osprey's eggshells to thin and fail long before hatching. Although the osprey population is slowly recovering, Florida Fish and Wildlife has kept this beautiful raptor on its list as a species of special concern.

Like most birds of prey, the osprey tends to return to the same nest year after year, and it is especially fond of nesting on power poles. Taking a cue from this behavior, Sanibel resident Mark "Bird" Westall, founder of the International Osprey Foundation, started constructing special nesting platforms in the mid-1970s to see if the osprey would take to them. Today you can see many of these nesting sites

Osprey landing   © Hung V. Do

around the islands, the most common design being a single pole with a sturdy square platform on top, approximately 30-40 feet above the ground. The platforms have proved popular with ospreys, though it doesn't keep them from building nests in unlikely places such as atop the buoys marking the Intracoastal Waterway or on the overhead sign structures directly over McGregor Blvd. approaching the Sanibel Causeway.

The osprey is learning to live with humans. It is one of the most widespread raptors in the world, found on all continents except Antarctica. It is sometimes mistaken for a bald eagle, though it is considerably smaller and has a mottled white head.

It can often be observed soaring along the edge of the causeway searching for prey. With a diet that is 99 percent fish (it has been known to eat snakes and small reptiles, though rarely), the osprey is commonly found hovering over almost any good-size body of water, from inland ponds to open tidal flats. It strikes the water with incredible speed, sometimes completely submerging its body. Once the osprey grasps a suitable prey, be it a sheepshead, seatrout, mullet, or any other local fish, it quickly turns the fish to face forward into the wind, making it more aerodynamic to carry. The osprey has been known to die after sinking its powerful talons into a fish too large for the bird to lift. Unable to extricate itself in time, its drowns with a large redfish, snook, or large-mouth bass attached.

Bald eagles sometimes prey on osprey offspring, but by and large the biggest threats to the osprey come from manmade chemical pollutants and degraded water quality, which results in loss of fisheries.

⬜ _____ **Bald Eagle** (*Haliaeetus leucocephalus*) Nicknames: eagle / Status: FL=species of special concern, threatened in the lower 48, IUCN=LC / Life span: to 30 years / Length: 28-38 in. (71-96 cm) / Wingspan: 72-96 in. (183-234 cm) / Weight: 9.1 lb (4.13 kg) / Nests on islands / Found: GB, IW, MZ.

Our national symbol, the bald eagle is always a bird lover's delight to observe. With a wingspan up to eight feet across, the majestic eagle soaring above the islands is a spectacular sight. Florida has the largest nesting population of bald eagles outside of Alaska. Although the National Fish and Wildlife Service still lists the bald eagle as threatened, it has been downgraded to a species of special concern in Florida.

Until the 1940s and the widespread use of DDT as a mosquito and insect control, the bald eagle flourished in the United States. By the early 1960s the bald

©ThroughTheLensGallery.com

eagle population had collapsed to the point where it was one of the first animals listed when the Endangered Species Act was passed in 1973. Only the peregrine falcon suffered as dramatically from the use of DDT and other chemicals. After 20 years of sustained conservation efforts, the bird was reclassified to threatened on July 12, 1995. Although far below historic numbers, the bald eagle is on the road to recovery.

Its predominant diet is fish, although this large bird will also take waterfowl, squirrels, rabbits, muskrats, and cattle egret. The eagle will also feed on fresh carrion when the opportunity arises. The eagle and osprey do not get along. Not only has the eagle been known to take osprey chicks, but it also habitually steals captured fish from osprey in flight. It is not at all uncommon to see osprey aggressively shagging off any nearby eagle.

When soaring, the juvenile bald eagle can sometimes be mistaken for a turkey vulture or black vulture. The juvenile, whose coloration is a mottled brown, does not

©ThroughTheLensGallery.com

attain adult plumage until it is 5 years old. One of the best ways to distinguish an eagle from a vulture in flight is that the eagle soars with straight wings, almost like a plank, whereas the vulture's wings curve upward in the shape of a V.

The eagle uses the same nest year after year, adding a small amount of twigs and branches every year. Some nests become huge, weighing more than a ton.

The only viable threat to the bald eagle is man. The fine for shooting a bald eagle can be as much as $100,000 and a year in prison. The larger threat from man, however, is chemical pollution and habitat loss.

☐ Red-shouldered Hawk (*Buteo lineatus*) Nicknames: chicken hawk / Status: FL=stable, IUCN=LC / Life span: to 19 years / Length: 17-24 in. (43-61 cm) / Wingspan: 37-44 in. (94-111 cm) / Weight: 1.1 lb (0.5 kg) / Nests on islands / Found: UA, IW, MZ.

When you spot a hawk on Sanibel or Captiva, odds are that it is a red-shouldered hawk. Sightings of other hawks, such as the Cooper's hawk, peregrine falcon, and red-tailed hawk, are infrequent. The medium-size red-shouldered hawk is often seen in the Bailey Tract, the Sanibel Gardens Preserve, and along the trails behind the Sanibel-Captiva Conservation Foundation headquarters on San-Cap Road. It is a truly beautiful raptor.

©ThroughTheLensGallery.com

Mice, cotton rats, marsh rabbits, snakes, amphibians, worms, snails, and an occasional bird are all on the menu of the red-shouldered hawk. It is a perch hunter, sitting on high Australian pine branches or other lofty vantage points, then quickly pouncing on prey spotted below. It can often be heard, at a considerable distance, repeating a loud, rapid *keeyah, keeyah*. It has a disdain for the great horned owl, which has been known to raid red-shouldered hawk nests, and it will shag the owls off when discovered in its area.

The red-shouldered hawk not only reuses the same nest year after year, but also has been known to remain in the same territory, though multiple generations, for more than 45 consecutive years. It is generally monogamous and builds solitary nests.

Red-shouldered Hawk   © Hung V. Do

Great Horned Owl (*Bubo virginianus*) Nicknames: cat owl, hoot owl / Status: FL=stable, IUCN=LC / Life span: to 27 years / Length: 18-25 in. (46-63 cm) / Wingspan: 40-60 in. (101-152 cm) / Weight: 3 lb (1.36 kg) / Nests on islands / Found IW.

Chances are you will never actually see a great horned owl on Sanibel or Captiva. This nocturnal feeder comes out at dusk and retires just before sunrise. A far better way of knowing if there is a great horned owl in the area is by hearing it. Both males and females make a loud, resonant *Whoo! Whoowhoowhoo! Whoo!* call that is unmistakable.

Easily recognized by the two tufts of feathers on its head resembling ears and its large size, the great horned owl is a formidable predator. It is the only bird known to kill full-grown skunks, falcons, and domestic cats. It also eats marsh rabbits, rats and mice, insects, coots, and other owls. Because of its ability to tackle prey weighing more than itself, the great horned owl is scorned by the islands' other major raptors: osprey, red-shouldered hawks, and bald eagles. Crows have been known to mob the great horned owl's nest and kill their chicks.

©ThroughTheLensGallery.com

The great horned owl ranges from the High Arctic to Argentina. It is not common on the islands, though several nests are scattered around. A solitary nesting bird, the great horned owl is monogamous and aggressive. It has been known to strike at humans in defense of its nests. The powerful grip and long talons can inflict serious injury.

Eastern Screech Owl (*Otus asio*) Nicknames: squinch owl, death owl, shivering owl, mottled owl / Status: FL=Declining population, IUCN=LC / Life span: to 20 years / Length: 8-10 in. (16-25 cm) / Wingspan: 18-24 in. (45-61 cm) / Weight: 5.9 oz (.17 kg) / Nests on islands / Found: IW.

One of the smallest owls in North America, the eastern screech owl has been known to consume one-third of its body weight every day. It has a distinct call, similar to a horse's whinny, then descending in pitch to a drawn-out trill. Because of its size and its nocturnal habits, this owl, like the great horned owl, will more likely be heard and seldom, if ever, seen.

Eastern Screech Owl red phase   © Michael Hughes

The eastern screech owl has two distinctive color morphs: red and gray. The red phase seems to be more heat tolerant and is the color most often observed in South Florida. The screech owl's broad diet consists of insects, spiders, crayfish, mammals, amphibians, reptiles, fish, and small birds, including starlings and songbirds.

This small owl will nest in hollow cavities and dense foliage, as well as manmade bird boxes. Although it is fundamentally monogamous, the male owl has been known to take up with two females and remain in this avian ménage à trois throughout its lifetime. The screech owl suffers from loss of habitat and pesticide poisoning.

Barn Owl (*Tyto alba*) Nicknames: monkey-faced owl, white owl / Status: FL=stable with a slight decline, IUCN=LC / Life span: to 15 years / Length: 13-16 in. (32-40 cm) / Wingspan: 39-49 in. (100-125 cm) / Weight: 14-25 oz (.39.70 kg) / Nests on islands / Found: IW.

In *The Sanybel Light*, a memoir by long-time islander Charles LeBuff, the author tells the story of a barn owl chick found by his friend, Bob Sabatino, near the Sanibel Lighthouse. By the time it was an adult, the owl, named Hoot, had become quite tame, and Sabatino occasionally took it to the Sanibel Audubon meetings in the early 1970s. Sabatino would have Hoot fly over the top of the crowd, then come back and land on his heavily padded arm. Owls can be trained in much the same manner as falcons. It is a barn owl that is featured in the Harry Potter films, magically transforming itself into a schoolmarm upon landing at the head of the class.

©ThroughTheLensGallery.com

This species of owl is almost completely nocturnal, so the chances of seeing one on either Sanibel or Captiva is extremely slim. The barn owl is one of the most widely distributed birds in the world, occurring on every continent except Antarctica and having 46 different races worldwide.

It is successful for good reason; it has several features that are nothing short of amazing. It may well possess the most acute sense of hearing of any wild animal. It has asymmetrically positioned ear openings, and its disk-shaped face amplifies sounds in a similar fashion as those parabolic dishes seen in spy movies. It is able to locate field mice in complete darkness or find burrowing moles under the cover of a deep snow. Its call is either an unusual hissing sound or a high-pitched screech, both of which are very disconcerting in the dark of night.

The barn owl eats mostly rodents, small rabbits, and an occasional grackle or other small bird. It nests in attics, barns, and hollowed-out trees. It is susceptible to automobile collisions. It is also one of the only birds in the world where the female of the species is more attractive than the male.

☐ _____ **Turkey Vulture** (*Cathartes aura*) Nicknames: turkey buzzard / Status: FL=stable, IUCN=LC / Life span: to 16 years / Length: 25-32 in. (64-81cm) / Wingspan: 67-70 in. (170-178 cm) / Weight: 3.2 lb (1.45 kg) / Nests on islands / Found: GB, IW, MZ, UA.

© Hung V. Do

The turkey vulture is one of the easiest birds to spot on Sanibel and Captiva. All you really have to do is to look up. The only time you will not see them soaring above the islands is in the early morning before the rising thermals form. One consistent location for viewing vultures is high above the microwave tower located just west of Tarpon Bay Road. Later in the evening vultures can be seen roosting on that same tower.

A carrion feeder, the turkey vulture thrives on roadkill, red-tide incidents (feeding on washed-up fish carcasses), and other dead animals. When there is a shortage of carrion, it feeds on garbage, vegetables, and even pumpkins, so it is actually an omnivore. Even though the vulture—with its unsavory eating habits, bald head, and dark black body—is considered unattractive by most birders, it plays an important role in the ecosystem. It quickly removes dead chicks from rookeries and feeds on stillborn livestock and other large carcasses such as deer and bear. This niche behavior greatly reduces the risk of diseases spreading from the decaying flesh. The vulture makes up the biological cleaning crew of the wilderness.

Whereas the black vulture feeds by sight, the turkey vulture feeds by both sight and smell. It has the most sophisticated olfactory sense of any bird in the world, able to spot and smell carrion from heights of up to 200 feet.

The turkey vulture tends to be less social than its close cousin, the black vulture. Although the turkey vulture is easily and frequently spotted soaring overhead, almost no one ever sees its nests. This is in large part because it nests either on the ground in dense cover such as Brazilian pepper or white mangrove thickets where it builds a minimal nest of raked stones, dried leaves, and wood chips, or in hollowed-out tree stumps with narrow entrances.

It has several other unique behaviors, including a propensity to defecate on its own legs, using the evaporation of the water to cool down. When alarmed, the turkey vulture has been known to throw up on its attackers.

Because of its tendency to feed on roadkill, the turkey vulture is often hit by automobiles. It is also sometimes killed by predators such as panthers in an effort to keep the vulture off of fresh kills.

❏ _____ **Black Vulture** (*Coragyps atratus*) Nicknames: black buzzard / Status: FL=stable, expanding into the Northeast, IUCN=LC / Life span: to 25 years / Length: 24-27 in. (60-68 cm) / Wingspan: 54-60 in. (137-152 cm) / Weight: 4.8 lb (2.18 kg) / Nests on islands / Found: GB, IW, MZ.

The black vulture commonly soars with the turkey vulture and is hard to distinguish from its close cousin when more than 100 feet high. As it gets closer to the ground, the black vulture's grayish-black head and whitish wing tips become easier to distinguish. Another difference between the two birds is the

©ThroughTheLensGallery.com

wing shape in flight. Whereas the turkey vulture tends to keep its wings in a distinctive V shape, the black vulture keeps its wings flatter, flapping far more often than do turkey vultures.

There are other differences. The black vulture does not have the well-developed sense of smell of the turkey vulture. As a result, it often lets a solitary turkey vulture discover the kill, then gangs up to chase the solitary bird off and take over the carcass. It also sometimes preys on live chicks in heron and pelican rookeries.

Although its wingspan and body are shorter, the black vulture weighs more than the turkey vulture and is more aggressive. It tends to be less common along the coastline than inland but is readily found soaring above Sanibel and Captiva.

It nests on the ground, preferring open spaces amidst dense saw-palmetto thickets.

❏ _____ **Double-crested Cormorant** (*Phalacrocorax auritus*)

Nicknames: shag / Status: FL=stable and expanding its range, IUCN=LC / Life span: to 22 years / Length: 28-35 in. (70-90 cm) / Wingspan: 45-48 in. (114-123 cm) / Weight: 4 lb (1.81 kg) / Nests on islands / Found: GB, IW, MZ.

Related to the pelican family, the cormorant is commonly seen throughout the islands. Often found near marinas and boat docks, it has also been known to steal small fish from anglers before they can land them. An accomplished swimmer, the cormorant can dive to 25 feet and hold its breath for well over a minute. It eats mostly fish, catching them with its beak while underwater.

Although the cormorant was affected by the use of DDT and similar pesticides, it has recovered, and the population is expanding into the interior of North America where it has been known to decimate fish farms. It is sometimes killed by fishermen who blame the bird for declining fish populations in freshwater lakes. The cormorant is often mistaken for the anhinga, especially when swimming, but the cormorant has a much thicker neck and a noticeable hooked bill. It nests in colonies, most of the time exclusively with other cormorants.

Anhinga (*Anhinga anhinga*) Nicknames: snakebird, water turkey, darter / Status: FL=stable, IUCN=LC / Life span: Life span: to 11 years / Length: 30-37 in. (75-95 cm) / Wingspan: 45-48 in. (114-123 cm) / Weight: 2.7 lb (1.22 kg) / Nests on islands / Found: IW, MZ.

One of the most photographed birds on Sanibel, the anhinga can be seen at almost any time of the day along Wildlife Drive in the "Ding" Darling refuge drying its wings. The name *anhinga,* which comes from the Tupi-speaking natives of the Amazon basin, means "evil spirit of the woods." Locally it is often referred to as the snakebird because of its ability to swim through the water with only its long, snakelike neck exposed.

When in full breeding plumage, the male anhinga sports a stunning black and white neck, back, and forewings that resemble piano keys. The female anhinga has a brown neck and breast. Because of its similar size and feeding habits, the anhinga is easily confused with the cormorant. Unlike the cormorant, however, the anhinga is an excellent flyer and can sometimes be seen soaring with wood storks and vultures high above the islands.

©ThroughTheLensGallery.com

The anhinga, a distant relative to the pelican, has evolved a unique style of fishing. Unlike the cormorant, the anhinga has no natural oils in its feathers. That, coupled with its dense bone structure, allows the anhinga to sink once its feathers become saturated with water. Also unlike the cormorant, the anhinga seldom grasps its prey but instead impales the pinfish or sand trout on its dagger-like beak, which comes complete with serrations on the top bill, preventing the fish from slipping off once the anhinga resurfaces. The anhinga carefully flips the minnow off of its beak and swallows it whole.

Its unusual perching behavior, with its large wings spread wide open, occurs because the anhinga becomes completely waterlogged after foraging. Sometimes, when startled and still too wet to fly, the anhinga will simply fall back into the water creating a loud, unexpected splash.

Although its principal diet is fish, the anhinga has been known to eat baby alligators, water snakes, leeches, and frogs. Monogamous and colonial, it often nests with egrets and herons.

Yes, it did make it down.   ©ThroughTheLensGallery.com

Mottled Duck (*Anas fulvigula*) Nicknames: Florida duck, summer mallard / Status: FL=stable, IUCN=LC / Life span: to 13 years / Length: 17-24 in. (44-61 cm) / Wingspan: 30-33 in. (76-83 cm) / Weight: 2.3 lb (1.04 kg) / Nests on islands / Found: IW.

Often seen in pairs, the mottled duck is readily observed in the Bailey Tract in the early morning and evenings. It tends to fly just above the treetops and can be heard making a distinctive *quack, quack, quack* as it travels. Both male and female mottled ducks bear a resemblance to a female mallard duck.

Mottled duck family   © Blake Sobczak

The mottled duck is a game bird in Florida and is heavily hunted in the St. Johns River marshes in north central Florida, as well as other wetlands across the state. More than 13,000 mottled ducks are harvested annually. On Sanibel the mottled duck is far tamer than the migratory blue-winged teal and if approached slowly, will not fly away. It feeds primarily on small crustaceans, insects, and mollusks but will also filter-feed on vegetation. In shallow water it can be observed tipping, with its head buried in the muck and only its tail feathers sticking out of the water.

It is monogamous, mating very early in life, and it keeps solitary nests in dense vegetation. On the mainland the mottled duck has even been known to nest in tomato fields. It is in danger of losing its identity as a result of hybridization with feral mallards across the state. The chicks and eggs are preyed upon by snakes, alligators, snapping turtles, and hawks.

☐ _____ **Common Moorhen** (*Gallinula chloropus*)
Nicknames: Florida gallinule, pond chicken / Status: FL= stable to slightly declining, IUCN=LC / Life span: to 10 years / Length: 13-14 in. (32-35 cm) / Wingspan: 21-24 in. (54-62 cm) / Weight: 12 oz (0.34 kg) / Nests on islands / Found: IW, MZ.

This widely distributed member of the rail family ranges from Argentina into southern Canada. Unlike its secretive cousins, the clapper rail and the king rail, the moorhen is not a shy bird. It is easily approached and photographed, often without need of a telephoto lens.

Using its oversized yellow-green feet, it works its way through cattails and rushes along the edges of lakes and ponds. Lacking webbed feet, the moorhen has a curious swimming stroke, appearing to bob its head with every stroke. A close relative, the purple gallinule, is a beautiful purple version of the moorhen but is seldom seen on Sanibel, preferring the habitat of the Everglades and other wetlands.

One easy way to identify the moorhen is by its distinctive candy-corn bill, which has a yellow tip and red beak in the shape of a candy corn protruding from its unique red frontal shield. The moorhen is a very vocal bird—hence the nickname pond chicken—making a variety of clucks, screams, squeaks, and pips.

Common Moorhen ©ThroughTheLensGallery.com

The moorhen is preyed upon by weasels, raccoons, and bobcats, and its nests are targeted by snakes. Its biggest problem is continued loss of wetlands habitat. It is common in Florida but a species of special concern in several midwestern and northeastern states.

🔲 _____ **Laughing Gull** (*Larus atricilla*) Nicknames: black-headed gull / Status: FL=stable, increasing its range, IUCN=LC / Life span: to 19 years / Length: 15-18 in. (39-46 cm) / Wingspan: 36-47 in. (92-120 cm) / Weight: 11.5 oz (.33 kg) / Nests on islands / Found: GB, MZ.

Known for its distinctive, laugh-like call, the laughing gull is the most common seagull on Sanibel and Captiva. It dons a black cap during breeding season, but during most of the year is far less conspicuous, with a white head, gray wings, and blackish markings. The juvenile coloration is a mottled gray before reaching adult plumage in three years.

©Rob Pailes, Santiva Images

This gull gathers along the spoil islands of the causeway, as well as almost anywhere along the beaches. It feeds on fish, crustaceans, insects, carrion, eggs, young birds, and refuse. It frequently raids unattended picnic grounds when the unsuspecting tourists head out for a swim. It may also sit atop a pelican's head waiting for it to strain out the saltwater and feed on the overflowing minnows.

The laughing gull is monogamous and a strong colonial nester. In nearby Tampa Bay there are islands where up to 10,000 laughing gulls mate and nest at one time.

Laughing Gull   © Joseph Blanda, M.D.

© Rob Pailes, Santiva Images

☐ _____ **Snowy Plover** (*Charadrius alexandrinus*) Nicknames: Cuban snowy plover / Status: FL=threatened, IUCN=LC / Life span: to 11 years / Length: 6-7 in. (15-17 cm) / Wingspan: 13 in. (34 cm) / Weight: 1.22 oz (.05 kg or 34-58 g) / Nests on islands / Found: GB.

The snowy plover is a very small, delicate-looking shorebird that is suffering from coastal overdevelopment. Human disturbances, such as unleashed dogs, children, and in some areas, automobiles being driven on the beaches, have all contributed to the rapid decline of this once familiar species. Arguably Florida's most threatened bird, some estimates put its total number between 220 and 400 nesting pairs.

© Rob Pailes, Santiva Images

The snowy plover is often mistaken for the piping plover but has dark legs and an all-black beak as opposed to the yellow-orange legs and orange and black bill of the piping plover. The snowy plover is quite a bit smaller than the killdeer or Wilson's plover.

It feeds on small crustaceans and soft invertebrates such as sand flies. Its nest

Male Snowy Plover   © Rob Pailes, Santiva Images

consists of some shallow scrapes of assorted shells upon which two to three pale, dotted eggs are laid, sometimes up to two broods annually. Young plovers leave the nest within three hours of hatching.

The plover's only defense is camouflage, flattening itself against the ground when a predator or a person approaches. Predation to the nests comes from dogs, gulls, rodents, snakes, and ghost crabs. Its primary threat is continued coastal development and loss of suitable beach dune habitats. On Sanibel plover nesting areas are sometimes marked off by stakes and yellow police tape. Under no circumstances should dogs, children, or adults be allowed into these roped-off areas, as the tiny eggs of the snowy plover are all but impossible to spot and are easily stepped on.

☐ _____ **Wilson's Plover** (*Charadrius wilsonia*) / Nicknames: ringneck, thick-billed plover / Status: FL=stable, IUCN=LC / Life span: to 10 years / Length: 8 in. (20 cm) / Wingspan: 14-16 in. (35-40 cm) / Weight: 1.9 oz (53 g) / Nests on islands / Found: GB, MZ.

© Rob Pailes, Santiva Images

Named after an early ornithologist, Alexander Wilson, who first discovered the bird in 1913 at Cape May, New Jersey, this plover is considerably larger than the snowy plover. The primary differences are the neckband, which for the Wilson's plover continues all around the bird's neck—hence the nickname ringneck. Another noticeable difference is the thicker, longer black bill, allowing the Wilson's plover to feed on larger prey, such as fiddler crabs, crustaceans, and insects.

The primary habitat for the Wilson's plover is along the water's edge, where it looks for coquinas, marine worms, and other prey. Like its cousin the killdeer, both the male and female feign a broken wing when its nest or chicks are approached by animals or beachcombers. The Wilson's plover is monogamous and a solitary nester. Its primary threat is continued beach-front development, which results in loss of suitable nesting habitat.

☐ _____ **Killdeer** (*Charadrius vociferus*) Nicknames: kildee, meadow plover / Status: FL=thriving because of its ability to adapt to urban environments, IUCN=LC / Life span: to 11 years / Length: 8-11 in. (20-28 cm) / Wingspan: 18-19 in. (46-48 cm) / Weight: 3.2 oz (90 g) / Nests on island / Found GB, IW.

© Sara Yunsoo Kim Photography

Perhaps most famous for its loud, familiar call, *killdeeahdeedee,* the killdeer's scientific name aptly describes its behavior: *vociferous,* meaning loud and vocal. Often found in the Sanibel Gardens Preserve or the Bailey Tract, the killdeer is a fairly large plover that frequents uplands, as well as beaches. Larger than the Wilson's plover, the killdeer is most easily recognized by its double-banded neck and its distinctive call.

One of the most successful of all plovers, the killdeer is an example of an animal that not only has learned to adapt to the ways of man, but also flourishes in any number of urban or suburban environments. It nests in baseball fields, gravel rooftops, railroad yards, and scores of similarly unlikely locations. Because of this adaptation, the killdeer is prone to pesticide poisoning and traffic and window collisions, among a host of other metropolitan dangers. Despite some losses, the killdeer population continues to expand, reaching all the way from the northern fringe of Chile to British Columbia.

Killdeer chick   © Sara Yunsoo Kim Photography

The killdeer's diet consists almost entirely of insects, but it will also take small crustaceans and an occasional seed. It is a solitary nester and will feign a broken wing if you approach too near to its nesting locale.

☐ _____ **Fish Crow** (*Corvus ossifragus*) Nicknames: crow / Status: FL=stable, IUCN=LC / Life span: to 14 years / Length: 14-16 in. (36-40 cm) / Wingspan: 33 in. (84 cm) / Weight: 7-12 oz (.19-.34 kg) / Nests on islands / Found: UA, GB, IW, MZ, CW.

Fish crow with pretzel © Joseph Blanda, M.D.

The fish crow, although slightly smaller, is all but impossible to discern from the American crow. That being said, the American crow is almost never found on Sanibel and Captiva, so the chances are that any crow you see on the islands is a fish crow. One distinctive difference is in the call; the fish crow is famous for its nearly constant *cah, uh-uh*.

The fish crow is unique in that it is one of very few birds endemic to North America. It does not have the range of the American crow, extending only as far north as Tennessee, while the American crow's range extends all the way to the Northwest Territories. The American crow far outnumbers the fish crow. Unlike its cousin, however, the fish crow does not appear to be as vulnerable to the West Nile virus, which in some regions has decimated American crow populations.

A highly adaptable bird, the fish crow feeds on garbage, eggs, insects, carrion, ticks from livestock, various berries, and some fruit. Like all crows, jays, and ravens, the fish crow appears to be capable of learned behaviors. the fish crow, for example, has learned to pick up a mollusk, fly high above a rock pile or highway and release it, breaking the shellfish open so the bird can feed on it. While not quite at the same level as the tool-using green heron, it is a fascinating example of avian intelligence.

Huge flocks of fish crows, called *murders*, roost on islands in and around St. Petersburg and Tampa where they number in the thousands. The fish crow has adapted well to the habits of *Homo sapiens* and because of that is expanding its range throughout the Southeast.

🔲 _____ **Mourning Dove** (*Zenaida macroura*) Nicknames: turtle doves, Carolina dove, wood dove / Status: FL=thriving, Florida's population alone is estimated at 50 million birds, IUCN=LC / Life span: to 31 years / Length: 12 in. (30 cm) / Wingspan: 17-19 in. (37-48 cm) / Weight: 4.3 oz (.12 kg) / Nests on islands / Found: UA, IW.

©ThroughTheLensGallery.com

With a total population in the United States of approximately 350 million birds—even with an annual harvest of more than 20 million doves by hunters (2 million are taken in Florida alone)—the mourning dove is in no imminent danger of extinction. Although impressive, these numbers pale in comparison with its extinct cousin, the passenger pigeon, whose numbers at the time of European contact have been estimated at 5 to 7 billion.

The mourning dove has two very distinctive characteristics that distinguish it from its European relative, the Eurasian collared dove: it is the dove responsible for the familiar *ooah, woo, woo, woo* call; and it whistles when it takes flight.

A highly adaptable bird, the mourning dove has flourished under the environmental changes brought on by mankind. It has learned to live comfortably in urban, suburban, and agricultural settings. On Sanibel and Captiva the mourning dove is ubiquitous, seen perched on telephone wires, sign posts, and almost any tall tree.

It feeds predominantly on grains and seeds, and it can be found filling its crop with sandy grit along almost any unpaved road. The grit assists in digesting the various seeds and fruits the dove thrives on. It is also famous for its "crop milk" or "pigeon's milk," which it regurgitates and feeds to its chicks for the first few weeks after hatching.

The mourning dove is preyed upon by falcons, bobcats, and sportsmen. It is monogamous, often pairing for life, and it nests in individual nesting sites, often in very unusual places.

☐ _____ Eurasian Collared-Dove (*Streptopelia decaocto*)

Nicknames: collared turtle dove / Status: FL=thriving, rapidly expanding its current range northward, IUCN=LC / Life span: to 5 years / Length: 11-12 in. (29-31 cm) / Wingspan: 14 in. (35 cm) / Weight: 5-6 oz (.15-.17 kg) / Nests on islands / Found: UA, IW.

Note the distinctive collar © Charles Sobczak

Like the cattle egret, but in this case directly introduced by man, the Eurasian collared-dove is rapidly expanding its range across North America. Originally from western India, this is a bird that has flourished because of repeated human introductions. It was first imported into Turkey in the 1600s, then went on to spread into the Balkans, Greece, Italy, North Africa, and finally swept over all of Europe where it is firmly entrenched. It can also be found across North Africa as far west as Morocco where, as elsewhere, it prefers living in proximity to human development.

It came to Florida via the Bahamas, where approximately 50 doves were released in 1974. The species reached the Florida Keys in the late 1970s and has been moving north and west ever since. They now breed west of the Mississippi, and there are established pockets of Eurasian collared-doves in southern California. Within the next 20 to 40 years this dove will probably inhabit every state in the lower 48, as well as Mexico, Central America, and southern Canada.

The Eurasian collared-dove is slightly larger than the native mourning dove and can be readily distinguished from that bird by the black ring extending half-way around its nape and by its tail, which is squared-off with white outer feathers. Unlike the mourning dove, it does not whistle when taking flight but has been known to make a catbird-like mew when taking off and landing, as well as a similar but much quicker *cacoocuk* when roosting. This dove is monogamous and makes a solitary nest.

Its diet is almost identical to the mourning dove, consisting chiefly of seeds, grains, and occasional insects. This dove has already interbred with the native ringed turtle doves, and there is some speculation that it may be interbreeding with the mourning dove as well. Because of its growing numbers, the Eurasian collared-dove has become an important item in the winter diet of Florida hawks, including the red-shouldered hawk.

❏ _____ **Common Ground-Dove** (*Columbina passerina*)

Nicknames: eastern ground-dove / Status: FL=declining populations throughout the Southeast and along the gulf coast, IUCN=LC / Life span: to 7 years / Length: 6-7 in. (15-18 cm) / Wingspan: 11 in. (27 cm) Weight: 1.1 oz (31 gm) / Nests on islands / Found: GB, IW, MZ.

© Blake Sobczak

The translation of its scientific name accurately describes this beautiful, small bird: sparrow-like dove. Most often seen in pairs or groups of four, it is usually happened upon by accident as it feeds along the bike path of the Indigo Trail in the "Ding" Darling refuge or along shell roads throughout the islands. Because of its diminutive size, it is easy to distinguish from either of the two larger doves.

The underside of the common ground-dove has a reddish hue, and its wings have gray, brown, and purplish spots. It is an attractive bird and relatively common throughout the islands.

When disturbed it tends to fly a short distance and land, only to do the same thing again and again until it finally turns and flies behind you. Like its larger cousins, the ground-dove feeds on seeds, grains, and small berries. It is monogamous, and it is widely believed that pairs mate for life.

❏ _____ **Red-bellied Woodpecker** (*Melanerpes carolinus*)

Nicknames: zebra woodpecker, ladderback, orange sapsucker / Status: FL=stable to slightly expanding its range, IUCN=LC / Life span: to 12 years / Length: 9 in. (24 cm) / Wingspan: 13-17 in. (33-42 cm) / Weight: 23 oz (65-91 gm) / Nests on islands / Found IW, MZ.

Anyone with a home on Sanibel or Captiva may be all too familiar with the habits of this medium-size woodpecker. In the spring, during the breeding season, it loves to hammer on tin roofs, hollow trees, or anything loud that might attract a mate but will assuredly drive the homeowners half-crazy. This noisy bird also makes a trill-like sound that is fairly easy to identify, resembling a rolling *churrr, churr, churr* sound, like a gargled chirp.

This species is misnamed because it doesn't have much of a red belly. Its underside has a slightly rosy hue, but it is far easier to identify from its partially red head and beautiful back markings, which resemble a black and white ladder, hence its nickname, ladderback.

One amazing characteristic of the woodpecker is the length of its tongue. Although shorter than that

© Rob Pailes, Santiva Images

of some species, the male red-bellied woodpecker's tongue can be up to four inches long, protruding deep into holes and crevices where it pulls out arthropods, a primary part of the woodpecker's diet. It also eats seeds, nuts, sap, and fruit and has been known to feed on tree frogs and small lizards.

The red-bellied woodpecker loves nesting boxes and can be found using them in the Sanibel Gardens Preserve, the Bailey Tract, and other locations around the islands. It sometimes competes with starlings for the best nesting boxes, and it's not unusual to see the two species quarreling over them. This woodpecker is sometimes taken by hawks, and its nests, when in trees rather than nesting boxes, can be raided by palm rats and snakes. It is monogamous and mates for life.

Displaying its red belly   © Hung V. Do

Pileated Woodpecker (*Dryocopus pileatus*)

Nicknames: lord-god, good-god, woodchuck, cock-o-the-woods / Status: FL=stable, IUCN=LC / Life span: to 12 years / Length: 16-19 in. (40-49 cm) / Wingspan: 26-30 in. (66-76 cm) / Weight: 9-12.5 oz (.25-.35 kg) / Nests on islands / Found: IW, MZ.

©ThroughTheLensGallery.com

This is the infamous woodpecker that was the role model for the cartoon character, Woody the Woodpecker. Its unmistakable call is a loud, ringing *kukkukkuk*. A fairly large bird, about the same size as a fish crow, the pileated can be seen flying around the islands and is noted for a series of quick, rapid wing flaps followed by a pause that always results in the bird quickly losing altitude.

With its bold red crest and large black bill, the pileated woodpecker is a very attractive bird. It could be mistaken for the ivory-billed woodpecker, which is slightly larger, has a bone-white bill, and is in all likelihood extinct.

In flight   © Joseph Blanda, M.D.

The pileated is a formidable drilling machine, known to peck so deep into smaller trees that the tree breaks in half. With its very strong beak and a special shock-absorbing head, the pileated working on a hollow log can produce a noise that can carry for blocks on a still morning. Particularly irritating to homeowners is the pileated's obsession with drilling holes into the outside of houses, wood siding, window frames, pilings, you name it. There are plenty of island residents who will tell you what they think about this accomplished woodsmith, though some of what they say might not be repeatable.

The pileated feeds extensively on ants, beetles and beetle larvae, seeds, and fruit. It is monogamous and known to nest in wooden bird boxes (you can generally tell if a pileated is using the box if the entranceway has been chiseled open to the size of your fist), hollowed-out telephone poles, and larger trees. Its eggs and chicks are sometimes preyed upon by snakes, rats, and raccoons, but for the most part it has few natural enemies once it reaches adult size. Because it prefers taller trees, the pileated is vulnerable to lightning strikes.

☐ _____ **Northern Mockingbird** (*Mimus polyglottos*)
Nicknames: mockingbird, eastern mockingbird / Status: FL=stable, IUCN=LC / Life span: to 14 years / Length: 8-10 in. (21-26 cm) / Wingspan: 12-14 in. (31-35 cm) / Weight: 1.59-2.05 oz (45-48 g) / Nests on island / Found: UA, IW, MZ.

"Mockingbirds don't do one thing but make music for us to enjoy...but sing their hearts out for us. That's why it's a sin to kill a mockingbird."
Made famous by Harper Lee's riveting tale of racism and intolerance in *To Kill a Mockingbird*, this small passerine (perching bird) is Florida's state bird and

its most beloved singer. Scientific observation has confirmed that the scope and beauty of its songs are nothing short of amazing. A northern mockingbird, which might live to be 14 years old, will add variations to its own song throughout its entire adult life. It has been noted to sing more than 400 song types and has a unique ability to mimic other species' songs, hence the name.

© Joseph Blanda, M.D.

The male has two distinct sets of songs: one for spring and another for the fall. It is sheer joy to sit back and take in the lovely serenade of this magnificent songbird perched high atop a telephone pole in the early evening. On moonlit nights the mockingbird has been known to sing straight through until dawn.

Florida's state bird, the mockingbird has adapted well to *Homo sapiens*, expanding its range all the way into Alaska by learning to live in proximity to human development. This bird exemplifies wildlife's ability to adapt to the new habitat of urban areas. It can be found throughout the islands and is easily distinguished from its close cousin, the catbird, by its gray and white plumage.

The mockingbird feeds predominantly on insects, berries, and invertebrates. Monogamous and breeding for life, the mockingbird is a bird you will want to slow down and listen to if you happen upon one singing. It is a true delight.

___

Blue-gray Gnatcatcher (*Polioptila caerulea*)

Nicknames: none / Status: FL=stable, IUCN=LC / Life span: to 4 years / Length: 4 in. (10-11 cm) / Wingspan: 6 in. (16 cm) / Weight: .18-.25 oz (57 g) / Nests on islands / Found IW.

© Hung V. Do

Sometimes called a miniature mockingbird, the blue-gray gnatcatcher is similar in coloration and, like the mockingbird, loves to mimic other bird songs. Although a number of these diminutive birds are year-round residents, the population greatly increases during the winter months with the southern migration of additional gnatcatchers. Thus, it is far easier to find this bird during the tourist season.

Of course, if you do see a blue-gray gnatcatcher, don't expect it to stay still for very long. Like many of the smaller birds, it is a hyperactive creature, flitting around the understory in a constant search for midges, gnats, spiders, and small insects. This is one of very few birds on Sanibel that feeds on the notorious no-see-um. It not only picks insects off of branches and vegetation but also can sally insects in flight.

The gnatcatcher is monogamous and a solitary nester. Because of its small size, it is vulnerable to insecticides and related chemical pollutants. It also has to deal with cowbird parasitism, wherein the much larger cowbird female lays her eggs in the gnatcatcher's nest,

Blue grey gnatcatcher   © Clair Postmus

eliminating any chance of survival for the gnatcatcher's offspring and forcing it to rear a chick nearly 10 times the size of an adult gnatcatcher.

☐_____ **European Starling** (*Sturnus vulgaris*) Nicknames: blackbird / Status: FL= thriving, IUCN=LC / Life span: to 15 years / Length: 8-9 in. (20-23 cm) / Wingspan: 12-16 in. (31-40 cm) / Weight: 2.12-3.39 oz. (60-96 g) / Nests on islands / Found: UA, IW, MZ.

In 1890, and again in 1891, some 100 starlings were released in Central Park, in New York City. It was an ill-conceived effort by a misguided literary guild to introduce all the birds of Shakespeare's works into the New World. Today, the European starling ranges from Alaska to northern Mexico and numbers in excess of 200 million. It is continuing to spread southward into Central America and over time will more than likely inhabit all of South

© Sara Yunsoo Kim Photography

America.

©ThroughTheLensGallery.com

The sad part of this tale is that the starling's expansion comes at the expense of many native birds, including the Eastern bluebird, great crested flycatchers, and all of the indigenous woodpeckers. The problem is that the starling is a cavity nester, and because of its sheer numbers, it uses so many of the available nesting sites that the other native birds cannot find suitable habitats to raise their own broods.

One major factor in the success of the starling is its ability to adapt to urban and suburban settings. It has learned to forage in dumpsters and picnic areas, even going so far as picking insects off of car radiators in supermarket parking lots.

The starling feeds on seeds, insects, fruit, and various berries. It is mostly monogamous, but individual males can be polygamous.

❑ _____ **House Sparrow** (*Passer domesticus*) Nicknames: English sparrow, weaver finch / Status: FL=thriving, IUCN=LC / Life span: to 15 years / Length: 6 in. (14 cm) / Wingspan: 7-10 in. (19-25 cm) / Weight: .92-1.13 oz (26-32 g) / Nests on islands / Found: UA, IW.

©ThroughTheLensGallery.com

Birders can find a well-established flock of these imported sparrows at Bailey's General Store at the corner of Tarpon Bay Road and Periwinkle Way. There, as in other urban settings, the sparrow flits about the rafters and spends most of the day foraging for insects, bread crumbs, and whatever else it can find in and around the parking lot. Well adapted to human beings, the house sparrow is another runaway import whose population numbers in the hundreds of millions.

Originally introduced from England into New York City in 1850 and 1851, possibly by the same literary group that brought the European starling over, this small brown sparrow now ranges from the Northwest Territories of Canada to Tierra del Fuego in Chile. The house sparrow is not as controversial an import as is the starling, however, since it is not a cavity nester and prefers strictly urban environments. It is a flying mouse in that it is hardly ever found

Female House Sparrow
©ThroughTheLensGallery.com

away from human agricultural or urban settings. The house sparrow loves fast-food joints, gas stations, and grocery stores. There are well-established colonies of these birds living inside large chain stores such as Home Depot and Lowe's.

The house sparrow feeds on seeds and grains. Its biggest threats are housecats, sparrow hawks, and encounters with vehicles. The sparrow is monogamous and nests in loosely formed colonies. Its call is a consistent *chirrup, chirrup, chirrup*. The male of this species wears a far more interesting feather pattern than the females.

❒ _____ **Northern Cardinal** (*Cardinalis cardinalis*)
Nicknames: none / Status: FL=stable, IUCN=LC / Life span: to 15 years / Length: 8-9 in. (21-23 cm) / Wingspan: 10-12 in. (25-31 cm) / Weight: 1.48-1.69 oz (42-48 g) / Nests on island / Found: UA, IW, MZ.

Northern Cardinal   © Hung V. Do

The brilliantly colored northern cardinal holds the record for being named a state bird, having achieved that honor in seven states: Illinois, Indiana, Kentucky, North Carolina, Ohio, Virginia, and West Virginia. (The meadowlark comes in second with six states, and the mockingbird, Florida's state bird, is a close third with five.) On Sanibel and Captiva, the northern cardinal is always a delight to see, especially during the spring when the male takes on its richer breeding plumage, giving its bright red color an almost fluorescent hue. The female has a duller coloration that sometimes resembles a cedar waxwing. The cardinal raises up to three broods during the breeding season, which runs from March through August.

The male northern cardinal can often be found pecking at itself in rearview mirrors, tinted windows, and even hubcaps. Extremely territorial, the male will

Female Northern Cardinal   © Hung V. Do

shag off rivals that stray into its well-defended area. The cardinal feeds primarily on seeds and berries, and contributes to the dissemination of poison ivy throughout Sanibel and Captiva by eating the seeds of the ivy then scattering them via its digestive tract.

The cardinal is monogamous and a solitary nester. It is occasionally subject to parasitic cowbird hatchlings, and its nests are sometimes raided by fish crows, grackles, snakes, and rats. The cardinal is expanding its range westward and northward across the United States.

☐ _____ **Common Grackle** (*Quiscalus quiscula*) Nicknames: jackdaw, Florida grackle, crow, blackbird / Status: FL=stable to expanding, IUCN=LC / Life span: to 22 years / Length: 11-13 in. (28-34 cm) / Wingspan: 14-18 in. (36-46 cm) / Weight: 2.6-5 oz (74-142 g) / Nests on islands / Found: UA, IW.

The grackle is one of the most common birds found on Sanibel. Like the starling, sparrow, and its cousin, the boat-tailed grackle, the common grackle is most often found in and around parking lots, dumpsters, and similar urban or suburban settings. Readily identified by several telltale signs, the common grackle is an easy bird to add to your island wildlife list.

One of those signs is the bird's distinct call: a short, high-pitched squeak that sounds like a metal gate opening that is in desperate need of oil. Other identifiable details are the pale yellow eyes and the oil-slick coloration, especially on the male. The grackle is easy to

© Hung V. Do

©ThroughTheLensGallery.com

distinguish from the similar-size starling by the color of its bill—the grackle's bill is solid black, whereas the starling has a long and pointed yellow bill.

The common grackle engages in an odd behavior called anting. It allows ants to crawl all over its body or sometimes catches the ants, squishes them in its beak, then rubs them all over its feathers in a practice believed to reduce parasites. The common grackle will sometimes resort to lemons or mothballs when it cannot find the ant-based formic acid.

The grackle is an opportunistic feeder. It eats insects, mice, seeds, berries, and refuse and has been observed wading into the water to catch minnows. For the most part the grackle is monogamous, but some males are known to be polygamous. It nests in colonies with other blackbirds. Large flocks sometimes cause problems in agricultural areas.

□ _____ **Boat-tailed Grackle** (*Quiscalus major*) Nicknames: jackdaw / Status: FL=stable to expanding, IUCN=LC / Life span: to 12 years / Length: 10-15 in. (26-37 cm) / Wingspan: 15-20 in. (39-50 cm) / Weight: 3.28-8.44 oz (92-239 g) / Nests on islands / Found: UA, IW.

Similar to but quite a bit larger than the common grackle, the boat-tailed grackle is not as often seen on the islands. Easy to recognize by its unusually long, keel-shaped tail, the boat-tailed grackle is Florida's largest blackbird. The female of this species is much browner in color, resembling a cowbird.

The boat-tailed grackle is one of the few birds that are not monogamous, and it has developed an unusual mating system similar to that of American elk and other ungulates. A single bird becomes the dominant male and defends his personal harem in a form of avian polygamy. Although the dominant male may get almost 90 percent of the copulations in his harem, we now know, thanks to modern DNA testing, that he actually sires only 25 percent of the offspring. The female grackle steps out repeatedly on the male while off foraging for food. This behavior helps to keep the gene pool far more diverse than it would first appear.

Like the other blackbirds, the boat-tailed grackle is an opportunistic feeder. It eats small fish, snails, aquatic and terrestrial insects, small birds, bird and reptile eggs, berries, grains, and seeds.

© Hung V. Do

Prairie Warbler (*Dendroica discolor*) Nicknames: Florida prairie warbler / Status: FL=stable, IUCN=LC / Life span: to 10 years / Length: 4.75 in. (12 cm) / Wingspan: 7.5 in. (19 cm) / Weight: .3 oz. (8.5 g) / Nests on islands / Found: IW, MZ.

In a classic case of poor name selection, the prairie warbler is seldom found on prairies. This tiny warbler much prefers the dense understory of mangroves and shrubbery. The prairie warbler is now believed to be of two different races, one slightly larger and living in the mangrove forests. Although the islands have a resident population, these birds are joined every winter by many more migrant birds, which makes spotting a prairie warbler much easier during the winter months.

© Judd Patterson Photography

This is a very small, quick bird, so it is more difficult to photograph than, say, a sun-drying anhinga. Like all warblers, the prairie warbler has a lovely song. You are far more likely to hear one than to see it. It eats mostly spiders and insects, which it gathers from the branches and leaves of the red mangrove.

The prairie warbler is monogamous, though the males are sometimes polygamous. It is a solitary nester, raising one to two broods per year. It is preyed upon by larger birds, snakes, lizards, and other nest predators.

❏ _____ **Common Yellowthroat** (_Geothlypis trichas_)

Nicknames: Maryland yellowthroat / Status: FL=stable, IUCN=LC / Life span: to 11 years / Length: .45 in. (11-13 cm) / Wingspan: 6-7 in. (15-19 cm) / Weight: .32-.35 oz (9-10 g) / Nests on islands / Found: IW.

Because the common yellowthroat is so small, its eggs, chicks, and even the adults are often preyed upon by loggerhead shrikes, kestrels, and other predatory birds. Weighing in at a third of an once—roughly the weight of three pennies—and with its habit of staying well beneath the understory, the yellowthroat is a very difficult bird to spot.

Whereas some bird books identify this tiny bird as monogamous, others state that it is possibly polygamous, while still others admit that the true nature of its breeding behavior remains to be defined. It is prolific enough to be on the menu of an unusual host of predators, including largemouth bass, chuck-will's-widow, and cowbird parasitism. It also suffers from manmade perils such as the straightening of rivers and the loss of wetland habitats. Because of its diminutive size, this bird is especially vulnerable to pesticides and agricultural chemicals.

©ThroughTheLensGallery.com

❏ _____ **Carolina Wren** (_Thryothorus ludovicianus_)

Nicknames: Florida wren / Status: FL=stable to declining, IUCN=LC / Life span: to 9 years / Length: 5-6 in. (12-14 cm) / Wingspan: 7 in. (16 cm) / Weight: .64-.78 oz (18-22 g) / Nests on islands / Found: UA, IW.

© Joseph Blanda, M.D.

Anyone owning a home on Sanibel or Captiva is probably familiar with this energetic little brown bird. The Carolina wren is not only comfortable with human enterprises, but it also takes full advantage of them. You may find these small songbirds building their deep, circular nests around your home in minnow buckets, bike helmets, or under the rafters. Other unlikely nesting locations may include car radiators, mailboxes, or even in clothes hanging on the line.

The Carolina wren is famous for its *teakettle, teakettle, teakettle* song. One captive male was observed to sing his melody 3,000 times in a single day.

This bird is a busybody and extremely inquisitive. It will enter enclosed areas through an open door, turn over pieces of paper, and forage through just about anything in its search for insects, small invertebrates, and seeds.

Monogamous and mating for life, a pair of Carolina wrens can have up to three broods in a given year if conditions are favorable. Because it prefers to forage in the understory in and around human habitation, the Carolina wren is especially vulnerable to being preyed upon by domestic cats and dogs, as well as snakes, rats, and larger birds.

☐ _____ **Blue Jay** (*Cyanocitta cristata*) Nicknames: jaybird / Status: FL=stable to expanding north and west, IUCN=LC / Life span: to 17 years / Length: 10-12 in. (25-30 cm) / Wingspan: 13-17 in. (34-43 cm) / Weight: 2.47-3.5 oz (70-100 g) / Nests on islands / Found: UA, IW.

A member of the crow family, the blue jay is a fairly common sight on the islands. Known for its loud call, *jay, jay, jay,* or sometimes *thief, thief, thief,* this very attractive bird is also an excellent mimic, known to imitate the cry of the red-shouldered hawk and the osprey to the point where even an experienced birder cannot tell the difference.

A fairly large bird, the blue jay often raids the nests of smaller birds, such

© Sara Yunsoo Kim Photography

as the Carolina wren, prairie warbler, and common yellowthroat. It will take both the eggs and sometimes the chicks. This characteristic is somewhat offset by the blue jay's tendency to go after other large predators that would be far more likely to take the adult bird of these same species. That includes eagles, hawks, and owls, which the blue jay harasses to no end when they fly into its territory.

Its diet includes just about anything smaller than itself: carrion, eggs, chicks, acorns, nuts, frogs, fish, snails, small mammals, seeds, and even green and Cuban anoles. Monogamous but not always for life, the blue jay tends to switch partners every few years, allowing for a number of different couplings over its 17-year life span. It is a solitary nester. Hawks and owls prey upon the adult blue jay.

Blue Jay
© Joseph Blanda, M.D.

☐ _____ **American Oystercatcher** (*Haematopus palliatus*)
Nicknames: mantled oystercatcher, brown-backed oystercatcher / Status: FL=declining, species of special concern, IUCN=LC / Life span: to 14 years / Length: 16-17 in. (40-44 cm) / Wingspan: 30-36 in. (76-91 cm) / Weight: .87-1.5 lbs (.39-.68 kg) / Nests on islands / Found: MZ, GB.

An unmistakable bird, both for its distinctive coloration and its large red bill, the American oystercatcher can be a difficult bird to locate on Sanibel and Captiva. It can sometimes be found working the oyster bars in Tarpon Bay or around Buck Key just east of Captiva. There are approximately 400 nesting pairs in all of Florida, with the largest concentration occurring on Cedar Key during the winter months, where flocks of more that 1,000 have been reported.

Feeding   © Sara Yunsoo Kim Photography

Oystercatcher eating a marine worm © Rob Pailes, Santiva Images

The oystercatcher is a very specialized bird, feeding almost exclusively on mollusks, including oysters, clams, and other bivalves. It has also been known to eat amphipods, crabs, barnacles, echinoderms, and, rarely, small fish. It uses its long, strong bill to pry open bivalves and, failing that, will hammer and chip away at the shellfish until the living organism can be consumed.

Initially, the bird's decline could be attributed to overhunting, but it is no longer considered a game bird in any part of its range. Its biggest threat now is nesting-site and habitat loss, especially along the coastlines where it spends the entirety of it life. Other threats include predation by eagles and hawks, and its nests, generally

In flight © Sara Yunsoo Kim Photograhy

on beaches or oyster bars, are sometimes preyed upon by gulls, raccoons, and otters. The oystercatcher is monogamous and a solitary nester.

❏ _____ **Mangrove Cuckoo** (*Coccyzus minor*) Nicknames: none / Status: FL=rare but not formally endangered, common in the Caribbean and Mexico, IUCN=LC / Life span: to 5 years / Length: 11-13 in. (28-32 cm) / Wingspan: 16 in. (40 cm) / Weight: 2.29-2.5 oz (65-72 g) / Nests on islands / Found: MZ.

Many South Florida birders consider a confirmed sighting of a mangrove cuckoo to be the Holy Grail of birding. A very attractive, long, and elegant-looking bird, the mangrove cuckoo is secretive and, because of its foraging environment deep in the red and black mangroves, it is extremely difficult to spot. It is a true tropical species that only recently has found a permanent foothold in Florida, the only place in the continental United States where this bird can be found. More common in the Keys, the mangrove cuckoo has been seen along Wildlife Drive, though rarely.

The mangrove cuckoo feeds on insects and small vertebrates. Because of its reclusive nature, little is known about the Florida population.

Mangrove Cuckoo

© Clair Postmus

Black Skimmer
© Judd Patterson Photography

Migratory Birds
Winter – Summer – Fall – Spring

☐ _____ **American White Pelican** (*Pelecanus erythrorhynchos*)
Nicknames: none / Status: FL=stable to increasing slightly, IUCN=LC / Life span: to 31 years / Length: 60-63 in. (152-160 cm) / Wingspan: 96-110 in. (243-279 cm) / Weight: 15.4 lb (7 kg) / Nests: in the summer in Canada and the north-central Great Plains / Found: fall, winter, and early spring months in MZ

The white pelican is the largest and heaviest bird found on Sanibel. Before its eradication from both islands around 1910, the wild turkey (weighing as much as 24 pounds) would have held this title. The wild turkey was more than likely lost as a result of over-hunting. That being said, however, the white pelican would still have boasted a longer wingspan, measuring nine feet for a mature bird. The white pelican is one of only seven pelican species worldwide; the only other pelican native to North America is the familiar brown pelican. There is one pelican species in South America, the Peruvian pelican, which is similar in appearance to the brown pelican but more than twice as large.

Over the past 20 years the sightings of the white pelican

on Sanibel have increased dramatically. In the early 1990s it was found only on remote barrier islands and along oyster bars in northern Pine Island Sound. Today it can be seen regularly off the third culvert along Wildlife Drive in the J.N. "Ding" Darling National Wildlife Refuge, especially during a midwinter low tide.

A stunning bird to observe in flight, the white pelican has conspicuous black wingtips and trailing edges and carries one of the largest bills in the world. (The Australian pelican, which is seven pounds heavier and has the same coloration, does in fact have the largest bill of any bird species on earth!) During the nesting season the white pelican develops a large, conspicuous plate on its upper bill. The purpose of the plate is not entirely understood but is believed to be related to breeding displays.

Male Pelican in Breeding Plumage

© ThroughTheLensGallery.com

Unlike its brown cousin, the white pelican does not dive for its food. Instead it forms a communal group that herds its catch into shallow water or surrounds a school of minnows, then feeds on them by dipping its large bill into the water and scooping them up. Although it feeds on saltwater fish during the winter months, its primary diet consists of freshwater species such as perch, sunfish, suckers, and carp. As the white pelican's numbers have increased, it has come increasingly in conflict with the growing aquaculture industry in the southeastern United States.

Because of its commanding size, the white pelican has few natural predators. Like many other birds, this pelican was severely impacted by the widespread use of DDT and other pesticides beginning in the 1940s until DDT was banned in the United States in 1972. The white pelican is still recovering from the effects. Despite being a protected species, it is still the target of hunters, its single largest cause of mortality.

Magnificent Frigatebird (*Fregata magnificens*)

Nicknames: man-o'-war bird, pirate of the sea, hurricane bird / Status: FL=stable, IUCN=LC / Life span: to 19 years / Length 35-45 in. (89-116 cm) / Wingspan: 85-88 in. (217-224 cm) / Weight: 2.8-4.2 lb (1.3-1.9 kg) / Nests: in a large colony in Estero Bay and in the Keys / Found: mostly in the spring and summer months gliding high above the islands.

One of the most efficient flying birds in the world, the magnificent frigatebird rivals the albatross family in its ability to remain airborne for extended periods of time. Extremely light, and with an enormous wingspan, it has the lowest wing-loading ratio (weight to wingspan) of any bird in the world. Seemingly suspended in the breeze, the frigatebird resembles a kite or large black bat soaring high overhead.

The frigatebird is kleptoparasitic, a feeding characteristic most often found in insects but also observed in certain birds. This means that the frigatebird will often harass a gannet or boobie into disgorging its catch, then snatch it away from the other bird in midair—hence the nickname, pirate of the sea.

On the open ocean the frigatebird survives on squid, jellyfish, fish, and even young sea turtles. A truly spectacular flyer, the frigatebird has been observed synchronizing its

Male Frigatebird during breeding season   ©Judd Patterson Photography

speed and aligning its direction perfectly to snatch flying fish while the fish is airborne! In the Florida Keys, this foraging behavior makes the frigatebird a welcome sight for anglers searching for the pelagic fishes of the Gulf Stream (dolphin, wahoo, marlin, and tuna) because the frigate tends to follow these predators in hopes of feeding on their by-catch or capturing the flying fish fleeing before them.

Female Frigatebird in flight
©ThroughTheLensGallery.com

The male frigatebird has a large red pouch that it inflates during breeding season. The chicks of the frigatebird are pure white and extremely vulnerable to predation. They remain with the mother for more than a year after hatching, and because of the risk of being killed by other nesting frigatebirds, they are never left unattended. Because of this lengthy upbringing, the female frigate mates once every other year.

The frigatebird has been known to get swept up in major storms. In 1988 Hurricane Gilbert carried a flock of frigatebirds deep into North America, causing record sightings as far north as Ontario. Recent DNA testing has shown that the frigate is more closely related to the penguin than to the pelican family where most scientific literature still places it. Most predation to the frigatebird comes at the nesting site since it has no known predators once this large bird is at sea.

☐ _____ **Common Loon** (*Gavia immer*) Nicknames: great northern diver / Status: FL=stable, IUCN=LC / Life span: to 19 years / Length: 26-36 in. (66-93 cm) / Wingspan: 41-52 in. (105-133 cm) / Weight: 9.1 lb (4.1 kg) / Nests: along the far northern tier of North America / Found in the fall, winter, and spring on occasion in the back bay but far more common in the Gulf of Mexico well offshore.

Although a difficult bird to encounter inshore, the common loon is a frequent sighting in the Gulf of Mexico just off the islands during the winter months. In the gulf it prefers to inhabit the coastal waters between 30 and 100 feet in depth, diving for small fish and crustaceans. When in Florida the loon does not exhibit the beautiful black and white patterns it displays up north. Its winter plumage is a dull brown on the back and neck with a whitish underbelly. In the early morning and sometimes during the evening the wintering loon will give its distinctive cry in the gulf, an unmistakable and unforgettable yodel.

The loon can dive up to 250 feet deep, aided by a dense bone structure found mainly on land-based birds such as the ostrich and emu. To propel itself to such depths its hind legs are placed far back on its body, making it virtually unable to do more than waddle awkwardly on land. These two features combine to create an unusual form of loon mortality. If a loon mistakes a wet parking lot or stretch of

Common Loon in winter plumage © Sara Yunsoo Kim Photography

highway for a lake, then it will not be able to take flight again and unless rescued, will starve to death. Some birds have been forced down onto small ponds in inclement weather and because they need long runways to take flight again, they often succumb to starvation. The loon is also preyed upon by large sea mammals such as porpoise and sharks and along the California coast is sometimes taken by sea otters. The chicks are commonly victims of ravens, minks, snapping turtles, and northern pike.

Because it relies on small fish, the loon is also vulnerable to acid rain, which kills the phytoplankton and in turn starves out lake or pond minnows, causing a collapse in the food chain. Industrial pollutants, especially oil spills, take large numbers of loons annually. Lead poisoning from digesting lead sinkers or buckshot is another cause of mortality, as is entanglement in fishing nets and discarded fishing line. Despite these obstacles, the common loon is not endangered.

The loon is monogamous and a solitary nester. Its nests are always located just a few feet from the water's edge.

☐ _____ **Pied-billed Grebe** (*Podilymbus podiceps*) Nicknames: didapper / Status: FL= stable, IUCN=LC / Life span: to 5 years / Length: 12-15 in. (34-38 cm) / Wingspan: 17.7-24.4 in. (45-62 cm) / Weight: 9-20 oz (.25-.57 kg) / Nests: along the northern tier of North America from the Ohio Valley into far northern Canada / Found: in the late fall through the early spring in MZ; rarely seen in the gulf or along the beaches.

A small waterbird, the pied-billed grebe is a fairly common sighting along Wildlife Drive in the "Ding" Darling refuge in midwinter. It seldom takes flight when threatened or approached, preferring instead to dive for cover. Although it swims and behaves like a duck, the grebe does not have webbed feet; instead each toe has lobes that flare out when paddling.

Female Pied-billed Grebe
© Clair Postmus

Male Pied-billed Grebe
© ThroughTheLensGallery.com

This bird is seldom found far from shore and prefers much shallower water than does the loon or boobie. It is an omnivore and opportunistic, consuming equal amounts of minnows, crustaceans, and vegetative matter, as well as marine insects. During the winter tourist season the tiny pied-billed grebe should be an easy addition to your Sanibel and Captiva life list. The name *pied-billed* refers to the multicolored bill, which develops a dark ring during breeding season. When wintering on the islands, however, the grebe will not display this ring.

Red-breasted Merganser (*Mergus serrator*) Nicknames: sawbill, fish duck, hairy-head / Status: FL=stable, IUCN=LC / Life span: to 9 years / Length: 20-25 in. (51-64 cm) / Wingspan: 26-29 in. (66-74 cm) / Weight: 2.5 lb (1.2 kg) / Nests: in the far north all the way to the edge of the Arctic Ocean / Found: winter months in MZ.

A good-sized diving duck, the red-breasted merganser is quite common and prefers the saltwater estuaries to lakes and ponds when in Florida. The female merganser can often be found in midwinter feeding in the tidal flow located at

Male Red-breasted Merganser in flight   © Sara Yunsoo Kim Photography

Female Red-breasted Mergansers take wing   © Hung V. Do

the first three culverts along Wildlife Drive in the "Ding" Darling refuge. The male of the species tends to prefer the offshore habitat to the back bays and estuaries.

Its annual migration takes the merganser to the far north all the way to Hudson Bay and the coast of Greenland. In the summer, the male merganser sports a black head and crest with iridescent, greenish overtones and a clear white band around the neck. This breeding plumage is almost never apparent while the bird is wintering in Florida.

One of the fastest flying ducks, it has been clocked at more than 100 miles per hour. An extremely adept swimmer, it feeds primarily on fish but has been known to eat shrimp and crabs as well. The merganser is equipped with a serrated mandible, which greatly enhances its ability to hold on to slippery fish.

The red-breasted merganser is primarily monogamous and a solitary ground nester. Predation occurs mostly in the breeding grounds from gulls, coyotes, foxes, hawks, and owls. Because of the fishy flavor of its meat, the merganser is seldom a target of duck hunters.

Male Merganser in breeding plumage

© ThroughTheLensGallery.com

☐ _____ **Hooded Merganser** (*Lophodytes cucullatus*) Nicknames: fish duck / Status: FL=stable, IUCN=LC / Life span: to 11 years / Length 16-19 in. (42-46 cm) / Wingspan: 23-26 in. (58-66 cm) / Weight: 1-1.5 lb (.45-.68 kg) / Nests: in northern Florida all the way to southern Canada / Found: in the winter in MZ.

The hooded merganser is a unique looking bird and a rare sighting on Sanibel. The male has a large fan-shaped crest that is distinctly black and white, while the female more closely resembles a female red-breasted merganser, though smaller. The hooded merganser has a nictitating membrane on its eye that is similar

to that of the American alligator. This additional eyelid is transparent and protects the merganser's eyes while diving.

An excellent underwater swimmer and diver, the hooded merganser feeds on fish, crustaceans, and aquatic insects, as well as plants. Unlike the loon or the red-breasted merganser, this small bird can take off quickly from the water.

Male Hooded Merganser   © ThroughTheLensGallery.com

Its beak is serrated much like a steak knife, allowing it to hold firmly onto slippery fish or insects. It is a solitary nester. One clutch was found to hold 44 eggs. Both merganser species mate for life.

☐ _____ **American Coot** (*Fulica americana*) Nicknames: mud hen, pull-doo, pond crow, splatterer / Status: FL=stable, probably increasing, IUCN=LC / Life span: to 22 years / Length: 15 in. (38 cm) / Wingspan: 23-38 in. (58-71 cm) / Weight: 1.6 lb (.72 kg) / Nests: north of the Ohio Valley all the way into the southern Northwest Territories of Canada / Found: common in winter and spring in IW and MZ.

© Clair Postmus

The American coot is related to both the common moorhen and the purple gallinule. It is easy to distinguish from the moorhen by the all-white beak and solid black coloration.

This bird is widespread, found in all the lower 48 states, all of Mexico and Central America, and over half of Canada. It prefers freshwater to saltwater wetlands.

American Coot with Chick ©ThroughTheLensGallery.com

It is a game bird in Florida, often taken in the fall along with ducks, geese, and other waterfowl. On Sanibel it is quite common in the winter months.

The coot is primarily an herbivore, eating mostly leaves, seeds, and roots of aquatic plants. It can be spotted paddling quietly in ponds or diving to depths of up to 25 feet. Similar to the grebe, the coot does not have webbed feet like those of ducks, but wide lobes that flare out when it swims. The chicks are taken by snakes and snapping turtles, and the adult is a favorite food of bald eagles.

☐ _____**Blue-winged Teal** (*Anas discors*) Nicknames: blue-wing, summer teal, white-faced teal / Status: FL=Stable, IUCN=LC / Life span: to 23 years / Length: 14-16 in. (35-40 cm) / Wingspan: 22-24.5 in. (56-63 cm) / Weight: 8-19 oz (.23-.53 kg) / Nests: from Northern Texas all the way to Alaska / Found: from early fall through late spring in IW and MZ.

The blue-winged teal is one of the first birds to head south for the winter and one of the last to leave Florida in the spring. Because it waits so long to leave, this is one of the few birds you can find on the islands that begins to show its bright breeding plumage before its migration north. The female resembles the Florida mottled duck but is much smaller. The teal feeds primarily on aquatic vegetation and marine insects but will also graze on land, eating seeds and berries.

Two Male Blue-winged Teal © Joseph Blanda, M.D.

This bird can cover great distances in its migration, summering in northern Alberta and wintering in Colombia, a distance of more than 7,000 miles! Despite being heavily hunted on its annual migration southward, the blue-winged teal is possibly one of the most common wintering ducks on the islands. Easily observed at the Bailey Tract or in the Sanibel Gardens Preserve, flocks of up to 50 or 60 can often be found. Because it is targeted by hunters, the teal is extremely skittish; you are unlikely to get much closer to one than gunshot range.

Its primary threat is loss of wetlands habitat, both in the United States and in Central and South America where many of the birds winter. Tens of thousands are taken every year during duck-hunting season. Other mortality occurs to the nests and chicks from a variety of predators including otters, mink, fishers, snapping turtles, snakes, and birds.

☐ _____ **American Kestrel** (*Falco sparverius*) Nicknames: sparrow hawk, kitty hawk / Status: FL=the smaller Florida race is considered threatened, IUCN=LC / Life span: to 14 years / Length 8.6-12 in. (21-30 cm) / Wingspan: 20-24 in. (51-61 cm) / Weight: 2.8-5.8 oz (80-165 g) / Nests: in areas of Florida and has one of the largest raptor distributions of all New World birds, from Alaska to Tierra del Fuego / Found: during fall, winter, and spring in IW, MZ, UA.

The kestrel is the smallest member of the falcon family. It is a colorful bird of prey, with hints of blue, auburn, and white in the males. With 17 races spread across both continents, the kestrel has evolved a number of colorful variations in its plumage.

Although the American kestrel can be spotted on the islands year-round, its numbers increase dramatically during the winter months, making an encounter much more likely at that time of year. The kestrel

American Kestrel ©ThroughTheLensGallery.com

readily adapts to human changes in the landscape and is as comfortable on a baseball field as in a woodland. As a result of its easy adaptation, it is thriving across North and South America. The smaller, indigenous Florida race is the only threatened subspecies.

Though nicknamed the sparrow hawk, the kestrel feeds primarily on insects and small vertebrates, including frogs and mice. It does take small birds, sometimes in flight, but these are not its primary diet.

The kestrel has one unusual characteristic: after building its nest, it squirts feces on the cavity walls, allowing them to dry and reinforce the nest. With a collection of half-eaten animals lying on the bottom and walls covered in feces, its nest can become quite odiferous.

Perched American Kestrel   © Hung V. Do

Its primary threats are pesticides and lack of suitable nesting sites. The kestrel readily takes to wooden bird boxes, and there is currently a push nationwide to increase these artificial nesting sites throughout the kestrel's range.

☐ _____ **Merlin** (*Falco columbarius*) Nicknames: pigeon hawk / Status: FL=stable, IUCN=LC / Life span: to 11 years / Length: 9.4-11.8 in. (24-30 cm) / Wingspan: 20.9-26.8 in. (53-68 cm) / Weight: 5.6-8.5 oz (160-240 g) / Nests: in Florida but is much more commonly seen on the islands when the winter migrants return from northern Canada / Found: UA, IW, MZ.

Slightly larger than the kestrel, this swift falcon is one of many birds that is slowly but steadily adapting to human landscapes. Like many species, it at first dipped in population as woodlands and fields became parking lots and cities, but the birds that survived that gauntlet of change are now finding these urban settings teeming with viable prey such as mourning and Eurasian-collared doves, pigeons, and rats. The merlin is finding a new home in these ever-encroaching urban areas.

Merlin eating a shorebird

© Judd Patterson Photography

Over the past decade or two, the merlin has become a more common sight on Sanibel and Captiva. Although there are no known nesting pairs on the islands at this time, there is every reason to believe the merlin may begin nesting here.

One of only a handful of birds that does not build a nest, the merlin prefers to use old nesting sites, either from other raptors or sometimes from crows or other larger nesting birds.

The species comes in two colors: the male tends to be blue-gray above, while the female is brown. It does not accelerate in steep dives like the peregrine falcon but tends to hunt closer to the ground, preying on smaller passerines and rodents.

As an adult, the merlin is seldom taken by anything, but its chicks and eggs can fall victim to snakes, rodents, and other birds. For reasons unknown, DDT did not harm the merlin as severely as it did the peregrine falcon and bald eagle.

☐ _____ **Cooper's Hawk** (*Accipiter cooperii*) Nicknames: big blue darter, chicken hawk / Status: FL=stable, IUCN=LC / Life span: to 20 years / Length: 14.6-15.4 in. (37-39 cm) / Wing span: 24.4-35.4 in. (62-90 cm) / Weight: 7.8-14.5 oz (220-410 g) / Nests: throughout the lower 48 and across the southern tier of Canada / Found: in the winter in MZ, IW, UA.

Considered to be one of the world's most agile and skillful fliers, the Cooper's hawk readily cuts through tangles of bush, tree limbs, and heavy cover in search of prey. It specializes in taking down smaller birds, including doves, shorebirds, and grackles. This behavior comes at a price. In a study of more than 300 adult birds, 23 percent showed old, healed-over fractures in the bones of their chest and wishbone. It may well be assumed that another 5 to 10 percent did not survive the collision.

The Cooper's hawk is adapting to people. In the early part of the 20th century its population was in decline as forests were cut down to make way for farms and ever-growing urban and suburban environments. Recently the remaining birds have shown a tolerance to these changes and are moving into cities and suburbs with surprising frequency. There the Cooper's hawk can find ample prey in rock pigeons and mourning and Eurasian-collared doves. Its flying skills come in handy amidst the telephone poles, fences, and concrete of a modern city.

The Cooper's hawk can be readily distinguished from the slightly larger red-shouldered hawk by its broader wingspan and, when in flight, its straight, narrower tail feathers. It often tends to have a bluish or darker red tint to the back as well. The chicks are well

Cooper's Hawk perched
© Sara Yunsoo Kim Photography

protected but still fall victim to snakes and other raptors; the adults are seldom taken by anything other than the great-horned owl.

Cooper's Hawk in flight
© Sara Yunsoo Kim Photography

❐ _____ **Peregrine Falcon** (*Falco peregrinus*) Nicknames: duck hawk / Status: FL=endangered, IUCN=LC / Life span: to 19 years / Length: 16-20 in. (40-50 cm) / Wingspan: 43-46 in. (109-116 cm) / Weight: 1.3 lb (.58 kg) / Nests: in the High Arctic and throughout the Rocky Mountains / Found: mostly during the winter months in UA, IW, MZ.

The peregrine falcon, even more so than the bald eagle, was severely impacted by the widespread use of DDT and related chemicals. The fastest bird in the world, clocked at speeds approaching 200 miles per hour, proved no match against pesticide contamination throughout its range. The peregrine came dangerously close to extinction in North America by the late 1960s, with some estimates putting the entire population at that time at no more than 150 breeding pairs. The good news

Peregrine Falcon © Clair Postmus

about the peregrine is that it is fast recovering from its brush with extinction, and up to 2,000 migrate through the Florida Keys each year.

This beautiful bird has had more scientific research done on it than any other bird in the world, with its current bibliography exceeding 2,000 primary scientific papers. Admired by falconers from England to Saudi Arabia, the peregrine falcon has been trained to hunt for more than 1,000 years. The name *peregrine* means "wanderer," an excellent choice since some peregrines have been known to travel more than 15,000 miles (25,000 km) in a single year. On the other hand, some nesting peregrine pairs remain sedentary their entire lives.

Because of its ability to travel long distances and fly at an average speed of 25-35 mph, the peregrine inhabits every continent except Antarctica and can be found on many oceanic islands.

The peregrine falcon's primary diet is other birds. In urban settings it has become adept at killing pigeons, mourning doves, starlings, and a host of other city-dwelling species. In the wild it hunts ducks, shorebirds, seagulls, and even small geese. It also takes rodents, bats, and other small mammals. It dives on its prey at tremendous speeds, often killing the animal upon impact.

Aside from being killed by hunters and having its eggs fail from pesticide poisoning, the peregrine falcon has few other natural threats. There simply are no other birds fast enough to catch the peregrine. It is a solitary nester, sometimes settling on the window ledges of tall skyscrapers and bridges in cities.

Peregrine Falcon: the fastest animal on earth

© Hung V. Do

❏ _____ **Swallow-tailed Kite** (*Elanoides forficatus*) Nicknames: none / Status: FL=stable, but endangered in South Carolina, IUCN=LC / Life span: to 12 years / Length: 19-25 in. (46-64 cm) / Wingspan: 48 in. (122 cm) / Weight: 13-21 oz (.37-.60 kg) / Nests: throughout Florida and southern Alabama and Mississippi during the summer / Found: in the spring, summer, and fall in IW, MZ.

Swallow-tailed Kite   © Judd Patterson Photography

The swallow-tailed kite, like the magnificent frigatebird, is an impressive bird to witness in flight. In fact, you are most likely to spot and identify this bird when it is soaring high above. With its pure white body, large black-tipped wings and deeply forked black tail, this bird resembles an enormous, snowy barn swallow.

Unlike most of the migratory birds that arrive in Florida, the swallow-tailed kite comes up from Central and South America during the summer. In effect, Florida is its northern breeding grounds. Once a common nesting bird as far north as Minnesota, the swallow-tailed kite has suffered from extensive habitat loss through most of its former North American range.

©ThroughTheLensGallery.com

There is a small resident nesting population at Corkscrew Swamp on the mainland, and more than likely some of the birds found flying over Sanibel and Captiva originate from there. They predominantly eat flying insects including dragonflies, bees, and beetles but while in flight will also pick off snakes, crickets, cicadas, and small birds from the canopy top. A skilled flyer, the swallow-tailed kite can turn its tail feathers almost 90 degrees, allowing it to make sharp turns and quick dives. Its only long-term threat is habitat loss, although some efforts are under way to reintroduce the kite into its former northernmost ranges.

☐ _____ **Black Skimmer** (*Rynchops niger*) Nicknames: shearwater, scissorbill, sea-dog, razorbill / Status: FL=the local population of black skimmers are declining, IUCN=LC / Life span: to 20 years / Length: 15.7-19.7 in. (40-50 cm) / Wingspan: 42-50 in. (106-127 cm) / Weight: 7.5 oz-1 lb (.21-.45 kg) / Nests: on islands / Found: during the winter months in MZ, CW, GB.

Skimmer when feeding   © Clair Postmus

Note the extended lower beak   © Clair Postmus

The black skimmer's nickname sea-dog comes from the dog-like barking sounds the bird makes as it glides over the water's surface in search of minnows. The skimmer feeds in a most unusual fashion. It is the only bird in the world whose lower mandible (beak) is longer than the upper. It flies, generally in pairs or small groups, directly over the surface of the water with its extended lower bill slicing through the water. When it detects a fish or crustacean, it snaps its head down and snatches the creature directly from the water.

North and South America are home to three races of skimmer. The northern race, *Rynchops niger*, is the only one that frequents our coastline. Although its numbers in Florida are declining as a result of a lack of suitable nesting sites, the South American population, which prefers freshwater rivers and lakes to estuaries, is healthy. Two other species of skimmers inhabit Africa and India.

The skimmer tends to feed at dawn and dusk and has even been known to feed nocturnally. The best place to view the skimmer is along the causeway in the late afternoon or anywhere in the back bay. Another reliable viewing opportunity is just after dawn along the gulf beaches. It prefers very still water for skimming. It is monogamous and nests in colonies of other skimmers, generally on beaches, sandy islets, or sandbars.

☐ _____ **Ring-billed Gull** (*Larus delawarensis*) Nicknames: none / Status: FL=stable, IUCN=LC / Life span: to 27 years / Length: 16.9-21 in. (43-51 cm) / Wingspan: 41.3-46 in (105-115 cm) / Weight: 10.6 oz -1.9 lb (.30-.72 kg) / Nests: across the northern tier of the U.S. and well into northern Canada / Found: mostly during the winter in MZ, GB, UA.

The ring-billed gull is easy to identify. Look for the bright yellow bill with a clear black ring extending around both the upper and lower beaks. No other gull or tern has this distinctive characteristic. The ring-billed gull has adapted well to human landscapes and is frequently found in parking lots, near landfills, on golf courses, and in other urban locations.

This is a fairly large gull and has been known to interbreed and hybridize with smaller gulls such as the Franklin's, black-headed, and laughing gulls. It is an attractive bird, with

©ThroughTheLensGallery.com

lovely white spots mottled over the black tips at the end of its wings. It can be readily found along the beaches or sitting on the large exposed sandbars during low tide in the "Ding" Darling refuge.

This gull feeds on fish, carrion, shrimp, and crabs. Because it has adapted so well to humans, it also feeds on potato chips, Doritos, and bread crumbs, and has even been known to beg. Feeding the ring-billed gull, or any bird, makes it more aggressive and can create a nuisance bird. However tempting, feeding any wildlife should always be avoided.

The ring-billed gull is sometimes preyed upon by falcons and eagles, and its nests can be raided by Arctic foxes, coyotes, and bobcats. A colony nester, the adult ring-billed gull has been observed to return to nest within three feet of where it was born.

Note the obvious ring
© Rob Pailes, Santiva Images

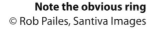 **Royal Tern** (*Sterna maxima*) Nicknames: big striker, redbill, cayenne tern / Status: FL=stable, but declining in some areas, especially California, IUCN=LC / Life span: to 28 years / Length: 17.7-19.7 in. (45-50 cm) / Wingspan: 49-53 in. (124-134 cm) / Weight: 12.3-16 oz (.35-.46 kg) / Nests: in a small area along the Eastern Seaboard during the summer / Found: GB, MZ, CW.

Royal Tern   © Clair Postmus

Sporting a cool hairdo, the royal tern is a fairly common sighting along the spoil islands of the causeway during the winter months. It crouches low against the wind and is often seen in flocks of 20 or more. One of the largest terns in North America, the royal can be found all the way to southern Argentina.

A typical flock of Royal Terns   © Hung V. Do

The royal tern is larger than its cousins, the sandwich and Forster's terns. It also has a yellow-orange bill, whereas the smaller sandwich tern has a black bill with a yellow tip.

The royal feeds mostly on small minnows, shrimp, and crustaceans, primarily by plunge diving, a similar technique to that used by the brown pelican. It hovers 40 to 60 feet in the air, then falls headfirst on its prey, sometimes going completely underwater. The royal is also known to raid the by-catch of pelicans and can sometimes be seen sitting on a pelican's head looking for strained-off minnows as the pelican empties its pouch of saltwater.

The royal tern is monogamous and a colony nester, most often with other species of terns. It is preyed upon by falcons, and its nests are vulnerable to mammals such as raccoons and weasels. Because it is so reliant on a stable minnow population, water-quality degradation can devastate local royal tern populations.

□_____ **Sandwich Tern** (*Sterna sandvicensis*) Nicknames: Cabot's tern / Status: FL=uncommon but stable, IUCN=LC / Life span: to 22 years / Length: 13.4-17.7 in. (34-45 cm) / Wingspan: 33.1-35.4 in. (84-90 cm) / Weight: 6.3-10.6 oz (180-300 g) / Nests: along the Atlantic coastline during the summer / Found: during the winter months in GB, MZ, CW.

Sandwich Tern   © Clair Postmus

Smaller than the royal tern, in the winter this tern is just as common as its larger cousin. The sandwich tern prefers to go farther out to sea than the royal and plunges from far greater heights. It feeds predominantly on fish, shrimp, and small squid.

Strictly a winter visitor, the sandwich tern returns each summer to the barrier islands of the Northeast. There, it nests in large colonies with hundreds, sometimes thousands, of other gulls and terns. The noise, odor, and commotion of these nesting sites can be quite chaotic. Parent terns appear to be able to find their offspring by their calls. The sandwich tern is monogamous.

Ninety-plus years ago the sandwich tern was sometimes harvested by market hunters with punt guns, greatly reducing the population. The bird was more common in Florida in the 1800s, then declined dramatically, but now is increasing in numbers throughout the state. Its only real threat at this time is the loss of suitable nesting sites.

□ _____ **Forster's Tern** (*Sterna forsteri*) Nicknames: none / Status: FL=stable but declining in some Midwest states, and in many states is now considered a species of special concern, IUCN=LC / Life span: up to 15 years / Length: 13-14.2 in. (33-36 cm) / Wingspan: 29-33 in. (73-83 cm) / Weight: 4.6-6.7 oz (130-190 g) / Nests: in the upper Midwest and lower central provinces of Canada / Found: in winter in GB, MZ, and along the Sanibel Causeway.

Forster's Tern   © Clair Postmus

The Forster's tern is one of three terns that are fairly common here during the winter months (the others being the royal, and sandwich, and least terns). The only one not mentioned here is the Caspian tern, which is the largest tern but quite rare on the islands. Unlike the other terns, the Forster's tern ranges no farther south than Central America. The bird is named after German naturalist Johann Reinhold Forster (1729-1798), who was the first to attempt to catalog all American vertebrates.

A small bird with a deeply forked tail, the Forster's tern is, like most terns, a plunge diver. It sometimes can be seen hovering above a school of minnows along the causeway, then dropping onto them and either picking them off the surface or completely submerging itself.

The Forster's tern forms loosely knit colonies with other terns when nesting. It lays its eggs in unusual floating nests. Large carp have learned to capsize the nests and eat either the eggs or the chicks. The adult Forster's tern is preyed upon by falcons. The Forster's tern also suffers from loss of suitable habitat resulting from the draining of wetlands in the wheat fields where they nest in the summer.

☐ _____ **Least Tern** (*Sterna antillarum*) Nicknames: sea swallow, pigeon de la mer, little tern / Status: FL=threatened, IUCN=LC / Life span: to 24 years / Length: 8.3-9.1 in. (21-23 cm) / Wingspan: 18.9-20.9 in. (48-53 cm) / Weight: 1.1-1.6 oz (30-45 g) / Nests: in Florida in the summer months, including Sanibel and Captiva; winters in Colombia and Venezuela / Found: only during summer in GB, IW, MZ, and the Sanibel Causeway.

True to its nickname sea swallow, this is the smallest tern in the Western Hemisphere. Weighing less than a robin, this tiny tern feeds on small fish, crustaceans, and sand eels. Its cap is similar to other terns, but its diminutive size and black-tipped yellow bill are the best methods of identifying this bird.

Like several other summer species, the least tern has made Florida its northern nesting site, although several small populations nest as far north as Massachusetts. Once hunted for its plumes, the least tern is still considered threatened in much of its range, and its population is being closely monitored. There is also a West Coast population that summers in California and winters deep into Mexico.

The least tern suffers from habitat and nesting-site loss. It prefers to nest on beaches where it is often in conflict with humans and their pets. If agitated by an unwanted intruder, the least tern has a nasty habit of hovering over the potential predator and defecating, so be forewarned. The least tern is monogamous but always nests in colonies with other terns.

© Rob Pailes, Santiva Images

Least Terns sharing a minnow   © Hung V. Do

☐ _____ **Common Nighthawk** (*Chordeiles minor*) Nicknames: bull bat / Status: FL=stable, IUCN=LC / Life span: to 9 years / Length: 8.7-9.4 in. (22-24 cm) / Wingspan: 20.9-22.4 in. (53-57 cm) / Weight: 2.3-3.5 oz (65-98 g) / Nests: on island during the summer / Found: IW, UA.

Known for its incessant frog-like call *beant* while flying high above the canopy at dusk, the common nighthawk is a more common summer visitor than it is during the cooler and far less insect-rich months of the year. When the light is still sufficiently bright to watch this bird, it can be readily identified by the two distinctive white markings on the underside of both wings.

The nighthawk, just like the chuck-will's-widow and the whip-poor-will, is almost exclusively an insect eater. Its mouth opens extraordinarily wide during feeding, and its aerial acrobatics are designed to glean insects continually from the air. It dines on beetles, flies, moths, dragonflies, and a host of other airborne bugs.

Common Nighthawk © Judd Patterson Photography

Another fascinating behavior of this insectivore occurs during late May and early June over the islands when the male begins its courtship behavior. It flies several hundred yards into the air, then commences a steep dive. Just six or seven feet from the ground the bird pulls out of the dive and as he flexes his wings downward, the air rushing through his wingtips makes a deep whirring noise, similar to the sound of a large rubber band being plucked. These dives are directed primarily at the female, but the male nighthawk has also been known to direct his dive at young nighthawks, intruders, and even people.

The common nighthawk is experiencing a decline in population throughout parts of its range, while adapting to outside lighting and using flat, gravel-topped roofs in other parts. It is not a threatened or endangered species, however, and the IUCN has it as a species of least concern. It is a solitary nester and generally monogamous.

❏ _____ **Black-bellied Plover** (*Pluvialis squatarola*) Nicknames: bull-head, black-breasted plover, beetlehead / Status: FL=stable, IUCN=LC / Life span: to 12 years / Length: 11 in. (28 cm) / Wingspan: 23.2-23.6 in. (59-60 cm) / Weight: 5.6-9.8 oz (160-277 g) / Nests: in the High Arctic in the summer / Found: during all but the midsummer months in GB, MZ, CW.

Nesting in the High Arctic along the extreme northern tier of Alaska, across the Yukon and Northwest Territories, all the way east to Baffin Island, the black-bellied plover migrates between the tundra and the tropics of Florida annually. It is the ultimate snowbird. One of the largest and most striking plovers, the black-bellied plover is a true survivor. Like most shorebirds, ducks, and geese, tens of thousands of plovers were killed by market hunters 90-plus years ago.

Market hunting was the northern version of Florida's plume hunting. Most of it occurred between the 1870s and the 1920s. Sometimes employing punt guns, a huge, multi-barreled shotgun that was 10 feet long and could shoot up to two

Black-bellied Plover in flight © Sara Yunsoo Kim Photography

pounds of lead BBs in a single blast, these meat hunters were capable of killing as many as 100 plovers in a single blast. They would then sell the bird meat, packing the dead animals in ice and shipping them via train to the large urban markets of Chicago, St. Louis, Boston, and New York.

As the flocks of ducks, geese, snipes, and plovers plummeted, the states passed game limits, and the market hunters were forced either to find another business or to hunt illegally, which many did well into the 1950s. Luckily, the black-bellied plover was plentiful enough to endure this gauntlet of over-harvesting and is slowly on its way to recovery.

This plover feeds along the coastline and tidal flats, eating mostly marine worms, insects, mollusks, and crustaceans. Warier than most, the black-bellied plover acts as a sentinel bird amidst mixed flocks of feeding or roosting shorebirds, often alerting all to possible danger with

Black-bellied Plover feeding on the beach © Charles Sobczak

its distinctive three-note whistle. Gulls, arctic foxes, and owls prey upon its nesting sites. The adult bird is sometimes taken by falcons.

☐ _____ **Semipalmated Plover** (*Charadrius semipalmatus*)
Nicknames: ringneck / Status: FL=stable, IUCN=LC / Life span: to 9 years /
Length: 6.7-7.5 in. (17-19 cm) / Wingspan: 14-15.25 in. (35-39 cm) / Weight:
1.7 oz (47 g) / Nests: in the Subarctic across all of Alaska to Newfoundland /
Found: in the winter months in MZ, GB, CW.

The term *semipalmated* refers to the partial webbing between this bird's toes. Most shorebirds, such as the similar-looking snowy and piping plovers, have unwebbed toes. Because of this feature the semipalmated plover can swim across small water channels when foraging. The chicks have also been observed swimming short distances to small islets or across shallow lakes.

Semipalmated Plover　　　© ThroughTheLensGallery.com

The best way of distinguishing the semipalmated from other plovers is its darker back and orange-yellow legs, as compared with the light back and gray legs of the snowy and the larger size and bill, along with the dark back and dull pink legs of the Wilson's. Never easy to separate, all of these smaller shorebirds present one of the most difficult avian categories to identify, even for the most ardent birders.

Like all plovers, the semipalmated eats predominantly mollusks, worms, and insects. It forms loose colonies amidst other plovers and is preyed upon by hawks, owls, and mammals, mostly in its nesting grounds in the far north.

☐ _____ **Spotted Sandpiper** (*Actitis macularious*) Nicknames: tip-up, teeter snipe, teeter tail / Status: FL= stable, IUCN=LC / Life span: to 9 years / Length: 7-7.9 in. (17-20 cm) / Wingspan: 14.6-15.7 in. (37-40 cm) / Weight: 1.2-1.8 oz (34-50 g) / Nests: just north of the Mason-Dixon Line all the way to northern Alaska / Found: mostly in the winter months in GB, MZ, CW.

The spotted sandpiper has several unique characteristics. The first of these is the teetering walk that gives the bird its nicknames. No one thus far has been able to explain the reason for this behavior, but it makes the bird relatively easy to identify. Another interesting characteristic of the spotted sandpiper is that it is polyandrous, meaning that the female bird mates with several different males in a single season.

The female spotted sandpiper behaves, in many ways, more like the male of most species. She is larger than the male, is the first to arrive at the breeding grounds and aggressively stakes out the nesting site, quickly attracts a male mate, then,

Spotted Sandpiper © Clair Postmus

after laying her eggs, leaves most of the parenting to the male. Enigmatically, in other populations, the spotted sandpiper is monogamous and the female helps care for the chicks. These adaptations appear to be directly related to varying environmental conditions, many of which are not well understood.

The spotted sandpiper eats marine invertebrates and insects almost exclusively. It is not uncommon to find this bird in urban or suburban settings, feeding along streams, rivers, and ponds. Its eggs and chicks are preyed upon by a variety of predators, from weasels to owls to jaegers.

☐ _____ **Greater Yellowlegs** (*Tringa melanoleuca*) Nicknames: telltale snipe / Status: FL=stable, IUCN=LC / Life span: unknown / Length: 11.4-13 in. (29-33 cm) / Wingspan: 23.6 in. (60 cm) / Weight: 3.9-8.3 oz (111-235 g) / Nests: across the northern tier of Canada, generally in mosquito-infested bogs and wetlands / Found: during the winter months in MZ, GB, CW.

©ThroughTheLensGallery.com

The greater yellowlegs is one of a very small handful of birds that does not have an established life span allocated to it by the Patuxent Wildlife Research Center of the U.S. Geological Survey (which posts all of the estimated life spans of various species). The reason is simple. The greater yellowlegs nests in inhospitable, mosquito-infested muskeg swamps, and even dedicated scientists are reluctant to venture into these areas to study this fairly common shorebird.

Because 24 species of plovers and various members of the sandpiper family spend most or part of the winter in coastal Florida, they can be difficult to tell apart.

One method of distinguishing the greater from the lesser yellowlegs is by the relative length of the bill. On the greater yellowlegs, the bill is roughly 2-2.5 times longer than the depth of the head, whereas the lesser yellowlegs' bill is only 1-1.5 times longer. The lesser is roughly half the weight of the greater yellowlegs.

Another distinction is the call. Both yellowlegs act as sentinel birds for other shorebirds, but the greater yellowlegs has a rapid, *teu, teu, teu* alarm, whereas the lesser has a shorter and softer *tu, tu* call. That being said, it is extremely easy to confuse these two birds, especially from a distance.

The greater yellowlegs is a probe feeder. It uses its long bill to prod the soft mud of tidal flats or the loose sand along the edge of the surf. It eats aquatic and terrestrial insects, particularly flies and beetles. It has also been known to take small fish and seeds.

It is a solitary nester. The chicks and eggs are preyed upon by weasels, hawks, and other small northern predators, and the adult is sometimes taken by falcons.

☐ _____ **Lesser Yellowlegs** (*Tringa flavipes*) Nicknames: telltale snipe / Status: FL=stable, IUCN=LC / Life span: to 4 years / Length: 9.1-9.8 in. (23-25 cm) / Wingspan: 23.2-25.2 in. (59-64 cm) / Weight: 2.4-3.3 oz (67-94 g) / Nests: across the northern tier of Canada and Alaska all the way to the Arctic Ocean / Found: during the winter months in GB, MZ, CW.

Lesser Yellowlegs   © Sara Yunsoo Kim Photography

Like its larger cousin, the lesser yellowlegs migrates an unbelievable distance annually. It nests in the High Arctic and winters in Tierra del Fuego, a distance of more than 9,000 miles each way. It's difficult to imagine this three-ounce bird making that round-trip every year, but a number of them somehow manage to do so.

The lesser yellowlegs is a fairly common to abundant bird on the islands during February and March, and can often be spotted off of Wildlife Drive in the "Ding" Darling refuge amidst large groups of other shorebirds on the north side of the cross-dike. It can be distinguished from other shorebirds by its long, bright yellow legs.

It breeds farther north than its greater yellowlegs cousin, where it encounters predators such as snowy owls, Arctic foxes, and skuas (also known as jaegers). Unlike the greater yellowlegs, the lesser yellowlegs forms loose colonies at its breeding grounds.

☐ _____ **Piping Plover** (*Charadrius melodus*) Nicknames: none / Status: FL=Threatened, IUCN=NT / Life span: to 14 years / Length: 6.7-7.1 in. (17-18 cm) / Wingspan: 14-15.5 in. (35-39 cm) / Weight: 1.5-2.2 oz (43-63 g) / Nests: in the Great Plains during the summer / Found: from May through August in GB.

Piping Plover　　© Sara Yunsoo Kim Photography

Very similar in size and appearance to the snowy plover, the piping plover is estimated to number 450 in the entire state of Florida. The easiest way to distinguish between the snowy and the piping is by the piping's bright yellow legs and multicolored beak with an orange base and black tip. Because its coloration resembles the sand it forages over, the piping plover is very difficult to see, even when it is mere yards in front of you.

Unlike some of the other sandpipers, the piping plover prefers feeding along the upper segments of the beach, hanging closer to the vegetation line. There it feeds on fly larvae, beetles, and crustaceans. The piping plover was once a relatively common shorebird. It has suffered primarily from habitat loss because of human intrusion into much of its former range: beaches and beach dunes. The bird has been unable to adapt to a species that loves the beach as much as it does—namely, *Homo sapiens*. It also suffers from irregular releases of dams, which can result in the loss of entire broods.

Piping Plover nesting　　© Sara Yunsoo Kim Photography

Ruddy Turnstone © Rob Pailes, Santiva Images

☐ _____ **Ruddy Turnstone** (*Arenaria interpres*) Nicknames: calico-back, rock plover, brant bird / Status: FL=stable, IUCN=LC / Life span: to 14 years / Length: 6.3-8.3 in. (16-21 cm) / Wingspan: 19.7-22.4 in. (50-57 cm) / Weight: 3-6.7 oz (84.190 g) / Nests: in the extreme High Arctic along the shoreline of the Arctic Ocean from Baffin Island to the North Slope / Found: during the winter months in GB, MZ, CW.

An unmistakable and attractive shorebird, the ruddy turnstone can be readily found along the gulf beaches from early fall through late spring. Sometimes non-breeders remain on the islands year-round. The ruddy turnstone's coloration runs from a rusty brown to a bold brown and white pattern when in flight. Its bill is much shorter than that of the yellowlegs and many other shorebirds and has a slight upturn. The turnstone uses its wedge-shaped bill to flip and turn over stones (hence its name), shells, pieces of seaweed, and other rack-line debris found along the beach in search of its favorite prey.

The turnstone eats primarily insects, mollusks, worms, and bird eggs. It has been observed feeding on such unlikely meals as coconut meat and picnic crumbs. This small shorebird is tolerant of human activity and does not hesitate to raid a beach encampment. It also frequents fishing piers, docks, and bridges where it feeds on discarded fish scraps.

The ruddy turnstone migrates almost as far as the yellowlegs, but goes only as far south as northern Argentina. Preyed upon by any number of creatures along the northern tier, the adult bird is sometimes taken by falcons.

☐ _____ **Sanderling** (*Calidris alba*) Nicknames: sand snipe, beach bird, whiting / Status: FL=stable, IUCN=LC / Life span: to 12 years / Length: 7.1-7.9 in. (18-20 cm) / Wingspan: 13.8 in. (35 cm) / Weight: 1.4-3.5 oz (40-100 g) / Nests: high in the Arctic on Baffin Island and farther north / Found: during all but the heart of summer in MZ, GB, CW.

Sanderlings running along the beach.   © Sara Yunsoo Kim Photography

This is the small, pale shorebird that spends most of its day running in and out of the breaking waves along the shore. Some non-breeding adults remain in Florida year-round, so it may be observed even in the summer on rare occasions. It is the single most common shorebird in the world, found on many temperate and most tropical beaches worldwide. The Spanish name for this bird bears mentioning: *playero blanco*, or white sandpiper.

Like several long-distance flying shorebirds, some individual sanderlings fly farther than most New World birds, traveling from the southern tip of South America to Ellesmere Island in northern Canada. It dines on marine invertebrates including the common sand flea and the tiny shellfish coquina, dashing in and out of the breaking waves in search of these aquatic animals. Although still fairly common worldwide, the sanderling is in decline as a result of habitat loss. It is polyandrous and nests in colonies.

© Rob Pailes, Santiva Images

☐ _____ **Western Sandpiper** (*Calidris mauri*) Nicknames: peep / Status: FL=stable, IUCN=LC / Life span: to 9 years / Length: 5.5-6.7 in. (14-17 cm) / Wingspan: 10.2-14.6 in. (26-37 cm) / Weight: .8-1.2 oz (22-35 g) Nests: primarily along the western shore of Alaska / Found: from late fall through mid-spring in GB, MZ, CW.

Despite its small size, usually weighing less than an ounce, the western sandpiper makes a nearly 20,000-mile journey every year. Unlike many shorebirds, the western sandpiper summers along the west coast of Alaska. In migration, huge flocks come up the west coast of the United States and Canada to nesting

Western Sandpipers feeding   © ThroughTheLensGallery.com

sites along the Bering Sea, sometimes nesting in eastern Siberia as well. Estimates are that more than 6.5 million of these tiny sandpipers pass through the Copper River Delta in Alaska every late spring and early fall.

Along the beach this shorebird is easy to confuse with the nearly identical least sandpiper. Leg color is the key difference; the western has black legs, whereas the least sandpiper's are more yellowish. The western sandpiper is far more common along the Pacific coast, but a fair number of them come as far east as southern Pennsylvania. It feeds on aquatic insects, worms, and crustaceans. It is fed upon, especially the chicks and eggs, by mink, weasels, and other terrestrial predators.

☐ _____ **Least Sandpiper** (*Calidris minutilla*) Nicknames: peep / Status: FL=stable, IUCN=LC / Life span: to 16 years / Length: 5.1-5.9 in. (13-15 cm) / Wingspan: 10.6-11 in. (27-28 cm) / Weight: .07-1.1 oz (19-30 g) / Nests: along the northern tier of North America from the Aleutian Islands to Newfoundland / Found: during the winter months in GB, CW, MZ, IW.

Very similar to its tiny cousin, the western sandpiper, the least sandpiper is commonly seen along the beaches during the winter. Unlike the western, it also inhabits mudflats and inland ponds, so when you spot a sandpiper in these areas, it is in all probability a least sandpiper.

Least Sandpiper　　　© Rob Pailes, Santiva Images

The smallest shorebird in the world, the least sandpiper generally weighs less than an ounce. Its scientific name *minutilla*—meaning very small—aptly describes this tiny bird.

For such a small creature, the least sandpiper migrates all the way from northern Alaska to the Brazilian rain forests, where it winters. Not necessarily needing coastal shorelines, the least will also winter in open fields, along rivers, and any productive wetlands.

The eggs and chicks are preyed upon by gulls, foxes, and a host of other hungry animals. The adult falls victim mostly to habitat loss. Although the least sandpiper numbers are stable, recent surveys have shown the eastern U.S. population to be in decline.

🗆 _____ **Dunlin** (*Calidris alpina*) Nicknames: red-backed sandpiper, sand-snipe / Status: FL=stable to declining for unknown reasons, IUCN=LC / Life span: to 12 years / Length: 6.3-8.7 in. (16-22 cm) / Wingspan: 14.2-15 in. (36-38 cm) / Weight: 1.7-2.3 oz (48-64 g) / Nests: in the High Arctic around the northern fringe of Hudson Bay / Found: from early fall through late spring in MZ, GB, CW.

A small sandpiper with a long, slightly decurved beak, the dunlin is common to the tidal flats and sandbars along either side of Wildlife Drive in the "Ding" Darling refuge. It leaves the islands for only a few months a year, making a beeline to its tundra nesting grounds near Baffin Island, as well as both James and Hudson bays. Known worldwide, the dunlin has a distinct population that nests along the northern and western

Dunlin   Courtesy Wikipedia Commons by Mdf.

edge of Alaska, then migrates southward to Japan and China for the winter. It is also common in Europe and Asia. The dunlin is one of the fastest-flying sandpipers, with some flocks having been clocked at speeds up to 100 miles per hour.

The name dunlin is derived from combining two Old English words: *dunn*, meaning a brownish, gray color; and *lin* or *ling*, meaning something small. This accurately describes this bird, whose winter plumage and size match its name. During its brief breeding season the dunlin takes on a rufous or reddish-brown back, hence the nickname red-backed sandpiper. It feeds on marine worms and insects that it gleans from the mud with its long bill in a repetitive, rapid movement that resembles the motion of a fast-stitching sewing machine. Dunlin chicks and eggs are taken by numerous northern predators, and the adult is a favorite prey for falcons during its long and tenuous migrations.

❑ _____ **Marbled Godwit** (*Limosa fedoa*) Nicknames: none / Status: FL=declining, IUCN=LC / Life span: to 13 years / Length: 15.6-18.9 in. (42-48 cm) / Wingspan: 32 in. (81 cm) / Weight: 10.1-16 oz (285-454 g) / Nests: in the Great Plains of North Dakota, Montana, and central Canada; winters along the coast / Found: MZ.

Whereas many shorebirds are difficult to distinguish from one another, the marbled godwit does not present any identification problems, even to the most inexperienced birder. Not only does the bill of the marbled godwit extend outward and tilt upward to an absurd degree, but also its coloration is equally distinctive. The bill has a creamy pink base that ends with a dusky tip. That, along with the bird's large size, makes it an unmistakable sighting.

The godwit uses its long beak to probe deep into the tidal mudflats where it ferrets out marine worms, mollusks, and crustaceans. In the Great Plains, where these food sources cannot be

© Rob Pailes, Santiva Images

found, the godwit switches its diet to grasshoppers, insects, seeds, and berries.

The marbled godwit population has been in decline for some years now, and a sighting of this bird is a fairly uncommon event in the "Ding" Darling refuge or elsewhere on the islands. This bird is a victim of the large commercial wheat farms that now dominate its former range. Most of its prime habitat has been converted to agricultural activity, and the population of this beautiful bird has suffered accordingly. The few natural predators it has include falcons, owls, and eagles.

❑ _____ **Whimbrel** (*Numenius phaeopus*) Nicknames: Hudsonian curlew / Status: FL=stable, IUCN=LC / Life span: to 13 years / Length: 17.3 in. (44 cm) / Wingspan: 31-33 in. (78-83 cm) / Weight: 10.9-17.4 oz (310-493 g) / Nests: in the High Arctic from Alaska to Hudson Bay / Found: MZ.

The whimbrel and the marbled godwit have one thing in common: an unmistakable snout. Both of these large shorebirds have long bills; whereas the godwit's beak turns up, the whimbrel's takes a marked downturn. The whimbrel, probably because of its choice of wintering grounds, is doing far better than the godwit, but is still a fairly uncommon sighting on Sanibel or Captiva.

The whimbrel's primary diet consists of fiddler crabs and other crustaceans. It uses its long decurved beak to pry deep into the hiding holes of fiddler crabs and extract them. An unusual behavior follows a successful probe. The whimbrel will often take the squirming crab down to the water's edge, dip it several times in the saltwater to wash off the mud, break off the claws and legs, and consume the crab. In the High Arctic where it nests, the bird changes its diet to insects, seeds, and berries.

One of many shorebirds that migrates vast distances every year, the sturdy whimbrel is unusual in that it makes its 2,500-mile-long flights nonstop! How a one-pound bird accomplishes what a 747 jet aircraft can do is an amazing example of animal endurance.

©ThroughTheLensGallery.com

The whimbrel suffers from some predation to its young in the High Arctic, mostly from Arctic fox, skaus, snowy owls, and weasels. The adult bird is subject to predation by falcons, hawks, and an occasional alligator.

☐ _____ **Willet** (*Catoptrophorus semipalmatus*) Nicknames: stone curlew, bill-willie, white-wing curlew, pill-willet / Status: FL=stable, IUCN=LC / Life span: to 10 years / Length: 13-16.1 in. (33-41 cm) / Wingspan: 27.6 in. (70 cm) / Weight: 7.1-11.6 oz (200-330 g) / Nests: in the northwestern Rocky Mountains and the Great Plains of North Dakota, Montana, and central Canada / Found: MZ, GB.

Two Willets in flight   ©ThroughTheLensGallery.com

Slightly smaller than either the whimbrel or the marbled godwit, the willet more closely resembles the greater yellowlegs. The primary difference is that the willet's legs are blue-gray and easily distinguished from the bright yellow of the yellowlegs. Its name comes from its call, a

Shorebirds in "Ding" Darling
©ThroughTheLensGallery.com

Willet   ©ThroughTheLensGallery.com

distinctive *pill-will-willet*. Another sure way of spotting this bird is the striking black wing patches and white stripes that are displayed the moment it takes wing.

The willet is a probing shorebird, using its sturdy, straight beak to dig into soft mudflats in search of crabs, crustaceans, and marine worms. It has also been observed taking small fish, which is not a common menu item among shorebirds. On the plains, where it nests in the same general areas as the marbled godwit, the willet switches its diet to insects, grasshoppers, seeds, and berries.

The willet suffered heavy losses during the era of market hunting around the turn of the 20th century. The giant punt guns took willets and other large shorebirds out by the tens of thousands. Today the willet suffers from habitat loss to farming but is doing better than most shorebirds in adapting to a world filled with people. Natural predation comes from ferrets, large hawks, and red fox in the north, as well as alligators, falcons, and eagles in Florida.

☐ _____ **Red Knot** (*Calidris canutus*) Nicknames: robin snipe, red-breasted snipe, American knot / Status: FL=declining, IUCN=LC / Life span: to 15 years / Length: 9.1-9.8 in. (23-25 cm) / Wingspan: 20.5-22 in. (52-56 cm) / Weight: 4.8 oz (135 g) / Nests: in the extreme High Arctic along the edge of the Arctic Ocean / Found: MZ, GB.

©ThroughTheLensGallery.com

As it approaches breeding season, the dull gray red knot turns a beautiful chestnut color, and its wings, once dullish gray, become a dappled brown and black. The red knot has the longest yearly migration of any bird in the world, flying annually some 18,600 miles from its summer breeding grounds in the Arctic to its wintering home in Tierra del Fuego. Not all red knots make this tenuous journey, as a sizable population elects to winter in Southwest Florida.

© Joseph Blanda, M.D.

Yet another victim of market hunters, the red knot was once the most abundant shorebird in North America. Because of its tendency to form large flocks during its migration, the market hunters targeted red knots every spring and autumn until this once populous bird was almost lost. Today it suffers from water pollution, especially along the Chesapeake and Delaware bays where it once fed almost exclusively on the eggs of the horseshoe crab. Because of water-quality degradation and over-harvesting by fisherman, the horseshoe crab population in the Chesapeake has plummeted dramatically, and the eggs that were once abundant are now scarce, creating a decline in the red knot population as well. This is a classic example of how a break in the food chain can affect unrelated species.

The red knot is a beach and mudflat feeder. Behaving a bit like the curlew and a bit like a sandpiper, it works the edge of the surf zone looking for coquinas and sand fleas, while in the mud flats it pries into the mud looking for marine worms and crustaceans. In the High Arctic the eggs and chicks are taken by land-dwelling predators such as fox and mink, and the adult is taken by falcons, eagles, and owls.

❏ _____ Short-billed Dowitcher (*Limnodromus griseus*)

Nicknames: red-breasted snipe / Status: FL=stable, IUCN=LC / Life span: to 8 years / Length: 9.8-11.4 in. (25-29 cm) / Wingspan: 18-22 in. (45-55 cm) / Weight: 3.2-4.2 oz (90-120 g) / Nests: near James Bay and across northern Quebec, as well as northern Manitoba and Alberta / Found: during all but a few summer months in MZ, GB; some non-breeding individuals can be found on the islands year-round.

If you are having trouble distinguishing this bird from its close cousin, the long-billed dowitcher, don't be disappointed. Even experienced birders have trouble telling these two dowitchers apart, since only the female long-billed dowitcher has a longer bill. Only the calls, which are distinct, can be used to tell one species from the other.

© Sara Yunsoo Kim Photography

In fact, the identification of the various shorebird species found in Florida is a lifelong pursuit. There is a saying among birders that describes it well: "Shorebirds aren't for sissies." There are so many variables among the 24-plus species of sandpipers and plovers, including juvenile plumage, breeding plumage, and localized variations, that it is well beyond the scope of this work to delineate one from the other. For a better understanding of these species, each with its own

Dowitcher
© Rob Pailes, Santiva Images

environmental niche, refer to books such as *Stokes Beginner's Guide to Shorebirds* by Donald and Lillian Stokes or *The Shorebird Guide* by Michael O'Brien et al.

The dowitcher breeds in the muskegs of the taiga to the edges of the boreal forests. It dines on fly larvae, insects, snails, and seeds. During the winter months it forages for marine worms and insects, as well as crustaceans and mollusks. It uses its long beak to pry deep into the soft mud in a sewing-machine manner. The nests and chicks are taken by owls, foxes, and both pomarine and parasitic jaegers, as well as a host of other northern predators. The adult is sometimes taken by falcons and owls.

☐ _____ **Black-necked Stilt** (*Himantopus mexicanus*) Nicknames: none / Status: FL=stable to increasing slightly, IUCN=LC / Life span: to 12 years / Length: 13.8-15.4 in. (35-39 cm) / Wingspan: 28 in. (71 cm) / Weight: 4.8-7.8 oz (136-220 g) / Nests: on island in the summer / Found: IW, GB, MZ.

Only the flamingo rivals this bird in having the longest legs in proportion to its body. When the stilt takes flight, its long pinkish-red legs trail behind the bird, giving it a most unusual and unmistakable look. The stark contrasts of the black-and-white markings also help to make this an easy bird to identify.

There are five species of stilts in the world, with the most endangered of them being the Hawaiian subspecies, called the ae'o. In Hawaii a deadly combination of over-hunting, habitat loss, and introduced predators such as rats and feral cats reduced the entire population of stilts to fewer than 400 birds by the mid-1940s. With careful management and habitat restoration, the Hawaiian stilt has recovered to a stable population of more than 1,400.

The stilt is a very noisy bird. When approached, an agitated stilt will yap incessantly until the person or predator passes. Its call, as opposed to its graceful feeding habits, lacks any pretense of refinement. The stilt arrives on Sanibel in early summer to nest. It can generally be found

Black-necked Stilt © Hung V. Do

from late April through September in the Bailey Tract of the "Ding" Darling refuge, as well as any number of other inland locations. It can be found along the beaches, but not as readily. Rarely, it can be seen foraging in the mangrove flats.

The stilt eats primarily small fish, crustaceans, and marine worms. It uses its thin, needle-like beak to prod deep into the soft bottom in search of prey. Its eggs, which are laid directly on the ground or on floating vegetation, are vulnerable to snakes and rats. The adult is sometimes taken by hawks and falcons.

☐ _____ **Belted Kingfisher** (*Ceryle alcyon*) Nicknames: eastern belted kingfisher / Status: FL=stable to a slight decline, IUCN=LC / Life span: to 5 years / Length: 11-13.8 in. (28-35 cm) / Wingspan: 18.9-22.8 in. (48-58 cm) / Weight: 4.9-6 oz (140-170 g) / Nests: from northern Florida to the northern tier of North America from Alaska to Newfoundland / Found: during most of the year except late spring and summer in IW, MZ, UA.

The distinctive loud and rattling call of the belted kingfisher generally announces its arrival or departure from a roosting site. A plunge diver that often hovers in the air studying its potential meal before diving, the kingfisher prefers fresh to saltwater environments. This is a bird that has taken advantage of human activities and can readily be found along highways where drainage swales and ponds have been dredged. The kingfisher is often spotted sitting on a telephone pole or power line over these small bodies of water waiting for an errant minnow or tadpole to get close to the surface.

The belted kingfisher is one of only a handful of avian species in which the female is more brightly colored than the male. There are 93 different species of kingfishers worldwide, including the famous Australian kingfisher, the kookaburra. The best places to find these birds locally are around inland lakes or along the banks of the Sanibel River.

The kingfisher lives year-round throughout most of the United States,

Kingfisher with minnow © Hung V. Do

but some do migrate south during the winter months. Its nests are robbed by grackles, various snakes, and tree-climbing mammals, while the adult is taken by alligators and falcons. The kingfisher is unusual in that, like the cliff swallow, it digs tunnels and makes cavities in riverbanks where it builds its nests and raises its offspring. It is adapting well to human-designed changes in the landscape, and despite some regional losses, it is fundamentally successful.

☐ _____ **Tree Swallow** (*Tachycineta bicolor*) Nicknames: white-bellied swallow / Status: FL=thriving, IUCN=LC / Life span: to 12 years / Length: 4.7-5.9 in. (12-15 cm) / Wingspan: 11.8-13.8 in. (30-35 cm) / Weight: .06-.09 oz (16-25 g) / Nests: in the northern tier of the U.S. all the way into the Northwest Territories / Found: flocking during the winter months, sometimes in the hundreds, in IW.

Two Tree Swallows   © Sara Yunsoo Kim Photography

Over the past decade the tree swallow population, along with a number of other swifts and swallows, has been steadily increasing on Sanibel and Captiva. During the peak winter months, November through May, hundreds, if not thousands, of tree swallows can often be spotted forming what appears to be insect-like swarms above the center of the islands. A common sighting in the Bailey Tract and Sanibel Gardens, this agile flyer can be found early in the morning or at sunset feeding on midges and insects midair. The tree swallow is readily distinguished from its cousin, the barn swallow, by the lack of the deeply forked tail and the rufous coloration.

The tree swallow nests farther north than any other American swallow. It uses other birds' feathers to line its cavity nest. The feather lining is believed to help prevent various ectoparasites such as mites and provide additional warmth to the growing chicks. The tree swallow winters as far south as Panama and Cuba but does not make it into South America.

It is doing well in part because of its unique ability among swallows to survive on seeds and fruit, as well as insects. On the islands it feeds on wax myrtle trees when insects are scarce because of strong winter cold fronts. Nests of the tree swallow are sometimes invaded by predatory birds, including shrikes, and there is some mortality caused by snakes, but by and large the tree swallow has a stable to increasing population across all of North America.

American Robin (*Turdis migratorius*) Nicknames: robin redbreast / Status: FL=stable, IUCN=LC / Life span: to 14 years / Length: 7.9-11 in. (20-28 cm) / Wingspan: 12.2-15.7 in. (31-40 cm) / Weight: 2.7-3 oz (77-85 g) / Nests: in northern Florida all the way to sections of the Arctic Ocean off the Northwest Territories / Found: only during the winter months in IW, MZ, UA.

There is probably not a reader out there who doesn't know what a robin looks like, let alone what it eats. Known for pulling worms out of the ground with its stout, strong beak, the robin is a prime example of a bird that has transitioned well to urban and suburban environments. A large distinctive bird, it is known up north as the quintessential harbinger of spring. On the islands it tends to arrive in large, sometimes enormous, flocks.

© Sara Yunsoo Kim Photography

The robin is one of the leading causes for the proliferation of poison ivy and Brazilian pepper on Sanibel and Captiva. Known for occasionally eating over-ripe fruit, it has sometimes been found disoriented and unable to fly after consuming too many fermented berries. In essence, the robin has a drinking problem.

Some robins have been known to survive to 14 years, but in the wild most do

© Clair Postmus

not survive more than six years. Because of its tendency to forage on the ground, it is quite often preyed upon by snakes, rats, and weasels. It is also prone to pesticide and herbicide contamination from the extensive use of lawn chemicals that get into the robin's food chain. Chemicals that keep the weeds down can do an equally good job of keeping the birds down and should be used sparingly if at all.

Gray Catbird (*Dumetella carolinensis*) Nicknames: black mockingbird / Status: FL=stable, IUCN=LC / Life span: to 17 years / Length: 8.3-9.4 in. (21-24 cm) / Wingspan: 8.7-11.8 in. (22-30 cm) / Weight: .08-2 oz (23-56.5 g) / Nests: in southern Georgia all the way to New England / Found: throughout most of autumn, winter, and late spring in IW, MZ.

© Hung V. Do

Related to the thrushes and mockingbirds, the catbird can also string together its own varied and personal song. It is more widely known for its *meow*-like cry, which it sings incessantly during the winter evenings to establish its feeding territory. Some songs may last up to 10 minutes and can be every bit as endearing as the mockingbird's.

Found almost exclusively in the understory, the catbird, with its dark gray body and black cap, is difficult to spot in dense thicket. In fact, its scientific name, *Dumetella*, means small thicket. It is best spotted in upland areas mid-island and along the Indigo Trail in the "Ding" Darling refuge. It can sometimes be seen flitting from one side of the path or road to the other, then quickly disappearing into the underbrush. At times these fleeting glances of the catbird allow you to notice the rufous under-tail coverts. The catbird is fond of the fruit produced by female gumbo limbo trees in the spring.

The catbird is taken by red-shouldered hawks, falcons, and snakes. It is thriving but has yet to truly transition into urban environments like its close cousin, the mockingbird.

❏ _____ Red-winged Blackbird (_Agelaius phoeniceus_) Nicknames:

Florida redwing, redwing / Status: FL=stable, IUCN=LC / Life span: to 15 years / Length: 6.7-9.1 in. (17-23 cm) / Wingspan: 12.2-15.7 in. (31-40 cm) / Weight: 1.1-2.7 oz (32-77 g) / Nests: in northern Florida all the way to the muskeg taiga of northern Canada / Found: IW along the Sanibel River and residential lakes and ponds.

Male Red-winged Blackbird
© ThroughTheLensGallery.com

Female Red-winged Blackbird   © Hung V. Do

Once more common on the islands than it appears to be today, the red-winged blackbird has a familiar _conk-la-reeeee_ call that is a sure tip-off that it's in the area. This attractive bird has a local population that climbs considerably during the winter months, but there may be small year-round populations found across Southwest Florida. The female looks very different from the male, more like an oversized female house sparrow than a blackbird.

The red-winged blackbird is highly polygynous; some males have been recorded to have as many as 15 separate mates in a given breeding season. Fiercely territorial and aggressively protective of its nest, the red-winged blackbird will attack horses, cattle, and people if they come too close. The male will often use its bright red shoulder patches to intimidate anyone threatening its territory or nest.

Although the red-winged blackbird has not moved into strictly urban environments, it has flourished in recent years by adapting to the many agricultural changes in the landscape. It now nests in alfalfa, wheat, and barley fields, as well as rice plants. Its most familiar nesting site is in cattails where it weaves an intricate nest out of willow bark and cattail leaves. It also appears to be learning to acclimate to golf courses, suburban ponds, and lakes.

It feeds on many of the by-products of our civilization: corn, rice, oats, and barley, as well as native foods from ragweed and cocklebur seed to insects such as grasshoppers and dragonflies. Because it often nests over ponds, fledglings are sometimes taken by bass, snakes, and other aquatic predators. The adult falls victim to hawks and falcons.

☐ _____ **Ovenbird** (*Seiurus aurocapillus*) Nicknames: golden-crown thrush, wood wagtail / Status: FL=stable to increasing, IUCN=LC / Life span: to 11 years / Length: 4.3-5.5 in. (11-14 cm) / Wingspan: 7.5-10.2 in. (19-26 cm) / Weight: 0.6-1 oz (16-28 g) / Nests: just south of the Mason-Dixon Line all the way north into Newfoundland and the Northwest Territories / Found: IW, UA on both islands.

A member of the warbler family, this small bird is more likely to be heard than seen. Known for its repetitive *teacher, teacher, teacher* song, it scurries about the ground in search of insects hiding in the leaves and debris on the forest floor. It gets its name from its covered nest, which with its dome and side entrance resembles a Dutch oven.

Ovenbird　　　　　　　© Clair Postmus

For a small bird, weighing in at roughly three pennies, the ovenbird, like many small warblers, suffers from high mortality—although it has been known to live as long as 11 years under ideal conditions. In the wild it has been estimated that half of all ovenbirds perish every other year, making its actual life span much shorter than it at first appears.

The ovenbird's nest is raided by squirrels, chipmunks, and snakes. Because the adult bird primarily forages on the ground, it too is a common prey for any number of small terrestrial predators.

☐ _____ **Eastern Towhee** (*Pipilo erythrophthalmus*) Nicknames: red-eyed towhee, ground robin, white-eyed towhee / Status: FL=stable to slightly declining for unknown reasons, IUCN=LC / Length: 6.8-8.2 in. (17.3-20.8 cm) / Wingspan: 7.9-11 in. (20-28 cm) / Weight: 1.1-1.8 oz (32-52 g) / Nests: in central and northern Florida to Minnesota / Found: in the winter months in IW.

An uncommon find on the islands, this bird is still sighted with some frequency during the winter months when its mainland numbers swell from northern visitors. An oversized sparrow with very interesting eyes, the eastern towhee is a forest floor dweller that is far easier to hear than it is to see. This bird has several eye-color variations lending it the nicknames, white-eyed and red-eyed towhee.

It was once in the same species as the spotted towhee from the western states but is now considered a separate species. Historically, the two species were linked but the great ice sheets split the North American continent down the middle some 18,000 years ago, creating isolated populations that gave rise to two distinct species. As in the Galapagos, where Charles Darwin found individual islands to harbor

Male Eastern Towhee   © Judd Patterson Photography

similar but distinct species, geologic events such as glaciation will often isolate, then give rise to new species.

The eastern towhee is an omnivore, feeding on a variety of forest food. They eat seeds from ragweed, smartweeds, grasses, acorns, blueberries, wheat, and corn, as well as insects such as millipedes, centipedes, and woodland snails.

A common victim of cowbird parasitism, the female eastern towhee often finds herself raising a far larger chick than she had bargained for. The adult bird is taken by a wide variety of predators, but overall the population appears to be stable across most of the United States, with some slight declines along the Eastern Seaboard.

❒___ **Great Crested Flycatcher** (*Myiachrus crinitus*) Nicknames: southern crested flycatcher, freight-bird / Status: FL=stable, IUCN=LC / Life span: to 13 years / Length: 6.7-8.3 in. (17-21 cm) / Wingspan: 13.4 in. (34 cm) / Weight: 1-1.4 oz (27-40 g) / Nests: from central Florida through the Upper Midwest / Found: in the winter due to the increase of migrants into Florida in IW, UA.

©ThroughTheLensGallery.com

The great crested flycatcher inhabits the treetops and is seldom found in the understory and virtually never on the ground. Unlike its cousins, the eastern and gray kingbirds, it does not like perching on telephone lines. It sits on high exposed limbs and sallies out to catch insects in midair. Although it has been known to eat some seeds and berries, the majority of its diet consists of flying insects.

This bird has benefited, as has the white-tailed deer, from forest fragmentation, and it is thriving within its rather large range. It migrates as far south as Central America, and its

numbers across Florida increase dramatically during the cooler winter months.

The great crested flycatcher is unusual in that its nest usually contains at least some crinkly material, formerly snakeskin but now commonly plastic wrappers, cellophane, or onion skins. No one has really ever been able to explain this strange behavior. It is a cavity nester and will readily occupy an old woodpecker nesting hole or sometimes take to man-made bird boxes. The nests are preyed upon by other birds, snakes, and tree-climbing mammals. Because of its flying prowess, the adult is seldom targeted by falcons.

Flycatcher with dragonfly
© Clair Postmus

☐ _____ **Gray Kingbird** (*Tyannus dominicensis*) Nicknames: pipiry flycatcher / Status: FL=stable, IUCN=LC / Life span: to 11 years / Length: 9 in. (22 cm) / Wingspan: 14.5-16 in. (37-40 cm) / Weight: 1.5 oz (42 g) / Nests: on Sanibel in the summer; winters in South America / Found: MZ, UA on both islands.

A neo-tropical species, the gray kingbird is a fairly common sighting here during the summer. It is unusual in that it comes only as far north as Florida to nest. It is fond of perching on power lines, and that is the most likely place to find one. It is also comfortable hanging around baseball fields and golf courses.

It looks similar to the eastern kingbird, which has the same migration pattern but continues all the way north to the Yukon and Northwest Territories of Canada. Both birds are mostly gray, but the eastern kingbird displays dark black on the head and back, while the gray kingbird is gray throughout these areas. Whereas the

Courtesy Wikipedia Commons

eastern kingbird has a white tip on its black tail, the gray kingbird is solid black. At a distance, these two are easy to confuse.

The gray kingbird eats mostly insects while in Florida but returns to fruits and berries once it heads back to the Amazon basin for the winter. It aggressively defends its range, as well as its nest. It has been known to shag off large hawks, crows, and blue jays and does not show any fear of these enemies. The kingbird is taken by a vast array of South American predators, especially large hawks and snakes, but the adult has few natural enemies in Florida.

❑ _____ **Loggerhead Shrike** (*Lanius ludovicianus*) Nicknames: butcher bird, French mockingbird, catbird / Status: FL=stable, IUCN=LC / Life span: to 12 years / Length: 7.9-9.1 in. (20-23 cm) / Wingspan: 11-12.6 in. (28-32 cm) / Weight: 1.2-1.8 oz (35-50 g) / Nests: throughout Florida year-round; expands into southern Canada in the summer / Found: throughout the year but more common in the winter months, in IW, UA.

The loggerhead shrike is an amazing example of nature doing the unexpected when it finds a niche not being utilized by other creatures in a given environment. It belongs in the *Passeriformes* order, which includes most of the songbirds such as the warbler, cardinal, and sparrow. These birds, commonly called passerines and known for their singing and perching abilities, are hardly considered predators in the same sense as hawks, owls, and eagles, but the loggerhead shrike is a songbird predator, and an excellent one at that.

The nickname butcher bird aptly describes this unusual bird. Lacking the strong feet and powerful talons of a raptor, the shrike has devised another method of holding and devouring its prey. It catches mice, frogs, insects, and other birds, then impales the catch on a large thorn or barbed-wire fence and rips it apart with its strong beak. If you examine the shrike closely, you will note that the beak is shaped much more like a hawk's than that of a typical songbird.

In appearance, the loggerhead shrike vaguely resembles and is roughly the

Loggerhead Shrike   © Clair Postmus

same size as a mockingbird. It has a distinctive black eye band that makes it easy to spot. The shrike is not a common sighting on the islands and can be found far more readily on the mainland. There is a resident Florida population but the winter population swells every year with the return of the migratory birds from the northern tier of their range.

Because it is an aggressive predator, the adult shrike is rarely targeted by other prey. The chicks suffer from some snake and rodent predation, and the entire Eastern Seaboard population is suffering from habitat loss and pesticide and herbicide overuse.

□ _____ **Eastern Phoebe** (*Sayornis phoebe*) Nicknames: pee-wee, tick bird, bridge bird / Status: FL=expanding its range, IUCN=LC / Life span: to 10 years / Length: 5.5-6.7 in. (14-17 cm) / Wingspan: 10.2-11 in. (26-28 cm) / Weight: 0.6-0.7 oz (16-21 g) / Nests: from southern Georgia year-round all the way into the Northwest Territories in the summer / Found: during the winter only in IW, UA.

Eastern Phoebe   ©ThroughTheLensGallery.com

Named for its call, an easily recognized *fee-bee, fee-bee,* this bird has the honor of being the first bird ever banded in America. That banding was done in 1804 by a naturalist whose name has since become synonymous with birding in America, John James Audubon. He tied a small silver thread around one leg of a migratory phoebe in an attempt to learn whether or not the bird would return to the same nesting site the following spring.

The bird in fact did return, and the eastern phoebe is now known to be extremely site-specific when nesting. This species has also benefited from man-made changes to the landscape. It is fond of using any number of human structures such as bridges, overpasses, culverts, and building ledges for nesting sites. It cements its cup-like nest to concrete walls or ceilings, then lines it with moss, fine grass, or leaves. This adaptation has made urban changes a godsend for the population of this small bird.

The phoebes eat mostly insects but will also dine on very small fish, berries, and fruit. Its nests are sometimes raided by other predatory birds, and it has suffered some cowbird parasitism. The adult phoebe is taken on occasion by kestrels and merlins.

☐ _____ **Cedar Waxwing** (*Bombycilla cedrorum*) Nicknames: cedar bird, seal, cherry robin, Canadian robin / Status: FL=stable, IUCN=LC / Life span: to 8 years / Length: 5.5-6.7 in. (14-17 cm) / Wingspan: 8.7-11.8 in. (22-30 cm) / Weight: 1.1 oz (32 g) / Nests: north of the Mason-Dixon Line up into north-central Canada / Found: during fall, winter and spring in IW, UA.

© Sara Yunsoo Kim Photography

Never a common bird on the islands, the cedar waxwing is nonetheless a spectacular sighting once encountered. Its gorgeous coloration—brownish above, yellow belly, and white under-tail coverts—makes it easy to identify. Slightly smaller than a cardinal, but with a similar crest, the markings of this bird through a pair of good binoculars make it a welcome sight. The adult waxwing extrudes a waxy, reddish substance from the feather shafts of its secondary flight feathers, perhaps as a signal of age or social status, but no one has been able to determine exactly why. The waxwing ventures all the way to central Canada in the summer and as far south as the northern edge of South America during the winter months.

© Sara Yunsoo Kim Photography

The waxwing survives almost entirely on fruit and berries. That characteristic sometimes dooms parasitic cowbird chicks because when the cowbird lays its eggs in a waxwing's nest, the food that the waxwing brings to the young cowbirds does not contain enough of the insect protein they need to thrive. The cedar waxwing has been known to ingest fermented berries not only to the point of intoxication, but also to the point of death from alcohol poisoning.

It builds solitary nests but will sometimes roost in loose colonies. Its nests can be raided by any number of winged and four-legged predators, and the adult is sometimes taken by falcons.

Indigo Bunting © Clair Postmus

☐ _____ **Indigo Bunting** (*Passerina cyanea*) Nicknames: indigo bird, swamp bluebird / Status: FL=stable, IUCN=LC / Life span: to 9 years / Length: 4.7-5.1 in. (12-13 cm) / Wingspan: 7.5-8.7 in. (19-22 cm) / Weight: 0.4-0.6 oz (12-18 g) / Nests: from northern Florida to the northern edge of the lower forty-eight / Found: during the spring and fall migrations in IW.

A neo-tropical traveler, the indigo bunting is most commonly seen in late April and May and again in August through October as it flies to and from its northern nesting grounds. The indigo winters in the Caribbean, southern Mexico, and Central America. It is a joy to see, but as is the case with so many passerines, it is best observed through a pair of binoculars.

An interesting characteristic of the indigo bunting is that it migrates at night. Scientists still do not completely understand how this tiny bird is able to do so, but they believe the bird has somehow learned to navigate by starlight. Another fascinating aspect is its song. Each individual bunting's song is unique to its locale. Males as close together as a few hundred yards have different songs, sometimes retaining these through two or three generations, then slowly changing them over the decades.

The indigo bunting is an omnivore, eating a wide variety of seeds, grains, and wild berries, as well as insects and their larvae. It is semi-monogamous and a solitary nester. Because it forages around fields, it is vulnerable to pesticide and fertilizer poisoning. It also suffers from cowbird parasitism and habitat loss.

❏ _____ **Painted Bunting** (*Passerina ciris*) Nicknames: nonpareil / Status: FL=declining, IUCN-NT / Life span: to 9 years / Length: 4.7-5.1 in. (12-13 cm) / Wingspan: 8-8.5 in. (20-21 cm) / Weight: 0.5-0.7 oz (13-19 g) / Nests: along the Eastern Seaboard to North Carolina, and a separate race nests in east Texas through Arkansas / Found: during the spring and fall migrations in IW, UA.

© Judd Patterson Photography

Perhaps the single most colorful bird that passes through Florida, the male painted bunting is a curious palate of blue, lime-green, red, and gray. The female is more of a greenish-yellow color and nowhere near as brilliantly colored as the male.

There are two distinct populations of the painted bunting: an eastern and a western race. The birds coming through Florida generally winter in Cuba and Central America, while the western race winters in Northern Mexico. Some birds remain in South Florida for the winter, although not specifically on Sanibel or Captiva.

These birds have one extremely rare characteristic, which is even more unexpected given the small size of this animal: the male is very territorial and aggressive toward other male buntings. Fights between rival males can become extremely animated, involving fierce pecking, beating each other with their wings, and grappling, sometimes resulting in the death of the defeated bird, a highly unusual outcome among avian rivals.

The painted bunting is approaching threatened status primarily because of habitat loss in its eastern population. It prefers dense thickets and mixed pine and hardwood forests. It is not adapting well to human alterations to the environment, although it can often be spotted on the islands in urban locations.

☐ _____ **Yellow-rumped Warbler** (*Dendroica coronata*) Nicknames: myrtle warbler, Audubon's warbler / Status: FL=stable, IUCN=LC / Life span: to 8 years / Length: 4.7-5.5 in. (12-14 cm) / Wingspan: 7.5-9.1 in. (19-23 cm) / Weight: 0.4-0.5 oz (12-13 g) / Nests: throughout Canada and in the Rocky Mountains during the summer / Found: during the winter months in IW, GB.

Far and away the most abundant wintering warbler in Florida, the yellow-rumped warbler is a common sighting on the islands from October through April. A clue to its abundance lies in one of its nicknames, the myrtle warbler. It is the only warbler able to digest the waxes found in bayberries and wax myrtle trees, both of which are common on the islands.

©ThroughTheLensGallery.com

An extremely versatile feeder, the yellow-rumped warbler takes advantage of a wide array of habitats and the various foods it might encounter there. Sometimes found on beaches picking through the rack line, sometimes skimming insects from the surface of rivers and ponds, even gleaning insects from piles of manure, this warbler is adept at taking a meal anywhere it can.

The summer breeding plumage is much more colorful than its plainer winter coats, but it seldom molts into that plumage before arriving in its nesting area. That being said, its yellowish rump can still be

©ThroughTheLensGallery.com

found during the winter months, though it is far more subdued in color.

Like all smaller birds, some predation occurs at the nest, both to the chicks and eggs, and the adult yellow-rumped warbler is occasionally taken by kestrels and merlins. Overall this very adaptable bird is thriving and is not likely to be placed on any threatened lists anytime soon.

Yellow Warbler (*Dendroica petechia*) Nicknames: Cuban golden warbler, golden warbler, wild canary, summer yellow-bird / Status: FL=stable, IUCN=LC / Life span: to 10 years / Length: 4.7-5.1 in. (12-13 cm) / Wingspan: 6.3-7.9 in. (16-20 cm) / Weight: 0.3-0.4 oz (9-11 g) / Nests: north of the Mason-Dixon Line to Alaska, as well as a remnant nesting population in the Florida Keys / Found: in the winter in MZ, IW.

© Sara Yunsoo Kim Photography

This nearly solid yellow warbler can sometimes be confused with the goldfinch, but has a softer coloration that includes streaks of light brown. Like most warblers, the yellow warbler has a beautiful song that almost always begins with a rapid *sweet, sweet, I'm so sweet* followed by a dozen variations on that call. This is truly one of the most stunning of all the warblers.

Although the yellow warbler suffers from cowbird parasitism, it has evolved a fascinating countermeasure to deal with the problem. If a cowbird lays an egg in a yellow warbler's nest, the female quickly builds a new nest over the old one, entombing the cowbird's egg beneath it. If the cowbird lays another egg in the nest, the yellow warbler responds in kind by building yet another nest on top of the second egg. This process has been observed to create nests that are up to six layers high. Eventually the cowbird elects to choose another host bird for its egg deposit.

The yellow warbler forages in bushes, shrubs, and trees. It eats mostly insects, caterpillars, and fruit. It suffers from the use of herbicides and pesticides, which results in the poisoning of the bird and its chicks. As is true of all warblers, the adult is taken by kestrels and merlins, but the bird is in far more danger from habitat loss and the behavior of man than any of its other predators.

© Joseph Blanda, M.D.

☐ _____ **Palm Warbler** (*Dendroica palmarum*) Nicknames: yellow palm warbler, western palm warbler / Status: FL=stable, IUCN=LC / Life span: to 6 years / Length: 4.7-5.5 in. (12-14 cm) / Wingspan: 7.9-8.3 in. (20-21 cm) / Weight: 0.2-0.5 oz (7-13 g) / Nests: in far northern Canada and Newfoundland / Found: from September through April in IW.

A winter resident of the islands, the palm warbler in a way belies its namesake. During the summer it migrates to the distant north, far from its winter palms, breeding in the open boreal coniferous forest as far north as the open tundra. The palm warbler is the second most abundant winter warbler; only the yellow-rumped warbler can be as easily spotted. Although the palm warbler has a yellow rump as well, it is easily separated from the yellow-rumped warbler by its brown cap and yellow eyebrow and throat. It is also known to bob its little tail continuously.

Its primary diet consists of insects, beetles, caterpillars, and grasshoppers, but during cold fronts when insects can prove scarce, it turns to small fruits and seeds for nourishment. The adult is sometimes taken by kestrels and merlins, but by and large it has a fairly stable population throughout Florida.

Palm Warbler perched
© Hung V. Do

Black-and-white Warbler (*Mniotilta varia*) Nicknames: none / Status: FL=stable, IUCN=LC / Life span: to 11 years / Length: 4.3-5.1 in. (11-13 cm) / Wingspan: 7.1-8.7 in. (18-22 cm) / Weight: 0.3-0.5 oz (8-15 g) / Nests: from the mid-south all the way into upper Canada to the Northwest Territories / Found: every month of the year except June in IW.

© Hung V. Do

An absolutely stunning black-and-white pattern greets the lucky birder who happens upon one of these warblers. This pop-art streaking makes the black-and-white warbler one of the easiest small birds to identify, since no other buntings, vireos, or other small birds have such a distinctive feather pattern.

The black-and-white warbler feeds unlike any other warbler. Its unusual extended hind toe and claw allow it to feed in much the same manner as a nuthatch, scurrying up and down trees, sometimes upside down, searching for its primary food, insects. It also has a longer bill, enabling it to take insects from deep bark and tree crevices.

It has one of the longest migrations of any warbler, summering as far north as the southern edge of the Yukon and wintering

©ThroughTheLensGallery.com

as far south as northern Peru. It suffers heavily from cowbird parasitism, habitat loss, and forest fragmentation. Despite these factors, it is a fairly common and beautiful little bird found in Florida during the winter.

☐ _____ **White-eyed Vireo** (*Vireo griseus*) Nicknames: none / Status: FL=stable, IUCN=LC / Life span: to 7 years / Length: 4.3-5.1 in. (11-13 cm) / Wingspan: 6.7 in. (17 cm) / Weight: 0.4-0.5 oz (10-14 g) / Nests: in the Southeast as far north as southern Iowa / Found: mostly during the peak winter months in IW.

©ThroughTheLensGallery.com

Identified by its whitish-colored eye, this little bird wears a pair of yellow spectacles around that bright white iris. It is a fairly common winter resident on the islands but prefers to feed in thick underbrush, making it difficult to spot. It does not sing as much during the summer breeding season, saving its lovely song, which usually begins with a sharp *chick*, for Floridians to enjoy. The white-eyed vireo's migration range extends as far south as the Yucatan and as far north as Iowa.

Feeding mostly on insects, snails, and spiders, the vireo has also been known to take small lizards, fruits, and berries. It is subject to cowbirds laying their eggs in its nests, but overall is doing quite well throughout its range.

☐ _____ **Ruby-throated Hummingbird** (*Archilochus colubris*) Nicknames: none / Status: FL=stable, IUCN=LC / Life span: to 9 years / Length: 2.8-3.5 in. (7-9 cm) / Wingspan: 3.1-4.3 in. (8-11 cm) / Weight: 0.1-0.2 oz (2-6 g) / Nests: in northern Florida to southern Canada / Found: throughout all but the summer months in IW, UA.

The islands' smallest bird, the ruby-throated hummingbird is an amazing creature. One of the few birds able to truly hover and the only bird able to fly backwards and upside down, the ruby-throated hummingbird beats its wings so fast it creates a humming sound. When in flight its feet virtually disappear into its tiny body, making it more aerodynamically perfect.

This bird is found on the islands only on occasion and is far more commonly seen in the summer throughout its northern range. Despite its tiny size, the

Male Ruby-throated Hummingbird
© Joseph Blanda, M.D.

ruby-throated hummingbird stores enough fat to enable it to fly nonstop across the 600-mile expanse of the Gulf of Mexico twice a year.

The hummingbird is found only in the Americas, from Tierra del Fuego to Alaska. There is an amazing 325 species of hummingbirds, though the vast majority of these birds live in Central and South America.

Unlike humans, the hummingbird is able to see things in the ultraviolet color spectrum, which lies far above our eyesight capabilities. This allows the hummingbird to spot the flowering plants upon which they rely for nectar. Fascinating to observe at feeders, it seems to be attracted to the color red. Sadly, this is also a cause of mortality, since it is attracted to the red tops of certain power-line capacitors and is electrocuted when attempting to feed on them.

The hummingbird is an important pollinator, but it also eats nectar-eating insects and tiny spiders. The high-energy diet of nectar is essential to its metabolic needs, with some hummingbirds known to have heart rates as high as 1,260 beats per minute. That is roughly 1,200 beats faster than the heartbeat of a well-trained athlete. As if that isn't enough of an amazing feat, it has been calculated that when flying forward, a hummingbird's wing can exceed 4,500 beats a minute, or 75 beats per second.

The ruby-throated hummingbird will readily come to artificial feeders, attracted by sugar water. Only white granulated sugar has been proven safe to use: a ratio of one cup sugar to four cups water is the most common recipe.

The hummingbird is seldom preyed upon as an adult, but the size of its tiny eggs—smaller than jellybeans—and chicks make them vulnerable to being eaten by predators as small as lizards, mice, and tiny snakes. Some of the South American species, especially the highly specialized birds, are endangered, but the ruby-throated hummingbird appears to be doing well throughout its range, possibly in part because of the innumerable feeders put out across the backyards of North America every summer.

The Rest of the Birds

The following birds have been seen on Sanibel and Captiva with some regularity. Because there are more than 291 species of birds that have been officially documented on the two islands, there is simply not sufficient room to give detailed information and photographs for each of them. Following is a checklist of seventy-two additional species that can be found on Sanibel and Captiva. For photos and more information on these birds go to www.allaboutbirds.org which is the official Web site of the Cornell Lab of Ornithology.

☐ _____ **American Bittern** (*Botarus lentinginosus*) Nicknames: stake driver, thunder pump, sun-gazer, Indian hen / Status: FL=stable, IUCN=LC / Life span: to 8 years / Length: 23.6-33.5 in (60-85 cm) / Wingspan: 36.2 in (92 cm) / Weight: 13.1-17.6 oz (370-500 g) / Nests on mainland Florida / Found: IW fall through spring-rare.

☐ _____ **Least Bittern** (*Ixobrychus exilis*) Nicknames: none / Status: FL=stable, IUCN=LC / Life span: n/a / Length: 11-14.2 in (28-36 cm) / Wingspan: 16.1-18.1 in (41-46 cm) / Weight 1.8-3.6 oz (51-102 g) / Nests on island / Found: IW year round-rare.

☐ _____ **Glossy Ibis** (*Plegadis falcinellus*) Nicknames: black curlew, bronze curlew / Status: FL=stable, IUCN=LC / Life span: to 21 years / Length: 18.9-26 in (48-66 cm) / Wingspan: 36 in (91 cm) / Weight: 17.6-28.2 oz (500-800 g) / Nests on mainland Florida / Found: year round-rare.

☐ _____ **American Wigeon** (*Anas americana*) Nicknames: baldpate, gray duck / Status: FL=stable, IUCN=LC / Life span: to 20 years / Length: 16.5-23.2 in (42-59 cm) / Wingspan: 33.1 in (84 cm) / Weight: 19-46.9 oz (.54-1.33 kg) / Migratory, nests in northern U.S. and Canada / Found: MZ, IW fall through spring.

☐ _____ **Northern Shoveler** (*Anas clypeata*) Nicknames: spoonbill, spoon-billed wigeon / Status: FL=stable, IUCN=LC / Life span: to 18 years / Length: 17.3-20.1 in (44-51 cm) / Wingspan: 30 in (76 cm) / Weight: 14.1-28.9 oz (400-820 g) / Migratory, nests in western U.S. and Canada / Found: MZ, IW fall through spring.

☐ _____ **Northern Pintail** (*Anas acuta*) Nicknames: sprig, sprigtail, spike, spiketail / Status: FL=stable, IUCN=LC / Life span: to 22 years / Length: 20.1-29.9 in (51-76 cm) / Wingspan: 34 in (88 cm) / Weight: 1-3.2 lb (.50-1.45 kg) / Migratory, nests in northern plains and Canada / Found: MZ, IW fall through spring.

☐ _____ **Green-winged Teal** (*Anas crecca*) Nicknames: greenwing, common teal / Status: FL=stable, IUCN=LC / Life span: to 20 years / Length: 12.2-15.4 in (31-39 cm) / Wingspan: 20.5-23.2 in (52-59 cm) / Weight: 4.9-17.6 oz (140-500 g)/ Migratory, nests mostly in Canada / Found: IW, MZ fall through spring-rare.

☐ _____ **Lesser Scaup** (*Aythya affinis*) Nicknames: bluebill, bullhead, raft duck, little bluebill, blackhead / Status: FL=stable, IUCN=LC / Life span: to 18 years / Length: 15.4-18.1 in (39-46 cm) / Wingspan: 26.8-30.7 in (68-78 cm) / Weight: 1-2.4 lb (.45-1.1 kg) / Migratory, nests mostly in Canada / Found: MZ, IW in the winter in spring-rare.

❏ _____ **Northern Harrier** (*Circus cyaneus*) Nicknames: marsh hawk / Status: FL=stable, IUCN=LC / Life span: to 16 years / Length: 18.1-19.7 in (46-50 cm) / Wingspan: 40.2-46.5 in (102-118 cm) / Weight: 10.6-26.5 oz (300-750 g) / Migratory, nests across northern tier of U.S. and deep into Canada / Found: IW, MZ, UA fall through spring.

❏ _____ **Sharp-shinned Hawk** (*Accipiter striatus*) Nicknames: little blue darter / Status: FL=stable, IUCN=LC / Life span: to 19 years / Length: 9.4-13.4 in (24-34 cm) / Wingspan: 16.9-22 in (43-56 cm) / Weight: 3.1-7.7 oz (87-218 g) / Migratory, nests from the Mason/Dixon line north to Canada / Found: IW, MZ fall through spring-rare.

❏ _____ **Broad-winged Hawk** (*Buteo platypterus*) Nicknames: none / Status: FL=stable, IUCN=LC / Life span: to 16 years / Length: 13.4-17.3 in (34-44 cm) / Wingspan: 31.9-39.4 in (81-100 cm) / Weight: 9.3-19.8 oz (265-560 g) / Migratory, nests in northern Florida to Canada / Found: IW, MZ in the winter and spring-rare.

❏ ___ **Short-tailed Hawk** (*Buteo brachyurus*) Nicknames: none / Status: FL=stable, IUCN=LC / Life span: n/a / Length: 16 in (40 cm) / Wingspan: 35 in (90 cm) / Weight: 14-20 oz (400-500 g) / Nests in the mainland of Florida / Found: MZ, UA, IW year round but rare.

❏ _____ **Red-tailed Hawk** (*Buteo jamaicensis*) Nicknames: buzzard / Status: FL=stable, IUCN=LC / Life span: to 28 years / Length: 17.7-52.4 in (45-65 cm) / Wingspan: 44.9-52.4 in (114-133 cm) / Weight: 1.5-2.86 lb (0.69-1.3 kg) / Nests in the mainland of Florida / Found: IW, MZ, UA only during the winter and spring-rare.

❏ ___ **Clapper rail** (*Rallus longirostris*) Nicknames: saltwater marsh hen / Status: FL=stable, IUCN=LC / Life span: to 7 years / Length: 12.6-16.1 in (32-41 cm) / Wingspan: 19 in (48 cm) / Weight: 5.6-14.1 oz (160-400 g) / Nests in the mainland of Florida / Found: MZ, IW year round but rare.

❏ _____ **King Rail** (*Rallus elegans*) Nicknames: freshwater marsh hen, mud hen / Status: FL=declining, IUCN=LC / Life span: n/a / Length: 15-18.9 in (38-48 cm) / Wingspan: 20 in (51 cm) / Weight: 10.8-13.1 oz (305-370 g) / Nests on island / Found: IW, MZ - rare.

❏ ___ **Virginia Rail** (*Rallus limicola*) Nicknames: marsh hen / Status: FL=stable, IUCN=LC / Life span: n/a / Length: 7.9-10.6 in (20-27 cm) / Wingspan: 12.6-15 in (32-38 cm) / Weight: 2.3-3.4 oz (65-95 g) / Migratory, nests along the northern tier of the lower 48 into southern Canada / Found: IW, MZ during winter and spring.

❏ ___ **Sora** (*Porzana carolina*) Nicknames: Carolina crake, meadow chicken, ortolan / Status: FL=stable, IUCN=LC / Life span: n/a / Length: 7.9-9.8 in (20-25 cm) / Wingspan: 14 in (35 cm) / Weight: 1.7-4 oz (49-112 g) / Migratory, nests north of the Mason-Dixon line / Found: IW, MZ during winter and spring-rare.

❏ ___ **Limpkin** (*Aramus guarauna*) Nicknames: crying bird, courlan / Status: FL=stable, IUCN=LC / Life span: n/a / Length: 25.2-28.7 in (64-73 cm) / Wingspan: 39.8-42.1 (101-107 cm) / Weight: 31.7-45.9 oz (0.9-1.3 kg) / Nests in the mainland of Florida / Found: IW year round but rare.

❑ _____ **Solitary Sandpiper** (*Tringa solitaria*) Nicknames: tip-up, wood sandpiper / Status: FL=stable, IUCN=LC / Life span: n/a / Length: 7.5-9.1 in (19-23 cm) / Wingspan: 22 in (56 cm) / Weight: 1.1-2.3 oz (31-65 g) / Migratory, nests in northen Canada / Found: IW, MZ, UA in the fall and spring as it flies between North and South America.

❑ _____ **Semipalmated Sandpiper** (*Calidris pusilla*) Nicknames: peep / Status: FL=stable, IUCN=LC / Life span: to 19 years / Length: 5.1-5.9 in (13-15 cm) / Wingspan: 11.4-11.8 in (29-30 cm) / 0.7-1.1 oz (21-32 g) / Migratory, nests in the high Arctic / Found: GB, IW, MZ in the fall and spring.

❑ ____ **Stilt Sandpiper** (*Calidris himantopus*) Nicknames: none / Status: FL=stable, IUCN=LC / Life span: n/a / Length: 7.9-9.1 in (20-23 cm) / Wingspan: 18 in (47 cm) / Weight: 1.8-2.5 oz (50-70 g) / Migratory, nests in the Arctic / Found: IW, MZ, GB during the winter and spring-rare.

❑ _____ **Wilson's Snipe** (*Gallinago delicata*) Nicknames: common snipe, Jack snipe, English snipe / Status: FL=stable, IUCN=LC / Life span: to 9 years / Length: 10.6-12.6 in (27-32 cm) / Wingspan: 16.1-17.3 in (41-44 cm) / Weight: 2.8-5.1 oz (79-146 g) / Migratory, nests along the northern tier well into Canada / Found: IW in the winter only.

❑ _____ **Herring Gull** (*Larus argentatus*) Nicknames: none / Status: FL=stable, IUCN=LC / Life span: to 28 years / Length: 22-26 in (56-66 cm) / Wingspan: 53.9-57.5 in (137-146 cm) / Weight: 1.75-2.75 lb (.80-1.25 kg) / Nests across Canada in the Maritimes / Found: migratory, GB, MZ, CW during the winter and spring.

❑ _____ **Bonaparte's Gull** (*Larus philadeplphia*) Nicknames: surf gull / Status: FL=stable, IUCN=LC / Life span: n/a / Length: 11-15 in (28-38 cm) / Wingspan: 29.9-31.5 in (76-80 cm) / Weight 6.3-7.9 oz (180-225 g) / Nests in northern Canada / Found: migratory, GB, MZ, CW during winter and spring.

❑ ____ **Caspian Tern** (*Sterna caspia*) Nicknames: none / Status: FL=staple, IUCN=LC / Life span: to 29 years / Length: 18.5-21.3 in (47-54 cm) / Wingspan: 47.2-53.1 in (120-135 cm) / Weight: 1.15-1.75 lb (530-782 g) / Nests in Newfoundland and central Manitoba, Canada / Found: migratory, GB, MZ, CW during winter and spring.

❑ ___ **Yellow-billed Cuckoo** (*Coccyzus americanus*) Nicknames: rain crow / Status: FL=stable, IUCN=LC / Life span: to 5 years / Length: 10.2-11.8 in (26-30 cm) / Wingspan: 15-16.9 in (38-43 cm) / Weight: 1.9-2.3 oz (55-65 g) / Nests in the southern U.S. during the summer, winters in South America / Found: passes through during migration north, MZ, IW during the spring-rare.

❑ _____ **Chuck-will's-widow** (*Caprimulgus carolinensis*) Nicknames: Dutch whip-poor-will, Spanish whip-poor-will / Status: FL=stable, IUCN-LC / Life span: to 14 years / Length: 11-12.6 in (28-32 cm) / Wingspan: 22.8-24 in (58-61 cm) / Weight: 2.3-6.6 oz (66-188 g) / Nests in northern Florida, possibly on Sanibel and the Southeast / Found: migratory, IW, MZ, UA during all but the winter months.

❏ _____ **Whip-poor-will** (*Caprimulgus vociferus*) Nicknames: none / Status: FL=stable, IUCN=LC / Life span: to 4 years / Length: 8.7-10.2 in (22-26 cm) / Wingspan: 17.7-18.9 in (45-48 cm) / Weight: 1.5-2.3 oz (43-64 g) / Nests east of the Mississippi across the Midwest and Northeastern U.S. / Found: migratory, UA, IW during the spring.

❏ _____ **Chimney Swift** (*Chaetura pelagica*) Nicknames: chimney swallow, chimney bat, chimney sweep / Status: FL=stable, IUCN=LC / Life span: to 14 years / Length: 4.7-5.9 in (12-15 cm) / Wingspan: 10.6-11.8 in (27-30 cm) / Weight: 0.6-1.1 oz (17-30 g) / Nests on the mainland Florida all the way to southern Canada / Found: migratory, passes through to and from South America, IW, MZ, UA in the spring.

❏ _____ **Yellow-bellied Sapsucker** (*Sphyrapicus varius*) Nicknames: none / Status: FL=stable, IUCN=LC / Life span: to 6 years / Length: 7.1-8.7 in (18-22 cm) / Wingspan: 13.4-15.7 in (34-40 cm) / Weight: 1.5-1.9 oz (43-55 g) / Nests in the upper Midwest well into Canada / Found: migratory, IW, MZ, UA during the winter and spring.

❏ _____ **Downy Woodpecker** (*Picoides pubescens*) Nicknames: sapsucker / Status: FL=stable, IUCN=LC / Life span: to 12 years / Length: 5.5-6.7 in (14-17 cm) / Wingspan: 9.8-11.8 in (25-30 cm) / Weight: 0.7-1 oz (21-28 g) / Nests on mainland Florida and throughout most of the U.S. to Alaska / Found: IW, UA year round but rare.

❏ _____ **Northern Flicker** (*Colaptes auratus*) Nicknames: yellowhammer, highhole, golden-winged woodpecker / Status: FL=stable, IUCN=LC / Life span: n/a / Length: 11-12.2 in (28-31 cm) / Wingspan: 16.5-20.1 in (42-51 cm) / Weight: 3.9-5.6 oz (110-160 g) / Nests throughout North America and on the islands / Found: IW, MZ, UA year round.

❏ _____ **Eastern Wood-Pewee** (*Contopus virens*) Nicknames: none / Status: FL=stable, IUCN=LC / Life span: to 7 years / Length: 5.9 in (15 cm) / Wingspan: 9.1-10.2 in (23-26 cm) / Weight: 0.4-0.7 oz (10-19 g) / Nests in northern Florida to the upper Midwest / Found: migratory, IW, MZ, UA in the spring.

❏ _____ **Acadian Flycatcher** (*Empidonax virescens*) Nicknames: green-crested flycatcher / Status: FL=stable, IUCN=LC / Life span: to 11 years / Length: 5.9 in (15 cm) / Wingspan: 9.1 in (23 cm) / Weight: 0.4-0.5 oz (11-14 g) / Nests east of the Mississippi from northern Florida to southern Minnesota eastward / Found: migratory, IW, MZ, UA during the spring.

❏ _____ **Blue-headed Vireo** (*Vireo solitarius*) Nicknames: solitary vireo / Status: FL=stable, IUCN=LC / Life span: to 7 years / Length: 5.1-5.9 in (13-15 cm) / Wingspan: 7.9-9.4 in (20-24 cm) / Weight: 0.5-0.7 oz (13-19 g) / Nests across southern Canada / Found: migratory, IW, MZ, UA during the winter and spring.

❏ _____ **Red-eyed Vireo** (*Vireo olivaceus*) Nicknames: hanging bird, preacher bird / Status: FL=stable, IUCN=LC / Life span: to 10 years / Length: 4.7-5.1 in (12-13 cm) / Wingspan: 9.1-9.8 in (23-25 cm) / Weight: 0.4-0.9 oz (12-26 g) / Nests throughout the lower U.S. except in the western and southwestern states / Found: migratory to and from South America, IW, MZ, UA in the fall and spring.

❏ _____ **Black-whiskered Vireo** (*Vireo altiloquus*) Nicknames: none / Status: FL=stable, IUCN=LC / Life span: n/a / Length: 5.9-6.3 in (15-16 cm) / Wingspan: 10 in (26 cm) / Weight: 0.6-0.8 oz (17-22 g) / Nests on island / Found: migratory, IW, MZ, UA winters in South America.

❏ _____ **American Crow** (*Corvus brachyrhynchos*) Nicknames: common crow, southern crow, corn crow / Status: FL=stable, IUCN=LC / Life span: to 14 years / Length: 15.7-20.9 in (40-53 cm) / Wingspan: 33.5-39.4 in (85-100 cm) / Weight: 11.1-21.9 oz (316-620 g) / Nests on mainland Florida and throughout the U.S. / Found: IW, GB, MZ, CW, UA year round.

❏ _____ **Purple Martin** (*Progne subis*) Nicknames: black martin, gourd martin, house martin / Status: FL=stable, IUCN=LC / Life span: to 13 years / Length: 7.5-7.9 in (19-20 cm) / Wingspan: 15.4-16.1 in (39-42 cm) / Weight: 1.6-2.1 oz (45-60 g) / Nests on islands / Found: migratory, IW, MZ, UA during the winter months.

❏ _____ **Northern Rough-winged Swallow** (*Stelgidopteryx serripennis*) Nicknames: sand martin, gully martin, gully bird / Status: FL=stable, IUCN=LC / Life span: to 6 years / Length: 4.7-5.9 in (12-15 cm) / Wingspan: 10.6-11.8 in (27-30 cm) / Weight: 0.4-0.6 oz (10-18 g) / Nests from Central Florida north to Canada / Found: migratory, IW, MZ, UA at any time of the year.

❏ _____ **Bank Swallow** (*Riparia riparia*) Nicknames: sand martin / Status: FL=stable, IUCN=LC / Life span: to 8 years / Length: 4.7-5.5 in (12-14 cm) / Wingspan: 9.8-11.4 in (25-29 cm) / Weight: 0.4-0.7 oz (10-19 g) / Nests across the northern U.S. deep into Canada and Alaska / Found: migratory, IW, UA, MZ during the fall and spring.

❏ _____ **Barn Swallow** (*Hirundo rustica*) Nicknames: none / Status: FL=stable, IUCN=LC / Life span: to 8 years / Length: 5.9-7.5 in (15-19 cm) / Wingspan: 11.4-12.6 in (29-32 cm) / Weight: 0.6-0.7 oz (17-20 g) / Nests from northern Florida through most of the U.S. and southern Canada / Found: migratory, IW, UA, MZ year round.

❏ _____ **House Wren** (*Troglodytes aedon*) Nicknames: eastern house wren, Jenny wren / Status: FL=stable, IUCN=LC / Life span: to 9 years / Length: 4.3-5.1 in (11-13 cm) / Wingspan: 5.9 in (15 cm) / Weight: 0.4 oz (10 g) / Nests from the Mason Dixon line into southern Canada / Found: migratory, IW, UA, MZ, GB all year but rare in the winter.

❏ _____ **Sedge Wren** (*Cistohorus platensis*) Nicknames: short-billed marsh wren / Status: FL=stable, ICUN=LC / Life span: n/a / Length: 3.9-4.7 in (10-12 cm) / Wingspan: 5.5-6 in (14-15 cm) / Weight: 0.3 oz (8.5 g) / Nests in the Midwest of the U.S. / Found: migratory, IW, UA, MZ, GB only in the winter.

❏ _____ **Marsh Wren** (*Cistohorus palustris*) Nicknames: long-billed marsh wren, Tomtit / Status: FL=stable, IUCN=LC / Length: 3.9-5.5 in (10-14 cm) / Wingspan: 5.5-7 in (14-16 cm) / Weight: 0.3-0.5 oz (9-14 g) / Nests in the upper U.S. into the plains of Canada / Found: migratory, IW, MZ, GB, UA only in the winter.

❐ _____ **Ruby-crowned Kinglet** (*Regulus calendula*) Nicknames: none / Status: FL=stable, IUCN=LC / Life span: to 5 years / Length: 3.5-4.3 in (9-11 cm) / Wingspan: 6.3-7.1 in (16-18 cm) / Weight: 0.2-0.4 oz (5-10 g) / Nests across all of Canada and Alaska / Found: IW, MZ, GB, UA only in the winter.

❐ _____ **Veery** (*Catharus fuscescens*) Nicknames: Wilson's thrush / Status: FL=stable, IUCN-LC / Life span: to 10 years / Length: 6.7-7.1 in (17-18 cm) / Wingspan: 11-11.4 in (28-29 cm) / Weight: 1-1.9 oz (28-54 g) / Nests along the U.S. / Canadian border / Found: migrates to South America, IW, MZ, UA in the fall.

❐ _____ **Wood Thrush** (*Hylocichla mustelina*) Nicknames: brown thrush, swamp sparrow, branch bird / Status: FL=stable, IUCN=LC / Life span: to 9 years / Length: 7.5-8.3 in (19-21 cm) / Wingspan: 11.8-13.4 in (30-34 cm) / Weight: 1.4-1.8 oz (40-5- g) / Nests in northern Florida all the way into the upper Midwest / Found: migratory, IW, UA, MZ in the fall.

❐ _____ **Brown Thrasher** (*Toxostoma rufum*) Nicknames: brown thrush, sandy mocker, thrash, fence corner bird / Status: FL=stable, IUCN=LC / Life span: to 12 years / Length: 9.1-11.8 in (23-30 cm) / Wingspan: 11.4-12.6 in (29-32 cm) / Weight: 2.2-3.1 oz)61-89 g) / Nests on the mainland of Florida north well into central Canada / Found: uncommon but can be found year round in IW, MZ, UA.

❐ _____ **Orange-crowned Warbler** (*Vermivora celata*) Nicknames: none / Status: FL=stable, IUCN=LC / Life span: to 8 years / Length: 4.3-5.5 in (11-14 cm) / Wingspan: 7.5 in (19 cm) / Weight: 0.2-0.4 oz (7-11 g) / Nests in the Rockies and high plains well into Canada and Alaska / Found: migratory, found in the winter and spring, IW, MZ, UA.

❐ _____ **Nashville Warbler** (*Vermivora ruficapilla*) Nicknames: none / Status: FL=stable, IUCN-LC / Life span: to 10 years / Length: 3.9-4.7 in (10-12 cm) / Wingspan: 6.7-7.9 in (17-20 cm) / Weight: 0.2-0.4 oz (7-11 g) / Nests in southern Georgia all across the U.S. and into southeastern Canada / Found: migratory, generally only in the spring, IW, MZ, UA.

❐ _____ **Magnolia Warbler** (*Dendroica magnolia*) Nicknames: none / Status: FL=stable, IUCN-LC / Life span: to 8 years / Length: 4.3-5.1 in / Wingspan: 6.3–7.9 in (16-20 cm) / Weight: 0.2-0.5 oz (6-15 g) / Nests across southern Canada / Found: migratory, most common in the spring, IW, MZ, UA.

❐ _____ **Black-throated Green Warbler** (*Dendroica virens*) Nicknames: none / Status: FL=stable, IUCN-LC / Life span: to 6 years / Length: 4.3-4.7 in (11-12 cm) / Wingspan: 6.7-7.9 in (17-20 cm) / Weight: 0.2-0.4 oz (7-11 g) / Nests across southern Canada / Found: migratory, most common in the spring, IW, MZ, UA.

❐ _____ **Blackburnian Warbler** (*Dendroica fusca*) Nicknames: none / Status: FL=stable, IUCN-LC / Life span: to 8 years / Length: 4.3-4.7 in (11-12 cm) / Wingspan: 7.9-8.3 in (20-21 cm) / Weight: 0.3-0.5 oz (9-13 g) / Nests from Maine through northeastern Canada / Found: migratory, common in the spring and fall, IW, MZ, UA.

❒ ___ **Yellow-throated Warbler** *(Dendroica dominica)* Nicknames: Sycamore Warbler / Status: FL=stable, IUCN=LC / Life span: to 5 years / Length: 5.1-5.5 in (13-14 cm) / Wingspan: 8.3 in (21 cm) / Weight: 0.3-0.4 oz (9-11 g) / Nests in northern Florida throughout the Southeast to southern Illinois / Found: IW excluding the summer months.

❒ ___ **Pine Warbler** *(Dendroica pinus)* Nicknames: pine-creeping warbler / Status: FL=stable, IUCN=LC / Life span: to 6 years / Length: 5.1-5.5 in (13-14 cm) / Wingspan: 7.5-9.1 in (19-23 cm) / Weight: 0.3-0.5 oz (9-15 g) / Nests in northern Florida to the Great Lakes region / Found: migratory but can be spotted year round, IW, MZ, UA.

❒ ___ **Northern Parula** *(Parula americana)* Nicknames: Southern parula warbler / Status: FL=stable, IUCN=LC / Life span: to 5 years / Length: 4.3-4.7 in (11-12) / Wingspan: 6.3-7.1 in (16-18 cm) / Weight: 0.2.0.4 oz (5-11 g) / Nests in central Florida north to southeastern Canada / Found: migratory, but can be spotted year round, IW, MZ, UA.

❒ ___ **Blackpoll Warbler** *(Dendroica striata)* Nicknames: none / Status: FL=stable, IUCN=LC / Life span: to 8 years / Length: 5.5 in (14 cm) / Wingspan: 8.3-9.1 in (21-23 cm) / Weight: 0.4-0.5 oz (12-13 g) / Nests across northern Canada into Alaska / Found: migratory, found most often in the spring, IW, MZ, UA.

❒ ___ **American Redstart** *(Setophaga ruticilla)* Nicknames: flamebird / Status: FL=stable, IUCN=LC / Life span: to 10 years / Length: 4.3-5.1 in (11-13 cm) / Wingspan: 6.3-7.5 in (16-19 cm) / Weight: 0.2-0.3 oz (6-9 g) / Nests across the eastern U.S. and well into Canada / Found: migratory, best spotted in the spring and fall, IW, MZ, UA.

❒ ___ **Prothonotary Warbler** *(Protonotaria citrea)* Nicknames: golden swamp warbler, swamp yellowbird / Status: FL=stable, IUCN=LC / Life span: to 8 years / Length: 5.25 in (14 cm) / Wingspan: 8.5 in (22 cm) / Weight: 0.5 oz (13 g) / Nests in northern Florida to north of the Ohio River Valley / Found: migratory, most often seen in the spring, IW, MZ.

❒ ___ **Worm-eating Warbler** *(Helmitheros vermivorus)* Nicknames: none / Status: FL=stable, IUCN=LC / Life span: to 8 years / Length: 4.3-5.1 in (11-13 cm) / Wingspan: 8.5 in (22 cm) / Weight: 0.4-0.5 oz (12-14 g) / Nests in the southeastern U.S. / Found: migratory, stays in Florida both winter and spring, IW, MZ, UA.

❒ ___ **Northern Waterthrush** *(Seiurus noveboracensis)* Nicknames: none / Status: FL=stable, IUCN=LC / Life span: to 9 years / Length: 4.7-5.5 in (12-14 cm) / Wingspan: 8.3-9.4 in (21-24 cm) / Weight: 0.5-0.9 oz (13-25 g) / Nests in northern Canada and Alaska / Found: migratory, stays in Florida for winter and spring, IW, MZ, UA.

❒ ___ **Louisiana Waterthrush** *(Seiurus motacilla)* Nicknames: large-billed waterthrush, water wagtail / Status: FL=stable, IUCN=LC / Life span: to 12 years / Length: 5.5 (14 cm) / Wingspan: 9.4 (24 cm) / Weight: 0.7-0.8 oz (19-23 g) / Nests throughout the southeastern U.S. / Found: migratory, best found in the winter and spring, IW, MZ, UA.

❒ ___ **Hooded Warbler** *(Wilsonia citrina)* Nicknames: none / Status: FL=stable, IUCN=LC

/ Life span: to 8 years / Length: 5.1 in (13 cm) / Wingspan: 8 in (21 cm) / Weight: 0.3-0.4 oz (9-12 g) / Nests in the northeastern U.S. / Found: migratory, best sighted during the spring and fall migration, IW, MZ, UA.

❒ _____ **Summer Tanager** (*Piranga rubra*) Nicknames: summer redbird / Status: FL=stable, IUCN=LC / Life span: to 8 years / Length: 6.7 in (17 cm) / Wingspan: 11-12 in (28-30 cm) / Weight: 1.1 oz (30 g) / Nests from central Florida through the southeast and southwest / Found: migratory, best sighted in the spring and fall as it goes to and from South America, IW, MZ, UA.

❒ _____ **Scarlet Tanager** (*Piranga olivacea*) Nicknames: none / Status: FL=stable, IUCN=LC / Life span: to 10 years / Length: 6.3-6.7 in (16-17 cm) / Wingspan: 9.8-11.4 in (25-29 cm) / Weight: 0.8-1.3 oz (23-28 g) / Nests in the Midwest and the southeast U.S. / Found: migratory, best sighted in the spring and fall as it flies to and from South America, IW, MZ, UA.

❒ _____ **Swamp Sparrow** (*Melozpiza georgiana*) Nicknames: none / Status: FL=stable, IUCN=LC / Life span: to 6 years / Length: 4.7-5.5 in (12-14 cm) / Wingspan: 7.1-7.5 in (18-19 cm) / Weight: 0.4-0.8 oz (11-24 g) / Nests in the upper Midwest into Canada / Found: migratory, generally seen only in the winter, MZ, IW, UA.

❒ _____ **Rose-breasted Grosbeak** (*Pheucticus ludovicianus*) Nicknames: none / Status: FL=stable, IUCN=LC / Life span: to 13 years / Length: 7.1-8.3 in (18-21 cm) / Wingspan: 11.4-13 in (29-33 cm) / Weight: 1.4-1.7 oz (39-49 g) / Nests in the upper Midwest into Canada / Found: migratory, best spotted in the spring, IW, MZ, UA.

❒ _____ **Blue Grosbeak** (*Passerina caerulea*) Nicknames: none / Status: FL=stable, IUCN=LC / Life span: to 10 years / Length: 5.9-6.3 in (15-16 in) / Wingspan: 11 in (28 cm) / Weight: 0.9-1.1 oz (26-31 g) / Nests across the southern tier of the U.S. / Found: migratory, best seen in the spring, IW, MZ, UA.

❒ _____ **American Goldfinch** (*Carduelis tristis*) Nicknames: wild canary, thistle bird, Eastern goldfinch / Status: FL=stable, IUCN=LC / Life span: to 10 years / Length: 4.3-5.1 in (11-13 cm) / Wingspan: 7.5-8.7 in (19-22 cm) / Weight: 0.4-0.7 oz (11-20 g) / Nests from central Georgia north and across most of the U.S. and southern Canada / Found: migratory, best seen in the winter, UA, MZ, IW.

❒ _____ **Brown-headed Cowbird** (*Molothrus ater*) Nicknames: none / Status: FL=stable, IUCN=LC / Life span: to 16 years / Length: 6.3-8.7 in (16-22 cm) / Wingspan: 12.5-15 in (32-38 cm) / Weight: 1.3-1.8 oz (38-50 g) / Nests in northern Florida well up into Canada / Found: can be seen throughout the year but rare, IW, MZ, UA, GB.

❒ _____ **Baltimore Oriole** (*Icterus galbula*) Nicknames: northern oriole, Bullock's oriole / Status: FL=stable, IUCN=LC / Life span: to 11 years / Length: 6.7-7.5 in (17-19 cm) / Wingspan: 9.1-11.8 in (23-30 cm) / Weight: 1.1-1.4 oz (30-40 g) / Nests throughout most of the eastern U.S. and into southern Canada / Found: migratory, best found in the spring on its way north from South America, IW, MZ, UA.

American Avocet   © Judd Patterson Photography

Accidentals, Vagrants and Casuals.

Most of the following list was taken from the September, 2007, *Birds* pamphlet put out by the staff of the J.N. "Ding" Darling National Wildlife Refuge. Other additions were made by Vince McGrath, lifelong birder and wildlife naturalist at *South Seas Plantation* as well as SCCF's "Wildlife Project" official bird list. The following birds have been seen on Sanibel and/or Captiva and are considered to be one of the following:

Accidentals: Species that are represented by a single or several records but have a normal range that is distant from this region. Therefor these birds are not expected to become established in this range. Sometimes these birds are carried to Sanibel and Captiva by a storm or weather event. Other times their appearance might be a result of an accidental release (such as in the case of various parrot or parakeet sightings) or the bird or flock of birds might have become lost or disoriented during their seasonal migration and landed here in error.

Vagrants: Species with a natural range that is close to this region, that can be expected to be observed in the region on rare occasions. Vagrants would include sightings of Muscovy ducks from the mainland or the appearance of white-crowned pigeons or sooty terns from the Florida Keys.

Casuals: Species that have either a natural range that borders the region, or an extremely limited range within this region, and that may be expected to be recorded infrequently on an annual basis or over a period of several years in a nearby range.

Because the chances of seeing any of these birds on Sanibel and Captiva should be considered a very rare occurrence, only their formal name, scientific name and other common names are given here, along with an adjacent check box. To learn more about these birds, including identification of these accidental species, go to www.allaboutbirds.org. If you should come across a species that is not on this list, or found elsewhere in this book, try to take a photograph of the bird and report your sighting to "Ding" Darling by calling them at (239)472-1100 or writing to Refuge Manager, J.N. "Ding" Darling NWR, 1 Wildlife Drive, Sanibel, FL 33957. Be sure to include a photograph of the bird, where it was seen and the date you observed it. The staff at "Ding" Darling makes every effort to keep abreast of all recorded and validated species found on Sanibel and Captiva Islands and appreciates your help in this regard.

There are an additional 112 birds included in this list.

☐ _____ **Horned Grebe** (*Podiceps auritus*) Nicknames: none.

☐ _____ **Northen Gannet** (*Morus bassanus*) Nicknames: none.

☐ _____ **Masked Booby** (*Sula dactylatra*) Nicknames: Atlantic blue-faced booby.

☐ _____ **Greater Flamingo** (*Phoenicopteridae Flamingos*) Nicknames: flamingo

☐ _____ **Fulvous Whistling Duck** (*Dendrocygna bicolor*) Nicknames: fulvus tree duck, Mexican squealer.

☐ _____ **Snow Goose** (*Chen caerulescens*) Nicknames: blue goose.

☐ _____ **Muscovy Duck** (*Cairina moschata*) Nicknames: royal duck.

☐ _____ **Wood Duck** (*Aix sponsa*) Nicknames: summer duck, woodie, squealer, swamp duck, acorn duck.

☐ _____ **Gadwall** (*Anas strepera*) Nicknames: gray duck, gray mallard.

☐ _____ **Eurasian Wigeon** (*Anas penelope*) Nicknames: none

☐ _____ **Mallard** (*Anas platyrhynochos*) Nicknames: greenhead, gray mallard, Susie.

☐ _____ **Cinnamon Teal** (*Anas cyanoptera*) Nicknames: none.

☐ _____ **Surf Scoter** (*Melanitta perspicillata*) Nicknames: skunkhead, coot, sea coot.

☐ _____ **Black Scoter** (*Melanitta nigra*) Nicknames: common scoter, American scoter, coot, black coot, sea coot, black duck.

☐ _____ **Canvasback** (*Aythya valisineria*) Nicknames: can.

☐ _____ **Redhead** (*Aythya americana*) Nicknames: pochard.

☐ _____ **Ring-necked Duck** (*Aythya collaris*) Nicknames: ringbill, ring-billed duck, blackjack, blackhead.

☐ _____ **Bufflehead** (*Bucephala albeola*) Nicknames: butterball, dipper, spirit duck.

☐ _____ **Ruddy Duck** (*Oxyura jamaicensis*) Nicknames: butterball, bull-necked teal.

☐ _____ **Swainson's Hawk** (*Buteo swainson*) Nicknames: none.

☐ _____ **Broad-winged Hawk** (*Buteo platypterus*) Nicknames: none.

☐ _____ **Mississippi Kite** (*Ictinia mississippiensis*) Nicknames: none.

☐ _____ **Short-tailed Hawk** (*Buteo brachyurus*) Nicknames: none.

☐ _____ **Black rail** (*Laterallus jamaicensis*) Nicknames: Jamaican crake, little black crake.

☐ _____ **Purple Gallinule** (*Porphyrio martinica*) Nicknames: blue Peter, mud hen, pond chicken, bonnet-walker.

☐ _____ **Sandhill Crane** (*Grus canadensis*) Nicknames: whooper.

☐ _____ **American Avocet** (*Recurvirostra americana*) Nicknames: none.

☐ _____ **Long-billed Curlew** (*Numenius americanus*) Nicknames: sickle bill.

☐ _____ **White-rumped Sandpiper** (*Calidris fuscicollis*) Nicknames: peep.

☐ _____ **Upland Sandpiper** (*Bartramia longicauda*) Nicknames: none.
☐ _____ **Pectoral Sandpiper** (*Calidris melanotos*) Nicknames: grass snipe, creaker.
☐ _____ **Parasitic Jaeger** (*Stercorarius parasiticus*) Nicknames: none.
☐ _____ **Pomarine Jaeger** (*Stercorarius pomarinus*) Nicknames: none.
☐ _____ **Lesser Black-backed Gull** (*Larus fuscus*) Nicknames: Scandinavian lesser black-backed gull.
☐ _____ **Great Black-backed Gull** (*Larus marinus*) Nicknames: none.
☐ _____ **Gull-billed Tern** (*Sterna nilotica*) Nicknames: none.
☐ _____ **Roseate Tern** (*Sterna dougallii*) Nicknames: none.
☐ _____ **Common Tern** (*Sterna hirundo*) Nicknames: mackerel gull.
☐ _____ **Sooty Tern** (*Sterna fuscata*) Nicknames: none.
☐ _____ **Black Tern** (*Chlidonias niger*) Nicknames: none.
☐ _____ **Bridled Tern** (*Sterna anaethetus*) Nicknames: none.
☐ _____ **Rock Pigeon** (*Columba livia*) Nicknames: rock dove, city pigeon.
☐ _____ **White-crowned Pigeon** (*Patagioenas leucocephala*) Nicknames: baldpate, white-hooded pigeon.
☐ _____ **White-winged Dove** (*Zenaida asiatica*) Nicknames: Eastern white-winged dove.
☐ _____ **Monk Parakeet** (*Myiopsitta monachus*) Nicknames: Quaker parakeet.
☐ _____ **Budgerigar** (*Melopsittacus undulatus*) Nicknames: budgie, parakeet, shell parakeet.
☐ _____ **Rose-ringed Parakeet** (*Psittacula krameri*) Nicknames: green parakeet.
☐ _____ **White-winged Parakeet** (*Brotogeris vericolurus*) Nicknames: none.
☐ _____ **Black-billed Cuckoo** (*Coccyzus erythropthalmus*) Nicknames: none.
☐ _____ **Smooth-billed Ani** (*Crotophaga ani*) Nicknames: parrot blackbird, black witch, tickbird, Cuban parrot.
☐ _____ **Barred Owl** (*Strix varia*) Nicknames: swamp owl, hoot owl.
☐ _____ **Short-eared Owl** (*Asio flammeus*) Nicknames: none
☐ _____ **Red-headed Woodpecker** (*Melanerpes erythrocephalus*) Nicknames: white-wing, redhead.
☐ _____ **Hairy Woodpecker** (*Picoides villosus*) Nicknames: sapsucker.
☐ _____ **Eastern Wood-pewee** (*Contopus virens*) Nicknames: none.
☐ _____ **Least Flycatcher** (*Empidonax minimus*) Nicknames: none.
☐ _____ **Vermillion Flycatcher** (*Pyrocephalus rubinus*) Nicknames: none.
☐ _____ **Western Kingbird** (*Tyrannus verticalis*) Nicknames: none.
☐ _____ **Scissor-tailed Flycatcher** (*Tyrannus forficatus*) Nicknames: none.
☐ _____ **Yellow-throated Vireo** (*Vireo flavifrons*) Nicknames: none.
☐ _____ **Bell's Vireo** (*Vireo belli*) Nicknames: none.
☐ _____ **Philadelphia Vireo** (*Vireo philadelphicus*) Nicknames: none.
☐ _____ **Solitary Vireo** (*Vireo solitarius*) Nicknames: none.
☐ _____ **Cliff Swallow** (*Petrochelidon pyrrhonota*) Nicknames: none.
☐ _____ **Cave Swallow** (*Petrochelidon fulva*) Nicknames: Caribbean cave swallow.
☐ _____ **Tufted Titmouse** (*Baeolophus bicolor*) Nicknames: Peter bird, Peto bird, tomtit.
☐ _____ **Eastern Bluebird** (*Sialia sialis*) Nicknames: Florida bluebird.
☐ _____ **Swainson's Thrush** (*Catharus ustulatus*) Nicknames: olive-backed thrush.
☐ _____ **Gray-cheeked Thrush** (*Catharus minimus*) Nicknames: none.
☐ _____ **Hermit Thrush** (*Catharus guttatus*) Nicknames: Eastern hermit thrush, swamp sparrow.
☐ _____ **American Pipit** (*Anthus rubescens*) Nicknames: water pipit, titlark, prairie sparrow.

❏ _____ **Blue-winged Warbler** (*Vermivora pinus*) Nicknames: none.
❏ _____ **Golden-winged Warbler** (*Vermivora chrysoptera*) Nicknames: none.
❏ _____ **Tennessee Warbler** (*Vermivora peregrina*) Nicknames: none.
❏ _____ **Nashville Warbler** (*Vermivora ruficapilla*) Nicknames: none.
❏ _____ **Cerulean Warbler** (*Dendroica cerulea*) Nicknames: none.
❏ _____ **Chestnut-sided Warbler** (*Dendroica pensylvanica*) Nicknames: none.
❏ _____ **Bay-breasted Warbler** (*Dendroica castanea*) Nicknames: none.
❏ _____ **Kentucky Warbler** (*Oporornis formosus*) Nicknames: none.
❏ _____ **Wilson's Warbler** (*Wilsonia pusilla*) Nicknames: none.
❏ _____ **Connecticut Warbler** (*Oporornis agilis*) Nicknames: none.
❏ _____ **Townsend's Warbler** (*Dendroica townsendi*) Nicknames: none.
❏ _____ **Cape May Warbler** (*Dendroica tigrina*) Nicknames: none.
❏ _____ **Mourning Warbler** (*Oporornis philadelphia*) Nicknames: none.
❏ _____ **Canada Warbler** (*Wilsonia canadensis*) Nicknames: none.
❏ _____ **MacGillivray's Warbler** (*Oporornis toimiei*) Nicknames: none.
❏ _____ **Yellow-breasted Chat** (*Icteria virens*) Nicknames: none.
❏ _____ **Western Tanager** (*Piranga ludoviciana*) Nicknames: none.
❏ _____ **Roufus-sided Towhee** (*Pipilo erythrophthalmus*) Nicknames: none.
❏ _____ **Chipping Sparrow** (*Spizella passerina*) Nicknames: none.
❏ _____ **Lark Sparrow** (*Chondestes grammacus*) Nicknames: none.
❏ _____ **Field Sparrow** (*Spizella pusilla*) Nicknames: none.
❏ _____ **Le Conte's Sparrow** (*Ammodramus leconteii*) Nicknames: none.
❏ _____ **Savannah Sparrow** (*Passerculus sandwichensis*) Nicknames: none.
❏ _____ **Swamp Sparrow** (*Zonotrichia leucophrys*) Nicknames: none.
❏ _____ **Lincoln's Sparrow** (*Melospiza lincolnii*) Nicknames: none.
❏ _____ **Henslow's Sparrow** (*Ammodramus henslowii*) Nicknames: none.
❏ _____ **Sharp-tailed Sparrow** (*Ammodramus caudacutus*) Nicknames: none.
❏ _____ **Seaside Sparrow** (*Ammodramus maritimus*) Nicknames: none.
❏ _____ **Song Sparrow** (*Melospiza melodia*) Nicknames: none.
❏ _____ **Grasshopper Sparrow** (*Ammodramus savannarum*) Nicknames: none.
❏ _____ **White-throated Sparrow** (*Zonotrichia albicollis*) Nicknames: none.
❏ _____ **White-crowned Sparrow** (*Zonotrichia leucophrys*) Nicknames: none.
❏ _____ **Bobolink** (*Dolichonyx oryzivorus*) Nicknames: ricebird.
❏ _____ **Dickcissel** (*Spiza americana*) Nicknames: none.
❏ _____ **Eastern Meadowlark** (*Sturnella magna*) Nicknames: field lark, Southern meadowlark.
❏ _____ **House Finch** (*Carpodacus mexicanus*) Nicknames: none.
❏ _____ **Purple Finch** (*Carpodacus purpureus*) Nicknames: none.
❏ _____ **Pine Siskin** (*Carduelis pinus*) Nicknames: none.
❏ _____ **Yellow-headed Blackbird** (*Xanthocephyalus xanthocephyalus*) Nicknames: none.
❏ _____ **Shiny Cowbird** (*Molothrus bonariensis*) Nicknames: glossy cowbird.
❏ _____ **Orchard Oriole** (*Icterus spurius*) Nicknames: none.

Prince of Peace
© AlanMaltz.com

The Mammals of Sanibel and Captiva

The world population of mammals is estimated to number around 5,400 species, and new species are still being discovered in remote regions of the world, such as the jungles of Borneo and the impenetrable swamps of northern Colombia. Since 1993 scientists have discovered some 400 new species, most of which are bats and rodents. This is not surprising since bats represent almost 25 percent of all mammalian species, topped only by rodents, which command an astounding 40 percent.

Mammals have the smallest number of distinct species of any group of living organisms covered in this book. In short, we are in the minority on this planet. The primary reason for this lack of diversity is a function of time. When you envision any phylum of living organisms as a tree, you can understand that the longer the tree grows, the wider its spread and the more branches and stems it develops. Mammals are the new kids on the block, having first appeared as tiny rodent-like creatures during the Triassic period, extending from 251 to 199 million years ago. Most of the other trees of life beat our appearance by more than 150 million years.

North America, excluding Mexico and Central America, is not overly rich in mammalian species, in large part because of the absence of the many bat and rodent species found in most tropical and subtropical climates. Africa, which is 20 percent larger than North America, has 1,100 known mammalian species, almost twice as many as North America. The U.S. and Canada are home to approximately 643 species, consisting of 37 separate families, from whales to shrews. Florida has 98 different species. The largest order is Cetacea—whales, dolphins, and porpoises—numbering 21 species. Sanibel and Captiva can claim a scarce 22 species, including dogs, cats, and the species reading this book (*Homo sapiens*).

There used to be more, but an entire subclass of mammals, the Pleistocene megafauna—the woolly rhinoceros, mastodon, giant camel, saber-toothed tiger, cave bear, among others—all vanished from Florida's landscape in the past 10,000 years. In more recent times Sanibel and Captiva have lost several species that were once fairly common here, including the black bear, white-tailed deer, pilot whale, Caribbean monk seal, and, possibly, the panther. We have added a number of introduced species, particularly since the completion of the Sanibel Causeway in 1963, including the opossum, black rat, armadillo, Norwegian or brown rat, and house mouse.

Although the number of mammals may not be large, the diversity and biology of the mammals we have are amazing—especially our two familiar aquatic species: the bottle-nosed dolphin and the endangered West Indian manatee.

By sheer population, humans are the single most represented mammalian species on the islands. The resident population of Sanibel stands at 6,347, while Captiva adds another 437 for a combined total of approximately 6,784 full-time residents. This total does not take into account the thousands of tourists and guests who fill the motels, resorts, rental condominiums, and spare bedrooms during the peak winter months, nor does it factor in the numerous day-trippers who drive over the causeway to visit the islands. When you add those numbers to the equation, the population of the two islands can swell to more than 31,000 people on any given day in March.

While that may seem like a lot of people, it is important to consider density. For example, Sanibel (17.5 square miles) is only 5½ square miles smaller than Manhattan, but it has 1,628,448 fewer people. Closer to home, Marco Island, (17.1 square miles) which is similar in size to Sanibel, has a population of 15,791 residents, more than twice Sanibel's population, and approximately 2 percent open space. Sanibel has more than 30 times as much open space (64 percent of the island). Captiva, including undeveloped Buck Key and Patterson Island, fares equally well, with more than 333 acres of preserve on Buck Key and Patterson Island, as well as a substantial section of South Seas Resort along its eastern, mangrove-covered edge.

This is not to say we haven't had an impact on the island's wildlife, because we have. Development has impacted the vast majority of Florida's now-crowded coastline, but all things considered, Sanibel and Captiva have done very well to fend off the rush of development over the past 60 years.

Here then, are our fellow mammals.

©ThroughTheLensGallery.com

Island Mammals

☐ _____ **Opossum** (*Didelphis virginiana*) Nicknames: Virginia opossum, common opossum, 'possum / Status: FL=stable, IUCN=LC / Life span: to 7 years / Length: 15-20 in., not including the tail (38-51 cm) / Weight: 9-13 lb (4-6 kg) / Reproduces: does not establish a nest but tends to wander, carrying the young along, raising two litters yearly, with up to 10 tiny opossums in each litter / Found: nocturnal, MZ, GB, IW, UA.

North America's only marsupial, the opossum, along with the armadillo, is a fairly recent immigrant to Sanibel and Captiva. Unknown to either island before the building of the causeway in 1963, both the opossum and the armadillo are widely believed to have hitchhiked to the island in the root balls of large ornamentals such as royal and Canary date palms. However it got here, the opossum is now firmly established

© Wikipedia Commons

on the islands and represents an animal that has done extremely well by hanging onto the coattails of the world's most invasive species, *Homo sapiens*.

The opossum is a native of South America, migrating into North America more than 2 million years ago over the Isthmus of Panama. Around the early 1600s, when the first European settlers were arriving in the northeastern United States, the opossum's range extended only as far north as Virginia, but it has since dramatically expanded. This is in large part a result of the animal's ability to adapt to the changes humans make to the environment and to increasingly moderate winters (i.e., climate change—which is also attributed to human activity).

In 1608, Captain John Smith, upon discovering this unusual animal, described it as such:

> *"An Opassom hath an head like a Swine, and a taile like a Rat, and is the bignes of a Cat. Under her belly she hath a bagge, wherein she lodgeth, carrieth, and sucketh her young."*

Unknown in Europe, the opossum was such a curiosity that in the early 1500s the explorer Pinzón brought one back to present to the Spanish court of King Ferdinand and Queen Isabella. The royals were amazed to find a creature that raised its young in a pouch and had 13 teats and a prehensile tail. Because the opossum also came with a foul odor—secreted involuntarily from its scent glands whenever it "plays 'possum," or pretends to be dead—it quickly fell out of favor with the royal court.

There are more than 75 species of opossum in the New World, but only one of these, the common opossum, has made it to North America. The rest range from southern Chile to Central America and vary in size from the tiny Formosan mouse opossum, weighing less than an ounce, to the largest member of the family, the

Virginia opossum, which now thrives on Sanibel and Captiva. There are aquatic opossums, tree-dwelling opossums, and shrew opossums. Although of the same order (*Marsupialia*) as the kangaroo and koala bear, the opossum is not directly related to the Australian orders of marsupials. Various opossum species have been introduced into New Zealand, where the invasive bushy-tailed opossum now numbers more than 60 million.

The opossum is not considered a very intelligent creature, having a brain size roughly six times smaller than a similar-size raccoon. It has a good sense of hearing and an acute sense of smell but relatively poor eyesight. Oddly enough, the opossum has more teeth (50) than any other mammal in North America.

An omnivore, the opossum will eat just about anything, including garbage, carrion, frogs, snakes (the opossum is immune to rattlesnake and cottonmouth snake bites!), small mammals, worms, fruit, insects, and grubs. It should never be fed or handled, as it is capable of inflicting a painful bite.

The wild opossum seldom lives beyond two years. It is heavily preyed upon by owls, bobcats, hawks, panthers, raccoons, dogs, coyotes, and foxes. Because it is slow moving and nocturnal, its single largest source of mortality today is deadly encounters with vehicles. It tends to freeze when approached by an automobile and will sometimes play dead as the car gets closer, never a good choice to make.

⬜ _____ **Armadillo** (*Dasypus novemcinctus*) Nicknames: long-nosed armadillo, nine-banded armadillo, Hoover hogs, road pizza, possum on the half shell / Status: FL=stable, IUCN=LC / Life span: to 15 years / Length: 15-23 in. (27-57 cm body only) / Weight: 12-22 lb (5-9.5 kg) / Reproduces: in long deep burrows in beach ridges / Found: nocturnal, IW, MZ, UA.

Another causeway import, the nine-banded armadillo is fairly common throughout the islands. The name *armadillo* means "little armored one" in Spanish. Like the opossum, the armadillo is an immigrant from South America, probably coming into Central America and Mexico during the same time frame as the opossum, roughly 2 million years ago. Its northern migration into the United States is a far more recent event, having been first noted north of the Rio Grande River in 1880. Once into Texas, the species continued drifting north and east, reaching the Florida Panhandle in the 1920s.

© Wikipedia Commons

A second East Coast population was established after a pair escaped from a small zoo in Cocoa, Florida. The two populations met in the early 1970s, and now the species is firmly entrenched from the Florida Keys to the Georgia border. It

Crossing an island road   ©ThroughTheLensGallery.com

continued to expand its range to the north and east, eventually inhabiting most of the lower United States to just north of the Ohio River Valley. Found only in the New World, the 20 species of armadillo range in size from the 130-pound South American giant armadillo to the tiny and endangered fairy armadillo. The three-banded armadillo, native only to South America, has the unique ability to roll itself up completely when threatened, looking like an oversized, plated, soft ball.

The armadillo can become a lawn and garden problem. Primarily an insectivore, it uses its long, powerful snout and sharp claws to ferret out grubs and worms from the soil. Its erratic digging patterns can make quick work of a well-manicured lawn. The best way to handle this behavior is with some patience and the knowledge that it eats more than 200 pounds of insects a year, meaning it will leave you with fewer cockroaches, termites, ants, and other troublesome insects to contend with. It also eats amphibians, reptiles, fungi, tubers, and carrion.

Although it can coil itself into a ball, this behavior offers little protection from bobcats, panthers, and alligators that are able to reach the armadillo's unprotected belly or crunch through its shell. Because of its high reproductive rate and the protection its shell offers, however, the armadillo is thriving. One fascinating aspect of its reproduction is that the nine-banded armadillo always gives birth to four identical offspring.

The biggest cause of mortality is from automobile collisions. When startled, the armadillo has an even worse response to oncoming cars than the opossum: it usually either stands upright to sniff the oncoming vehicle or jumps straight into the air, making a collision with the car inevitable.

Commonly eaten in South America and said to taste like pork, very few armadillos are hunted or consumed in North America. Although mostly nocturnal, it will venture out of its burrow at dusk and dawn and can be spotted on rare occasions. Sadly, its nickname, road pizza, indicates the most likely sighting you will have of a nine-banded armadillo on the islands.

⬚ _____ **Marsh Rabbit** (*Sylvilagus palustris*) Nicknames: marsh hare / Status: FL=stable statewide but endangered in the Lower Keys, IUCN=LC / Life span: to 7 years / Length: 17 in (43 cm) / Weight: 2.2-2.6 lb (1-1.2 kg) / Reproduces: in abandoned burrows of gopher tortoises and armadillos or in dense thickets / Found: at twilight in IW, UA.

© Charles Sobczak

One of the most peculiar habits of the marsh rabbit is its tendency to let go with a strange, lizard-like squeal when startled. It is a bizarre sound coming from such an adorable little rabbit.

Commonly seen eating grass and other vegetation along the bike paths, the marsh rabbit is the bread and butter of many of the island's predators, especially bobcats, hawks, and owls. Although a member of the cottontail family, the marsh rabbit does not have a fluffy white tail. It has smaller ears than does the cottontail and prefers wetter environments. The marsh rabbit will actually swim across tidal passes to inhabit other barrier islands. It ranges all the way north to Virginia and west to Alabama.

The marsh rabbit eats a wide variety of vegetation. It is also known to eat its own excrement. This uncommon practice, called *coprophagy,* allows it to re-digest certain plants and extract vital nutrients from its own fecal pellets. The practice is similar to a cow chewing its cud.

©ThroughTheLensGallery.com

The marsh rabbit is a game animal in Florida, as it is in most of its range. Because a subspecies, *Sylvilagus palustris hefneri* (named after Hugh Hefner of *Playboy* fame), located in the lower Florida Keys, is endangered, the marsh rabbit is not hunted south of the Everglades.

It would be easy to think that the marsh rabbit is also prone to roadkill, but in fact it is rare to see them hit by automobiles. Like the white-tailed deer, the marsh rabbit appears to be adapting to the automobile. Its primary cause of mortality is predation, including being taken by alligators when swimming.

☐ _____ **Mexican Free-tailed Bat** (*Tadarida brasiliensis*)
Nicknames: Brazilian free-tailed bat / Status: FL=stable but a species of special concern in several states, IUCN=LC / Life span: to 18 years / Length: 3.5 in. (9 cm) / Wingspan: 12.5 in. (32 cm) / Weight: 0.43 oz (12.3 g) / Reproduces: in caves, under overpasses, in crevices, and in bat houses / Found: nocturnal, IW, UA.

The acoustical surveys done by the Florida Bat Conservancy have confirmed only three bat species living on Sanibel. The bat has an amazing tale of adaptation. It may come as a surprise that nearly one-quarter of all known mammals are bats. Worldwide there are 951 species of bats, ranging in size from the tiny bumblebee bat of Thailand (aka Kitti's hog-nosed bat), which is the smallest mammal in the world at two grams, to the flying foxes of Samoa, weighing in at 3.3 pounds and commanding a wingspan of 6.6 feet! The only known mammal capable of sustained flight, the bat has colonized the entire world, migrating as far as 2,300 miles across open ocean.

Tadarida brasiliensis - Free-tailed bat

© Jennifer Smith

It is rare to see any of the three bat species that inhabit Sanibel. The Mexican free-tailed bat is so named because its tail hangs free and extends past its back uropatagium (the flap of skin behind its body that ties the two wings together). Although scarce on the islands, it is quite common in mainland Florida. One cave near Gainesville harbors some 10,000 bats. While that number may sound impressive for a single roost, Bracken Cave, near San Antonio, Texas, holds an unbelievable 20 million bats. With each Mexican free-tailed bat capable of eating 3 grams of insects every evening, the San Antonio roost alone consumes more than 66 tons of bugs a night!

The bat eats insects and does so by the millions. The Mexican free-tailed bat has been observed to fly as high as two miles in search of flying insects. It uses echolocation, much like the dolphin, to find food, emitting super-high-frequency sounds to detect tiny insects in flight. The Mexican free-tailed bat will often feed in total darkness without incident. It is an important part of insect control, but sadly that also makes it vulnerable to human efforts to control insects. Vast colonies have been destroyed by overuse of pesticides.

A bat cannot glide. Its wings are nowhere near as aerodynamically perfect as bird wings, and it must constantly flap to remain airborne. It is sometimes called a flying rat or flying mouse, but because of its low reproductive rate should more accurately be called a flying shrew, which breeds far less often than rats or mice.

The bat has few predators. Because it lives on the ceilings of caves and in tight crevices, its young are generally difficult for most predators to access, and the adult is all but impossible to prey upon while flying. Its largest sources of mortality come from collapsing or flooding caves, the sealing up of caves by people, and extensive pesticide use.

☐ _____ **Northern Yellow Bat** (*Lasiurus intermedius*) Nicknames: yellow bat / Status: FL=stable, IUCN=LC/ Life span: to 20 years / Length: 2.8 in. (7 cm) / Wingspan: 14-16 in. (35-40 cm) / Weight: 0.5-1.1 oz (14-31 g) / Reproduces: in hanging Spanish moss and cabbage palms / Found: nocturnal, IW, MZ, UA.

Larger than the Mexican free-tailed bat, the northern yellow bat is probably more common than its cousin. Its name is derived from the yellow coloration of its fur.

Another insectivore, the northern yellow bat consumes vast quantities of insects, including mosquitoes. It can sometimes be spotted under streetlights, eating the insects that are attracted to the light.

This bat is a solitary nester and prefers natural cover such as trees and moss to the caves and concrete overpasses that many other bats are fond of. It often roosts in Spanish moss or dead palm fronds. The practice of trimming cabbage palms in urban settings is detrimental to the yellow bat because it destroys its roosting habitat. Around the turn of the century when there was an industry for collecting Spanish moss for mattresses and upholstery, one gatherer counted more than 50 northern yellow bats per acre in a grove of moss-covered live oaks.

Northern Yellow Bat © Jennifer Smith

Because it nests in trees, the yellow bat faces some predation from snakes and raccoons. For the most part, however, this bat is common throughout Florida.

☐ _____ **Big Brown Bat** (*Eptesicus fuscus*) Nicknames: brown bat / Status: FL=stable, IUCN=LC / Life span: to 19 years / Length: 4.33-5.12 in. (110-130 mm) / Wing span: 12.99 in. (330 mm) / Weight: 0.81 oz (23 g) / Reproduces: on islands / Found: nocturnal in MZ, UA, IW.

The big brown bat's name is somewhat misleading. It not very big, weighing in at less than an ounce. It is actually smaller than the northern yellow bat. None of the wild bats of North America is much heavier than an once.

Like the other two species on Sanibel, the big brown bat is primarily an insectivore, feeding on a vast array of flying insects from termites, flying ants,

Big Brown Bat   © Jennifer Smith

mosquitoes, and beetles, to mention just a few. It is considered a beneficial species as are all bats in that it consumes enormous quantities of insects throughout its unexpectedly long lifetime.

The big brown bat is not common anywhere in Florida, but is found in limited numbers everywhere except the Keys. It has a tremendous range, running from southern Canada all the way to northern South America. It is common in cities, towns, and rural areas and is rarely found in heavily forested habitats. It does not migrate south, but hibernates for the winter throughout its northern range. It prefers nesting in tree cavities, but also takes readily to buildings, bridges, and bat houses.

Brown bat young are preyed upon by snakes, raccoons, and feral cats. The adult is sometimes taken by owls and falcons as it leaves its roost early in the evening.

◻ _____ **River Otter** (*Lutra canadensis*) Nicknames: common otter / Status: FL=stable but extirpated in 11 states and endangered in 13 more, IUCN=LC / Life span: to 20 years / Length (including tail): 26-42 in. (66-106 cm) / Weight: 11-30 lb (5-14 kg) / Reproduces: near water in suitable dens; will often use another animal's burrow or find natural holes in riprap and tree roots / Found: diurnal in MZ, IW.

There are 12 species of otters worldwide. The mammal appears on every continent except Australia and Antarctica. The longest of the freshwater species is the giant otter of the Amazonian basin, weighing up to 66 pounds; the shorter but heavier sea otter of the north Pacific coastline can weigh up to 90 pounds. Throughout its range, otter populations are declining as a result of continued habitat loss and the harvesting of its meat and fur.

The only aquatic member of the weasel family, the otter is renowned for its playfulness. Curious and entertaining to observe, it is a favorite at zoos and

©ThroughTheLensGallery.com

River Otter　　　　　　　　　　　　　　　　　　　　　　　© AlanMaltz.com

aquariums. Children seem to gravitate to the otter naturally, as they do with the dolphin. In the wild, the otter is far less playful but is still known to slide down a muddy embankment repeatedly or engage in other behavior that can only be described as having fun. Aside from primates, the sea otter is the only mammal known to use tools when harvesting food.

The diet of the river otter that inhabits Sanibel and Captiva is largely made up of fish, both fresh and saltwater species. It prefers slower-moving fish such as gar, panfish, and catfish, but will catch just about any fish it can. It also eats crawfish, horseshoe crabs, frogs, coots, ducks, beetles, and on rare occasions, muskrats and marsh rabbits.

An otter is capable of holding its breath for up to four minutes, diving as deep as 60 feet and swimming as fast as six miles per hour. Its fur is so dense that its skin never gets wet. Young otters, even though they are born with webbed feet and will eventually spend most of their lives in the water, must be taught how to swim by their parents. The otter is very vulnerable to water quality issues and will quickly abandon any polluted lakes or streams. Poor water quality has been a major factor in the otter's decline worldwide.

The river otter is slowly being reintroduced into states where it once was plentiful, including Iowa, Kansas, Kentucky, Nebraska, New Mexico, North and South Dakota, Ohio, Oklahoma, Tennessee, and West Virginia. It was formerly found in all of these states, but over the past few centuries has been trapped for its high-quality fur, causing localized extinctions. Most states now protect the otter.

The otter is preyed upon by alligators, bobcats, coyotes, and wolves. Because of its unusual method of running, arching its back high into the air as it runs, it is very vulnerable to automobile collisions. Oil spills are especially troublesome for the otter.

The Exxon *Valdez* spill in Prince William Sound killed more than 1,000 sea otters and dozens of river otters within days.

On Sanibel and Captiva the otter is a rare sighting. It sometimes frequents the Captiva marinas and can be seen around Buck Key and in the Bailey Tract of the "Ding" Darling refuge. Hurricane Charley in 2004 had a negative impact on the local otter population, though the specific reasons for this are still unclear. Further studies will be needed to determine the true impact hurricanes have on these engaging aquatic mammals.

❒ _____ **Raccoon** (*Procyon lotor*) Nicknames: common raccoon, coon, masked bandit / Status: FL=stable, IUCN=LC / Life span: up to 20 years in captivity / Length: 16-28 in. (41-71 cm w/o tail) / Height: 9-12 in. (23-40 cm) / Weight: 8-20 lb (3.6-9 kg) / Reproduces: in hollow logs, shallow burrows, under buildings / Found: predominantly nocturnal, MZ, IW, GB, UA.

If there is one wild mammal you can expect to see on Sanibel or Captiva, it is the raccoon. Intelligent, curious, and persistent, the raccoon has adapted well to the behavior of humans. Because of this, and in large part owing to the raccoon's ability to access both residential and commercial refuse containers, its population on the islands is artificially higher than could be sustained with natural foraging alone.

In the wild, the raccoon eats insects, lizards, acorns, plants, worms, nuts, and fruit. It will take young marsh rabbits, raid bird nests for both eggs and chicks, and dig up sea turtle nests to reach the eggs. The raccoon also eats the small black dates found in the fall on cabbage palms, as well as the figs of the strangler fig. On the islands it subsists predominantly on residential and commercial garbage, ferreting out everything from old milk cartons to greasy chicken wings.

Family of Raccoons   ©ThroughTheLensGallery.com

The raccoon found in the southern part of Florida is much smaller than its northern counterpart. It also tends to have longer legs to help dissipate heat. In Colorado one raccoon was verified to weigh 62 pounds, while most island raccoons seldom exceed 10 pounds. The raccoon is a very distant relative of the giant panda and the bear, but it is much more closely related to the similar-looking coati and

ringtail, found in Central and South America. The coati's range extends into the desert Southwest of North America.

The raccoon is one of the primary carriers of rabies in the United States. It is also prone to picking up canine distemper. If you see a raccoon behaving strangely, especially if it appears to be disoriented or unusually aggressive, call the Sanibel Police Department (use 239-472-3111, the non-emergency number, rather than 911 unless you've been bitten) or CROW (Clinic for the Rehabilitation of Wildlife, 239-472-3644) and report the animal. Never approach or attempt to capture a wild raccoon as it has very sharp teeth, strong jaws, and can inflict a vicious bite. If you are bitten by a raccoon, you will have to undergo rabies treatments.

The lifespan of a wild raccoon is much shorter than that of a captive raccoon. The young are preyed upon by owls and eagles, while the adult is taken by alligators and bobcats. Many of the young, who are weaned by 16 weeks, simply starve to death. Raccoon litters range from two to five kits; 90 percent fail to survive past the age of two. Much of the adult and juvenile mortality comes in the form of automobile collisions, which on Sanibel occur predominantly along San-Cap Road.

The age-old adage "Speed kills!" should be amended on Sanibel and Captiva to "Speed kills wildlife!" Please obey the posted speed limits, especially at night, dusk, and dawn when island wildlife is most active.

Look for raccoons just about anywhere, but especially along Wildlife Drive at dusk where some of them descend from cabbage palms and strangler figs to forage along the waterfront for horseshoe and blue crabs.

☐ _____ **Gray Squirrel** (*Sciurus carolinensis*) Nicknames: squirrel / Status: FL=stable, IUCN=LC / Life span: to 10 years / Length: 9-12 in. (23-30 cm) / Tail length: 7.5-10 in. (19-25 cm) / Weight: 14-18 oz (400-510 g) / Reproduces: in the forks of trees, mostly live oaks / Found: IW, UA.

Although very common in greater Southwest Florida, the gray squirrel is rarely if ever seen on Sanibel and Captiva. Because it is so prevalent on the mainland, however, it is entirely likely there are gray squirrels on the islands, probably arriving via landscape materials such as large live oaks or in the canopies or root balls of other landscape trees. In the 1988 second-edition printing of *The Nature of Things on Sanibel*, island naturalist George Campbell included the gray squirrel as a definite resident, and the wildlife biologists at the "Ding" Darling refuge and Sanibel-Captiva Conservation Foundation felt this species should be included here as well.

Though the gray squirrel does not appear to have a well-established resident population anywhere on the islands, there are areas that could support a population, such as the neighborhoods of Gumbo Limbo, the Dunes, or Beachview. There is also a large, native stand of live oaks that lies in an inaccessible (to the general public) region of the "Ding" Darling refuge that could harbor a gray squirrel colony.

The gray squirrel is a member of the *Rodentia* order of mammals, which compriseing 30 families, 389 genera, and some 1,702 species—more than 40 percent of all mammals. Other members of the order include the beaver, gopher,

Gray Squirrel   © Joseph Blanda, M.D.

mouse, rat, porcupine, paca, capybara and chinchilla. Of some 4,500 species of mammals worldwide, rodents and bats together represent 64 percent of the total!

Predominantly vegetarian, the gray squirrel survives on acorns, buds, seeds, fungi, and fruit. It will eat insects and insect larvae and an occasional bird egg, but the does not have a major impact on nesting birds or their chicks. The squirrel is preyed upon by bobcats, feral cats, and snakes. The single largest cause of mortality among adult squirrels is hunting; an estimated 500,000 gray squirrels are harvested annually.

☐ _____ **Sanibel Island Rice Rat** (*Oryzomys palustris sanibeli*)
Nicknames: rice rat / Status: FL=species of special concern, IUCN=SSC / Life span: to 5 months / Length: 6-8 in. (15-20 cm) / Tail length: 4-5 in. (10-12 cm) / Weight: 2.8-4.5 oz (80-130 g) / Reproduces: in wetlands areas / Found: IW, UA.

There is only one subspecies whose scientific name includes Sanibel (*sanibeli*), and that honor goes to a member of the rice rat genus. This small, inconspicuous rodent survives on grasses, roots, and seeds in the Bailey Tract of "Ding" Darling, as well as other interior wetland locations. Once fairly common, the Sanibel

Sanibel Rice Rat   © Sabrina Lartz

Island rice rat has seen a dramatic decline in population in recent years because of habitat loss and other factors that are still not clear to the biologists studying them.

Overall, the New World rice rats have not fared well. The Jamaican, Curaçao, and Nelson's rice rats are extinct. Several more of the 23 subspecies are believed to be extinct but have not been officially declared as such. The chances of actually seeing a Sanibel Island rice rat are slim. In years of trapping, the Sanibel-Captiva Conservation Foundation has managed to locate only four of them. The staff at the "Ding" Darling refuge has met with a bit more success, but the numbers are not encouraging.

A small, reclusive animal that predominantly feeds at night, the Sanibel Island rice rat was first identified as a subspecies of the Oryzomys genus in 1955. Given the present trend, it is a sad testament to our commitment to conservation that this indigenous subspecies, the only animal named after Sanibel Island, is heading toward extinction.

A captured Sanibel Rice Rat   © Sabrina Lartz

❑ _____ **Hispid Cotton Rat** (*Sigmodon hispidus*) Nicknames: cotton rat / Status: FL=stable, IUCN=LC / Life span: to six months / Length: 8-14 in. (20-36 cm) / Tail length: 3-6.5 in. (7-16 cm) / Weight: 2.75-4.25 oz (80-120 g) / Reproduces: in the interior wetlands and mangrove regions / Found: IW, MZ, UA.

Hispid Cotton Ray

Unlike the Sanibel Island rice rat, the hispid cotton rat is doing fairly well here. It is the most commonly trapped rodent in small animal surveys and appears to be adjusting to the many changes development has wrought on these barrier islands. Although plentiful, the hispid cotton rat is highly unlikely to take up residence in your garage, storage shed, or home as it much prefers a natural habitat.

Hispid Cotton Rat   Courtesy CDC

The name *hispid* refers to this rat's grizzled appearance. It ranges from the southern United States to the northern edge of Colombia and Venezuela.

The hispid cotton rat survives mostly on green vegetation. It cuts grass plants into sections to reach the heads and can cause major destruction to domestic crops such as sugar cane and sweet potatoes. On the mainland where it is still plentiful, the hispid rat eats insects and at times suppresses the local quail population by consuming vast numbers of quail eggs.

Like the marsh rabbit, the cotton rat is heavily preyed upon. Its average life span of six months reflects the level of predation this small mammal endures from raccoons, hawks, owls, bobcats, otters, snakes, and alligators. It makes up for its high mortality with an incredible rate of reproduction. It is capable of reproducing at six weeks of age, and if left unchecked, it would soon overrun the island.

☐ _____ **Black Rat** (*Rattus rattus*) Nicknames: ship rat, roof rat, palm rat, house rat / Status: FL=thriving, IUCN=LC / Life span: to 18 months / Length: 6.2-8.6 in. (16-22 cm) / Tail length: 7.4-9.5 in. (19-24 cm) / Weight: 2.5-10.5 oz (70-300 g) / Reproduces: anywhere it can, often in roofs / Found: IW, MZ, UA.

Agile climbers

It is impossible to underestimate the damage wrought to mankind and to any number of local environments by the black rat. For starters, it was the black rat that carried the Oriental rat flea (*Xenopsylla cheopsis*), which in turn carried the bubonic plague. Ravaging Europe from 1347 through 1352, the so-called Black Death killed an estimated 25 million people. As if that isn't enough, the black rat is also a carrier of lassa fever, murine typhus, ratbite fever, and leptospirosis.

Not only is the black rat a known disease carrier, but it also destroys vast amounts of food supplies through contamination and is responsible for the extinction of thousands of species worldwide. The black rat originally came from India and has spread to every continent except Antarctica. Beginning about 20,000 years ago, possibly related to human migrations, the black rat spread to the

Black Rat babies in nest

Middle East, then eventually into Europe. It reached the other continents during the Age of Exploration (3200 BC-1779 AD). Its nickname "ship rat" aptly describes the black rat's success as a stowaway; the early explorers unwittingly brought this adaptable rodent to nearly every one of their destinations. Once established, the black rat would wreak havoc on the native ground-dwelling birds, small mammals, reptiles, snakes, and insects.

The black rat, the Norwegian rat, and the house mouse, in large part thanks to their close relationships to humans, must now be considered the most successful mammals on earth, vastly outnumbering the 6.7 billion people on this planet.

The black rat tends to be nocturnal, so the best chance to see one is in the evening, particularly around dumpsters or crossing Periwinkle late at night. During the day the black rat often nests in palm trees. It can have up to five litters a year.

On Sanibel, the poisons used to try to control the black and Norwegian rats can sometimes be responsible for the death of owls, hawks, bobcats, and other creatures through an indirect chain of events. For a healthy predator, a poisoned rat is an easy target. When it kills and eats the rat, it consumes the same poison the rat has ingested. Even if the predator survives the initial poisoning, repeated consumption of poisoned rodents will eventually kill the animal. The use of any animal poisons on Sanibel and Captiva is strongly discouraged. Instead, try electric (aka the rat *"zapper"*) or mechanical traps, available at most hardware stores.

The black rat is preyed upon by all the islands' major predators. It lives a little more than a year in the wild. There is a relationship between black rat populations and raccoons. In the early 1990s, when the island raccoon population was decimated by canine distemper, the black and brown rat populations exploded, causing a massive pest problem in homes and condominiums throughout the islands.

☐ _____ **Norwegian Rat** (*Rattus norvegicus*) Nicknames: brown rat, Norway rat, wharf rat, common rat / Status: FL=thriving, IUCN=LC / Life span: to 18 months / Length: 10 in. (25 cm) / Tail length: 10 in. (25 cm) / Weight: 9-12 oz (250-350 g) / Reproduces: throughout the islands / Found: IW, MZ, GB, UA.

Despite its most common name, the Norwegian rat is originally from China. How this misnaming came about is unclear, but the name originated in England in the 1700s.

Slightly larger than its very close cousin, the black rat, the Norwegian rat is far more tolerant of cold and therefore has a much greater range. The Norwegian

Norway Rat   © Wikipedia Commons

rat is a sewer rat. It also inhabits back alleys, thrives along railroad tracks and in granaries, farms, landfills, junk yards—just about every environment that people inhabit is also inhabited by the Norwegian rat.

The Norwegian rat does not carry bubonic plague, but does harbor several other diseases and parasites, including Weil's disease, ratbite fever, cryptosporidiosis, viral hemorrhagic fever, Q fever, and hantavirus pulmonary syndrome. It serves as a host for *Toxoplasma gondi*, the parasite that causes toxoplasmosis, and appears to be a carrier for trichinosis.

In an ironic twist of fate, however, the Norwegian rat has probably saved more lives than it has taken. This is the original lab rat. Its use for this purpose came about in the early 1800s after breeders created a line of albino mutants to be used for dog baiting, a practice in which a large number of live rats were put inside a pit with a terrier. Men would place bets on how long it would take the dog to destroy all of the rats. In 1828, in an experiment on fasting, the first of these pure white Norwegian rats was put to use in the lab.

Norwegian lab rat

Today the lab rat is used every day in thousands of experiments worldwide. It has helped advance research in almost every possible medical field, from cancer to the study of genetics. Since the 1800s several more subspecies of the Norwegian rat have been created, including a hairless variety.

The Norwegian rat is nocturnal. It can be found in the same areas as the black rat. Although these two types of rats inhabit much the same territory, they do not interbreed. The Norwegian rat tends to stick closer to the ground, burrowing and nesting under homes and sheds, whereas the black rat is a skilled climber and inhabits cabbage palms and attics. If any of these rats gains entry into your home or shed, it should be trapped immediately, as it can chew wiring and cause electrical fires, among a host of other rat-related problems.

❒ _____ **House Mouse** (*Mus musculus*) Nicknames: mouse / Status: FL=thriving, IUCN=LC / Life span: to 12 months / Length: 3-3.9 in. (7.5-10 cm) / Tail length: 2-3.9 in. (5-10 cm) / Weight: 0.35-0.88 oz (10-25 g) / Reproduces: throughout the islands / Found: GB, IW, MZ, UA.

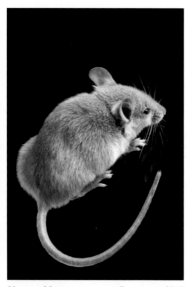

House Mouse   Courtesy CDC

Widely thought to have originated in northern India, the house mouse is ubiquitous throughout the civilized world. Like the black and the Norwegian rat, this tiny animal has ridden on the coattails of *Homo sapiens* for more than 10,000 years. The mouse is mostly nocturnal and will eat just about anything. In the wild it feeds on grains, grasses, and seeds. It is so small, almost always weighing under an ounce, that it does not require water to survive; it is able to obtain all the moisture it needs directly from food.

Every predator on the island, from rats to herons to raccoons, kills and eats the house mouse. It is interesting to note that the house mouse will kill a rat when given a chance; it will only partially eat the rat, however. The mouse is used even more than the rat for medical and scientific research. It is far less expensive to feed, and because of its small size, it is easier to cage.

Although it does carry diseases and takes a considerable toll on human food supplies worldwide, it is not considered as harmful as the rat. As an invasive species, however, the mouse can be as devastating as the rat. In the late 19th century, for example, the house mouse was introduced by whalers to Gough Island, a breeding place for 20 species of southern Atlantic seabirds. Since its introduction there, this clever rodent has learned how to attack albatross chicks that weigh 100 times more than a single mouse; it does so by attacking the chicks en masse, behaving much like a school of piranhas, with each mouse taking one bite at a time until the chick bleeds to death. Today, more than 700,000 mice kill an estimated 1 million chicks a year on Gough Island.

The difference between the two native rodents and the three introduced species cannot be greater: the native

House Mouse Courtesy CDC

Sanibel Island rice rat and the hispid cotton rat do not harbor any lethal diseases and live in harmony with their surroundings, whereas the black rat, Norwegian rat, and house mouse are all harmful invasives, a direct result of being transported into another environment by humans. Stories such as what has happened on Gough Island should make us ever more aware of the ramifications of bringing exotic animals and invasive plants into new environments.

☐ _____ **Bobcat** (*Lynx rufus*) Nicknames: wildcat / Status: FL=stable, IUCN=LC / Life span: to eight years / Length: 28-47 in. (70-120 cm) / Height: 20-24 in. (50-60 cm) / Weight: 16-30 lb (7-14 kg) / Reproduces: in dens in deep bush / Found: IW, MZ, UA.

Upclose with a male bobcat   © AlanMaltz.com

An estimated 700,000 to 1.5 million bobcats are live in North America. In the far north the bobcat is replaced by the slightly larger Canadian lynx, which has longer legs, huge feet, and denser fur, all of which are helpful for surviving in the boreal forests of northern Canada. The male bobcat commonly grows to 30 pounds; the largest ever recorded in the wild was 48.9 pounds. The bobcat is a game animal in Florida, trapped and hunted for its fine-quality fur.

Unlike so many of the world's cats, the bobcat population is not in trouble. Although in a few states, such as Ohio, Indiana, and New Jersey, the bobcat is considered endangered, for the most part this feline is thriving. Even in areas where it is not found, because of protections now in place across North America, the bobcat is steadily returning to its entire original range.

Female bobcat   © Sandy Ramseth

Sanibel has a healthy bobcat population. Although most sightings occur at dawn and dusk, the bobcat can sometimes be spotted midday. Its fur pattern varies by region; there have even been 10 confirmed cases of "melanistic" or black bobcats in Florida. The Sanibel bobcat tends to have less of the mottled fur pattern common to most of these animals. That accounts for the vast majority of misidentifications on the islands, mistaking the bobcat for the Florida panther. Although historically the panther may have ranged on Sanibel, the chances of one prowling around the island unnoticed at this point are virtually nil.

Like most wild cats, the bobcat is a carnivore and operates as an adept ambush predator. It is capable of jumping yards into the air, sometimes taking waterfowl right out of the air. During lean times it has been known to take down white-tailed deer weighing eight times more than the bobcat. It kills innumerable rats, mice, raccoons, opossums, armadillos, birds, snakes, feral and domestic cats, and just about anything and everything that can supply the daily protein it requires for survival.

Bobcat cub   © Sandy Ramseth

Only a handful of predators feed upon the bobcats. While cubs may be taken by coyotes, male bobcats, wolverines, and badgers, adults need only to fear wolves, pumas (in Florida these are called panthers), and large alligators. The bobcat has been known to attack people, but in most cases it involves a mother attempting to protect her litter. There has never been a recorded fatal bobcat attack.

It breeds year-round, but tends to favor April through September. On average it has one litter per year, with one to six kittens per litter. The bobcat is not capable of being domesticated.

☐ _____ **Feral Cat** (*Felis catus*) Nicknames: housecat, domestic cat / Status: Domesticated and abundant / Life span: to 14 years / Length: 18 in. (46 cm) / Tail length: 11.8 in. (30 cm) / Weight: 5.5-16 lb (2.5-7 kg) / Reproduces: it can have litters in the wild / Found: IW, GB, MZ, UA.

Feral Cat   © Wikipedia Commons

For the moment, the feral cat population on Sanibel and Captiva appears to be in decline. The exact reasons for this decline are unclear and further study is needed.

The origins of the housecat go back 9,500 years. Originally thought to have been domesticated in ancient Egypt, recent DNA studies indicate that all housecats are derived from as few as five self-domesticated African wildcats (*Felis silvestris lybica*). It turns out they domesticated us. Anyone who owns a cat can understand the irony of that statement.

A skilled predator, similar in hunting style to both the bobcat and the panther, a feral cat can decimate local populations of marsh rabbits, cotton rats, birds, anoles, insects, and mice. The wild housecat has been documented to hunt more than 1,000 different species for food. It relies on its multidirectional ears and acute sense of hearing to hunt, which it does mostly at night. Its retractable claws and well-padded feet make it silent and virtually undetectable to some unsuspecting foraging rodent.

The introduction of the housecat into certain ecosystems has been nothing short of cataclysmic. The feral cat, especially on remote oceanic islands, has single-handedly caused the eradication or extinction of dozens of species. One notable example is the Stephens Island wren, indigenous only to an island located just off of New Zealand. This small flightless bird fed exclusively on insects. Its entire population was destroyed within five years of the arrival of semi-feral cats, originally brought onto the island by the lighthouse keeper in 1892 to control rodents. By the time the wren was extinct, the island swarmed with more than 100 cats.

People still come out to Sanibel to dump their unwanted cats and kittens along the side of the road. This behavior is generally a death sentence for the cat—or should it survive, a death sentence for scores of shorebirds, passerines, and threatened Sanibel rice rats. Some people take to feeding feral cats, which can be a mixed blessing. Should the food source stop for any reason, the cat will quickly return to its predatory instincts and resume killing. Sadly, even a well-fed cat will sometimes kill out of instinct. If you have a feral or semi-feral cat in your area, it is best to have the cat trapped and removed from the environment.

☐ _____ **Gray Fox** (*Urocyon cinereoargenteus*) Nicknames: Florida fox / Status: FL=stable, IUCN=LC / Life span: to 10 years / Length: 31.5-41.3 in. (80-112 cm) / Tail length: 11-17.5 in. (27-44 cm) / Weight: 7.9-15 lb (3.6-6.8 kg) / Reproduces: not presently confirmed as a breeding population / Found: IW.

A handful of recent sightings along with one authentic photograph have confirmed the presence of the gray fox on Sanibel. In all probability, the gray fox inhabited both islands around the turn of the 20th century, but most were eliminated in the 1920s through the 1950s as varmints.

How the current gray fox got on the island remains a mystery. Foxes swim, which could bring them to the island via the passes (Cayo Costa to North Captiva, then down from Captiva to Sanibel) or across from Pine Island. Conceivably, one could have walked across the causeway during the night.

The gray fox is easily distinguished from its close relative, the red fox, by the lack of distinctive black boots, or dark markings along the lower half of all four legs. It is also considerably more aggressive than the red fox and will dominate that species in any given territory. This canid is unique in that it is one of only two dog species in the world that climbs trees. The other tree-climbing canine is the Asian raccoon dog.

The gray fox feeds on marsh rabbits, mice, rats, anoles, and birds. Its hunting technique is similar to that of the bobcat. In the wild it is preyed upon by panthers and alligators, and the kits are sometimes taken by owls and coyotes.

Gray Fox   © Al Tuttle

It has yet to be determined if this species will in fact take root here or if there is even a breeding pair. It is more likely that this animal will remain an accidental on Sanibel.

Domesticated Dogs (*Canis lupus familiaris*) Nicknames: rover / Status: FL=thriving, IUCN=domesticated / Life span: some breeds to 20 years / Length: 3.75 in.-8.2 ft (9.5-250 cm) / Weight: 4 oz-343 lb (113 g-155.6 kg) / Reproduces: at the foot of the bed / Found: GB, IW, MZ, CW, UA.

Phoebe, a domesticated poodle   © Blake Sobczak

Recent DNA evidence shows that all dogs, from the tiniest Yorkshire terrier at 113 grams, to the massive English mastiff at 343 pounds, came from the gray wolf some 15,000 years ago. Though it seems improbable, that adorable little poodle has the DNA of a wolf.

The dog is ubiquitous throughout the islands. Having been around humans for centuries, it has been bred to handle any number of chores—from bloodhounds tracking criminals to huskies pulling sleds and all points in between. The dog has reasonably good eyesight, very good hearing, and a sense of smell that is nothing short of astonishing. It is this sense of smell that is the primary reason why the dog should be kept on a leash whenever it is taken outside, especially on the beaches. Dogs are still wolves, and despite our best intentions, we should always consider them a threat to wildlife.

Its olfactory ability can sometimes lead an unleashed dog directly to a fresh sea turtle nest, and within seconds an entire sea turtle clutch can be destroyed. Even if the dog doesn't uncover the eggs, the strong canine scent left behind will likely lead raccoons to the nest later that evening. Dogs also tend to chase shorebirds, which, after flying across the Gulf of Mexico, are sometimes far too exhausted for such behavior. If a dog should catch an adult plover or sandpiper, one shake of the dog's head will kill the bird.

Pet owners are also tempted to unleash their dogs while walking them in wildlife preserves. An injured marsh rabbit is quickly killed by an unchecked dog. Leashes are for the dog's safety as well—alligators love eating dogs, even large ones.

☐ _____ **Florida Black Bear** (*Ursus americanus floridanus*)

Nicknames: bear / Status: FL = species of special concern, IUCN = LC / Length: 4-6 ft (1.2-1.8 m) / Height at shoulder: 2.5-3 ft (.76-.91 m) / Weight: 150-300 lb (68-136 kg) / Life span: to 27 years / Breeds: in the early summer with the female giving birth to twins or triplets midwinter / Found: IW, UA, MZ.

The story of Sanibel's solitary black bear began with an unexpected critter-cam photo taken at 5:34 a.m. on June 27, 2011. The photo was taken in the Bailey Tract of J.N. "Ding" Darling National Wildlife Refuge and was the first authenticated sighting of a black bear on Sanibel in all of recorded history.

Courtesy Paul Tritak & the staff at J.N. "Ding" Darling NWR

Over the next 12 months, the bear was spotted everywhere from the Wulfert area in the western part of the island to the 40-acre park abutting the Sanibel Lighthouse on the eastern end. It was near the lighthouse where the bear was shot with a tranquilizer dart by Florida Fish and Wildlife and removed from the island on June 21, 2012. At that time the bear was positively identified as a 3½-year old male weighing approximately 250 pounds.

How the bear arrived on Sanibel is a matter of speculation. Some believe it might have come across the causeway during the night, but the most likely scenario is that the bear swam to Sanibel from Pine Island, a distance of slightly more than a mile.

Historically, there are no confirmed records of the black bear living on Sanibel. There were deer, turkey, and rattlesnakes, all of which are now extirpated, but the Sanibel bear of 2011 was a first. The theory is that it was a young, wandering male looking for new habitat. Sanibel, with ample forage and thousands of acres of open space, provided an ideal environment. Because of the long-term likelihood of an automobile collision or a dangerous encounter with an islander, Fish and Wildlife elected to remove and relocate the bear.

What happened after the bear's relocation is comical. After being taken from Sanibel to Chassahowitzka National Wildlife Refuge, located 50 miles north of Clearwater, the bear started tracking south toward Tampa. After repeated 911 calls reporting a bear lurking near Busch Gardens, Sanibel's black bear was spotted hiding in an oak tree along Busch Boulevard on July 3, 2012, a mere 12 days after his capture near the Sanibel Lighthouse. Authorities darted him a second time and relocated the urban-loving bear to Apalachicola National Forest near Tallahassee, where he still resides.

The black bear is an omnivore. More than 85 percent of its diet consists of herbs, grasses, fruit, acorns, nuts, and tubers. It is very fond of honey and bee larvae, a trait that often brings it into direct conflict with Florida's beekeepers. It also eats termites, carpenter ants, and other colony-building insects. Less commonly, the black bear will take white-tailed deer and smaller mammals such as opossums and raccoons. It will readily feed on carrion and garbage, and has been known to chase panthers off of a fresh kill.

Black bear grazing © Judd Patterson

The black bear is considered a species of special concern in Florida, and hunting it has been banned since 1993. Over the past 40 years, the black bear has made an incredible recovery in Florida. Once considered "threatened," the state's black bear population has rebounded from a low of approximately 200 animals in 1970 to the current population of more than 3,000. Special Bear Management Units spanning seven distinct geographical districts have been established to assure the long-term management and survival of Florida's largest land predator.

☐ _____ **Coyote** (*Canis latrans*) Nicknames: coydog, prairie wolf, American jackal, bandit dog, brush wolf, song dog, Wile E. Coyote, coyotl (Aztec) / Status: FL = expanding its range, IUCN = LC / Length: 28-38 in. (71-96 cm) / Height at shoulder: 12-15 in. (30-38 cm) / Weight: 25-33 lb (11.5-15 kg) / Life span: to 15 years / Breeds: in early winter with the pups born in the spring / Found: IW, UA, GB, MZ.

The name coyote is one of very few words that have come to us from the Aztec language. The Aztec name for this adaptive and intelligent member of the Canidae family was coyotl, meaning God's dog. Prior to the 1930s the coyote was almost never seen east of the Mississippi River. Anyone familiar with old Western movies should appreciate the fact that the native habitat for this small canid was the open ranges and grasslands of the western plains, where its familiar pose—howling at the night sky—is embedded in our collective psyche. Today the coyote has made it all the way to Cape Cod, Massachusetts, and one was actually observed in New York City's Central Park. The eastern population now tends to be larger in size than the western.

The coyote is a recent arrival to Southwest Florida and Sanibel. The first documented evidence of one on Sanibel occurred on February 17, 2011, when a coyote was spotted and photographed by a visitor in the eastern impoundment of J.N. "Ding" Darling National Wildlife Refuge. There have been dozens of sightings since that time at various locations on the island. The coyote is well adapted to surviving in urban, suburban, and exurban environments, and Sanibel fits this model perfectly.

Coyote crossing tidal flat   © Sean Allott

There is ongoing controversy among biologists and residents as to whether these canids should be trapped and removed from Sanibel or left alone. There are valid arguments on both sides. No doubt the coyotes on Sanibel are killing both the cotton hispid rat and the endangered Sanibel rice rat, but they are also decimating the invasive black rat and the troublesome raccoon populations.

Coyotes did get here on their own, and although not native to the area, they are expanding their range naturally. Urban sprawl has provided the coyote with ample cover, as well as additional food sources such as garbage, roadkill, rabbits, and rodents. Small domestic dogs and cats are favorite prey for the coyote. The only animal capable of preying on an adult coyote in Southwest Florida is the panther, which is not documented on Sanibel. Coyote pups might fall prey to alligators, great horned owls, and rattlesnakes. Aside from human trapping or poisoning, the coyote has few natural predators to keep its population in check. Throughout Southwest Florida, if you live along the fringes of wooded areas or in subdivisions with large lot sizes, it's probably a good idea to take your pets in at night and be on the lookout for this newcomer.

Wild coyote   © Judd Patterson

Marine Mammals

❑ _____ **West Indian Manatee** (*Trichechus manatus*) Nicknames: sea cow, sea siren / Status: FL=endangered, IUCN=EN / Life span: to 60 years / Length: 10-15.2 ft (3.1-4.6 m) / Weight: 880-3,300 lb (400-1,500 kg) / Reproduces: in San Carlos Bay to the upper Caloosahatchee River / Found: BB.

© Wikipedia Commons

Until 1768 there were five species of *Sirenia* (manatees) in the world. First discovered and scientifically identified by German naturalist Georg Steller in 1741 off of three subarctic islands in the Steller Sea, the Steller Sea cow was the largest of the five species. Feeding exclusively on giant kelp, this 10-ton manatee did not have teeth but crushed the algae using two huge bony plates. It was too large to submerge itself and thus became an easy target for seal and whale hunters in the north Pacific. Growing to a length of 27 feet, the slow-moving, docile Steller's Sea cow was hunted to complete extinction within 27 years of its discovery.

The West Indian manatee is the second-largest member of this order. The female once obtained a length in excess of 15 feet and a weight approaching two tons. Today the average is 10-12 feet in total length. The other three remaining species are the West African manatee, similar in habits and size to the West Indian; the Amazonian manatee, which inhabits the freshwater system of the greater Amazonian basin; and the dugong, which has a whale-shaped tail and is closely related to the extinct Steller Sea cow.

The closest land-based relatives to the manatee are two very different mammals: the elephant and the hyrax, a rabbit-size herbivore from Africa. The manatee adapted to its salt and freshwater environment beginning in the Miocene period, some 26 million years ago.

The manatee is an herbivore, eating a variety of aquatic vegetation from turtle grass to freshwater reeds. An adult can consume up to 65 pounds of vegetation a day. Because it roots out these grasses, it also consumes vast amounts of sand. This gritty diet wears down its front teeth, which are replaced from back to front throughout its life; the manatee is one of only a few mammal species on earth that has this adaptation. The shark has a similar tooth replacement system, although for different reasons.

Because of its docile nature and the ease with which *Homo sapiens* have been able to harvest the manatee, all five species have been dramatically impacted by man. Ample archeological evidence proves that the West Indian manatee has been

Manny   © AlanMaltz.com

hunted unabatedly since the arrival of the first Paleo-Indians 12-14,000 years ago. This continuous harvesting, until the passage of the Endangered Species Act (1973) and the Marine Mammal Protection Act (1972), has greatly reduced the manatee's former range and placed the animal on the Endangered Species red list of the IUCN.

The meat of the manatee is said to be delicious, similar in texture and taste to the finest cuts of beef. The Calusa, Cuban fishermen, and early Sanibel settlers all ate manatee. The Native Americans used manatee hide for war shields, canoes, and shoes, the fat for oil, and the bones for "special potions." Hunting the manatee in the United States was officially banned in 1893, but poaching this gentle giant continues today.

The number-one cause of manatee death today is boat collisions. Because of its slow speed and large size, almost every adult manatee in the state has been scarred by boat propellers on its head, back, or tail. Biologists use these ubiquitous scars to identify individual manatees in any given range. Since a manatee swims at less than five miles per hour, it is no match for boats with 300-horsepower engines speeding across an estuary at 60 miles an hour. Laws requiring boaters to slow down in manatee zones are instrumental in saving this species.

Another major cause of manatee deaths is red tide and extreme cold spells, the latter of which can put large adults into a state of shock that often results in hypothermia. Because of its enormous size, the manatee is almost never taken by sharks, saltwater crocodiles, or alligators. We are its only real threat.

One reason the manatee population cannot recover easily is the animal's incredibly slow reproductive rate. It has one calf every two years and, depending on availability of mates, may go years without having a calf at all. A highly intelligent mammal, the manatee requires extended nursing periods to teach the calf where to find food, when to migrate to warm waters, and what dangers to avoid.

The combination of a docile nature, slow speed, delicious meat, and low reproductive rate has not been a prescription for success when competing with a smart, fast, and hungry hominoid.

Estimates are that between 1,500 and 2,500 manatees are living in the coastal areas of Florida. In 2007 the United States Fish and Wildlife Service attempted to upgrade the status of the manatee from endangered to threatened. There was an immediate outcry from organizations such as Save the Manatee Club, which argued that changing the status would result in far less regulation and would certainly contribute to increased manatee mortality throughout its range.

In winter one of the best places to see manatees is approximately 50 minutes north of Sanibel and Captiva at the 17-acre Manatee Park, near the warm outflow of the Florida Power and Light plant off of Palm Beach Blvd. (State Road 80). Attracted by the warm water, manatees gather by the hundreds in the power-plant discharge canal that flows into the Orange River, a tributary of the Caloosahatchee. Although the water is stained from tannic acid, the chances of seeing one of these rare animals is almost 100 percent as they seek shelter from winter cold fronts from mid-October through the end of March. Go to www.leeparks.org for a complete printout of hours, directions, and additional information.

On Sanibel and Captiva manatees are more difficult to find. Perhaps the best spots are along Roosevelt Channel on Captiva (behind Tween Waters Inn, McCarthy's Marina, and near Buck Key) or in the canal system along Shell Harbor on Sanibel, especially during the fall and late spring months. Because the local waters are often muddy, the only part of the manatee you are likely to see are its small head and nostrils and large, paddle-like tail.

A typical Tarpon Bay manatee sighting   ©ThroughTheLensGallery.com

☐ _____ **Bottle-nosed Dolphin** (*Tursiops truncatus*) Nicknames: flipper, porpoise, dolphin, common bottlenose dolphin / Status: FL=stable, IUCN=LC / Life span: to 45 years / Length: 7.5-9.5 ft (2.28-2.9 m) / Weight: 330-1,400 lb (150-650 kg) / Reproduces: in the back bays and estuaries / Found: BB, Gulf.

©ThroughTheLensGallery.com

Any visitor to Sanibel and Captiva would be hard pressed not to spot a bottle-nosed dolphin over the course of a week's stay. The dolphin is often observed swimming in the gulf just off the beaches or can be spotted inshore while kayaking or canoeing through the "Ding" Darling refuge, in Tarpon Bay, or along the bay side of Captiva. The dolphin can also be readily observed from the causeway, where it gathers to feed in the huge tidal flows along the Caloosahatchee River. It is always a delight to watch and shows little fear of man.

Worldwide there are 32 different species of toothed whales, the family (*Delphinidae*) to which the bottle-nosed dolphin belongs. The largest member of this extensive family is the orca, or killer whale, which can reach lengths of 30 feet and weigh as much as 9,000 pounds. The orca will attack and eat dolphins given the opportunity.

The dolphin is an extremely social animal, living in groups of 15 to 100 animals called pods. Several larger pods have been identified with as many as 1,000 members.

The dolphin has a unique and special relationship with man. Tales of bottle-nosed dolphins saving drowning sailors date back to Greek times, although recent studies indicate that this may be part of an instinctive behavior.

With a brain size larger than ours, the bottle-nosed dolphin has been studied extensively for decades. Highly intelligent, it has been trained to perform in places such as Sea World in Orlando, as well as to carry out tactical exercises including

©ThroughTheLensGallery.com

the detection of sea mines and enemy divers for the U.S. Navy. In some parts of the world the dolphin has actually learned to cooperate with local fishermen, driving schools of fish into their nets, then taking the escaping fish as a form of payment for services rendered.

The dolphin has a wide array of sounds and noises, including many in ranges far above the capacity of the human ear. An interesting study is being conducted by neurologists at Caltech University in California where scientists have verified that the dolphin has distinctly shaped brain cells (called von Economo neurons), which are found only in the great apes, elephants, and the whales. This may be biological evidence for behaviors that were once considered to be strictly human. These elongated neuron cells appear to be responsible for language, as well as empathy, trust, guilt, embarrassment, love, and humor.

Another amazing though seldom discussed fact about the bottle-nosed dolphin is its highly unusual sexual activity. Like humans, the dolphin is one of only a handful of species that has no set breeding or calving season, but mates and procreates any time of the year. Numerous studies of both wild and captive bottle-nosed dolphins have verified that this marine mammal engages in group sex, bisexuality, cross-species sex with the spotted dolphin, and homosexual activity. Some male pairs appear to partner for life, while the female dolphin, who may raise up to 10 calves in her breeding lifetime, will have a different father for every calf she births. Recent

Very Social Mammals   ©ThroughTheLensGallery.com

evidence indicates that as many as 1,500 species of wild animals engage in some form of homosexual or bisexual activity, including giraffes and chimpanzees. Some of this behavior may be related to social bonding and establishing dominance.

The dolphin eats mostly fish, but also takes squid and octopus. Along the west coast of Florida its predominant prey is mullet, which it stuns with its powerful tail, flipping the fish high in the air, then swimming back to dine on it. Several dolphins will sometimes be seen working together as a team to corral schools of striped mullet in a behavior similar to that of lion prides or wolf packs. High-frequency vocalizations help the dolphins coordinate these mullet hunts.

Although the temptation exists to feed this marine mammal, it is never advisable. It can make the dolphin dependent on humans for food and can lead to it becoming entangled in cast nets and fishing line, resulting in injury or sometimes death. Another concern is that the dolphin can and will bite. Feeding any wild animal, from shark to alligator, is not advisable.

In the wild, the dolphin has several natural predators. In Australia and New Zealand, scores of bottle-nosed dolphins display scarring from past shark attacks. In Florida the bottlenose has been known to be killed by bull, tiger, and hammerhead sharks, as well as killer whales. It is also infrequently killed when it gets entangled in crab-pot lines and gill and trawl nets. Water pollution, especially raw sewage that can bring on diseases, nutrient-rich dead zones from the overuse of fertilizers, and red tides also take their toll. The dolphin is also known for stranding itself, on beaches en masse, though no one has been able to sufficiently explain this bizarre and often fatal behavior. It is still killed and eaten in Japan and parts of China but is protected throughout most of its range.

One of the most difficult things for a self-centered species such as *Homo sapiens* to come to grips with is the concept that we may not be the most advanced or sophisticated species on the planet. While it is obvious that we, as tool makers and tool users, can out-compete and hence eradicate the entire world population of bottle-nosed dolphin, it is another thing entirely to admit that the dolphin has a better world to live in. It doesn't make tools because in its environment it doesn't need them. It has far more habitat than humans because the oceans cover more

On the Hunt　　　　　　　　　　　　　　　　　　　　　© Al Tuttle

than 70 percent of the globe. It has no gravity to contend with, ample food, few natural predators, a complex and rich social environment, and in all probability some kind of language, though we have yet to decode or understand it.

□___ **Atlantic Spotted Dolphin** (*Stenella frontalis*) Nicknames: mottled dolphin, spotted dolphin / Status: FL=stable, IUCN=insufficient data to determine status / Life span: to 50 years / Length: 7.5-7.6 ft (2.26-2.29 m) / Weight: 290-310 lb (130-140 kg) / Reproduces: in the Gulf and the Atlantic / Found: Gulf, offshore starting at 15 nautical miles.

In his book *The Nature of Things on Sanibel*, naturalist George Campbell's list of marine mammals includes Gervais beaked whale, goose-beaked whale, Atlantic killer whale, false killer whale, bottle-nosed dolphin, Curvier's porpoise, spotted porpoise, Atlantic dolphin, pilot whale, little piked whale, and Atlantic right whale. In 25 years of offshore fishing, I personally have seen only two of these: the very common bottlenose and the Atlantic spotted dolphin. The others may well be out there, but actually finding and seeing one may take a lifetime; therefore, only these two common dolphins are included in this work.

Atlantic Spotted Dolphin   Courtesy NOAA

The false killer whale (*Pseudorea crassidens*) was actually a fairly common sighting in the 1970s. In July 1976 a pod of 20 of these small whales were seen off the beaches of both Sanibel and Captiva only to later strand themselves on a barrier island to the north. To my knowledge there has never been a sighting of a false killer whale since.

Over the past decade, sightings of the spotted dolphin have become fairly common occurrences. Starting at roughly 18 miles from shore and extending into the deep Gulf, the chances of seeing one are very good. You are not likely to spot one from shore or in the back bay, however.

A spotted dolphin is smaller than the bottlenose. It is also far more curious and will sometimes come flying over to a moving boat from up to a mile away. It loves swimming in the bow, as well as jumping and diving in the wake of the boat, especially if you slow down to create a massive wake. It will sometimes come up to an anchored boat and roll on its side, as if to see what you are doing. It travels in pods of between 10 and 30 animals.

Sadly, the Pacific spotted dolphin has a bad habit of swimming with yellowfin tuna, a behavior that has resulted in the loss of more than 4 million of this species in the past 30 years. When the giant seine nets are set by commercial fisherman, the spotted dolphin swimming above the yellowfin tuna are also entrapped, often resulting in death. Today there are special devices that allow most of these dolphins to escape alive, and their numbers are recovering worldwide.

Yellow Rat Snake and Frog

© Blake Sobczak

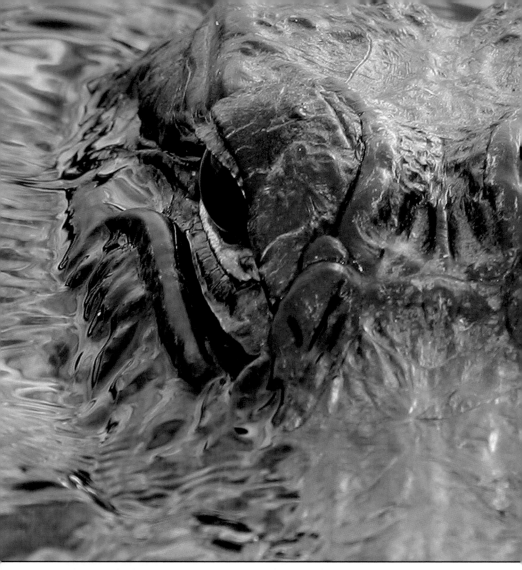

The Reptiles and Amphibians of Sanibel & Captiva

Florida leads the United States in the number of native reptiles and amphibians living within its borders. This isn't surprising when you consider the variety of microclimates within the state, most of them frost free. Add to that the fact that the lower third of Florida lies in a subtropical ecological zone, and it makes perfect sense. Reptiles and amphibians are cold blooded and their numbers increase in direct proportion to their proximity to the equator.

Worldwide there are 8,225 species of known reptiles in four groups: *Crocodilia*—alligators and crocodiles (23); *Sphenodontia*—the tuatara of New Zealand (2); *Squamata*—lizards, snakes, and worm-lizards (7,900); and *Testudines*—turtles and tortoises (300). There are slightly fewer amphibians, with 6,347 species in three orders: *Anura*—frogs and toads (5,602); *Caudata*—salamanders and newts (571);

©ThroughTheLensGallery.com

and *Apoda*—caecilians, which are limbless, earthworm-like newts (174).

Florida, including the numerous introduced species such as iguanas, Nile monitor lizards, and Burmese pythons, has some 184 species, divided into salamanders (26), frogs and toads (30), lizards (51), caecilians (1), snakes (47), turtles (26), and crocodilians (3). Sanibel and Captiva lack salamanders and caecilians, but the two islands fare very well overall with a total of 50 species, although the indigo snake is probably extirpated from both islands at this time. This total is divided into frogs and toads (9), lizards (13), snakes (12), turtles and tortoises (14), and crocodilians (2).

The two most fascinating local groups are the sea turtles and crocodilians. Sanibel experienced its first ever leatherback turtle nest in summer 2009, giving it the distinction of recording four of the world's eight known species of sea turtles nesting here. While we have only one crocodile, the "Refuge Croc" or "Wilma" as it is sometimes called, it is a large one. Our alligators are rebounding from an open harvest and are always a fascinating reptile to observe.

Several introduced species have been included in this section, though the chances of seeing some of these are remote. This section uses the standard zone abbreviations as throughout the rest of the book. You will find many lizards, frogs, and snakes without any weights given. This is typical in herpetology where far more emphasis is given to the length than to the weight of the animal.

This list was in large part produced from a master list provided by Chris Lechowicz, the herpetologist for SCCF. A downloadable PDF version of that list is available at the SCCF Web site (www.sccf.org; click on the Wildlife Projects tab).

Alligators & Crocodiles

American Alligator (*Alligator mississippiensis*)
Nicknames: gator, el lagarto (Spanish), alli / Status: FL=species of special concern, IUCN=LC / Life span: to 66 years / Length: 8.2-14.5 ft (2.5-4.4 m) / Weight: 160 (female)-1,200 lb (male) (72-544 kg) / Nests: on island / Found: IW, MZ, UA year-round.

The alligator, along with birds, survived the fifth extinction some 65.5 million years ago at the end of the Jurassic period. Its lineage goes back 230 million years. Despite the obvious difference in appearance, the alligator is more closely related to birds than to other cold-blooded animals such as turtles, snakes, and lizards. The alligator builds nests, lays eggs, and remains with its offspring for as long as a year after they are hatched—all characteristics commonly found in birds. Another similarity is that, like birds, the alligator, especially the American alligator, is very vocal.

Because the alligator was over-harvested for its hide and flesh, the species was placed on the endangered species list in 1967. At that time experts estimated that fewer than 400,000 alligators were left in the state of Florida. Restrictions on hunting, strong conservation efforts, and the alligator's ability to reproduce rapidly all helped to bring this primeval predator back, and 20 years later its status was changed to a species of special concern. Today an estimated 1-1.5 million alligators are living in Florida. Only Louisiana has more, with an estimated 1.5-2 million living in the swamps and bayous in the southern portion of the state.

Large Bull Alligator   ©ThroughTheLensGallery.com

The only other known species of alligator in the world is the Chinese alligator (*Alligator sinensis*), which has a wild population estimated at 150 animals and is expected to be extinct in the wild within the next decade. Of the 23 species of crocodilians left in the world, half are endangered or threatened. The only species currently thriving are the American alligator, the South American caiman, and the saltwater crocodile of Australia and Southeast Asia.

The American alligator has the strongest bite of any living animal, measured in laboratory conditions at 2,125 pounds per square inch. The only known animal to have ever exceeded that level of bone-crushing jaw power was Tyrannosaurus rex. The alligator can hold its breath and remain underwater for as long as six hours. It does this by shunting off the blood supply to its extremities and circulating all of its blood between its brain and heart. It can survive temperatures as low as 26° F but only for brief periods. Its optimum functioning temperature is 89° F.

The alligator has a high reproduction rate. After breeding in the spring, the male and female separate. The female generally lays one clutch of between 20 and 50 eggs, covering them with decaying vegetation that generates heat and serves as a form of incubation. The warmer eggs (90-93° F) become males, and the cooler eggs (82-86° F) become females. Hatchling mortality is very high, with 93 percent succumbing to predation before reaching sexual maturity around seven years of age. Almost every animal living in the wetlands habitat eats alligator eggs or hatchlings, including herons, egrets, raccoons, otters, snakes, bobcats, panthers, bears, fire ants, fish, crocodiles, and other alligators.

The alligator has a unique relationship with birds, and nowhere does that play out more dramatically than in bird rookeries. The alligator does not climb trees, but of course there are a host of island predators that do, including raccoons, bobcats, and rats. Because of the threat of these dexterous predators, most rookeries are located on islands surrounded by water or along wetlands where alligators are readily found. In an unusual symbiotic relationship, birds use the alligator as a reptilian sentinel guarding their nests. When a hungry raccoon attempts to swim to an island of nesting egrets and herons, the resident alligator stands ready to kill the predator long before it can reach its intended target. The alligator has little trouble drowning a predator as large as a Florida panther. The bobcat poses little

Hatchlings always stay close to mom   ©ThroughTheLensGallery.com

danger to a creature with a hide as thick and almost as effective as a bulletproof vest. There is a price to be paid for this service, however. The alligator is not above snatching fledglings from low-hanging branches, and if a nestling should end up on the ground or in the water below, the alligator quickly disposes of the wayward chick.

The alligator eats just about anything. It has the strongest digestive acids found in any living creature. Its stomach is capable of digesting hair, bone, and teeth into usable proteins. Its diet consists of fish, birds, turtles, snakes, mammals, and amphibians. Hatchlings also eat insects, snails, mollusks, frogs, mice, and rats. A mature bull alligator will eat deer, wild boar, cattle, and will even take down prey as large as black bears and horses.

People are often tempted to feed alligators, but this is not a good idea. Once this pattern is established, the animal equates humans with food, and anyone approaching the reptile is in grave danger.

You should never swim in any of Sanibel's freshwater lakes, ponds, or the Sanibel River. In the water, which is the alligator's domain, it takes only a small alligator to bite and drown a person. The alligator is capable of very quick attacks and can actually propel itself almost completely out of the water with a few swishes of its massive tail. Signs throughout the island warn of the dangers of these primitive but dangerous animals, and these warnings should be taken seriously. Since 1948 there have been more than 346 unprovoked alligator attacks on humans in Florida and 18 fatalities. (For more information about alligators and these attacks, read Alligators, Sharks & Panthers: Deadly Encounter's with Florida's Top Predator—Man, published by Indigo Press in 2007.)

On Sanibel, after two fatal attacks, one in 2001 and one in 2004, the alligator population was targeted with an open-permit harvest. More than 200 alligators have been removed from the interior wetlands in an effort to avoid another tragedy. Most of the larger bull alligators, some of them exceeding 12 feet in length, are now gone. A fair number of smaller alligators can still be found around the island, along with a few mature bulls up to 10 feet in length. The taking of so many of these apex predators has been a controversial environmental issue on Sanibel. The role the alligator plays in the wetlands environment is an important one, and its removal can upset the balance.

The recent increase of iguanas throughout the island has been tied to the decrease of mature alligators. Iguanas

©ThroughTheLensGallery.com

take readily to the water, where they are easy prey for the faster-swimming alligator. With the alligator population removed by trappers, the iguana population, as well as the far more troublesome West Nile monitor lizard, has skyrocketed.

With most of the larger alligators gone and the few remaining animals extremely weary of human contact, the island population appears to be undergoing a period of slow but steady recovery. One of the best locations to see alligators today is in the Bailey Tract of the "Ding" Darling refuge off of Tarpon Bay Road. Trappers were not allowed to harvest any alligators from federal lands, so this 160-acre preserve has become a safe haven for them. The alligator is also returning to a number of private lakes and ponds, but these are not as readily accessible to the public. The SCCF trail system running along the Sanibel River is another good location to spot an alligator.

🔲 _____ **American Crocodile** (*Crocodylus acutus*) Nicknames: American croc, saltwater croc, salty, croc / Status: FL=threatened, IUCN=VU / Life span: to 70 years / Length: 9.8-13 ft (3-4 m) / Weight: 380-840 lb (173-382 kg) female, 500-1,500 lb (226-678 kg) male / Nests: on island (infertile) / Found: IW,UA.

© Blake Sobczak

There is only one crocodile on Sanibel and Captiva Islands, and she is huge. Commonly referred to as "The Refuge Crocodile," this wayward female measures close to 13 feet in length and weighs almost half a ton. Her story, just like the story of the American crocodile in Florida, is fascinating.

The first official sighting of this animal occurred in 1980. Unofficial reports of her existence on the island date back to the 1970s, but no photographs or other proof of these sightings exist, so they remain in question. That wasn't the case on June 10, 1980. Following is an excerpt from the official memorandum of Charles LeBuff, the biological technician for the refuge at the time.

> "I received a radio call from Ede Stokes advising that George Weymouth had a crocodile under observation near stop number 10 (near the power line)… It was hauled out on the far bank of the canal along the exit loop. George had managed to get several photographs of it before it had reentered the water. Unable to relocate the reptile, we drove slowly along the road, and I saw an object that seemed out of place. I yelled at George, asking for binoculars, and telling him I might have the crocodile in view. I took about 14 photographs."

Although the photographs made it indisputable, the positive identification of a large crocodile by three leading wildlife experts would have sufficed. Over the decades, these sightings continued. The croc was seen again in 1981, vanishing for the next two years, then showing up again briefly in 1984. In December 1985 another large crocodile was found in a residential neighborhood on Pine Island (approximately 10 miles north of the refuge). The residents, fearful of this nine-foot behemoth, called Florida Fish and Wildlife and requested its removal.

Their first request was denied because the croc was found to be nonaggressive. By May 1986, after repeated complaints, F&W sent Officer Paul Molar, to capture and move the animal. He permanently marked it by removing the third scute from its tail. It was a female measuring 9 feet 4 inches and weighing 200-250 pounds. It was trucked about 70 miles south to Collier-Seminole State Park and released in an area known to have a breeding crocodile population.

A closer view shows the characteristic long flat head   ©ThroughTheLensGallery.com

Large male crocodile

Six months later she had migrated back to the area and was observed once again at the refuge. She mysteriously vanished from 1986 to 1988, then briefly reappeared in 1989. This pattern of appearing, then disappearing has continued ever since. In 1995 she built a nest in a resident's back yard but lacking a mate, her eggs were infertile. In 1998 the refuge personal deposited 15 yards of sand to build an artificial nesting site for her near the end of Wildlife Drive. Eventually she elected to use the new nesting site, but the croc and her eggs became such a draw that it was removed the same year.

All the while she continued to grow larger, feeding on turtles, raccoons, and small alligators. She is perhaps the largest female crocodile in Florida. At one point she actually chased off a female alligator and adopted 16 newly hatched baby alligators for five days. She has nested off and on over the past 20 years, but not a single egg has ever hatched. One theory is that she is simply too old and may have reached the end of her reproductive cycle. A more likely theory is that there is no available male croc in the region to fertilize her eggs. All crocodilians require a pairing to produce fertile eggs.

As of this writing, she is somewhere on Sanibel. She was seen repeatedly throughout the winter and spring of 2009 and made another infertile nest on the west end of the island. No doubt she will disappear and reappear again over time, though at this point she is probably nearing the end of her life span, which can exceed 70 years.

Statewide, the American crocodile population is slowly recovering. Florida represents the very northern edge of its survivable range. Unlike the alligator, the croc cannot tolerate cold weather. It inhabits the entire northern tip of South America down to Peru, all of Central America well up into the Sea of Cortez on the Pacific, Cuba and the Caribbean Islands, and the southern tip of Florida. It is capable of living its entire life in saltwater but can survive in both fresh and brackish waters as well. The alligator, on the other hand, dies after 10 to 12 hours of being submerged in saltwater.

In South America there have been official reports of 20-foot crocs. The largest skull ever measured was 28.6 inches long (72.6 cm) and came from a mature male estimated to be at least 22 feet long. That animal would have weighed close to 3,000 pounds. A crocodile this size could eat a horse. Whole.

Sadly, because of over-harvesting and hunting, the American crocodile is in trouble throughout its range. Venezuela banned the taking of crocodiles in 1972. Other nations such as Costa Rica and Cuba have followed suit, and in these locales the croc is making a slow but steady recovery from the brink of extinction.

Ironically, a major reason for the recovery of the American crocodile in Florida, where its numbers are now estimated at more than 1,500, is the nuclear power plant at Turkey Point, built in 1972 south of Miami near Homestead. The power plant encompasses some 3,300 acres of wetlands through which a series of canals were dug to assist in cooling the water used to keep the reactor core from overheating. Shortly thereafter, a handful of American crocodiles discovered these canals, which teemed with fish that thrived in the artificially warmed waters.

Like the endangered manatee that frequents the Florida Power and Light plant in North Fort Myers along the Orange River, the croc has found a safe haven at Turkey Point. The power plant has become the primary recovery engine for the entire Florida population, helping to upgrade the status of these impressive animals from endangered to threatened in 2007.

Juvenile crocodile   ©ThroughTheLensGallery.com

Despite its size, the crocodile is far less aggressive than the alligator toward humans. Aside from an injured croc named Zulu who killed the man who shot him in 1925 on the outskirts of Miami, there has never been a confirmed attack by any crocodile in the U.S., though there have been several confirmed fatal attacks in Mexico and Central America. You should never approach a crocodile in the wild. If its nest is anywhere near, the female crocodile will kill in defense of its eggs. The croc, like the alligator, is capable of explosive charges that occur almost faster than the human eye can follow. In the water the croc can obtain speeds of 20 miles per hour and is capable of launching its 2,000-pound body completely out of the water with its powerful tail.

Sadly, during an extended cold snap in early 2010, the refuge crocodile was found dead alongside the Sanibel River by SCCF staff member Dee Serage-Century. Dee found the croc during a walk along the East River Trail at SCCF on the afternoon of January 26, 2010. The croc died of exposure and old age. Her skeleton can now be viewed at the visitor center located at J.N. "Ding" Darling National Wildlife Preserve on Sanibel.

SCCF's resident Gopher Tortoise, Alice

© Maggie May Rogers / SCCF

Turtles and Tortoises

☐ _____ **Gopher Tortoise** (*Gopherus polyphemus*) Nicknames: Hoover chicken (from the days of the Great Depression), gopher, landlord of the sand / Status: FL=threatened, IUCN=VU / Life span: to 80 years / Length: 9.25-14.5 in. (23-37 cm) / Weight: 9-30 lb(4-13.6 kg) / Nests: on island / Found: IW, UA in or near its burrows.

Considered a keystone species, the gopher tortoise plays an important role in the lives of many other creatures. There are 300-400 species that use active or abandoned gopher tortoise burrows. These include the threatened indigo snake, gopher frogs, burrowing owls, the cotton mouse, rattlesnake, coachwhip snakes, and 32 species of spiders. An excellent excavator, the gopher tortoise digs burrows that have been documented to be as long as 47 feet and more than 18 feet deep, although the burrows on Sanibel, because of the high water table, are much shallower than this.

The gopher tortoise is strictly a land animal. It is related to the famous Galapagos tortoise, which can

© Eric B. Holt

Young gopher tortoise

grow to 880 pounds and is also strictly terrestrial. The easiest way to distinguish the gopher tortoise from another turtle is by the high, dark, rounded shell and the front feet, which are spade-like with heavy protective scales.

The gopher tortoise is known to stop traffic on occasion as it transits the islands. If you discover a turtle crossing a road and are unsure what kind it is, take it to the edge of the road and let it continue on but do not release it into any body of water because it could drown. There is an empty shell at the CROW clinic from a gopher tortoise that was placed into the Gulf of Mexico by a well-meaning but seriously misguided tourist who found it browsing on beach dune vegetation and thought it was a lost sea turtle. The combination of saltwater and wave action quickly drowned the poor gopher tortoise. The lesson we can take from this unfortunate incident is that in these kinds of circumstances, please leave wildlife alone.

No matter the species of turtle you help across any road or bike path, always ferry it along in the same direction it was heading. It may be following the scent of a mate, changing habitat, nesting, or looking for food. Returning the turtle to where it just came from will likely result in it turning around and re-crossing the same street or intersection a few minutes later, putting itself at risk again. It is now believed that some water turtles can see polarized light and use this ability to navigate over land to find other inhabitable bodies of water.

The gopher tortoise's natural range runs from extreme southwestern South Carolina across Georgia and into southeastern Louisiana. Its population has been severely impacted by development. Until July 30, 2007, when Florida rescinded the incidental take permits, the gopher tortoise was commonly plowed under by commercial and subdivision developers. It has moved from a species of special concern to its current status as threatened in Florida, and its population statewide is in decline. It has also been impacted by a respiratory illness called URTD (upper respiratory tract disease), which can result in death.

Although predominantly a herbivore, feeding on berries, grass, fruit and cactus flowers, the gopher tortoise has been known to scavenge carrion as well. It is preyed upon by a host of creatures, the smallest being the fire ant, which has been known to attack hatchlings. Other predators include gray fox, armadillos, snakes, and raptors. The slow-moving gopher tortoise was once a favorite with early island settlers who would, upon finding one, simply turn it over on its back and return later to bring it home for the kettle; hence, the comical but accurate nickname, Hoover chicken.

The best way to find a gopher tortoise on the islands is to find an active burrow. It has a home range of two to five miles but generally does not stray more than several hundred yards from its burrow to forage. If you do come upon one, please let it feed and do not pick it up or disturb it. It is one of only four species of land tortoise remaining in North America. The others are the desert tortoise of California, Nevada, and New Mexico; the Berlandier's tortoise of southern Texas; and the Bolson tortoise of Mexico, which was reintroduced into New Mexico in 2007.

☐ _____ Ornate Diamondback Terrapin (*Malaclemys terrapin macrospilota*) Nicknames: none / Status: FL=species of special concern, IUCN-NT / Life span: unknown / Length: 5-9 in. (12-23 cm) / Weight: 0.90-1.7 lb (300-1,400 g); the male is much smaller than the female / Nests: on island / Found: MZ

On Sanibel and Captiva, the ornate diamondback terrapin spends most of its life in and around the mangroves where it forages on carrion, snails, crabs, and salt-marsh plants. Along the Eastern Seaboard and down through Texas it lives in salt marshes. The terrapin is equipped with a special gland next to its eyes that allows it to secrete excess salt. It has one of the most heavily embossed shell patterns of any turtle and a unique spotted lavender skin. It is also becoming extremely rare.

The reason for its demise is simple: it is delicious. Until recently the terrapin was hunted in much of its

Juvenile terrapin　　　© Maggie May Rogers / SCCF

Juvenile terrapin
© Maggie May Rogers / SCCF

range for terrapin soup. It has also suffered from coastal development. Its biggest threat is crab traps, which it enters to forage on the bait, then drowns. There are five subspecies in Florida and two more in its greater range from southern New England to Corpus Christi, Texas.

Adult Diamondback terrapin in the mangroves   © Eric B. Holt

☐ _____ **Peninsula Cooter** (*Pseudemys peninsularis*) Nicknames: cooter, Florida river cooter / Status: FL=stable, IUCN=LC / Life span: to 12 years / Length: 12-15 in. (30-38 cm) / Weight: 6-8 lb (2.7-3.6 kg) / Nests: on island / Found: IW, UA.

Possibly Sanibel's most commonly seen turtle, the cooter is often observed basking on logs and banks or rising to the surface to breathe in almost any pond, river, or lake on the island. It is readily identified by bright, road-stripe yellow facial markings, although this can sometimes lead to confusion with the red-bellied turtle, which has a similar facial pattern. The name cooter may be derived from the African kuta, which means turtle in several dialects.

© Eric B. Holt

Cooter close up   © Maggie May Rogers / SCCF

Until very recently the cooter was commonly harvested for the dinner table in Florida. On July 20, 2009, however, U.S. Fish and Wildlife extended full protection to this species, so it is no longer legal to harvest wild cooters.

The mature cooter feeds on aquatic vegetation, while juveniles feed on aquatic insects and tadpoles. This turtle is a favorite food of adult alligators, which can easily crush the cooter's shell with powerful jaws. Hatchlings and juvenile cooters are fed upon by snakes, great blue herons, raccoons, and otters.

❏ _____ **Florida Snapping Turtle** (*Chelydra serpentina osceola*) Nicknames: common snapping turtle, snapper / Status: FL=stable, IUCN=LC / Life span: to 40 years / Length: 10-20 in. (25-50 cm) / Weight: 10-35 lb (4.5-16 kg) / Nests: on island / Found: IW, UA.

Aside from the sea turtles that nest along our beaches, the Florida snapping turtle and Florida soft-shell turtle are the two largest turtles on the islands. In captivity the snapping turtle has been known to grow to 75 pounds; a close relative, the endangered alligator snapping turtle, can reach an astonishing 200-plus pounds.

This turtle, especially when discovered on land, has a powerful bite and an ornery disposition. Picking one up by the carapace is ill advised, as its long neck is capable of reaching halfway back across its body. Picking it up by its tail can injure or kill it. Take extreme care if you come across one of these turtles while it is laying its eggs or crossing over land from one watershed to another.

Snapping Turtle nesting   © Courtesy Wikipedia Commons

The snapping turtle is an omnivore, consuming a wide variety of aquatic vegetation, as well as many invertebrates such as frogs, fish, reptiles (including other turtles and snakes), small birds, and mammals.

Alligators prey on the adult snapping turtle and the young are preyed upon by herons, otters, and even land-locked tarpon. Although nowhere near as common as the cooter, the snapping turtle can sometimes be seen basking on a log but is more likely to be seen in the spring when it comes up on land to lay its clutch of eggs. The snapping turtle, just like the cooter, is only recently protected from harvesting (July 20, 2009).

Juvenile snapping turtle   © Mark Kenderdine

☐ _____ **Florida Redbelly Turtle** (*Pseudemys nelsoni*) Nicknames: redbelly / Status: FL=stable, IUCN=LC / Life span: to 26 years / Length: 13 in. (34 cm) / Weight: Weight: 6-8 lb (2.7-3.6 kg) / Nests: on island / Found: IW, UA.

Very similar in appearance to the peninsula cooter, the redbelly (sometimes identified as red-bellied) turtle is not that common on Sanibel. The easiest way to distinguish it is its carapace, which has faded, wide, reddish markings on the costal scutes. When covered in moss or vegetation, however, the markings are difficult to see. You can also identify it by looking for a distinctive notch in its upper jaw, bordered by a cusp on either side. From a distance, however, this too is problematic.

Redbelly sunning on fallen log © Eric B. Holt

This turtle can survive in both fresh and brackish waters, but unlike the terrapin, it does not possess a salt gland. Strictly an herbivore, the redbelly consumes a wide variety of aquatic vegetation. It is heavily preyed upon by alligators, but in return it is known to lay its egg clutches inside alligator nests, relying on the female alligator to inadvertently protect the turtle eggs along with hers. The redbelly is sometimes seen basking on a log or a bank in almost any pond, river, or lake on Sanibel. It is not as common on Captiva because of the lack of freshwater ponds.

A good location for spotting many of the islands' turtles is in the two large lakes and the stretch of Sanibel River located to the west of Rabbit Road. Access to this half-mile-long stretch of water is easy because a section of the shared-use path runs along the pond's shore. Check out the bike-path maps in this book for details.

☐ ____ **Florida Box Turtle** (*Terrapene carolina bauri*) Nicknames: box turtle / Status: FL=species of special concern, IUCN=LC / Life span: to more than 100 years / Length: 6.5 in. (16.5 cm) / Weight: 5 lb (2.3 kg) / Nests: on island / Found: IW, UA.

Not a true tortoise, the Florida box turtle is semi-aquatic, at home in both terrestrial and aquatic habitats. In the water it prefers to remain in the shallows and does not appear to be a good swimmer. It has a life expectancy of more than 100 years.

Easily identified by its high, arching domed carapace with bright orange-yellow markings, the box turtle is commonly kept

Box Turtle © Maggie May Rogers / SCCF

as a pet. Collecting this turtle for the pet industry was recently outlawed, and the species is now protected throughout Florida. Because of the box turtle's popularity, Florida has imposed a two-turtle possession limit.

Box Turtle © Eric B. Holt

Its diet consists of insects, carrion, dung, and toxic fungi. The box turtle cannot be eaten by humans or other mammals because of the build-up of toxicity in its flesh from eating poisonous mushrooms and other fungi. Because of that, the box turtle is seldom preyed upon as an adult. That may be why it is so brightly patterned, much like other toxic and poisonous species. Some juveniles and hatchlings are taken by fire ants, herons, and skunks.

☐ ____ **Florida Softshell Turtle** (*Apalone ferox*) Nicknames: flatback, pancake turtle, river flyer / Status: FL= stable, IUCN=LC / Life span: to 30 years / Length: 6-25 in. (15-63 cm) / Weight: 20-50 lb (9-22.5 kg) / Nests: on island / Found: IW, UA.

A favorite food of the American alligator, the softshell turtle can be found in almost every pond and lake on Sanibel. It is easily recognized by its unusually long snorkel-like snout. Another means of identification is the flat, olive-black carapace, which resembles stretched leather. The largest Florida softshell on record topped the scales at 93 pounds (42 kg). The average size found around the islands is 25-35 pounds.

Florida softshell turtle close up   © Eric B. Holt

The softshell turtle is capable of pharyngeal breathing. This means it can bypass its lungs by taking in oxygen and releasing carbon dioxide through a special membrane that lines the throat, creating a direct gas exchange with the water. Think of it as a turtle gill device, giving the softshell the unique ability to remain underwater for extended periods of time.

The Florida softshell turtle is primarily a carnivore, dieting on insects, crustaceans, mollusks, fish, waterfowl, and amphibians. It has also been known to eat other turtles. Softshell eggs

Florida softshell turtle   © Eric B. Holt

and hatchlings are heavily preyed upon by otters, raccoons, skunks, and snapping turtles. Adults are fed upon by alligators and humans, as they are a favorite ingredient for making turtle soup.

On land the softshell turtle can be very aggressive and should never be handled. It is capable of delivering a nasty bite, and because of the habitat it thrives in, infection is a strong possibility.

Red-eared Slider (*Trachemys scripta elegans*)

Nicknames: red-eared terrapin, pond slider / Status: FL=stable (introduced species), IUCN=LC / Life span: to 40 years / Length: 8-12 in. (20-30 cm) / Weight: 3-5.5 lb (1.5-2.5 kg) / Nests: on island / Found: IW, UA.

Red-eared Slider resting on a log   © Eric B. Holt

Originally found west of the state of Mississippi, this small, colorful turtle early on became the most popular species for the turtle pet trade. In 1958, after several were released into the freshwater canals of Miami, the red-eared slider established a breeding population in Dade County. Over time, with the help of more and more releases from pet owners who grew tired of caring for them, this species has successfully moved into Collier, Orange, Marion, Duval, Lake, Hillsborough, Monroe, and Lee counties.

On Sanibel a sighting of this turtle is extremely rare. It may no longer have a breeding population here, though it has been authenticated in the past. The red-eared slider is easily identified by the distinctive red marking located directly behind its eye. This slider is an omnivore, feeding on crayfish, carrion, tadpoles, snails, crickets, and wax worms, as well as aquatic vegetation.

Although on the islands the red-eared slider does not appear to have a major impact on the environment, it is displacing native turtles in other regions. (Another commonly released reptile that is causing major concern in South Florida is the Burmese python, which can grow to a length of 20 feet and has been known to prey on women and children in its native Burma. Recent surveys indicate the Everglades population of this snake may be approaching 200,000.)

Yellow-bellied Slider (*Trachemys scripta scripta*)

Nicknames: slider / Status: FL=stable, IUCN=LC / Life span: to 35 years / Length: 5-13 in. (13-33 cm) / Weight: 3-5.5 lb (1.5-2.5 kg) / Nests: on island / Found: IW, UA.

Originally found only in northern Florida from Levy County north across the Panhandle, the yellow-bellied slider has been extending its range southward over the past 50 years. The Sanibel population was purposely introduced by a graduate student in the 1970s.

Since the ban on sales of the red-eared slider went into effect in fall 2008, people have begun farming the yellow-bellied slider in huge numbers, and the spread of this turtle through the pet trade will likely follow the same pattern as the red-eared slider. The indigenous yellow-bellied slider is believed to be interbreeding with the introduced red-eared slider, which has led to concern for the future of the yellow-bellied slider and motivated Florida to ban sales of the red-eared slider.

The yellow-bellied slider is a small turtle, rarely exceeding a foot in length in the wild. It is easy to distinguish from the cooter in that it has much more yellow on its face and carapace. Although it starts its life as an omnivore, by the time it reaches maturity almost 95 percent of its diet is derived from aquatic vegetation.

Belly of a Yellow-bellied Slider

© Eric B. Holt

Yellow-bellied Slider sunning on a log © Eric B. Holt

The yellow-bellied, like all turtles, is a common prey for the alligator. Eggs and hatchlings are preyed upon by a variety of species including herons, otters, other turtles, snakes, fire ants, and raccoons.

☐ _____ **Striped Mud Turtle** (*Kinosternon baurii*) Nicknames: three-striped mud turtle / Status: FL=stable, IUCN=LC / Life span: to 50 years / Length: 5 in. (12 cm) / Weight: 0.35-0.50 lb (160-230 g) / Nests: on islands / Found: IW, UA.

Juvenile Mud Turtle's belly pattern
© Eric B. Holt

One of the smallest turtles in the world, the striped mud turtle is rarely longer than five inches. Only the narrow-bridged musk turtle from North and Central America is as tiny. The striped mud turtle can readily be identified by the three distinctive stripes running across the top of the carapace. Its docile disposition and small size make it a favorite of the turtle pet trade. The striped mud turtle is now protected in the Keys but is still captured from the wild throughout most of the state. Because of its small size, the mud turtle is seldom used as food.

An omnivore, the mud turtle feeds on aquatic vegetation but will also eat insects, aquatic animals, and carrion. It is easily caught with small, baited hooks. In the wild even adults can be taken by herons, skunks, raccoons, and alligators.

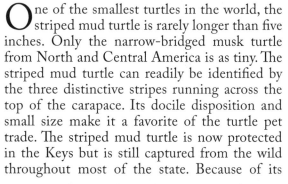

Striped Mud Turtle © Daniel Parker / SCCF

Loggerhead Sea turtle hatchling   © Sanibel-Captiva Conservation Foundation

Sea Turtles

❏ _____ **Loggerhead Sea Turtle** (*Caretta caretta*) Nicknames: loggerhead / Status: FL=threatened, IUCN=EN / Life span: to more than 100 years (maximum life span is still unknown) / Length: 36-42 in. (.92-1.1 m) / Weight: 250-350 lb (113-158 kg) / Nests: along the beaches during the summer / Found: GB

By far the most common of the four nesting sea turtles on Sanibel, the loggerhead turtle has been visiting the gulf beaches since the islands were formed some 5,000 years ago. With a history that goes back some 200 million years, long before the rise and fall of the dinosaur, it is easy to understand why people are so taken with sea turtles.

The loggerhead used to be much larger than is commonly found today. When Ponce de Leon arrived in Florida there were probably any number of these turtles weighing in at 1,000 pounds or more. Loggerheads of 600 to 800 pounds were quite common until the turn of the 20th century. Today, a loggerhead approaching 500 pounds is considered remarkable.

The range of the loggerhead is worldwide, though only in tropical or subtropical waters. It is found in the Mediterranean, Pacific, and Indian oceans. There are still a couple of sites where up to 10,000 females nest every year: one is in South Florida and another in Oman at the tip of the Saudi Arabian peninsula. Approximately 68,000-90,000 loggerhead turtle nests are recorded in the United States every year. The world population of the species is unknown.

The loggerhead is an omnivore, eating a variety of oceanic foods including jellyfish, Portuguese man o' war (a toxic jellyfish the loggerhead is immune to),

Loggerhead Sea turtle close up © Sanibel-Captiva Conservation Foundation

sponges, small fish, crustaceans, mollusks, crabs, and shrimp. Juveniles eat sea grasses and marine worms at first, moving to larger prey as their powerful jaws develop. The adult sea turtle has few natural predators. Sharks have been known to bite off turtle limbs but only an extremely large shark is capable of piercing the thick carapace.

The hatchlings are another story. Literally everything preys upon them for the first year of life. These predators include raccoons, dogs, herons, seagulls, crows, birds of prey, ghost crabs, shorebirds, snook, catfish, tarpon, shark, and even fire ants. To counter this constant predation, the female loggerhead can lay as many as four or five clutches of eggs each breeding season. Every clutch holds between 50 and 150 eggs, which helps the species tremendously because the mortality rate of sea turtle hatchlings is precariously close to 100 percent. Studies have shown that only one out of every 1,000 sea turtles makes it to adulthood.

Once heavily preyed upon by humans, all the world's sea turtles are now endangered. Although hundreds of thousands of these turtles were consumed in the United States for food, the larger threat to the population came from their nests being raided for eggs. Finding a sea turtle nest is not difficult since the female hauls herself up beyond the surf line and leaves a clearly evident crawl track. Eggs are still taken illegally throughout much of the Third World. Roughly the size of a large Ping-Pong ball, the egg is a free source of protein in a hungry world. This problem is exacerbated by the fact that the loggerhead nests only once every two to three years, so any additional pressure on its fecundity puts its long-term survival in jeopardy.

© Courtesy Wikipedia Commons

Other leading causes of mortality for the loggerhead are long-line fishing and shrimp trawlers. Once caught in a trawling net, a sea turtle would drown and get tossed back dead into the ocean since there was no longer a legal market for its meat. In 1989 the National Marine Fisheries Service required all U.S. shrimp boats to have turtle extruder devices (TEDs) installed on their nets. These large metal contraptions allow turtles and larger fish to escape entanglement in the trawling net pulled behind them.

TEDs have helped tremendously, but sadly many shrimp fleets throughout the world refuse to install them, or in some instances they fail to work correctly because of improper installation. Illegal taking of mature turtles still occurs throughout much of its range, and there are far too many beaches used by these turtles to secure all of them from egg poachers.

Thousands of sea turtles die annually from choking on plastic trash. To a sea turtle that feeds on jellyfish, a plastic bag or a six-pack ring floating offshore looks like food. Once ingested, this plastic can become lodged in the intestines, causing a slow and painful death. As if these gauntlets aren't enough, still another cause of loggerhead mortality is boat and propeller collisions. This is especially true in the early spring when the loggerhead comes to the surface to mate. Because of these and other impacts, the loggerhead turtle has suffered a 40 percent decline in population in the past decade.

Sanibel and Captiva islands, through the efforts of SCCF, are deeply involved in helping to save endangered sea turtles. In 1968 Charles LeBuff, a Sanibel wildlife expert and author, created Caretta Research and began keeping careful records of all false crawls and nesting sea turtles. In 1992 SCCF took over the work started by LeBuff and his volunteers, and that work continues today.

The numbers of sea turtle nests on Sanibel and Captiva peaked in 1998 and 2000 with 535 and 537, respectively. Those peak years were followed by a sharp decline that bottomed out in 2005 with only 212 nests recorded. The good news is that as of 2008, some 419 nests were recorded, though one good year is not enough time to determine if the island population is truly rebounding.

To volunteer on the turtle patrol or get involved with the sea turtle programs, go to www.sccf.org and click on Wildlife Projects or call SCCF at 239-472-2329. More than 100 volunteers are needed every year. Donations are also welcome, as fuel and Jeep maintenance costs for driving the beach every morning during turtle season can be substantial (the Jeeps rust out very quickly!). Saving the endangered sea turtle is everyone's responsibility.

HOW YOU CAN HELP TO SAVE THE ENDANGERED SEA TURTLES

© Sanibel-Captiva Conservation Foundation

Never dig or leave large holes in the sand. If you build a sandcastle, before leaving the beach be sure to fill in any holes you created. A female turtle can get trapped in a large hole, causing exhaustion and even death. Smaller holes are dangerous to the hatchlings, which can get stuck in them and become easy prey for seagulls, ghost crabs, and other predators or simply die of exposure from the relentless heat of the summer sun.

Turn your beach-side lights off and be sure to close your blinds and curtains at night if you live or rent along the beaches, especially in spring and summer. Sea turtle hatchlings often break free of their nests at night and head toward the brightest light. In pristine conditions that light is always the horizon line of the open ocean. With lighted condominiums and residences along the beach, these tiny hatchlings become confused and will often head inland. They stand little chance of survival against raccoons, birds, fire ants, and a host of other predators including the heat of the Florida sun, which will quickly dehydrate and kill them.

Never toss plastic bottles, garbage bags, six-pack rings, fishing line, or any refuse into the ocean or leave it on the beach where it can find its way to the water. Adult turtles confuse this kind of trash with jellyfish and suffer because of it. Hatchlings, seabirds, and fish can also become entangled in fishing line and other trash and drown.

Remove all of your beach chairs, umbrellas, and any other obstacles when you are done for the day. These objects can block or confuse an adult sea turtle making an evening crawl and are even worse hazards for the hatchlings heading toward the sea.

Never drive on the beach. Only the sea-turtle patrol and the Sanibel police are allowed to do so, and they are trained to look out for adult turtles, as well as possible nesting sites. An inexperienced driver can crush an unmarked nest in an instant.

If you happen to come across an adult turtle crawling to or from a nest, or laying its eggs, turn off your flashlight and never use a flash device on your camera to take a photo. This may confuse and disorient the turtle and cause it to abandon its nest and return to the sea. Keep your lights off, keep a safe distance back, and if possible, contact the proper authorities to report the sighting. If a female sea turtle has too many failed nesting attempts, then it may ultimately dump its eggs in the ocean.

If you are boating, especially in the spring and summer, watch out for surfacing turtles. If you see one near you, slow down and give it ample time to swim out of your way.

☐ _____**Green Turtle** (*Chelonia mydas*) Nicknames: soup turtle / Status: FL=endangered, IUCN=EN / Life span: to 80 years / Length: 3.2-5 ft (1-1.5 m) / Weight: 400-600 lb (181-272 kg) / Nests: on islands / Found: GB.

Green Turtle swimming over a coral reef   Courtesy Wikipedia Commons

The green turtle has, and always has had, a serious problem—it tastes fabulous. When a vulnerable animal has to nest on land every two to three years, crawls slightly faster than a snail, weighs in as much as 800 pounds, and tastes delicious, its chances of thriving in a planet filled with a subspecies of clever apes with an appetite and an ax, are not exactly high.

On Sanibel and Captiva the early settlers were particularly fond of the green turtle. Its nest was often raided for the eggs, and the adult was a common item on the settlers' menus. There is every reason to believe that the islands had as many green turtle nests as they currently have loggerhead nests, and that the predation around the turn of the 20th century severely diminished the green turtle population. Today, green turtle nests are a rare event, averaging less than one per year.

The green turtle is not named for the color of its carapace, which is actually black in the Eastern Pacific subspecies. The green turtle was given that name because that's the color of the fat and flesh found beneath the carapace.

One reason humans prefer the taste of the green turtle is its diet. Unlike the loggerhead, hawksbill, and the largest turtle of all, leatherback, the green turtle is an herbivore. It feeds on seagrass beds, algae, kelp, and seaweed. Its meat is still considered a delicacy and is a product of aquaculture in the Cayman Islands to

Green Turtle hatchling   © AlanMaltz.com

this day. Green turtle soup can still be found on menus in the Florida Keys and elsewhere in the world.

In the wild, without human predation, only the 20-foot-plus tiger shark has been known to feed on the adult green turtle. Its former range was possibly even greater than that of the loggerhead, extending well down into Australia, the Red Sea, Madagascar, and literally everywhere in between. Today the green turtle is in serious trouble throughout that range.

Like all marine turtles, the green turtle is an expert open ocean navigator, though the mechanism used for its long transoceanic voyages is still unknown. The current speculation is that it has trace elements of magnetic rock in certain parts of its brain, helping it to use the earth's magnetic field to locate nesting sites. It has been known to swim more than 1,400 nautical miles to return to the beach where it was born.

Oceanic pollution, shrimp and fish trawlers, egg raids, illegal hunting of adults, and habitat destruction throughout its entire range all conspire to make the future of the green turtle on this planet anything but certain. That's the trouble with tasting so good—it's not a healthy attribute in a planet filled with 6.7 billion mouths.

Green Sea Turtle hatchling
© Sanibel-Captiva Conservation Foundation

☐ _____ **Kemp's Ridley Turtle** (*Lepidochelys kempii*) Nicknames: bastard turtle / Status: FL=Endangered, IUCN=CR / Life span: to 50 years / Length: 24 in. (60 cm) / Weight: 100 lb (45 kg) / Nests: on islands (extremely rare) / Found: GB.

Courtesy NOAA

The Kemp's ridley sea turtle may well be one of the rarest animals in the world. The last time one is known to have nested on Sanibel was in 1996. This is one of the smallest of the world's sea turtles, and its numbers have been drastically reduced since Richard Kemp, a fisherman from Key West, first submitted the species for identification in 1906. It is similar to the olive ridley, another endangered species of sea turtle.

One of the most unique aspects of the Kemp's ridley turtle is a behavior called arribada, Spanish for arrival. At a certain time and date, determined by natural phenomena still not understood, hundreds of these turtles gather near a particular nesting beach near Rancho Nuevo, Mexico; then all come ashore to nest at exactly the same time.

In Mexico, the skins of these turtles became a popular material for cowboy boots, resulting in tens of thousands of the Kemp's ridley being taken during the past 70 years. In 1947 the number of nesting females at Rancho Nuevo was estimated at 89,000; by the mid-1980s that population had been reduced to fewer than 1,000. The turtle-skin boot business has now folded, thank heavens.

Kemp's Ridley turtle nesting
Courtesy FL Fish & Wildlife Service

Perhaps as a survival response to the slaughter of these turtles in Mexico, a few have begun to show up in new nesting locations. In 2007, Texas wildlife officials found 128 Kemp's ridley sea turtles nesting near Corpus Christi, and in 2009 some

10,594 hatchlings were safely released along the Texas gulf coast. Perhaps the few individuals that have crawled up to lay their clutches on Sanibel have done so in an effort to find a new safe haven.

The future of this small reclusive turtle remains in question. Predominantly a carnivore, the Kemp's ridley survives on mollusks, crustaceans, jellyfish, algae, seaweed, and sea urchins. Because it is smaller than most turtles, a fair number of adult ridleys are taken by sharks, large grouper, and other large fish.

Kemp's Ridley hatchling
Courtesy NOAA

◻ _____ **Leatherback Turtle** (*Dermochelys coriacea*) Nicknames: glass eater / Status: FL=Endangered, IUCN: CR / Life span: to 45 years / Length: 6-8.4 ft (1.8-2.5 m) / Weight: 1,100-2,000 lb (500-916 kg) / Nests: on islands (extremely rare) / Found: GB

On June 3, 2009, Linda Gornick, a volunteer with the SCCF Sea Turtle Research and Monitoring Program, discovered an unusual turtle crawl on the east end of Sanibel. She notified permittee Tom Krekel, who, upon further inspection, determined it was not a loggerhead crawl, but possibly a green turtle or, however implausible, a leatherback crawl. After seeing photos of the crawl, Florida Fish and Wildlife confirmed it was probably a green turtle that had made the unusual tracks up the beach.

The nest was appropriately marked and staked off, and the only thing left to do was to wait for hatching to begin. Two

Leatherback crawling from nest

months later the SCCF turtle patrol noted activity at the nest. SCCF's sea turtle coordinator Amanda Bryant and staff herpetologist Chris Lechowicz arrived at the nest the next morning and, noting a predatory ghost crab digging into the nesting site, elected to open the nest earlier than the standard three-day waiting period and confirm the presence of green turtle hatchlings.

They were both amazed to discover that it was not a green, a loggerhead, or a Kemp's ridley nest, but a leatherback turtle nest. They discovered 90 empty eggshells and rescued four live baby leatherback turtles, releasing all of them the following night.

Leatherback turtle hatchling   © Chris Lechowicz / SCCF

What is so amazing about this event is that from the earliest records of the Calusa Indians, through the early settlers, all the way through the research conducted by Charles LeBuff and his Caretta Research team, there had never been a documented leatherback sea turtle nest on either Sanibel or Captiva. In fact, there had never been a documented nest in all of Lee, Collier, or Charlotte counties. The closest and most recent leatherback nesting occurred in Sarasota County in 2001. The leatherbacks does nest in the Panhandle and along the East Coast of Florida. It also nests in South America, Africa, India, China, Australia, and Albania. There are only an estimated 34,000 nesting females left in the world.

One possible explanation for this solitary nest on Sanibel may go back to an experiment in the 1970s when a handful of East Coast hatchlings were released on Sanibel, though there is no way of positively tying the two events together since reliable DNA testing did not exist when the first set of hatchlings was released.

The leatherback turtle is a spectacular creature, the fourth-largest reptile in the world behind three crocodilians: the Nile and Indo-Pacific crocodiles and the rare freshwater gharial of the Indian subcontinent. The leatherback is not entirely cold blooded. In a mechanism similar to that of the great white shark, it has a counter-current heat exchanger that allows the turtle to maintain a body temperature as much as 32 degrees warmer than the surrounding water. This ability greatly extends the leatherback's range as far north as Newfoundland and as far south as the southern island of New Zealand.

It is also the deepest-diving and fastest-swimming reptile on earth. It has been documented to dive to a depth of 3,937 feet and obtain a speed of 22 miles per hour. Its front flippers can grow as large as 8.8 feet across, giving it the ability to fly through the water at more than four times the speed of the fastest Olympic swimmer!

The leatherback turtle feeds primarily on jellyfish. Its digestive system appears to be immune to the toxins found in jellyfish, some of which are fatal to humans. It cruises the open ocean in search of prey. One turtle was tracked covering 13,000 miles in 647 days. It has also been known to feed on tunicates and cephalopods such as squids and octopuses.

Like all sea turtles, the hatchlings suffer high predation, and only one or two leatherbacks in a thousand make it to breeding age. The leatherback turtle does not have a hard shell carapace for protection as do other sea turtles. Instead, its carapace is covered by a thick, leathery skin embedded with minuscule bony plates.

Because of its immense size, only the largest of sharks (great white, tiger, and bull) feed on the leatherback. It may also be attacked by killer whales, but this is not known for sure. Its largest threat comes from the harvesting of its eggs by humans, which in China and the Caribbean are considered to be aphrodisiacs. In Southeast Asia, egg harvesting has resulted in the complete eradication of nesting sites along most of the beaches the leatherback once frequented. It is also an accidental by-catch in commercial fishing vessels, long-lining fishing fleets, and because of its large size, shrimp trawlers. Turtle extruder devices are generally too small to work with leatherbacks.

Another cause of mortality is intestinal blockage following the ingestion of Mylar balloons and plastic bags, which resemble jellyfish in the open ocean. Chemical and bacterial water pollution also takes its toll on these marine giants. Efforts to save the critically endangered leatherback are taking place worldwide, but sadly, the future of these oceanic voyagers remains uncertain.

The Island's Snakes

Black Racer © Blake Sobczak

☐ _____ **Southern Black Racer** (*Coluber constrictor priapus*)
Nicknames: black racer, racer / Status: FL=stable, IUCN=LC / Life span: to 10 years / Length: 2-4.5 ft (0.61-1.4 m) / Weight: 0.75-1 lb (340-453 g) / Nests: on island / Found: IW, MZ, GB, UA.

The most commonly seen snake on Sanibel and Captiva, the southern black racer is also one of the most common snakes in Florida. One reason for the frequent sightings is that the black racer is a diurnal hunter, so it is out at the same time when most people are working in their yards, biking, or doing other activities that might bring them into contact with this snake. The black racer has one of the most extensive ranges of any North American snake, extending up to the Canadian border as far west as Washington and east to Maine.

The black racer is non-venomous but will inflict a nasty bite if grabbed. It will rattle its tail in the grass or dry leaves when cornered or threatened, imitating

Black racer eating a frog © Eric B. Holt

the eastern diamondback rattlesnake. It cannot be domesticated and should not be kept as a pet. It will continue to bite its captors throughout its entire life span.

Despite its scientific middle name (constrictor), the black racer is not a true constrictor. It tends to chase down, bite, then suffocate or crush its victims on the ground rather than coiling around them in true constrictor fashion. Its diet includes brown and green anoles, insects, moles, birds, frogs, eggs, smaller snakes, and rodents. It in turn is preyed on by red-shouldered hawks, owls, and larger snakes.

The black racer is extremely quick and at first appears capable of outrunning a human. This is an illusion created by the snake's small size relative to its quick speed. Regardless of its actual ground speed, its quickness and agility make it very difficult to catch. When spotted crossing a trail or road, it vanishes into the understory with amazing swiftness.

❒ _____ **Yellow Rat Snake** (*Elaphe obsoleta quadrivittata*)
Nicknames: rat snake / Status: FL=stable, IUCN=LC / Life span: to 20 years / Length: 4.5-7 ft (1.4-2.1 m) / Weight: 2-4 lb (0.9-1.80 kg) Nests: on island / Found: IW, MZ, GB, UA.

After the black racer, the yellow rat snake is the second most commonly seen snake on Sanibel and Captiva. It is an impressive predator. Growing to lengths of seven feet, with a circumference about the same size as a man's wrist, this snake can be quite startling when you happen upon one. It is non-venomous, however, and aside from a nasty bite, will not cause any real harm to a person. Nonetheless, it should never be picked up or handled.

The rat snake is a true constrictor. It seizes its prey, then coils its muscular body around the animal, slowly constricting the life out of it through suffocation. The yellow rat snake is one of the leading predators of invasive black and brown rats and is therefore very beneficial to wildlife. It also preys upon birds, frogs, lizards, eggs, insects, and small mammals. Extremely arboreal, the yellow rat snake can

Yellow Rat Snake © Maggie May Rogers / SCCF

often be spotted climbing into trees and up onto porches, rooftops, and rafters. It has nowhere near the speed of the black racer on the ground.

The yellow rat snake is preyed upon by hawks, ospreys, eagles, and owls. It is also eaten by raccoons, bobcats, and otters. Unlike the black racer, the yellow rat snake takes readily to humans, and after it becomes socialized, seldom bites. Various sub-species and color variations extend the range of the yellow rat snake across most of the eastern U.S., as far west as western Texas.

Yellow Rat Snake eating a Frog

© Charles Sobczak

Corn Snake
© Maggie May Rogers/ SCCF

☐ _____ **Corn Snake** (*Elaphe guttata guttata*) Nicknames: red rat snake / Status: FL=stable, IUCN=LC / Life span: to 23 years / Length: 3.9-5.9 ft (1.2-1.8 m) / Weight: 1.5-3 lb (0.68-1.3 kg) / Nests: on island / Found: IW, MZ, GB, UA.

© Mark Kenderdine

The corn snake is an extremely beautiful snake. Its name is derived from the maize-like pattern on its belly and its preference for corn fields. The name appeared as far back as 1676 when these colorful snakes were first discovered in America. Its docile nature, attractive skin pattern, and reluctance to bite make it a popular pet.

The range of the corn snake is much smaller than that of the black racer or yellow rat snake and does not extend much above the Mason-Dixon Line. It does survive at elevations up to 6,000 feet. In colder climates it hibernates during the winter.

When threatened, the corn snake coils up in much the same fashion as a rattlesnake. Its bite is swift and painful, and because of its heavily patterned coloration, it may easily be confused with the deadly rattlesnake. In yet another form of rattlesnake mimicry, the corn snake often rattles its tail, even though it lacks the rattle.

In the wild this small constrictor dines predominantly on rodents—mostly rats and mice—but will also take lizards, anoles, and frogs. The corn snake is preyed upon by all the major raptors, and juvenile snakes are taken by black racers. The best time for viewing one of these gorgeous snakes is early morning or near sunset. It tends to feed nocturnally and is seldom spotted midday.

Red Rat Snake

© Blake Sobczak

Ring-necked Snake (*Diadophis punctatus punctatus*)
Nicknames: none / Status: FL=stable, IUCN=LC / Life span: to 6 years / Length: 8-18.5 in. (20-47 cm) / Weight: 0.6-2 oz (17-56 g) / Nests: on island / Found: IW, MZ, UA.

Ring-necked snake sliding through a leaf © Blake Sobczak

One of the smallest snake found on the islands, the diminutive ring-necked snake is usually less than a foot in length. It is easily recognized by the distinctive red ring located just behind the head. Its range extends through all of Florida and across much of North America except in the higher elevations of the Rocky Mountains and the central plateau.

Although it has recently been discovered that the saliva of this species may have some toxicity, it is not considered poisonous and has no ability to inject its saliva into a human. This little snake can be easily picked up and seldom if ever attempts to bite. Its mouth is so small that even biting a baby finger is unlikely. When picked up, the ring-necked snake releases a strong, unpleasant musk smell. It does not make a good pet because as soon as it is placed into captivity, it refuses to eat and dies within a few weeks.

The ring-necked snake feeds upon insects, grubs, frogs, and newborn rodents. In the wild this tiny snake has an average life span of little more than a year. Because of its small size and defenseless nature, it is taken by a wide variety of predators, from hawks to rats, and is one of the favored preys of the coral snake and other larger snakes.

Ring-necked Snake   © Blake Sobczak

☐ _____ **Eastern Coachwhip Snake** (*Masticophis flagellum flagellum*) Nicknames: coachwhip / Status: FL=stable, IUCN=LC / Life span: to 17 years / Length: 6-8.5 ft (1.8-2.6 m) / Weight: 2-3 lb (.90-1.4 kg) / Nests: on island / Found: GB, IW.

Coachwhip coiled among leaves   © Mark Kenderine

With the absence of a viable population of indigo snakes on either Sanibel or Captiva, the coachwhip is now the longest snake found on the islands. The yellow rat snake is quite a bit heavier but shorter than the coachwhip.

Aptly named because its long, slender body resembles a bullwhip, the coachwhip is capable of bursts of speed up to 12 miles per hour. It is perhaps even more difficult to capture than the black racer. Its coloration is similar to that of a black racer across the first third of its head and body, but fades into a dark brown near the tail. Across its range, which is most of the southeastern U.S., the coachwhip exhibits a variety of color phases, from dark brown to pink.

The coachwhip is a daytime predator, focusing on lizards, small birds, and rodents. It tends to raise its head in cobra-like fashion when hunting, scanning the horizon in search of prey. Although it is non-venomous, under no circumstances should you attempt to catch a coachwhip. It is renowned for its aggressive nature and will inflict repeated and savage bites. In captivity it will strike incessantly at anyone approaching its glass terrarium to the point of harming itself. Because of that behavior, the coachwhip cannot be kept as a pet.

Once it reaches adult size, the coachwhip is seldom taken by birds of prey. Large snakes can be killed by rattlesnakes, and young snakes succumb to any number of predators, including raccoons, raptors, and bobcats. It prefers dry, upland environments and is best spotted along the high gulf ridges along West Gulf Drive. Its most common habitat is the vegetated dune area, where it hunts for shorebirds, passerines, anoles, and rodents.

☐ _____ **Peninsula Ribbon Snake** (*Thamnophis sauritus sackeni*) Nicknames: garter snake / Status: FL=stable, ICUN=NE / Life span: to 10 years / Length: 2.6-3.4 ft (0.79-1 m) / Weight: 1-1.5 lb (453-680 g) / Nests: on island / Found: IW, GB, UA.

Related to the common garter snake, the peninsula ribbon snake ranges throughout the eastern United States from the Mississippi to New England. The primary difference between the two snakes is that the garter snake is considerably stockier, and its striping is more pronounced.

The ribbon snake is most commonly seen along the Sanibel River and the bike path on San-Cap Road. It is an extremely shy snake that prefers dense underbrush and wetlands, and is seldom seen during the daytime. When captured it does not bite as readily as other snakes but does release an unpleasant musk odor. The ribbon snake does not do well in captivity and is seldom kept as a pet.

It feeds on crickets, small fish, and frogs. Alligators, snapping turtles, gar, birds of prey, and otters all prey upon the peninsula ribbon snake.

© Hung V. Do

☐ _____ **Florida Watersnake** (*Nerodia fasciata pictiventris*)
Nicknames: water snake, Florida banded water snake / Status: FL=stable, IUCN=NE/ Life span: to 9 years / Length: 4-5.2 ft (1.2-1.6 m) / Weight: 2-4.5 lb (.90-2 kg) / Nests: on island / Found: IW, UA.

Identify this snake by the lines on its head
© Blake Sobczak

Because of its aquatic nature, size, and coloration, the Florida watersnake is commonly confused with the venomous cottonmouth. Far too many of these harmless watersnakes are killed as a result of this mistaken identity. Cottonmouths and water moccasins are not found on the islands, so any snake resembling these poisonous snakes is probably a non-venomous watersnake or a mangrove snake and should not be harmed. When cornered the Florida watersnake does behave like a cottonmouth, coiling itself back as if to strike. Because it can grow quite large, its bite can be vicious. Sadly, many people kill all snakes out of fear. This is a tragedy because snakes play a vital role in keeping rodent populations down; no wild creature should be killed simply because we fear it.

The Florida watersnake ranges across most of the Southeast. It is a fairly heavy-bodied snake, with faint brown banding. The islands' watersnake has two color phases: blackish-green and reddish-orange. It feeds on a variety of aquatic prey including tadpoles, frogs, fish, juvenile turtles, and toads. Although it will survive in captivity, it can never really be handled as it tends to bite throughout its lifetime. In the wild it is preyed upon by crocodiles, alligators, gar, snapping turtles, and otters.

☐ _____ **Florida Brown Snake** (*Storeria victa*) Nicknames: brown snake / Status: FL=stable, IUCN=NE / Life span: to 7 years / Length: 12-19 in. (30-46 cm) / Weight: unknown / Nests: on island / Found: IW, UA.

The second-smallest snake on the islands, the Florida brown snake is only slightly larger than the ring-necked snake. It has a distinctive pattern, and some adult brown snakes have a light tan marking that rings the back portion of the head. It prefers a moist or aquatic habitat and can be found around ponds, drainage ditches, or homes where there is a source of water such as air conditioning units and garden hoses. It is not a common sighting on Sanibel or Captiva.

When captured this tiny snake will flatten its body and strike repeatedly, but its head and teeth are too small to inflict a serious bite. In time it does well in captivity and is therefore commonly kept as a pet.

The brown snake feeds on earthworms, slugs, and small invertebrates such as crickets and roaches. It is fed upon by other snakes, birds of prey, and small mammals such as rats.

Florida Brown snakes are tiny but a valuable part of the food chain.

© Eric B. Holt

☐ ___ Mangrove Water Snake (*Nerodia clarki compressicauada*)

Nicknames: mangrove snake, salt marsh snake / Status: FL=stable, IUCN=LC / Life span: to 20 years / Length: 30-37 in. (76-93 cm) / Weight: 1.2-2.2 lb (0.54-1 kg) / Nests: on island / Found: MZ, IW.

Red phase of Mangrove Water Snake   © Mark Kenderdine

Because of its size and coloration, the elusive mangrove water snake is virtually impossible to spot during the day. As evening approaches, especially in the fall, this small snake will come out of the mangroves in numbers along Wildlife Drive where it can be found absorbing the warmth of the road. Like all reptiles and amphibians, the mangrove snake is cold blooded and has to regulate body temperature by basking

Black Phase of a Mangrove Snake
©ThroughTheLensGallery.com

in the sun or absorbing the warmth of rocks or roadways when it is cold, and hiding in the shadowy understory or entering the water when it is too warm.

The mangrove snake is closely related to the Florida watersnake. It has a variety of color variations throughout its range: some varieties have a reddish hue, whereas others can be yellow and/or brown.

This snake is unusual in that it tolerates brackish water and prefers the habitat of red and black mangroves. It feeds on mangrove crabs, snails and slugs, small fish, and marine insects and worms.

In the wild it is preyed upon by raccoons, otters, ospreys, and larger fish such as snook and tarpon. The mangrove snake is not commonly kept as a pet.

☐ _____ **Eastern Indigo Snake** (*Drymarchon corais couperi*)
Nicknames: indigo snake, gopher snake / Status: FL=threatened, IUCN=LC-population declining / Length: 6-8.6 ft (1.8-2.6 m) / Weight: 8-10 lb (3.6-4.5 kg) / Nests: on island (possibly extirpated) / Found: IW, MZ, UA.

indigo Snake   Courtesy FL Fish & Wildlife Service

The eastern indigo snake is the largest non-venomous snake in North America. A long, thick-bodied snake, it can grow to nearly nine feet and weigh more than 10 pounds. Its coloration resembles that of a black racer, except that it has a rusty to blood-red hue under its chin as opposed to the brown hues of the black racer. It is also similar to the black racer in that the indigo snake is not a true constrictor. It catches its prey with powerful jaws and uses its body weight to pin down its prey, which, like all snakes, it swallows whole.

This beautiful species has been in steady decline in Florida for the past 30 years. A number of factors all seem to be coming into play. The indigo snake relies heavily on the burrows made by gopher tortoises, which because of habitat loss and URTD (upper respiratory tract disease) have suffered dramatic losses across the state. Another factor is the high demand for this species as a pet and hence the pressure put on the wild population by snake collectors. In the past decade the state of Florida placed a ban on taking wild indigos without a special permit.

On Sanibel the indigo snake was once quite common, but that is no longer the case. Despite numerous attempts to trap an indigo over the past several years, the staff at SCCF has yet to locate a single specimen. The last documented indigo on Sanibel was seen in 1999. This snake is, in all probability, extirpated from the islands. Anyone seeing a snake that could be an eastern indigo should take a photograph and report the location of the sighting to SCCF at 239-472-2329.

The indigo snake eats a variety of animals including reptiles and other snakes (especially yellow rat snakes), birds, and small mammals as large as marsh rabbits. Because of its size, the adult indigo snake is taken only by alligators, bobcats, and crocodiles. Birds of prey are unable to lift a 10-pound snake, and even the aggressive great-horned owl shies away from tackling such a formidable predator.

The indigo makes a fantastic pet. It tames readily and actually appears to enjoy being around people. Fortunately, it is fairly easy to breed in captivity, and it is these captive snakes that are meeting the demand in the pet trade.

☐ _____ Brahminy Blind Snake (*Rhamphotyphlops braminus*)

Nicknames: flowerpot snake, worm snake / Status: FL=invasive, introduced and thriving, IUCN=LC / Life span: to 2 years / Length: 2.5-6.5 in. (6.35-16.5 cm) / Weight: 1-4 oz (28-113 g) / Nests: on island / Found: UA, IW.

Originally introduced into the Miami area from Asia, this very small, completely blind snake is easily mistaken for an earthworm. One of the primary reasons for its success at establishing itself on every continent except Antarctica is that it is parthenogenetic. This term comes from combining the two Greek words, parthenos (virgin) and genesis (creation), meaning asexual reproduction. A very rare characteristic in vertebrates, shared by Komodo dragons, Nile monitor lizards, some sharks, and a handful of other reptiles and amphibians, it allows a single individual to establish a beachhead in any given environment by essentially

cloning itself, though the process is far more complex than that.

The Brahminy blind snake is totally blind and lives most of its life underground. It feeds on larvae, eggs, and the pupae of ants and termites. It is eaten by moles, armadillos, and opossum. Because of its subterranean habitat, it is very unlikely that you will find a Brahminy blind snake on Sanibel or Captiva, but it has become fairly well established on the island and is thriving somewhere beneath us.

© Courtesy Wikipedia Commons

☐_____ **Eastern Coral Snake** (*Micrurus fulvius fulvius*)

WARNING: VENOMOUS! Nicknames: American cobra, coral adder, thunder-and-lightning snake, candy-stick snake / Status: FL=stable, IUCN=NE / Life span: to 6 years / Length: 30-48 in. (0.76-1.2 m) / Weight: 8-15 oz (226-425 g) / Nests: on island / Found: IW, UA, GB.

© Eric B. Holt

With the eradication of the eastern diamondback from both islands, the eastern coral snake is the only venomous snake now found on Sanibel and Captiva. Its reclusive nature makes it difficult to spot, and, fortunately, it will generally flee long before it makes any attempt to bite a human being.

Because the islands do not have the coral snake mimic, the kingsnake, this short poem is not as applicable here as it is on the mainland, where people often mistake the two species: "Red to yellow, kill a fellow. Red to black, venom lack."

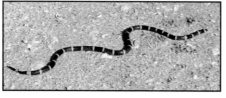

"No Friend to Jack"   © Eric B. Holt

On the islands, however, any candy-colored striped snake is a venomous coral snake and should never be picked up or handled. It produces a strong neurotoxin that is potentially fatal. Even a smaller coral snake is capable of biting a person between the fingers or toes; a larger one has very respectable fangs and can manage a deadly bite in any number of locations. With today's anti-venoms and rapid emergency response, it is unlikely that a person would die from a coral snake bite, but if you should come across one of these beautiful snakes, simply leave it alone and remove yourself from the area. They often come in pairs, and it's the coral snake you don't see that is more than likely going to become the problem.

The coral snake eats ring-necked snakes, anoles, small insects, and mice. Its small size makes it incapable of taking large prey. It is seldom fed upon by other snakes and animals with the exception of opossum, which is immune to most snake venom and has little trouble subduing a small coral snake.

The brightly patterned coloration of the coral snake is a common characteristic of toxic species throughout the world. The black, red, and yellow of a coral snake, just like the brilliant colors of Central America's poisonous frogs, ward off potential predators by boldly announcing their presence and their danger. It is as if to say, eat me if you dare!

© Courtesy Wikipedia Commons

Lizards

Green Anole   © Maggie May Rogers / SCCF

☐ _____ **Green Anole** (*Anolis carolinensis*) Nicknames: Carolina anole, American chameleon / Status: FL=in decline, IUCN=LC / Life span: to 4 years / Length: 6-8 in. (15-20 cm) / Weight: 0.05-1.5 oz (1.5-4 g) / Nests: on island / Found: IW, MZ, UA, GB.

Before the arrival of the brown anole from the Caribbean, the green anole was the only one found on Sanibel and Captiva. The more aggressive and invasive brown, or Cuban, anole has all but eliminated this emerald green lizard from the islands. Finding one today is a difficult undertaking. Its range extends throughout the Southeast from Mississippi to North Carolina.

It is easiest to spot when in its green coloration. Although not a true chameleon, the green anole is capable of swiftly changing color to brown, tan, or gray depending on the background material where the lizard is found. A brown-phase green anole is almost impossible to distinguish from the much more common brown anole. Look for the green anole's long, pointed snout, which differs from the blunt snout of the brown anole.

Because of its coloring, the green anole prefers foraging in the green foliage of bushes and trees, unlike the ground-dwelling brown anole. The green anole eats moths, ant larvae, flies, and crickets to mention a few of the many insects it preys upon. It in turn is part of the diet of herons, egrets, snakes, rats, and a number of different bird species, including grackles, merlins, and kestrels. The green anole makes an excellent pet and can live in captivity for more than seven years if cared for properly.

© Maggie May Rogers / SCCF

Brown Anole (*Anolis sagrei*) Nicknames: Cuban anole, Key West anole / Status: FL-Invasive, still expanding its range, IUCN=LC / Life span: to 5 years / Length: Length: 6-8 in. (15-20 cm) / Weight: 0.05-1.5 oz (1.5-4 g) / Nests: on island / Found: IW, MZ, UA, GB, CW.

Colorful dewlap expanded

©ThroughTheLensGallery.com

Although no one is certain when the brown anole arrived on Sanibel and Captiva, the consensus is that it was shortly after the completion of the original causeway. It probably hitchhiked over in the root balls and canopies of the many ornamental palms imported from the Miami area when the island was experiencing the rapid growth of the early 1970s. Once here, it quickly became the most prolific lizard on the islands. An invasive species, its sheer numbers now prohibit any viable attempts to contain its spread or effectively remove the species. Its range continues to expand across the Southeastern U.S.

The brown anole has a number of subtle color and pattern variations, but its dewlap, the throat fan you can often see the male extending when announcing its territory to other males, is always yellow or reddish-orange. It is one of the easiest reptiles to find on Sanibel and Captiva, occurring around condominiums, homes, pools, screen enclosures, and the bike path—virtually every island habitat harbors at least a few, if not scores of brown anoles.

It feeds mostly in the daytime and prefers foraging on the ground where it eats beetles, grasshoppers, spiders, and roaches. The brown anole is a favorite food for white and cattle egrets, as well as great blue herons. An injured lizard often succumbs to overwhelming attacks of fire ants, and it is also favored by many of the islands' indigenous snakes.

One of the many patterned variations of the Brown Anole

© ThroughTheLensGallery.com

☐_____ **Ground Skink** (*Scincella lateralis*) Nicknames: little brown skink / Status: FL=stable, IUCN=LC/ Life span: to 3 years / Length: 3.5-5 in. (9-13 cm) / Weight: n/a / Nests: on island / Found: IW, UA.

The smallest lizard found on Sanibel and Captiva and very uncommon here, the ground skink is most likely to be found beneath moist leaves, under logs, or hiding in woodpiles and debris. It feeds during the daytime, but its size and feeding habits make it a rare sighting. The ground skink is common throughout the Southeast and north to the Ohio River valley.

This somewhat comical lizard has been known to take a bite out of its own tail, mistaking it for a small centipede or insect. Like all skinks, its tail is quick to break off, allowing the animal to escape and leaving the predator with more of a snack than the meal it was originally in pursuit of. The ground skink is a favorite prey for smaller snakes such as the coral and ring-necked.

The home range of this diminutive skink may be as small as 20 square meters, wherein it consumes insects, spiders, and isopods such as woodlice and pill bugs.

☐_____ **Southeastern Five-lined Skink** (*Eumeces fasciatus*) Nicknames: blue-tailed skink, red-headed skink / Status: FL=stable, IUCN=LC / Life span: to 6 years / Length: 4.9-8.5 in. (12.5-21.5 cm) / Weight: n/a / Nests: on islands / Found: IW, GB, UA.

This relatively common skink is easily identified by its bright blue tail. It is the most colorful lizard native to Sanibel and Captiva and a true delight to observe when spotted. It is a fairly large lizard, growing close to nine inches long, and closely resembles the broad-headed skink. It likes to sun itself during the heat of the day and can sometimes be observed on pool decks and around other concrete or asphalt surfaces.

© Mark Kenderine

Adult male five-lined skink

It is incredibly agile and quick and nearly impossible to catch without a trap. It is commonly kept as a pet and can live up to 10 years in captivity. Although it will bite when captured, its mouth is too small to inflict serious damage.

The southeastern five-lined skink eats mostly insects but will also take young green and brown anoles. It is eaten by snakes, birds of prey, and small mammals. Like all skinks, the tail is easily broken off, allowing the lizard to escape when grabbed by the tail. Over time, the five-lined skink will regrow its lost tail.

Juvenile female five-lined skink

Six-lined Racerunner (*Aspidoscelis sexlineata*)

Nicknames: racerunner / Status: FL=stable, IUCN=NE / Life span: to 6 years / Length: 8-9.5 in. (20-24 cm) / Weight: n/a / Nests: on islands / Found: GB, IW, UA.

© Maggie May Rogers / SCCF

George Campbell, author of The Nature of Things on Sanibel, referred to this lizard as the Sanibel streaker. It is the fastest lizard on the island, capable of short bursts of speed approaching 20 miles per hour. That, coupled with its breakaway tail, makes this reptile virtually impossible to catch.

The tail of the six-lined racerunner makes up 70 percent of its total body length. Some studies have shown that this tail helps the lizard obtain its remarkable speed. A member of the teiid family of lizards, common only in the New World, the racerunner has approximately 200 members in its family, including the largest teiid, the three-foot tegu of South America.

Preferring drier upland habitats, the six-lined racerunner is most commonly seen in the upper reaches of the beaches and the beach dunes. In these more upland habitats the racerunner feeds on beetles, mosquitoes, flies, cockroaches, grasshoppers, and crickets. Because of its speed, the racerunner is seldom caught by anything other than birds of prey, which have no trouble swooping down on an unsuspecting lizard.

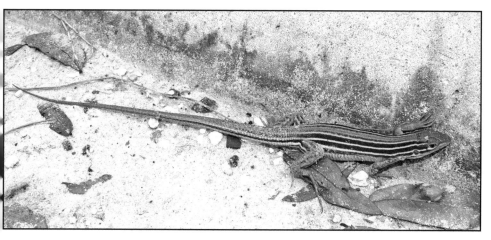

© Eric B. Holt

☐ _____ **Indo-Pacific Gecko** (*Hemidactylus garnotii*) Nicknames: fox gecko / Status: FL=invasive, increasing in population, IUCN=LC / Life span: to 13 years / Length: 5 in. (13 cm) / Weight: n/a / Nests: on island / Found: IW, UA.

An invasive species, probably arriving on Sanibel after the completion of the causeway in 1963, the Indo-Pacific gecko is the most commonly seen of all three introduced gecko species here. Originally from India, this gecko has spread across several continents with the help of Homo sapiens. It is also one of a very small group of animals that are parthenogenetic, or capable of asexual reproduction. Rarely exceeding five inches in length, this small lizard can be easily identified by its motion and its ability to cling to walls and ceilings, remaining upside down for hours. Sticky toepads allow the gecko to climb on surfaces as smooth as glass without difficulty.

The gecko moves very differently from the anole and racerunner. Its body tends to bend and twist more, and it is nowhere near as fast. It is mostly nocturnal, coming out near house or condominium lights during the evening to feed on the insects these lights attract. The Indo-Pacific gecko dines on moths, flies, and termites among a host of other insects. It is fed upon by larger lizards, as well as rats and snakes. Although considered invasive, this small gecko's impact on native species appears to be minimal.

Gecko at my window   © Blake Sobczak   **Gecko eating spider**

❒ _____ **Tropical House Gecko** (_Hemidactylus mabouia_)
Nicknames: Afro-American house gecko, cosmopolitan house gecko / Status: FL=invasive, spreading, IUCN=LC / Life span: to 10 years / Length: 5 in. (13 cm) / Weight: n/a / Nests: on islands / Found: IW, UA.

© Courtesy Wikipedia Commons

Similar in appearance to the Indo-Pacific gecko, the tropical house gecko is almost impossible to distinguish without a herpetologist's help. Originally from sub-Saharan Africa, this small gecko can now be found from Madagascar to Mexico. In its native habitat it is highly prized as a natural insect control, feeding on spiders, scorpions, cockroaches, anoles, and termites.

Strictly nocturnal, this gecko is most easily spotted after dark near an outside light. Like the Indo-Pacific gecko, special microscopic hairs on its footpads allow it to cling to almost any surface. Nowhere near as territorial as the anole, the tropical house gecko will sometimes work side by side with several other geckos, taking turns consuming the bugs that are attracted by an outdoor light.

❒ _____ **Tokay Gecko** (_Gekko gecko_)
Nicknames: bulldog gecko / Status: FL=invasive, increasing, IUCN=LC / Life span: to 10 years / Length: 11-15 in. (30-40 cm) / Weight: n/a / Nests: on islands / Found: UA, IW.

Released by pet owners or introduced via landscaping, the tokay gecko is the second-largest of the species, growing to more than a foot long. A nocturnal feeder, the tokay is renowned for its loud vocalizations, making a call that sounds like its name, tokeh, tokeh.

The nickname bulldog comes from its tenacious bite. The tokay has been known to keep biting down on a person for several days! The best way to get it to release its bite is to put the affected body part and the lizard underwater, where it will eventually give up or drown.

Tokay Gecko close up   Courtesy USGS

Originally from India, Bangladesh, and New Guinea, the tokay has now spread into Texas, Hawaii, and the Caribbean islands. It is not commonly found on Sanibel, though it can sometimes be spotted near the American Legion on Sanibel-Captiva Road and in many areas on the east end of Sanibel. It is known to be breeding on the island, as egg

Female Tokay Gecko

clusters have been verified. A very fast and strong gecko, the tokay feeds on other lizards, roaches, and small vertebrates such as mice and shrews.

☐ _____ **Green Iguana** (*Iguana iguana*) Nicknames: common iguana, bamboo chicken, chicken of the tree / Status: FL=invasive, increasing, IUCN=VU / Life span: to 20 years / Length: 3.5–6.5 ft (1-2 m) / Weight: 10-20 lb (4.5-9.1 kg) / Nests: on island / Found: IW, UA, GB, MZ.

© Rusty Farst

The current green iguana population on Sanibel and Captiva is a direct result of the release of this large Central and South American reptile by pet owners who no longer want the animal. After time, due in part to its long life span, the released reptiles find each other and propagate. Because of its size and ability to adapt to the climate and vegetation of the islands, a species like the green iguana can quickly get out of control.

On Gasparilla Island, approximately 25 miles north of Sanibel, the equally invasive and far more damaging spiny-tailed iguana has become a major concern to both environmentalists and residents. Unlike the green iguana of Sanibel and Captiva, which is an herbivore, the spiny-tailed iguana is an omnivore that eats not only

©ThroughTheLensGallery.com

native vegetation but also local birds, marsh rabbits, green anoles, young gopher tortoises, and snakes. Since 2006, Lee County has spent an average of $100,000 a year in an attempt to eradicate this invasive species from Gasparilla. To date, nearly 10,000 spiny-tailed iguanas have been caught and euthanized, mostly from the northern end of the island. The sheer numbers of these lizards, coupled with their high fecundity, make their removal a daunting and expensive task.

Echoing this program, the city of Sanibel has undertaken a green iguana eradication program on the islands. To date it has captured and euthanized more than 750 iguanas at a cost in excess of $50,000. Although nowhere near as devastating to wildlife as the spiny-tailed iguana, this huge lizard destroys ornamental vegetation, eating shrubs, orchids, fruits, mangoes, berries, and tomatoes. It also digs nesting burrows that can undermine sidewalks, seawalls, and foundations. It often leaves droppings in private swimming pools and is known to harbor salmonella bacteria.

The green iguana's high reproductive rate makes its eradication difficult. A single clutch can contain as many as 65 eggs. With the destruction of so many of the island's alligators after the death of an island resident in 2004, the green iguana has no natural predators other than bobcats to keep its population in check.

Although South Florida represents the northernmost part of its range, the iguana appears to be undergoing a process of natural selection. The more cold-tolerant members of the species are surviving, while the others die off during the winter. Eventually, the cold-resistant iguanas will continue to move northward, possibly as far as central Florida. Thus far, it has not been able to survive a hard freeze.

In Central and South America many people eat the green iguana. The level of harvest in some areas has become so severe that the ICUN is considering listing it as an endangered species. It is said to taste like chicken, especially when fried; hence, the nickname chicken of the tree.

Look for this exotic lizard in and around Beachview Country Club where the population is flourishing. If you see one, or a nesting female, report the sighting to the Sanibel Natural Resources Division at 239-472-3700, or keep the animal in sight and call the Sanibel Police Department at its non-emergency number, 239-472-3111. Do not attempt to kill or capture an iguana as it has sharp teeth and can deliver a nasty bite.

☐ _____ **Nile Monitor Lizard** (*Varanus niloticus*) Nicknames: leguaan (African) / Status: FL=invasive, expanding its range, IUCN=LC / Life span: to 15 years / Length: 4.5-7.5 ft (1.5-2.3 m) / Weight: 20-40 lb (9-18 kg) / Nests: in northern Cape Coral / Found: IW, MZ.

To date, only a handful of Nile monitor lizards have been authenticated on Sanibel. One was discovered floating dead in a pond on July 14, 2008. Considered by many herpetologists to be more potentially damaging than any other reptilian invasive, the spread of this species could have far-reaching ramifications throughout South Florida.

This powerful lizard is a carnivore. It is a distant relative of the Komodo dragon of Indonesia, the largest lizard in the world, known to obtain lengths of 10 feet and weigh more than 300 pounds. The Komodo has been known to kill children, goats, and dogs.

With a keen sense of smell, excellent speed, and sharp eyesight, the monitor lizard, once established on a barrier island, could quickly decimate a wide range of native animals. In Africa, where it originates, it is one

Courtesy USGS

NIle monitor lizard

of the leading predators of crocodile nests. On Sanibel it could turn its attention to alligator and sea turtle eggs. Equipped with sharp claws, it would have no trouble digging up loggerhead nesting sites and devouring all the eggs in a single night. A strong climber, this predator could do significant damage to bird rookeries and small mammal populations.

The Nile monitor has established quite a beachhead in northern Cape Coral where it can sometimes be spotted foraging for food during the day. These massive lizards were probably released as pets, though importing and keeping the Nile monitor in Florida is now allowed by special permit only. Every animal must also be identified with a microchip, ensuring that the owner will remain responsible for each lizard's continued captivity. A young Nile monitor lizard can be easily handled as a pet, but by the time it reaches two or three years of age, it is a ferocious lizard capable of killing a housecat with a single bite and swallowing it whole. Not surprisingly, the pet owner may want to remove this danger from the household.

The first reported sighting of a Nile monitor in this area was in 1990, and the population is now estimated at more than 1,000. It may lay up to 60 eggs in a clutch and is capable of parthenogenesis, which means that a single individual can reproduce without mating. In Africa this lizard is kept in check by other lizards and birds of prey that feed on the eggs and young. Larger lizards are sometimes killed and eaten by leopards and other wild cats. In Florida, alligators, panthers, and bobcats are its only natural predators.

If you see or suspect you see one of these lizards, which resemble giant brown anoles only much darker and without the dewlap, please call the Sanibel Police Department immediately at 239-472-3111 and report the sighting.

❐ _____ **Northern Curly-tailed Lizard** (*Leiocephalus carinatus*) Nicknames: lion lizard / Status: FL=invasive, slowly expanding its range, IUCN=NE / Life span: to 8 years / Length: 8-10.5 in. (20-27 cm) / Weight: n/a / Nests: on Captiva (unconfirmed) / Found: UA.

A recent immigrant to Captiva, the curly-tailed lizard is originally from the Caribbean, Cuba, Haiti, and Trinidad. Worldwide there are 28 different species of this small, relatively harmless lizard; most are found in the New World.

© Eric B. Holt

Because it loves to bask in the midday sun and is primarily diurnal, the curly-tailed lizard is easy to spot. When approached it quickly curls its tail and vanishes into the brush.

Thus far, it has not made it to Sanibel. Its range is limited to 'Tween Waters Inn on Captiva. Given an ample food supply of spiders, crickets, centipedes, and ants, there is every reason to believe this exotic, like the iguana and the brown anole, will continue to multiply and flourish on Captiva and eventually find its way to Sanibel as well. It has recently been verified that the curly-tailed lizard is reproducing on Captiva.

How this lizard arrived on Captiva is a matter of speculation. It was originally brought into South Florida and released into the sugarcane fields to fight pests. There is a fairly well-established population in the greater Miami area and in the Keys. It could have easily stowed away in root balls or large palms during the replanting of South Seas Resort after the devastation of Hurricane Charley or could have been released as an unwanted pet by an island resident. It is considered a good choice for a home terrarium and is fairly easy to keep as a pet.

The following lizards have only been seen on the islands a few times and do not appear to have established breeding populations.

☐ _____ **Red-headed Agama** (*Agama agama africana*)
Nicknames: rainbow agama / Status: FL=invasive, IUCN=NE / Life span: to 25 years / Length: 12-14 in. (30-35 cm) / Weight: n/a / Nests: does not appear to be nesting on islands / Found: rare, IW, UA.

This attractive lizard is originally from sub-Saharan Africa. Called the rainbow agama for good reason, it has a red head, orangish body, and bright blue hind legs and tail. This omnivore feeds mostly on insects such as beetles, cockroaches, moths, and termites, as well as spiders. Because there has been only a handful of sightings and this particular species does not have a major population base elsewhere in the state of Florida, we can assume that the few seen have probably been released household pets and hopefully will not become yet another troubling invasive on either island.

Red-headed Agama   © Chris Huh

☐ _____ **Knight Anole** (*Anolis equestris*) Nicknames: Cuban anole, Cuban night anole / Status: FL=invasive, expanding its range throughout the state, IUCN=LC / Life span: to 16 years / Length: 13-20 in. (33-51 cm) / Weight: n/a / Nests: does not appear to be nesting on the islands / Found: rare, IW, UA.

A full-size knight anole could easily be mistaken for an immature green iguana. One of the largest anoles in the world, this lizard could become a problem if it were to establish a viable population on either island. Its size, along with its omnivore diet, allows it to feed on other anoles, small birds, and mice. It is a very aggressive lizard and will fend off almost any intruder. Its bite can be very painful, and because it is extremely territorial, it bites more often than not. Thus far, only a few have been spotted on the islands, and hopefully it will not become a permanent invasive.

Courtesy Wikipedia Commons - Boston

Frogs and Toads

☐ _____ **Oak Toad** (*Bufo quercicus*) Nicknames: Anaxyrus quercicus (note: it is highly unusual for a species to have two different scientific names), hoppy toads / Status: FL=stable, IUCN=LC / Life span: to 3 years / Length: 0.75-1.25 in. (2-3 cm) / Weight: n/a / Found: IW, UA, MZ.

The oak toad is the smallest toad found in North America. It is capable of incredible population explosions; one study found an amazing 70 oak toads per acre near Orlando. There have been no recent sightings on Sanibel and Captiva, so this species may now be extirpated from the islands.

The oak toad is tiny and looks more like a small, hopping insect than a toad. Its size and inconspicuous coloration make it very difficult to spot. If you do happen upon one, you must be very careful not to harm it, especially if you pick it up for a closer look.

Oak Toad   Courtesy USGS

The oak toad prefers pine forests, shrub lands, and marshes, and proximity to a nearby water supply is important. In Florida this species is suffering from habitat loss due to urban sprawl. Its range extends throughout the Southeast. The oak toad is a carnivore and dines mainly on smaller insects. Most cockroaches are larger than this toad. It is heavily preyed upon by snakes, lizards, birds, and fire ants.

☐ _____ **Southern Toad** (*Bufo terrestris*) Nicknames: none / Status: FL=stable, IUCN=LC / Life span: to 5 years / Length: 3-4.5 in. (7.5-11.4 cm) / Weight: n/a / Found: IW, UA, MZ.

A fairly common toad found on both islands, the southern toad can sometimes be seen hopping around convenience stores late at night looking for a meal under the insect-attracting lights. On rainy nights you will see it out on roadways foraging or mating, and, especially in the spring and early summer, you can sometimes hear its continuous high-pitched trill throughout the night.

It is generally grayish to dark brown in color and looks like a typical toad. Its diet consists of beetles, larvae, cockroaches, and moths.

Southern Toad   © Blake Sobczak

It is preyed upon by snakes, raccoons, small mammals such as rats, and owls. The southern toad is a popular pet; it adapts well to handling and has no toxic secretions or other threats to children and pets. A close relative, the giant marine toad from Texas, can kill a dog or cat that is foolish enough to bite it. Luckily, this huge, poisonous toad has not made it to the islands.

☐____ **Cane Toad** (*Rhinella marina, formerly Bufo marinus*)
INVASIVE! Nicknames: marine toad, giant toad, sea toad / Status: FL = invasive, population increasing, IUCN = LC / Weight: 1-5 lb (.45-2.2 kg) / Life span: to 15 years / Reproduction: lays 8,000-25,000 eggs during the rainy season / Found: Collier and Lee counties, including Sanibel Island, all zones.

On July 17, 2013, during its monthly frog-call survey, the field biology staff of J.N. "Ding" Darling National Wildlife Refuge and SCCF (Sanibel-Captiva Conservation Foundation) heard an unusual frog call. Investigating the call, they discovered a population of giant toads, commonly referred to as cane toads, living in temporary wetlands near the intersection of Middle Gulf Drive and Fulgur Street on the eastern end of the island.

The staff surmised that the toads had hitchhiked to Sanibel, either as tadpoles surviving in standing water from a plant tarp or container, or as adults hiding in mulch, sod, or ornamental plants. By whatever method they arrived, the news was not something these field biologists were thrilled about. The cane toad is a troublesome invasive species and prolific breeder.

Originally from the forests of Central and South America, the cane toad has been used by natives in that region for food, as well as a poison, which is carefully rubbed on arrow tips when hunting. Called bufotoxin, this milky substance is released from the parotid gland located behind the eyes and is the toad's primary defense mechanism. It is often lethal to dogs, cats, raccoons, ring-tailed coatis, and various birds such as eagles and owls. Death by cane toad is extremely painful for any animal ingesting one. Symptoms include drooling, head-shaking, loss of coordination, and finally, convulsions and death. The victim's gums often turn dark red; a good indication the animal has eaten a poisonous cane toad.

The combination of its size, fecundity, and voracious appetite is what makes the cane toad especially troublesome for Sanibel and Captiva. It has been known to eat

Cane Toad   Courtesy Wikipedia Commons

insects, lizards, snakes, frogs, small mammals, garbage, various plants, pet food, and birds. The female, which is larger than the male, can lay up to 25,000 eggs at one time. A single string of these black eggs was measured at 66 feet long! On barrier islands such as Sanibel and Captiva, the cane toad could quickly overwhelm native species such as the southern toad, Eastern narrow-mouth frog, ring-necked snake, rice rat, and the green and brown anole. Although fatal human encounters are rare, licking a cane toad to get high from the chemicals in its secretion has been known to happen. It is not recommended.

The cane toad originally came to Florida in 1955 when a pet dealer in Miami accidentally released 100 of them. It is now firmly established throughout much of South Florida, including Monroe, Collier and Lee counties. The cane toad is yet another example of the inherent danger of introducing non-native reptiles, plants, or mammals into a new environment and stopping its spread across Florida will prove a daunting task. One limiting factor in Florida could be prolonged cold snaps, as the cane toad is not adapted to living in colder climates.

SCCF and the staff of J.N. "Ding" Darling are working diligently to control the spread of this toxic toad on Sanibel. They have asked that anyone who sees a cane toad or hears its distinctive call (for a sample, go to https://soundcloud.com/nature-sounds/cane-toad-bufo-marinus) to report it by calling 239-472-3984.

☐ _____ **Green Treefrog** (*Hyla cinerea*) Nicknames: American green treefrog, cowbell frog, bell frog, fried bacon frog / Status: FL=stable, IUCN=LC / Life span: to 5 years / Length: 2-2.5 in. (5-6 cm) / Weight: n/a / Reproduces: on island / Found: IW, UA.

Once far more populous than it is now, the small green treefrog has suffered tremendous losses at the hands of the larger and more aggressive Cuban treefrog. At this time it is not easy to find a green treefrog on Sanibel and Captiva, but some stable populations do still exist along the Sanibel River, especially on the SCCF hiking trails.

The green treefrog has a coastal range that extends all the way from Maryland to Corpus Christi, Texas. It also inhabits the Ohio River valley

© Eric B. Holt

all the way to southern Illinois. A pretty, lime-green color makes it very popular as a pet. It is also the state amphibian of both Georgia and Louisiana (oddly, Florida doesn't have a state amphibian).

The green treefrog is primarily nocturnal in nature. As a tadpole its diet consists of plants, algae, and aquatic insects, but once it undergoes its metamorphosis, it becomes a carnivore feeding on crickets, moths, and flies. The green treefrog is eaten by snakes and lizards, and the smaller ones are eaten by Cuban treefrogs.

© Mark Kenderdine

☐ _____ **Squirrel Treefrog** (*Hyla squirella*) Nicknames: rain frog, Morse-code frog / Status: FL=stable, IUCN=LC / Life span: to 6 years / Length: 0.9-1.75 in. (2.25-4.5 cm) / Weight: n/a / Reproduces: on islands / Found: IW, UA.

Named for its loud, persistent chatter in early spring, the squirrel treefrog has a call that resembles the chattering of a squirrel. During the mating season it also produces a unique sound a bit like sending Morse code, but with an alphabet that makes no sense. When the squirrel treefrog joins in with the oak toad on a rainy night in early spring, the noise can be deafening.

The squirrel treefrog is not as common on the islands as the green tree frog. Its range covers the southeastern U.S. from Virginia to the Texas gulf coast. It does not extend as far north as the green treefrog. It is easily mistaken for the green treefrog but

© Eric B. Holt

is quite a bit smaller and has more of a brownish hue. It has some chameleon-like characteristics, capable of changing its coloration in mere seconds from green to brown, spotted to plain, depending upon the surface it is resting upon.

Highly arboreal and nocturnal, this frog spends most of its adult life in trees, shrubs, and vines. It eats insects, including ants, beetles, moths, and termites. It is heavily preyed upon by Cuban treefrogs, snakes, small rodents, and birds.

☐ _____ **Cuban Treefrog** (*Osteopilus septentrionalis*) Nicknames: none / Status: FL=invasive, rapidly expanding its range, IUCN=LC / Life span: to 10 years / Length: 3-5.5 in. (7.5-14 cm) / Weight: n/a / Reproduces: on islands / Found: IW, UA.

© Eric B. Holt

The invasion of the Cuban treefrog is a case study in what happens when an interloper that is a prolific breeder enters a new environment through human commercial activity. First identified in the Florida Keys in the 1920s, this frog is now found throughout Florida and is rapidly moving up and into Georgia and the Carolinas, as well as westward toward the Texas coast. The Cuban treefrog spreads not only via ornamental plants, but also by motorized vehicles, trailered boats, and any number of other unusual methods.

This spread is nothing short of devastating to the native, indigenous frogs because the Cuban treefrog grows to twice the size of both the green and squirrel treefrogs and is capable of eating them. Furthermore, the Cuban treefrog tadpole is a superior competitor to native tadpoles, causing even more pressure on the indigenous species. It also appears to be negatively impacting certain smaller fish in the locales it has moved into.

The situation has become so dire that Dr. Steve Johnson, assistant professor of urban wildlife ecology at the University of Florida, wrote an article in which he instructs homeowners on how to euthanize and dispose of all the Cuban treefrogs they might encounter. This document is available on the Web site of the UF Institute of Food and Agricultural Sciences (http://edis.ifas.ufl.edu/UW259).

The Cuban treefrog readily gets into homes and condominiums, swims in toilets, can be found under sinks, has been known to short out electrical boxes, and generally wreaks havoc on the environment. Studies are now under way to explore the use of biological or chemical deterrents to halt or at least slow the continued spread of this invasive species.

The Cuban treefrog eats a wide variety of insects, but has also been known to consume Indo-Pacific geckos, green and brown anoles, and bird eggs, as well as some smaller hatchlings. It has become the prey of choice for yellow rat snakes, coral, and corn snakes and is heavily preyed upon by rodents.

You should always take care in handling the Cuban treefrog as its skin secretes a sticky substance that is extremely irritating to the mucous membranes of humans, such as the eyes, ears, and nose. People with allergies are especially vulnerable, and recovery from contact with a Cuban treefrog may take several hours. Although it has not been documented to be responsible in any dog or cat deaths, pets should be kept away from this potentially harmful frog. Given its ability to adapt and thrive in urban environments, the Cuban treefrog story will probably end with the frog winning.

☐ _____ **Greenhouse Frog** (*Eleutherodactylus planirostris planirostris*) Nicknames: none / Status: FL=invasive, IUCN=NE / Life span: to 5 years / Length 1-1.25 in. (2.5-3 cm) / Weight: n/a / Reproduces: on the islands / Found: IW, UA.

The greenhouse frog is another exotic, originally from the Caribbean and Cuba. Because it is even smaller than the native green and squirrel treefrogs, it does not appear to have anywhere near the negative impact of the Cuban treefrog. In fact, the greenhouse frog has also suffered from heavy predation by the Cuban treefrog.

Tiny exotic Courtesy USGS

This very small frog is unusual in that it skips the tadpole stage of development common with most amphibians. The female lays her eggs in rotting vegetation or under moist debris rather than in water. From those eggs come miniature, fully developed baby frogs. This is known as "direct development" and is extremely rare.

The greenhouse frog is not a treefrog and therefore is not equipped to climb on glass, plastic siding, or other slick surfaces. It stays in lawns, shrubs, and trees and feeds on a wide variety of small insects. It in turn is eaten by snakes, Cuban treefrogs, larger lizards, and rats.

☐ _____ **Eastern Narrow-mouth Frog** (*Gastrophryne carolinensis*) Nicknames: narrow-mouth frog / Status: FL=stable, IUCN=LC / Life span: to 4 years / Length: 1-1.5 in. (2-4 cm) / Weight: n/a / Reproduces: on the islands / Found: IW, UA.

Fairly common on Sanibel or Captiva, this small frog is easily recognized by its brown, blotchy skin color and distinctive pointed nose. In the past it has been considered a toad, but is actually a microhylid frog, which is a separate family. Its range extends across most of the Southeast from Texas to southern Maryland and north to the Ohio River valley. It is known to breed and propagate on Sanibel and Captiva and can commonly be heard on rainy nights.

It prefers living very close to moisture and is often found near ponds, under rotting logs, or hidden in debris piles. Strictly nocturnal, it is never seen in harsh sunlight. The narrow-mouth feeds on small insects and invertebrates, especially ants and termites. It is eaten by snakes, rodents, and larger lizards.

You'll likely hear this frog long before you ever find him
Courtesy USGS

❑ _____ **Pig Frog** (*Rana grylio*) Nicknames: southern bullfrog, lagoon frog / Status: FL=stable, IUCN=LC / Life span: to 6 years / Length: 3.25-6.5 in. (9-16 cm) / Weight: 2 oz (57 g) / Reproduces: on the islands / Found: IW, UA.

Courtesy USGS

This is the largest and loudest frog found on the islands. A mature pig frog, with its legs outstretched, can be more than 10 inches long. It is very similar in size and coloration to the slightly larger bullfrog, and both species are harvested for their prized frog legs.

It is considered a game animal, although no harvest limits or license is required to take one. In May 2008 the Florida Fish and Wildlife Commission issued an advisory on how many frog legs a person should eat per week because of mercury contamination. High levels of mercury have recently led to a ban on taking the pig frog in Everglades National Park and the Loxahatchee National Wildlife Refuge. Most of the frog legs served in restaurants are grown commercially, but thus far aquaculture attempts at raising the bullfrog and pig frog in Florida have not met with much success.

An exported exotic, the pig frog has been introduced into China, the Bahamas, and Puerto Rico where it is doing quite well. It is completely aquatic, seldom if ever leaving its pond, marsh, or lake. It is mostly nocturnal and tends to remain silent and hidden during the day, then starts croaking at dusk. Its loud, single calls can sound like a large pig grunting and are sometimes mistaken for alligators.

Its primary diet is crayfish, but it has also been known to dine on insects, tadpoles, fish, and other frogs. The pig frog is eaten by young alligators, herons, egrets, snakes, and freshwater fish such as bass and gar. The chances of seeing one are slim, but hearing them bellowing on a calm summer evening is quite easy, especially in the Bailey Tract of "Ding" Darling.

☐ _____ Southern Leopard Frog (*Rana sphenocephala*)

Nicknames: meadow frog, shad frog and herring hopper / Status: FL=stable, IUCN=LC / Life span: to 9 years / Length: 3.5-5 in. (9-14 cm) / Weight: n/a / Reproduces: on the islands / Found: IW.

Courtesy Wikipedia Commons

The southern leopard frog is similar in size and appearance to the northern leopard frog. This is the famous jumping frog described in detail by Mark Twain in his story "The Celebrated Jumping Frog of Calaveras County." When people think of what a frog looks like, they generally visualize the leopard frog. Its body is green, bronze, and blotchy brown, and it has a distinctive upper iris that is a beautiful gold color.

Both nocturnal and carnivorous, the leopard frog feeds on a variety of insects, earthworms, spiders, and centipedes. It breeds year-round. The tadpole is a strict vegetarian, feeding on rotting vegetation and algae for the first 90 days of its life.

Although quick to dive into deeper water when threatened by a predator, the leopard frog is heavily preyed upon by herons, snakes, raccoons, rats, and birds. It tends to do better in the cooler months than do most frogs and toads and can sometimes be heard croaking in the winter when most other amphibians are silent.

Courtesy USGS

The Case of the Disappearing Frogs

Squirrel Treefrog   © Mark Kenderdine

Nearly one-third of the world's 6,317 frog species are on the brink of extinction according to the Save the Frogs Foundation headquartered in Centerville, Va. Although several factors appear to be the leading causes of this mass extinction, the problem is complex and many scientist believe the root to be global climate change.

On of the leading causes of the decline in the world's frog populations is chytrid fungus and the disease it causes, chytridiomycosis. The disease is caused by a virulent, high transmissible fungus, (Batrachochytrium dendrobatidis or BD), that in some instances results in a one-hundred percent mortality. The fungus is suspected to have originated in the African clawed frogs, where it has been found in samples dating from the mid-1930s. The spread of the disease coincided with the advent of worldwide global jet transport, starting in the 1960s and continuing to the present.

The fungus kills the frogs by attacking its skin. The skin of a sick frog gets thicker resulting in the releasing of fatal toxins or by damaging the skin so badly that the frog's water and electrolyte balance, as well as their respiration, are affected. The frogs become sluggish, suffer loss of appetite, began trembling, sit out in the open sun to dehydrate and even worse, some frogs display no symptoms whatsoever and just suddenly die.

Some scientists have attempted to link the rise of chytrid fungus with climate change. The rising temperatures, especially at higher elevations such as the cloud forests of Costa Rica and the mountainous regions of Spain, are allowing the fungus to survive the winter. Warmer and drier climates are believed to stress amphibians, allowing the fungus to wipe out entire populations. The fungus has thus far caused the extinction of 74 of the 110 species of harlequin frogs in Central and South America.

Sadly, chytrid fungus isn't the only obstacle facing the world's amphibian populations. Because frogs and salamanders, as amphibians, have extremely thin and sensitive skin, they are very vulnerable to other kinds of environmental degradation. Water pollution is wreaking havoc on the frog population in places with little to no enforcement of pollution regulations such as in China and India. Amphibians are also susceptible to agricultural, industrial and pharmaceutical chemical pollutants. Atrazine, a herbicide commonly used in the U.S. appears to cause a variety of cancers and acts as an endocrine disruptor in frogs, causing tadpoles to become infertile.

Sanibel and Captiva have not been immune to this decline. In the past twenty years we have lost the Florida cricket frog (*Acris gryllus*), Florida chorus frog (*Pseudacris nigrita*), little grass frog (*Pseudacris ocularis*) and the Florida gopher frog (*Rana capito*). While the exact cause of their disappearance may be subject to any number of factors, the loss of bio-diversity in any environment is cause for alarm.

Frogs are a major food item for many of the island's predators. Wading birds, turtles, snakes and mammals all dine on frogs. In turn frogs help keep insect populations in check. The decline of frogs worldwide has been compared with the canaries in the coal mine. Are they the first harbingers of the next great extinction? Only time will tell.

The Fishes of Sanibel and Captiva

To date, more than 24,500 species of fish have been identified worldwide, and approximately two species a week are being added to the list. These species exist in environments that vary from shallow freshwater ponds to crushing depths in excess of 20,000 feet. They range in size from the 60-foot-long (18-meter) whale shark to the quarter-inch (8-mm) stout infantfish. Fish represent the largest segment of vertebrate animals found on earth. They are also the oldest vertebrates, starting their evolutionary journey some 525 million years ago during the Cambrian explosion of life.

In the southeastern Gulf of Mexico, from the beaches of Sanibel and Captiva to the edge of the continental shelf 175 miles west of Redfish Pass, there are more than 1,000 species of fish. These range from the pelagic yellowfin tuna, marlin, and dolphin to the deepwater Warsaw grouper, snapper, and tilefish. In the back bay, deep in the mangrove forests, and across the expansive grass flats, we have one of the most prolific biological systems on earth—the saltwater estuary. The rise and fall of the tides mix daily with the outflow of the Caloosahatchee River to the south and the Peace River to the north, creating a rich array of living organisms. From microscopic larval tarpon to eagle rays, from sea squirts to manatee, the backwaters of San Carlos Bay teem with life. The biological diversity of these estuaries is rivaled only by coral reefs and tropical rainforests. Per acre, they are one of the richest and most diverse ecosystems on the planet. Like so many natural treasures, they are also extremely fragile and vulnerable to chemical and effluent pollution, oil spills, urban stormwater runoff, and other abuses such as propeller scars across grass flats and illegal fishing and gill netting.

Across the state of Florida are another 230 species of inshore fish species, though nowhere near that many exist on the islands. In fact, before Tommy Wood and Charles LeBuff,

© Charles Sobczak

working with a developer and the Florida Fish and Wildlife Service, introduced largemouth bass and bream into several man-made ponds in the early 1960s, Sanibel and Captiva had only a handful of native freshwater species. Today these bass and bream inhabit nearly every freshwater body of water on the islands.

Choosing which fish to include in this section was not easy. The single most important factor was deciding which species were most likely to be observed—either in the water or on the other end of a fishing line—from shore. Though several of these species are seldom seen or caught from land, such as the little tuny (*Euthynnus alletteratus*) and the tripletail (*Lobotes surinamensis*), most of the others, including tarpon (*Megalops atlanticus*), are commonly found close enough to land to merit inclusion here.

One of the best ways to find fish is to find fishermen. From the Sanibel fishing pier at the tip of Point Ybel on the east end of Sanibel to the beaches of Captiva, experienced anglers will often guide you to the various species that abound in the waters surrounding these two islands. To facilitate this, and save space, I have added some abbreviations to the earlier list. Many of these abbreviations are also used in the shellfish section:

SFP—Sanibel Fishing Pier: Located at the east end of Sanibel, this short pier on Point Ybel harbors an amazing array of fish. Depending on the time of year you visit the pier you might see sheepshead, mangrove snapper, Spanish and king mackerel, shark, goliath and gag grouper, snook, redfish, and cobia, as well as baitfish such as pinfish, pigfish, scaled sardines, and glass minnows.

CWFP—Causeway Fishing Pier: Although this proposed fishing pier was not completed at the time of publication, the nearby seawalled sections of the causeway, located on both spoil islands, will suffice until the pier is completed. From the causeway, as well as the future causeway fishing pier, you will see many of the same fish as you see from the SFP, plus seatrout, black drum, permit, and pompano.

BB—Back Bay: This includes the seven spillways located under Wildlife Drive and the docks and launches of Sanibel and Captiva, including Tarpon Bay, Roosevelt Channel, and the entire eastern shoreline of Captiva. It includes all of Pine Island Sound, San Carlos Bay, and the mangrove-lined edges of Buck Key, Chino Island, and the Wulfert Keys. This region teems with pinfish, seatrout, redfish, snook, tarpon, blacktip shark, scallop hammerhead, and bull shark.

REDP—Redfish Pass: Created by two hurricanes in the 1920s, this pass separates Captiva from North Captiva. Running close to 25 feet deep, the pass harbors ladyfish, bluefish, Spanish and king mackerel, black grouper, mangrove snapper, snook, redfish, and several shark species.

GB—Gulf Beaches: This includes all of the gulf beaches of Sanibel, from the lighthouse to Blind Pass, as well as the entirety of Captiva's beaches from the northern side of Blind Pass to the tip of the island on Redfish Pass. The fish you can find here include snook, whiting, tarpon, several shark species, hardhead and gafftopsail catfish, flounder, and ladyfish.

OFFSR—Off Shore: You can see some species of fish from land, or better still, from the vantage point of a gulf-front condominium. These include the little tuny, king and Spanish mackerel, blue runner, cobia, and jack crevalle.

Because fishing rules and regulations are subject to change (such as who is required to have a license, slot limits, special species stamps, bag limits, and seasonal closures), they have intentionally been left out of this book. Species that are considered game fish (and this, too, is subject to change) have been identified with a star (★) in front of their names and require a saltwater or a freshwater license. Specific regulations can be found on the Internet at MyFWC.com or in the local tackle shops and general stores on the island where fishing licenses are sold. You may also purchase fresh-or saltwater fishing licenses online at www. wildlifelicense.com/fl/start.php.

While catch-and-release fishing is strongly encouraged, the recreational harvesting of the various species of game fish is also acceptable, as long as the fish meet the legal requirements and are brought home, cleaned, cooked, and enjoyed. Don't catch fish if you don't want to go through the trouble of cleaning and cooking them.

There are plenty of Web sites that offer advice on how to clean and cook your catch. One of these is www.sanibelislandfishingclub.com, which is the official site of the Sanibel Island Fishing Club. If you do practice catch-and-release fishing, please try to do as little harm as possible to your fish. Some important tips to ensure that you will release the fish uninjured so it will be able to fight again someday in the future can be found on page 329.

Snapper school   © Rusty Farst

Saltwater Minnows and Baitfish

☐ _____ **Atlantic Threadfin Herring** (*Opisthonema oglinum*)
Nicknames: gizzard shad, threadfins / Status: FL=stable, IUCN=NE / Life span: to 5 years / Length: 10-16 in. (25-40 cm) / Weight: 1-3 oz (28-56 g) / Spawns: in the inshore waters / Found: SFP, CWFP, BB, RP, GB, OFFSR.

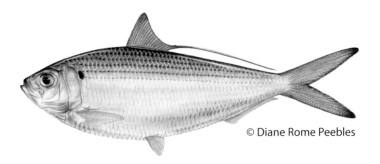

© Diane Rome Peebles

The threadfin herring is one of a select number of pelagic baitfish that provide forage for a wide variety of game fish and sharks in the waters surrounding the islands. It can often be seen in large schools from the Sanibel causeway, appearing like patches of rain falling on the surface of the water. During the heat of the summer it may school in great numbers beneath the shade of the causeway. This baitfish is readily identified by the long, thread-like extension running from the back of its dorsal fin to the base of its tail.

Anglers chum this popular baitfish to the back of their boats and capture it with large (up to 12 feet) cast nets. The threadfin is a commonly used bait for tarpon, snook, and shark. Immature threadfin can be used for seatrout, redfish, and Spanish mackerel. The threadfin has an enormous range, extending from the Chesapeake Bay to Brazil. It is an inshore species, seldom living in depths beyond 18 feet. In Mexico it is commercially harvested for human and animal consumption.

Threadfin, like most baitfish, dine on copepods, which are microscopic zooplankton. It will also take small fish, crabs, squid, shrimp, and algae. It can be hand caught using a Sabiki rig or very small (#12-14) gold hook. It is preyed upon by almost every fish in the gulf, as well as by pelicans, cormorants, anhingas, grebes, loons, and gulls.

☐ _____ **Scaled Sardine** (*Harengula juguana*) Nicknames: pilchard, greenback, whitebait / Status: FL=stable, IUCN=NE / Life span: to 3 years / Length: 8-14 in. (21-35 cm) / Weight: 0.75-1.5 oz (21-42 g) / Spawns: in the nearshore waters / Found: SFP, CWFP, MZ, BB, REDP, GB, OFFSR.

Often swimming in schools with threadfin herring, the scaled sardine, or whitebait as it is commonly referred to, is one of the most popular baitfish in Southwest Florida. In parts of Mexico, the Caribbean, and the northern coast of South America, the scaled sardine is harvested and canned for human consumption. It is not currently used as a human food source in the U.S. The scaled sardine ranges as far north as the coast of New Jersey to southern Brazil in waters from 15 to 120 feet deep.

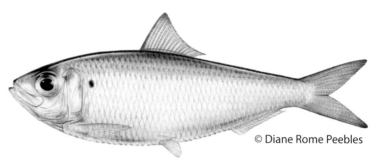

© Diane Rome Peebles

The scaled sardine feeds on zooplankton but will also take shrimp, squid, and small pieces of cut bait. This minnow is a very important link in the estuarine and coastal food webs. It is preyed upon by everything from sharks to king mackerel. Bottlenose dolphins feed heavily on mature schools of sardines, and herons, egrets, gulls, and pelicans feed on the smaller, immature schools.

All minnows are susceptible to water-quality degradation. When harmful algae blooms occur, the scaled sardine and threadfin herring are among the first fish to be impacted. If they are unable to flee the immediate area, entire schools can be destroyed in hypoxic events (often called dead zones). These dead zones occur when a rapid increase in nutrients (primarily nitrogen and phosphorus) create a condition called eutrophication. When the algae bloom created by the over-nutrification of the estuary begins to decompose, it uses all of the available oxygen, effectively suffocating all the living organisms within the immediate region (because these effects are manmade, they are often referred to as "cultural eutrophication"). Once these fish populations collapse, the birds, marine mammals, and fish populations that rely on this food source quickly follow suit.

Spanish Sardine (*Sarinella aurita*) Nicknames: smooth sardine, cigar minnows, gilt pilchard / Status: FL=stable, IUCN=NE / Life span: to 12 years / Length: 7-10 in. (18-25 cm) / Weight: 0.5-1 oz (14-28 g) / Spawns: in the nearshore waters / Found: SFP, OFFSR.

The Spanish sardine is found as far as 150 miles offshore in waters up to 1,000 feet deep, but is seldom seen in the back bays or estuaries. It is used extensively as a baitfish, packaged and frozen and is an excellent bait choice (cut into one-inch pieces) for grouper, redfish, and mangrove snapper.

A close relative, the *Sardinops sagax caerulea* was fished to complete extinction off the coast of California in the 1960s. This was the sardine that was the basis of the canning industry of Monterey, California, made

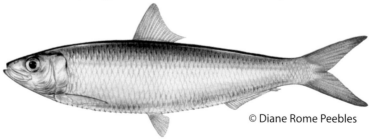

© Diane Rome Peebles

famous by John Steinbeck's *Cannery Row*. Another related species was fished to collapse off the coast of Peru. Much of that catch was converted to fishmeal and fish oil. The sardine is a valued food because it is very high in omega-3 fatty acids and easily canned.

Florida does not commercially harvest the Spanish sardine. Most of the frozen sardines anglers use are imported from Venezuela or the Far East. Large schools of sardines can be found off Captiva starting at 20-foot depths and extending to the continental shelf. The sardine is preyed upon by gannets, boobies, gulls, pelicans, and terns from above and jacks, sharks, tuna, and porpoises from below.

☐ _____ **Gulf Menhaden** (*Brevoortia patronus*) Nicknames: bunker, pogie, bugeye / Status: FL=stable, IUCN=NE / Life span: to 2 years / Length: 12-18 in. (25-45 cm) / Weight: .75-1 lb (340-453 g) / Spawns: in the nearshore waters / Found: BB, REDP, GB, OFFSR.

A heavily sought-after species, the gulf menhaden, along with two close relatives, the yellowfin and Atlantic menhaden, account for 40 percent of all commercial fish harvested in the U.S. In the Gulf of Mexico, especially off of Texas and Louisiana, gulf menhaden harvests average 400 to 600 kilotons a year. You won't find this fish listed on any menu,

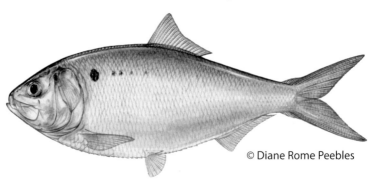

© Diane Rome Peebles

however, as it is a bony, oily fish with soft and unpalatable flesh. It is typically ground up into a high-protein feed for chicken, pigs, and cattle. Anyone who eats meat in the U.S. is indirectly eating reprocessed menhaden.

In his book *The Most Important Fish in the Sea: Menhaden and America*, published in 2007, H. Bruce Franklin argues that the commercial over-harvesting of menhaden along the Atlantic and in the gulf dramatically impacts the birds, marine mammals, and fish that once relied upon these plentiful filter feeders for sustenance. Franklin believes that these continued harvests will ultimately cause the collapse of the menhaden, as well as many other fisheries.

Until the net ban went into effect in 1994, the gulf menhaden was the absolute favorite local bait for catching tarpon. Anglers and guides would buy fresh or frozen "bunker" by the hundreds of pounds and chum extensively until the tarpon and shark swarmed around their boats. Now, however, it is an uncommon cast-net catch and cannot be readily caught on hook and line, making it all but impossible to find as a baitfish.

Offshore it is taken by bluefish, gulf-running redfish, snapper, tarpon, and marine mammals. Because of the menhaden's size, only the larger seabirds such as boobies and pelicans are capable of eating it.

☐ _____ **Bay Anchovy** (*Anchoa mitchilli*) Nicknames: glass minnow, silversides / Status: FL=stable, IUCN=NE / Life span: to 3 years / Length: 3-4 in. (7.5-10 cm) / Weight: n/a / Spawns: in the nearshore waters / Found: SFP, CWFP, BB, REDP, GB, OFFSR.

B ecause of its small size, the bay anchovy (aka glass minnow) is seldom if ever used as a baitfish. Throwing a cast net on a large school of these tiny anchovies is an unwelcome disaster. Their heads get stuck in the netting, and a single cast may result in hours of removing each

© Diane Rome Peebles

and every minnow hopelessly lodged in the monofilament mesh. Even when one is caught, it is so soft that it is virtually impossible to keep on the hook.

The bay anchovy plays a vital part in the food chain and is part of the diet of every game fish in the gulf. This filter feeder eats zooplankton and micro-crustaceans that are not edible by larger game fish. It forms the base of the food web that eventually ends with the gulf's apex predators: porpoises and sharks. Birds, especially terns, pelicans, and gulls, dine heavily on the bay anchovy and can be observed feeding on schools of them just off the causeway. If you see pelicans surface diving rather than plunge diving, the chances are that they are feeding on this fish.

The bay anchovy is easy to identify because it is nearly transparent. Small schools of them can be found running up and down the gulf beaches from the spring through the late fall. With the change of seasons, mile-wide schools of the bay anchovy migrate just offshore, attracting massive feeding frenzies of bonita tuna and Spanish mackerel. The bay anchovy is very tolerant of low salinity and can be found miles up the Caloosahatchee. It is found throughout the tropical and subtropical oceans.

☐ _____ **Pinfish** (*Logodon rhomboides*) Nicknames: pin perch, bream, butterfish, pins / Status: FL=stable, IUCN=NE / Life span: to 7 years / Length: 4-12 in. (10-30 cm) / Weight: n/a / Spawns: in the offshore waters / Found: SFP, CWFP, MZ, BB, REDP.

A nyone who has ever handled a live pinfish fish learns why it is so aptly named. Tiny points, called pins, stick out just a fraction of an inch beyond the dorsal fin and prick you repeatedly if you're not careful. Grabbing one of these the wrong way is like grabbing a pincushion with all the needles pointing out.

The pinfish is the bait of choice for many anglers. In the fall it is a popular bait for catching gag grouper, which favors pinfish and grunts as prey. Snook, redfish, seatrout, shark, tarpon, king

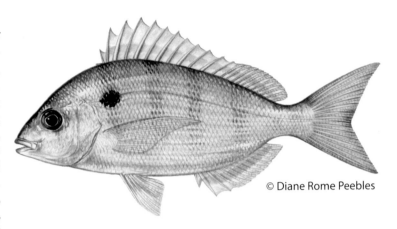

© Diane Rome Peebles

and Spanish mackerel, flounder, and cobia will all take pinfish. The bottlenose dolphin also preys on pinfish.

Catching pinfish for bait is best done by either hook and line with very small gold hooks (#12-14 Eagle Claw) and tiny pieces of squid, or by chumming, then throwing a cast net over grass beds between three and six feet deep. It needs a constant flow of fresh saltwater once caught or it will quickly die from lack of oxygen. Most bait stores carry frozen pinfish, but freshly caught live pins are preferred. A notorious bait stealer, the pinfish will pick an entire shrimp off your hook in seconds.

It is a prolific breeder: a single six-inch female will lay 90,000 eggs. Unlike the anchovy, sardine, and herring, the pinfish is not a schooling fish, though it does tend to congregate in certain areas. It forages in sea grasses and near potholes where it dines on small micro-crustaceans, fish eggs, and decaying plant material. In these submerged, grassy plains the pinfish plays a vital ecological role, keeping the shrimp and crab populations in check while constantly cleaning the algae and barnacle growth off sea grasses. The pinfish is rarely caught in the gulf.

☐ _____ **Pigfish** (*Orthopristis chrysoptera*) Nicknames: grunts / Status: FL=stable, IUCN=NE / Life span: to 1.5 years / Length: 5-15 in. (12-36 cm) / Weight: n/a / Spawns: in the offshore waters / Found: SFP, CWFP, MZ, BB, REDP.

Similar in many ways to the pinfish, the pigfish, or grunt as it is commonly called, is an excellent baitfish. It is easier to handle than pinfish, and many anglers consider it to be a superior bait, though it is nowhere near as plentiful as pinfish.

Like the pinfish, the pigfish does not school but can be found in the same habitat as pinfish: grass flats and along the edge of mangroves. It is also found offshore in waters up to 60 feet deep.

The pigfish is known for its constant pig-like grunting once removed from the water. It makes this telltale noise by rubbing together the teeth located deep in its throat.

It sometimes continues to grunt after being baited, which often leads to a very quick strike. Everything in the ocean eats the pigfish. Larger pigfish, in excess of 12 inches in length,

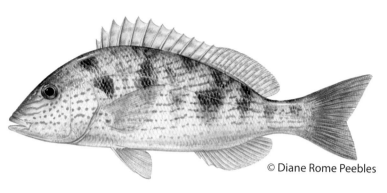

© Diane Rome Peebles

can make pretty good table fare as well. Offshore, its close relatives, the white grunt and tomtate, are commonly taken by anglers. The pigfish eats crustaceans, squid, and shellfish.

❑ _____ **Striped Mojarra** (*Diapterus plumieri*) Nicknames: mojarra, sand perch, sand brim / Status: FL=stable, IUCN=NE / Life span: to 6 years / Length: 4-12 in. (10-30 cm) / Weight: 4-36 oz (113-1,020 g) / Spawns: in the nearshore waters / Found: SFP, CWFP, MZ, BB, REDP.

With a range that extends from South Carolina to Brazil, the bulk of the striped mojarra population lives in the Caribbean basin. Unlike pinfish or pigfish, the mojarra is sometimes trawl-netted and used for fishmeal in much the same fashion as menhaden. Fairly common, but generally only cast-netted and seldom caught on hook and line, the mojarra is not as popular as other baitfish.

The mojarra tends to die when put into a bait well, even one with good circulation. Its flesh is far

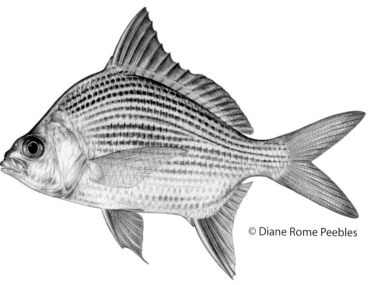

© Diane Rome Peebles

softer than pigfish, and, therefore, it does not stay on a hook as well. In the estuary it feeds on micro-crustaceans, detritus, aquatic insects, and micro-bivalves. It is readily taken by snook, seatrout, and redfish. It can grow to be more than two pounds but because of its soft flesh does not make good table fare.

☐ _____ ★**Striped Mullet** (*Mugil cephalus*) Nicknames: jumping mullet, finger mullet / Status: FL=stable, IUCN=NE / Life span: to 16 years / Length: 4-30 in. (10-76 cm) / Weight: 1-3 lb (0.45-1.3 kg) / Spawns: in the nearshore waters / Found: SFP, CWFP, MZ, BB, REDP, GB, OFFSR.

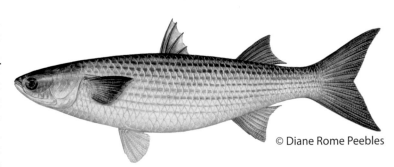

© Diane Rome Peebles

The striped mullet once formed the backbone of the Southwest Florida fishing industry. Before the regulation changes that banned the use of gill nets in 1994, hundreds of mullet boats worked the inshore and nearshore waters of the gulf. Most of these boats were not interested in the mullet for their meat, but for their roe, which could fetch as much as $100 a pound in Japanese fish markets. On a good night, a skilled mullet cast netter can make more than $1,000 from the sale of the valuable roe. The fish itself is sold as bait or for use as fishmeal.

Even after the net ban, fishermen from as far away as south Texas, using high-speed boats and mullet cast nets, came here to harvest mullet roe for the Asian markets. The state of Florida finally stopped issuing permits to out-of-state anglers for harvesting mullet in the early 2000s. Mullet fishing is still a viable commercial activity along the west coast of Florida, though not at the same level of harvest as before the net ban of 1994.

The mullet eats zooplankton, bottom-dwelling organisms, and detritus. It consumes vast amounts of marine algae and plant waste. This grazer of Southwest Florida forms the basis of the food chain created in large part by the falling leaves and detritus of the red mangrove.

Since the mullet is almost entirely an herbivore, it is nearly impossible to catch on hook and line. Some people claim you can catch one using frozen corn kernels. The best method, however, is by throwing a special, wide-meshed cast net aptly called a mullet net. Regular baitfish can swim through it because its mesh is very large; the sinkers used along the perimeter of the net are heavy, causing the net to sink quickly.

As food, the mullet is best smoked, as it has an earthy taste similar to freshwater suckers or carp. Cut mullet is a favorite for tarpon fishing in the spring and can also be used for shark, cobia, and bottom fishing. The adult mullet is a favorite of bottlenose dolphins, sharks, large snook, mackerel, and cobia. The smaller finger mullet (juvenile) is consumed by ladyfish, jacks, and a host of other predators.

The striped mullet is known for jumping. Frequently seen in the "Ding" Darling refuge, this leaping fish generally clears the water by at least a foot and tends to jump in patterns of three consecutive leaps. The striped mullet will often fly out of the water into the craft of an unsuspecting boater. Some people claim that the mullet

Striped Mullet captured by an Osprey   © ThroughTheLensGallery.com

jumps to escape predators, but studies have indicated that this is not the case. Other theories involve the removal of parasites from the gills of jumping mullet, but that too has not been verified. A more recent theory is that the mullet jumps to somehow obtain oxygen from the air. The trouble with this theory is that it does not appear to have any physiological mechanism that would allow it to take in this oxygen. Finally, some believe that the mullet jumps simply for the fun of it. The truth is, no one has been able to explain why the mullet jumps.

Saltwater Fish

❏ _____ **Hardhead Catfish** (*Arius felis*) Nicknames: sea catfish, hardhead, tourist trout / Status: FL=stable, IUCN=NE / Life span: to 5 years / Length: 1-2 ft. (30-60 cm) / Weight: 1-2.2 lb (.45-1 kg); Florida state record: 3 lb 5 oz., IGFA 12.2 lb / Spawns: in the nearshore waters / Found: SFP, CWFP, MZ, BB, REDP, GB, OFFSR.

Known to bite on just about anything tossed into the ocean, from squid to sardines, frozen shrimp to chicken legs, the hardhead catfish is truly Florida's tourist trout. It will bite on almost any size leader, from 100-pound test to shark-wire, and feed at any time of the day or night. If you cannot catch a hardhead catfish while fishing in Florida, your luck has completely run out.

The hardhead's range runs from Cape Cod, Massachusetts, to the Yucatan Peninsula. It is one of the most common larger fish in the estuary. Three large spines, one on the end of each front pectoral and the other on the dorsal fin, are dangerous, so the catfish should be handled with 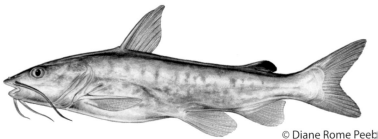 extreme care. The spines are covered in slime, serrated, and designed to penetrate easily; microscopic barbs along the spine make them incredibly difficult to remove. Infections are common, and anyone "stuck" by a catfish should seek medical attention.

© Diane Rome Peeb

The hardhead has evolved a unique parenting technique. After hatching, the male hardhead places the eggs, numbering between 20 and 65, in its mouth. The eggs will remain there until they hatch (around 30 days). After hatching, the larvae stay in the male's mouth for another two to four weeks when they began to venture out. They still return to the safety of the father's mouth for several more weeks until they are large enough to survive on their own. This unusual arrangement ensures a high survival rate and helps to offset the relatively small number of eggs the female catfish lays during spawning.

The hardhead is an opportunistic feeder, eating algae, sea grasses, sea cucumbers, gastropods, shrimps, crabs, and smaller fish. The catfish is eaten by sharks, cobia, and other large finfish. It is not generally considered table fare. Locally the hardhead catfish is considered a trash fish. Many tarpon hunters use the tail sections in the spring to fish for the silver kings; they consider it one of the best possible baits because, unlike many other cut baits, the other catfish leave it alone.

☐ _____ **Gafftopsail Catfish** (*Bagre marinus*) Nicknames: sail cat, gafftop, slime cat / Status: FL=stable, IUCN=NE / Life span: to 8 years / Length: 1.5-2.5 ft (45-76 cm) / Weight: 4-6 lb (1.8-2.7 kg); Florida state record: 8 lb 14 oz, IGFA 10 lb / Spawns: in nearshore waters / Found: SFP, CWFP, MZ, BB, REDP, GB, OFFSR.

Similar in many respects to the hardhead but considerably larger, the gafftopsail catfish is a much stronger fighter when hooked. It shares the same unusual parenting technique in which the male takes the female's eggs into its mouth immediately after spawning. Unlike the hardhead, the gafftopsail is not a bottom feeder but feeds throughout the water column and will often strike lures, spoons, and suspended baits.

The sail cat, as it is commonly called, feeds on minnows, shrimp, crustaceans, and invertebrates. It is fed upon by sharks, cobia, and large finfish such as tarpon. Its tail is used as cut bait in the same fashion as the hardhead. Its barbs are equally dangerous and considered venomous, so extreme care should be taken when handling the sail cat.

It ranges from Virginia to the northern tip of South America. Although regarded by many as a fairly good eating fish, the sail cat is seldom

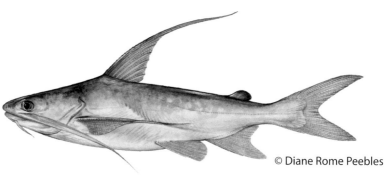

© Diane Rome Peebles

caught for table fare. If taken, however, it should be skinned, as the entire body is covered in a thick slime. Because the sail cat is a strong fighter—and aside from the dangers involved when attempting to de-hook it (it's sometimes easier and safer to cut the line right at the hook)—this is an exciting fish to catch and release.

❒ _____ **Ladyfish** (*Elops saurus*) Nicknames: big-eyed herring, ten-pounder, poor man's tarpon / Status: FL=stable, IUCN=NE / Life span: to 6 years / Length: 1.5-2 ft (45-60 cm) / Weight: 2-3 lb (.90-1.4 kg); Florida state record: 6 lb 4 oz, IGFA: 8 lb / Spawns: in the offshore waters / Found: SFP, CWFP, MZ, BB, REDP.

The nickname "poor man's tarpon" says volumes about this feisty, miniature relative of the tarpon. Once hooked, the frenetic ladyfish almost invariably takes to the air—leaping, flipping, twisting, and turning until the hook is thrown. Averaging around two pounds, the ladyfish is

© Diane Rome Peebles

considered to be a sport fish on light tackle. For anyone who has had the pleasure to hook one, it is always a fun, if not frantic, addition to a day of angling in the back bay. Its hyperactivity makes it slightly dangerous, however. It tends to toss lures back at you after being hooked, and it can be very difficult to unhook. Care should be taken when handling ladyfish though, unlike catfish, it does not have any venomous spines, nor does it have any teeth large enough to be a factor.

The ladyfish is an aggressive predator and will take just about any bait, live or artificial. It feeds on shrimp, greenbacks, pinfish, and even smaller ladyfish. It is heavily preyed upon by sharks, bottlenose dolphins, alligators, and birds. Its meat is bony and dry, so the ladyfish is almost never taken as a food fish.

It tends to congregate in the passes and on the outside of mangrove creeks. Its range extends from South Carolina, through the Caribbean, to the mouth of the Amazon.

▢ _____ **Lizardfish** (*Synodus foetens*) Nicknames: sea mat, soap fish / Status: FL=stable, IUCN=NE / Life span: to 2 years / Length: 10-16 in. (25-40 cm) / Weight: .60-1 lb. (272-452 g) / Spawns: in the offshore waters / Found: SFP, CWFP, BB, REDP, OFFSR.

The lizardfish is an inshore, as well as nearshore species. Inshore it is seldom longer than a foot, whereas in deeper water it can grow to 18 inches or more. Its range extends from southern Brazil to Massachusetts.

Best described as unattractive, the lizardfish has a mouth that is oddly wider than its sausage-shaped body. It varies widely in coloration, but its mottled olive and brown skin has an interesting pattern.

The lizardfish is considered by almost all anglers to be a junk fish. No one eats it, and aside from occasional use as cut bait for grouper, it is seldom used for anything else. When hooked, the lizardfish puts up hardly any struggle. It is predominantly a bottom feeder but will take a deep trolled lure offshore. It feeds on crabs, fish, and crustaceans and is eaten by groupers and sharks.

▢ _____ **Whiting** (*Menticirrhus littoralis*) Nicknames: gulf kingfish, gulf kingcroaker / Status: FL=stable, IUCN=NE / Life span: to 6 years / Length: 10-18 in. (25-46 cm) / Weight: 1-2 lb (453-907 g) / Spawns: in the nearshore waters / Found: SFP, REDP, GB.

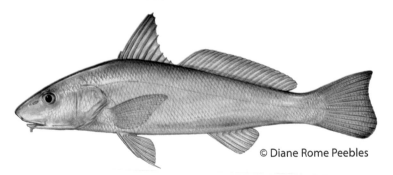

© Diane Rome Peebles

The whiting is a popular surf fish, predominantly caught along the gulf beaches and near passes. No state or IGFA records exist for whiting, but it is commonly caught and taken as a food fish all along the gulf coast. It feeds in and along the surf on small fish, sand fleas, crabs, and shrimp. The most common bait to use for catching it are sand fleas and fresh or frozen shrimp.

The whiting is best taken on very light spinning tackle. It is not a strong fighter and never jumps. Fall, winter, and spring appear to be the best times to find it along the beaches. It is almost never found in the estuary or in waters deeper than 12 feet. Anglers should be careful not to cast out too far as it prefers depths of three or four feet. The whiting is related to redfish, seatrout, and black drum. In northern waters another relative, the spot, is also a popular inshore fish to catch.

☐ _____ ★ **Bluefish** (*Pomatomus saltatrix*) Nicknames: tailor, choppers, snappers / Status: FL=stable, IUCN=NE / Life span: to 9 years / Length: 16-51 in. (40-130 cm) / Weight: 2-3 lb (.90-1.36 kg); Florida state record: 22 lb 2 oz, IGFA: 31 lb 12 oz / Spawns: in the offshore waters / Found: SFP, CWFP, BB, REDP, OFFSR.

Primarily a winter visitor, the bluefish is commonly found around Redfish Pass during the coldest months of the year. The bluefish found on the gulf coast of Florida is much smaller than the schools that work the Gulf Stream along the east coast, where the Florida record was taken. A strong fighter, the bluefish's nickname, "chopper," aptly describes this aggressive fish. Once worked into a feeding frenzy, the bluefish becomes almost piranha-like in its behavior.

It travels in schools and will attack shoals of mullet and other fish with unbelievable ferocity, killing and cutting up far more fish than they can eat. In New England, these schools are easily found by the large flocks of gulls, terns, and seabirds that follow the marauding bluefish. The bluefish also takes crustaceans and cephalopods (squid and octopus). Its distribution is worldwide, from the Indian Ocean to the North Atlantic.

Once located, the bluefish is as easy to catch as tossing in a shiny silver spoon or any live bait. Because it has small, sharp teeth, wire is recommended. Once in the boat, the bluefish has been known to bite, so care should be exercised at all times when handling this fish. Although a fair table fish when fresh, the bluefish's oily flesh does not freeze well.

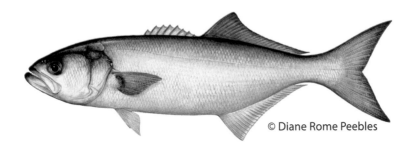

© Diane Rome Peebles

☐ _____ **Blue Runner** (*Caranx crysos*) Nicknames: runner, yellow mackerel / Status: FL=stable, IUCN=NE / Life span: to 11 years / Length: 10-22 in. (25-56 cm) / Weight: 0.75-1.5 lb (340-680 g); Florida state record: 8 lb 5 oz, IGFA: 11 lb 2 oz / Spawns: in the offshore waters / Found: SFP, CWFP, REDP, GB, OFFSR.

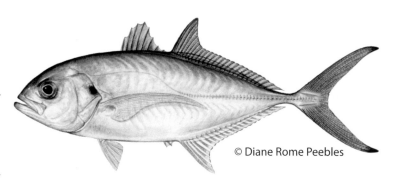

© Diane Rome Peebles

Sometimes mistaken for bluefish and vice versa, the blue runner is a member of the jack family. Aside from being roughly the same size on the gulf coast, however, the blue runner has little in common with the bluefish. The blue runner lacks the teeth of the bluefish and is nowhere near as aggressive. It feeds on small fish, shrimp, and other invertebrates.

Cut blue runner is an excellent bait for shark, tarpon, and mangrove snapper. Locally, the blue runner is the favored baitfish for king mackerel, where it is often slow trolled over artificial reefs and hard bottom. Light tackle and no more than 20-pound leader are all that is required to catch this attractive little fighter. It is seldom taken for food, but is reported to be excellent eating, though, like many jacks, tends to be oily and have a darker meat.

Its distribution is limited to the subtropical Atlantic, from western Africa to the Caribbean and north to Nova Scotia.

☐ _____ **Jack Crevalle** (*Caranx hippos*) Nicknames: jack, horse crevalle, common jack / Status: FL=stable, IUCN=NE / Life span: to 25 years / Length: 10-48 in. (25-124 cm) / Weight: 1-15 lb (.45-6.8 kg); Florida state record: 51 lb, IGFA: 54 lb 14 oz / Spawns: in offshore waters / Found: SFP, CWFP, MZ, BB, REDP, GB, OFFSR.

Commonly referred to as "jack," this is a frequent catch found almost anywhere in the waters surrounding Sanibel and Captiva. An aggressive fighter known to readily take surface plugs, spoons, and almost any kind of live or frozen bait, the jack is a popular sport fish, and for good reason. Its fight is typified by deep powerful runs and long, extended battles, especially with fish 10 pounds and above. Unlike ladyfish, the jack never jumps.

A schooling predator, the jack often attacks baitfish in canals, driving them against the seawalls and turning the water into a boiling froth. During these events almost any jig or spoon cast into the feeding jacks will result in an instant strike. The jack feeds predominantly on minnows and smaller fish, taking in crustaceans and invertebrates with far less frequency.

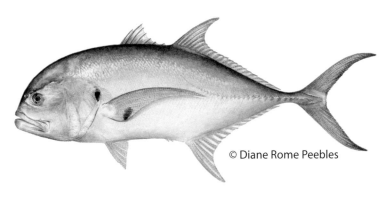

© Diane Rome Peebles

Mature jacks are heavily preyed upon by shark, tarpon, marlin, and other large finfish. Juveniles are taken by wading birds, as well as large snook and cobia. Tolerant of salinity changes, the jack roams far up the Caloosahatchee all the way to the Franklin locks. It is one of the most populous fish in the Atlantic Ocean, ranging from Newfoundland to the southern tip of Africa.

There have been confirmed reports of jacks weighing more than 32 kilograms (70 pounds). A jack this size should not be eaten, however, since it is prone to ciguatera poisoning. Smaller fish are sometimes taken as table fare but have a dark, oily flesh. The jack is excellent in fish stew and is very popular in India where its firm flesh is used in fish curry. In Florida, however, the jack is more popular as a testy game fish than a food fish.

☐ _____ ★**Pompano** (*Trachinotus carolinus*) Nicknames: cobblerfish, common pompano, Florida pompano / Status: FL=stable, IUCN=NE / Life span: to 4 years / Length: 14-25 in. (35-64 cm) / Weight: 1-3 lb (.45-1.36 kg); Florida state record: 8 lb 4 oz, IGFA: n/a / Spawns: in offshore waters/ Found: SFP, CWFP, BB, REDP, GB.

A popular game fish and gourmet dinner fare, the pompano is a much sought-after member of the jack family. The pompano feeds almost exclusively on crustaceans and shrimp. This diet helps give it a unique, almost nut-like flavor, making it the highest-priced marine food fish in the U.S. A tough fighter, the pompano is a wary feeder and can be difficult to catch.

The pompano is one of the smaller members of the Carangidae, or jack, family of fish. Worldwide there are 67 species of Carangidae, 23 of which are represented in U.S. coastal waters. They range in size from the greater amberjack, weighing in at more than 100 pounds, to the Atlantic leatherjacket, a minnow-sized jack sometimes accidentally taken in cast nets locally. Other familiar jacks include the lookdown, African pompano, almaco jack, permit, scad, and rainbow runner.

Catching pompano is an art. Light tackle and no more than 20-pound fluorocarbon leader is a must, along with small hooks (#1-#3 or smaller) and fresh shrimp. Jigging with a quarter-ounce yellow buck-tail jig in 6 to 15 feet of clear water will produce results, as will free-lining shrimp with little or no weight near the Sanibel Lighthouse or Redfish Pass at the turn of the outgoing tide.

Unlike some families of fish, such as snapper (Lutjanidae), jacks vary dramatically in food quality. Some are considered virtually inedible while others are

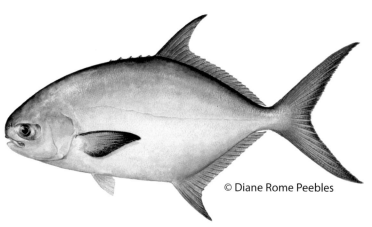

© Diane Rome Peebles

a renowned delicacy. As anyone who has eaten one will tell you, pompano falls under the later category. Pompano cooked (steamed) in paper is a popular recipe. Locally, fresh pompano at the island's many fine restaurants is always a delicious treat. If there is one fish you should try dining on while on Sanibel and Captiva, pompano is that fish.

☐ _____ ★**Permit** (*Trachinotus falcatus*) Nicknames: cobbler, Mexican pompano / Status: FL=stable, IUCN=NE / Life span: to 23 years / Length: 14-48 in. (35-122 cm) / Weight: 4-20 lb (1.8-9 kg); Florida state record: 56 lb 2 oz, IGFA: 56 lb 2 oz / Spawns: in the offshore waters / Found: CWFP, GB, OFFSR.

The permit is one of the most sought-after game fish in Florida. Anglers have been known to fly into the Keys from everywhere on the planet to catch one of these elusive members of the jack family. In the Florida Keys, the permit is stalked in flats boats while feeding over grass flats. It is most often taken with small crabs, but it is also targeted by fly fishermen, and, because of its cautious nature, is considered (along with bonefish) to be one of the hardest fish to catch on a fly. Because of its similar shape, the immature permit is readily

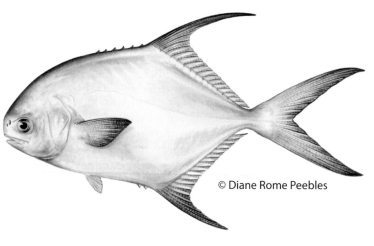

© Diane Rome Peebles

confused with the pompano. The best method of identifying one from the other is to remember that the belly of a pompano is yellow, and the back anal fin region of a permit is a distinct orange.

Locally the permit is almost never found in the back bay and estuaries. The most likely place to find large schools of permit are over the nearshore and offshore artificial reefs of Lee County. In the early spring though the summer permit congregate in large schools at the Doc Kline, Belton Johnson, Edison, and Pace's Place reefs. (For a complete list of these reefs go to http://www3.leegov.com/naturalresources/marine/autopage_T20_R6.htm.) Few anglers ever attempt to take them on a fly in deeper water, and the baits of choice are two- to three-inch crabs or fresh hand-picked shrimp.

The fish over these reefs tend to be large, averaging 15 to 35 pounds. Fluorocarbon leader, light tackle with good drag systems, and buried hooks are a must. The permit is a sight feeder and has sharp eyesight. Any sign of a hook and it will not bite. Extremely wary, the permit has to be approached slowly, and care must be taken not to spook the school.

Coming upon one of these schools, even if you are not trying to catch a permit, is a true marvel. They often number in the hundreds of fish per school, and their bright, silver sides flashing in the sunlight make for a fantastic sight.

In the wild the permit feeds on mollusks, crabs, and shrimp. It seldom feeds on small fish but has been known to do so on rare occasions. Once it reaches adult size, which can top 50 pounds, the only fish capable on feeding on permit are large sharks. A tireless fighter and considered good table fare, the permit will always be a top-notch catch in Florida waters.

★Spanish Mackerel (*Scomberomorus maculatus*)

Nicknames: none / Status: FL=stable, IUCN=NE / Life span: to 5 years / Length: 12-35 in. (30-91 cm) / Weight: 2-7 lb (.90-3.1 kg); Florida record: 12 lb, IGFA: 13 lb / Spawns: in the offshore waters / Found: SFP, CWFP, MZ, BB, REDP, GB, OFFSR.

Perhaps one of the most popular light tackle fish caught on Sanibel and Captiva, the Spanish mackerel has long been a favorite game fish throughout Florida. In the spring and fall large schools of Spanish mackerel can be seen from the beaches and off of either side of the causeway. Prone to jumping completely out of the water when feeding on anchovies and smaller minnows, it slashes across the water and is easy to identify because of its long body and deeply forked tail.

The Spanish mackerel ranges from Canada to the Yucatan. It feeds almost exclusively on small fish but will also take shrimp and squid. It has

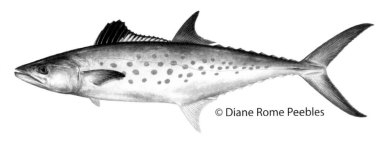

© Diane Rome Peebles

sharp teeth, and a foot of light wire leader (#2-#3 wire) is recommended, as the fish can cut through monofilament line in an instant. The Spanish mackerel is a strong fighter for its size. It makes great table fare if eaten fresh. Because its flesh is oily it does not freeze well.

Two of the best places to catch Spanish mackerel are the Sanibel fishing pier and the causeway pier. Free-lined herring, no larger than two inches, or small shrimp are the best baits to use. Use little (quarter-ounce split shot sinker) or no weight as the Spanish mackerel is not a bottom feeder, preferring to feed in the top half of the water column. Silver spoons and small white buck-tail jigs also work. The Spanish mackerel is fed upon by dolphins, sharks, cobia, tarpon, and its larger cousin, the king mackerel.

☐ _____ ★**King Mackerel** (*Scomberomorus cavalla*) Nicknames: kingfish, smoker / Status: FL=stable, ICUN=NE / Life span: to 14 years / Length: 2-4 ft (.60-1.2 m) / Weight: 5-20 lb (2.25-11.8 kg); Florida record: 90 lb, IGFA: 90 lb / Spawns: in the offshore waters / Found: SFP, CWFP, REDP, GB, OFFSR.

The king mackerel is an important commercial, as well as recreational fish. Literally millions of dollars are spent on international kingfish tournaments from the Carolinas to Brazil. In the Caribbean and South America the kingfish is considered the fish of choice when preparing çeviche, a Peruvian dish using raw fish that "cook" in lemon and lime juices. Commercially it is often salted, canned, or served as steak. Because of its oily flesh it should be eaten fresh. Freezing turns its flesh to a fishy-tasting mush.

The king mackerel is a fast and furious fighter. It strikes with amazing speed and has been

© Diane Rome Peebles

documented at speeds in excess of 50 miles per hour. Wire is mandatory as the kingfish has teeth that rival a barracuda's. A favorite method of catching a "smoker king" is slow trolling a blue runner over the offshore reefs in 20 to 50 feet of water. Because of its tremendous strikes, drags must be set feather light (two to three pounds of drag pressure), or the line will break instantly.

Other methods of taking the kingfish include the use of large diving plugs, silver spoons, and trolled surface baits. Large runs of king mackerel pass just a few miles off of Captiva every spring and fall during its annual migration; when running, this fish can be caught nonstop. Before the advent of spotting planes and large purse seines king mackerel schools would sometimes extend for five or six miles. Commercial limits have greatly aided in the return of this large predatory fish.

The kingfish feeds on everything in its way. It targets offshore schools of Spanish sardines all the way up to Spanish mackerel. Mature kingfish are taken by bottlenose dolphins and sharks.

Little Tunny (*Euthynnus alletteratus*) Nicknames: bonito, little tuna, false albacore / Status: FL=stable, ICUN=NE / Life span: to 10 years / Length: 14-36 in. (35-91 cm) / Weight: 3-7 lb (1.3-3.2 kg); Florida record: 27 lb, IGFA: 35 lb 2 oz / Spawns: in the offshore waters / Found: OFFSR.

Rarely seen in water less than 25 feet deep, the little tunny is the most common member of the tuna family found in the Gulf of Mexico. Farther offshore, starting in water 80 feet deep, the far more desirable blackfin tuna can be found, and farther still, starting around 100 miles offshore, the prized yellowfin tuna can be caught. Schools of little tunny rarely come close enough to shore to be seen from land.

The bonito, as it is often called, feeds predominantly on glass minnows and smaller schooling fish. As it feeds it slashes across the water, sometimes in schools numbering in the thousands. Offshore, these patches of feeding behavior look as if small sections of the gulf are in a rolling boil. Small white jigs no longer than two inches tossed into just such a feeding frenzy and retrieved as fast as possible will often result in hook-ups.

In the Keys the little tunny is a favorite bait for marlin and swordfish anglers. It was just such a bait that hooked the great marlin in Ernest Hemingway's novel, *The Old Man and the Sea*. Although a fun sport fish, the little tunny is seldom taken for

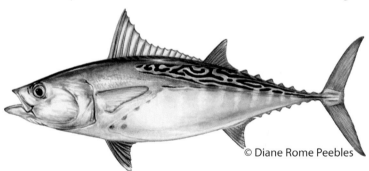

© Diane Rome Peebles

anything other than bait. Its flesh is dark red and has a strong flavor. As cut bait it is commonly used to catch shark, but if cut into one-inch cubes it will also take mangrove and yellowtail snapper. The little tunny roams most of the Atlantic, as well as the Mediterranean.

★**Tripletail** (*Lobotes surinamensis*) Nicknames: buoy fish, flasher, biajaca de la mar / Status: FL=stable, ICUN=NE / Life span: to 20 years / Length: 14-42 in. (.35-1.1 m) / Weight: 3-8 lb (1.3-3.6 kg); Florida record: 40 lb 13 oz, IGFA: 42 lb 5 oz / Spawns: in the offshore waters / Found: BB, REDP, GB, OFFSR.

A primitive fish and the only member of its family, Lobotidae, the tripletail has some unusual habits, making it one of the easiest fish to catch in the Gulf of Mexico. It is called buoy fish for good reason: it has the unusual habit of hanging around almost any floating or stationary object in the sea. Locally

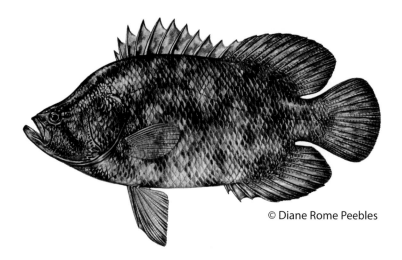

© Diane Rome Peebles

it is often targeted by anglers shortly after the stone-crab traps are set in mid-October every year.

Anglers run the traps with a light tackle rod in hand and a live well filled with shrimp. Once they discover a basking buoy fish, they turn the boat around, head upwind, and drift down unto the unsuspecting fish. A fresh shrimp cast out with no sinker within a few feet of this predator cannot be turned down. Once hooked, the tripletail is a powerful adversary. It dives, runs, and flops up and out of the water like a 10-pound pancake. The larger ones tend to wrap the trap line and escape, but the smaller ones come home for dinner.

A delicious eating fish, the tripletail, because it is so easy to catch, has been over-harvested by local anglers and is now a rare catch. Twenty years ago the tripletail was so plentiful that almost every buoy held one or more fish. Today, an angler might run 200 traps before spotting one. Ten years ago there were no size or catch limits on tripletail, which didn't help the survival rate. Recently Florida Fish and Wildlife adopted both slot and take limits on tripletail.

The tripletail eats small fish, shrimp, and crabs. It is often too large to be eaten by anything other than sharks and goliath grouper. A solitary wanderer, its range is worldwide in tropical waters.

❐ _____ ★**Sheepshead** (*Archosargus probatocephalus*) Nicknames: convict fish, sheephead / Status: FL=stable, ICUN=NE / Life span: to 25 years / Length: 10-24 in. (25-60 cm) / Weight: 1-4 lb (.45-1.8 kg); Florida record: 15 lb 2 oz, IGFA: 21 lb 4 oz / Spawns: in the inshore waters / Found: SFP, CWFP, MZ, BB, REDP, GB, OFFSR.

The sheepshead is a very popular game fish on Sanibel and Captiva. One reason is that the sheepshead fishery coincides with the arrival of the winter residents. During the warmer summer months the sheepshead is a rare catch, because most of the fish head to the deeper, cooler waters offshore. In the

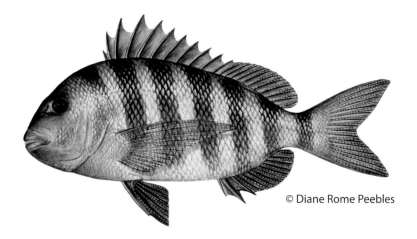

© Diane Rome Peebles

wintertime large numbers return and congregate along pilings, bridges, ledges, and reefs where they can be readily targeted.

Knowing the fish is down there and catching one are two different things, however. There is an old island saying about catching sheepshead: "You have to set the hook just before they bite!" The sheepshead is a notorious bait stealer, and time and again a clever "convict fish" will pick the shrimp off your hook before you have any chance of catching it. A good way to fool the sheepshead is by using a #4 or #5 hook, light 20-pound fluorocarbon leader, and small pieces of shrimp that totally bury the hook. The mouth of a sheepshead is incredibly hard, and looks similar to the mouth of a sheep—hence, the name. Because of this, setting a hook into this fish is problematic.

The sheepshead feeds on oysters, shellfish, barnacles, shrimp, and crabs. Its strong teeth and hard mouth are capable of breaking barnacles into pieces, after which it eats the living organism inside. It never eats minnows.

It is preyed upon, especially as juveniles, by a wide variety of finfish, including snook, redfish, tarpon, and sharks. The sheepshead ranges from the Carolinas to the northern coastline of Brazil. It is a delicious eating fish with white, firm meat. Its black and white markings are the reason for the nickname convict fish.

❒ _____ ★**Cobia** (*Rachycentron canadum*) Nicknames: ling, crab eater, sergeant fish, lemon fish, bonita, black salmon / Status: FL=stable, ICUN=NE / Life span: to 15 years / Length: 2.5-6.5 ft (76-200 cm) / Weight: 12-90 lb (5.4-41 kg); Florida record: 130 lb 1 oz, IGFA: 135 lb 9 oz / Spawns: in offshore waters / Found: SFP, CWFP, BB, REDP, GB, OFFSR.

A worldwide wanderer, the cobia can be found cruising in almost every tropical and subtropical ocean in the world. Although it seldom jumps, the cobia is considered one of the strongest and most tenacious fighting fish in the world, with battles between large fish and angler sometimes lasting hours. Lacking a swim bladder, the cobia behaves much like a shark in that it is constantly in motion. It is the only known member of the family

Rachycentron, although it may be distantly related to remoras (aka shark suckers).

© Diane Rome Peebles

The cobia is most often found during spring and fall migrations up to and back from the northern reaches of the gulf. Like the tripletail, the cobia is often fond of hanging around marine buoys, channel markers, bridges, and other structures. There it lies in hiding and ambushes prey such as crabs, crustaceans, minnows, and other finfish. A mature cobia weighs more than 50 pounds and has few natural predators aside from large sharks, but juvenile cobias are preyed upon by large dolphins, porpoise, goliath grouper, and other big fish.

Catching a cobia almost always requires stout tackle and heavy leader. Line test should be a minimum of 20 pounds, leader test 60 pounds or more, and number 5/0-7/0 hooks are advisable. The cobia lacks teeth so a wire leader is unnecessary. The Sanibel fishing pier and the causeway pier are likely spots to target cobia, especially in the spring and fall. Cobia also congregate over the numerous artificial reefs offshore and can sometimes be found cruising the back bays and estuaries, often in pairs.

This is not a common fish to encounter but a magnificent fighter once hooked. Its meat is highly prized and considered by many chefs to be one of the most desirable fish to cook because it is very firm and grills well. The cobia has a large, thick bloodline that must be completely removed before eating, as it will give the meat an unpleasant taste.

❏ _____ ★**Gulf Flounder** (*Paralichthys albigutta*) Nicknames: flounder, flatfish / Status: FL=stable, IUCN=NE / Life span: to 5 years / Length: 12-27 in. (30-71 cm) / Weight: 1-3 lb (.45-1.4 kg); Florida record: 20 lb 9 oz, IGFA: 20 lb 9 oz / Spawns: in the offshore waters / Found: SFP, CWFP, MZ, BB, REDP, GB, OFFSR.

The gulf flounder, or flounder as it is more often called, is not a common catch on Sanibel or Captiva. It prefers the cooler waters of the northern gulf. The world record was taken in Nassau

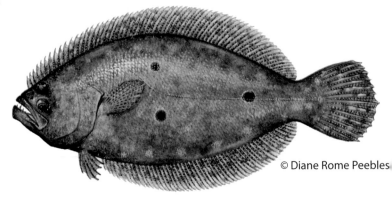

© Diane Rome Peebles

Sound in northeast Florida, in 1975. When caught locally, the flounder seldom exceeds 16 inches in length and tends to weigh little more than a pound.

The flounder can also be found offshore in depths of up to 400 feet. It is in the deeper water where anglers find larger specimens. This fish is unusual looking in that both eyes are on one side of its body. Perhaps even more unusual, when it is born the flounder resembles any other small fish larva, but shortly after it matures enough to take up its life along the bottom, one eye migrates to the upper side of the body, and the bottom side, which rests on the sand, is left sightless.

A delicious eating fish, the flounder is more often than not an accidental fish caught when fishing for sheepshead, seatrout, and other species. It is a bottom dweller and is most often hooked with minnows or shrimp sitting on the bottom. The flounder will sometimes take jigs and on very rare occasions strikes a slowly retrieved lure. It is preyed upon by stingrays, nurse sharks, snook, and grouper. It ranges from New England to the upper Caribbean.

> ☐ _____ ★**Gray Snapper** (*Lutjanus griseus*) Nicknames: mangrove snapper, snapper / Status: FL=stable, ICUN=NE / Life span: to 21 years / Length: 10-30 in. (25-75 cm) / Weight: 0.75-14 lb (.34-6.3 kg); Florida record: 17 lb, IGFA: 17 lb / Spawns: in the offshore waters / Found: SFP, CWFP, MZ, BB, REDP, GB, OFFSR.

The gray, or mangrove snapper as it is often called, is one of the most populous game fish in the Gulf of Mexico. Almost every artificial-reef census conducted has

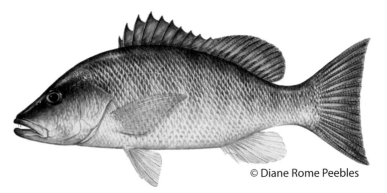

© Diane Rome Peebles

recorded this fish, sometimes in staggering numbers. The story is the same inshore: the mangrove snapper can be found under almost every dock and bridge, along the deeper cuts of tidal rivers, and in all the passes.

Although the mangrove snapper is the only local inshore species, the offshore waters hold additional snapper species including mutton, dog, lane, vermillion, red, yellowtail, and cubera. The cubera is the largest member of the snapper family with the state record standing at 116 pounds.

The snapper taken inshore is generally less than 16 inches long. It readily takes to small pieces of shrimp, cut bait, or squid. It responds well to chumming but this will also bring in unwanted fish such as catfish and jack. Light tackle with fluorocarbon leader (15-pound test) and small hooks (#2-3) work best. Avoid heavy sinkers and use small split shot weights as the mangrove snapper will readily come up into the water column.

Offshore the best way to target the larger snapper is by fishing at night. Chumming is mandatory, and medium spinning tackle is needed to pry the fish out of the wrecks and reefs it prefers. Catching snapper in the five-pound range is common in deeper water.

The snapper is a wary fish. It feeds predominantly at night, and its vision in the daytime makes it difficult to fool. Any indication of a hook and line will give it lockjaw. At night it readily feeds on shrimp, crabs, small fish, and even plankton. It is heavily preyed upon by larger grouper, sharks, cobia, tarpon, and larger cubera snapper. The mangrove snapper is a good eating fish that also freezes well.

❑ _____ ★**Goliath Grouper** (*Epinephelus itajara*) Nicknames: jewfish, giant grouper, guasa / Status: FL=threatened (goliath grouper is a protected species), IUCN=CR / Life span: to 37 years / Length: 1-8 ft (.45-2.4 m) / Weight: 5-800 lb (2.25-362 kg); Florida record: 680 lb, IGFA: 680 lb / Spawns: in the offshore waters / Found: SFP, CWFP, MZ, BB, REDP, GB, OFFSR.

Only the great hammerhead shark is larger than this immense grouper. In the 1800s there were reported catches of goliaths that weighed an unbelievable 1,500 pounds! A goliath this size would be more than 10 feet long and capable of swallowing a 50-pound fish whole! Sadly, because of over-harvesting by spear fishermen using explosive power heads, the goliath grouper population in Florida's waters was brought to the brink of extinction. There is a **complete ban** on the taking of any goliath grouper, juvenile or adult, in the state of Florida. The IUCN (World Conservation Union) has recently placed the goliath grouper on its critically endangered list. In Florida the fish is recovering from decades of excessive fishing.

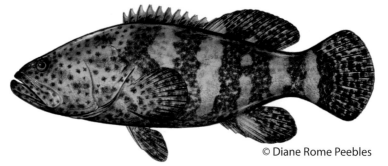
© Diane Rome Peebles

The goliath grouper is vulnerable to red tide and water pollution, and can sometimes be found washed up on the beach. It is sometimes caught by shark fishermen at night from the Sanibel and causeway fishing piers. The adult grouper has sharp spines in its first dorsal fin, which it erects when alarmed. Because of its size and power, the goliath should be handled with the utmost care.

Although many of the biggest goliaths are found well offshore, it is almost as common inshore. A large school of goliaths is known to live under the causeway spans, though catching one on normal tackle is impossible. Catch-and-release fishing for goliath grouper should be discouraged because of possible damage to the internal organs of the fish. It should never be taken up and out of the water, as doing so can cause serious injury or death to the fish.

The goliath eats almost anything it wants to eat or can catch. Its primary food is crab, fish, octopus, and slower-moving bottom fish such as burrfish, toadfish, lizardfish, and stingray. Underwater it makes a loud, booming noise when approached; this is believed to be a warning to anyone or anything getting too close.

Today, because of its recovery, it is not at all uncommon to catch juvenile goliath grouper inshore. It feeds in the mangroves, under docks and bridges, and is often taken when fishing for gag grouper. If caught, it must be released. If the fish has a tag, note the information on the tag, leave the tag on the fish, then safely return it to the water. Researchers at Florida State University are conducting a long-term study of the Florida goliath grouper population and can be notified of these tagged fish and any catch-and-release events by e-mailing the information to ifre@bio. fsu.edu.

★**Gag Grouper** (*Mycteroperca microlepis*) Nicknames: black grouper, gag, grass grouper / Status: FL=stable, IUCN=NE / Life span: to 27 years / Length: 12-45 in. (30-120 cm) / Weight: 3-50 lb; Florida record: 80 lb 6 oz IGFA: 80 lb 6 oz / Spawns: in the offshore waters exclusively on the shelf edge (50 to 150 m)/ Found: SFP, CWFP, MZ, BB, REDP, GB, OFFSR.

The only grouper common to the inshore waters, the gag grouper locally goes by the name black grouper. This is a misnomer because the real Florida black grouper (*Mycteroperca bonaci*) is not only never found inshore in Southwest Florida, it is a rare catch in the deeper, offshore waters as well. One reason for this misnomer is that the only other common grouper is the red grouper, which is seldom caught in water less than 30 feet deep, and people differentiate the two by their predominant coloration: red or black.

The gag grouper is a common catch inshore. An ambush predator, it often sits in deep cuts along the edge of mangroves waiting to rush

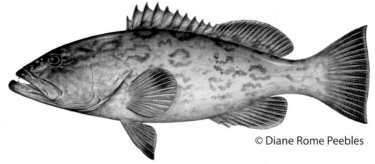

© Diane Rome Peebles

out and devour an unsuspecting shrimp or crab. It also roams the deeper grass flats, feeding on small minnows and crustaceans. A strong fighter when hooked, the gag will quickly wrap itself around mangrove roots or bury itself in rocks if given half a chance.

Starting in late October, large numbers of gag grouper come to within a few miles of Captiva in a prespawning aggregate. This seasonal migration runs through the end of January and can make for quite a day of nearshore angling. The bait of choice is pinfish or pigfish. The gag is fed upon by sharks and cobia. Inshore, juveniles are taken by a host of other predators, including herons and ospreys.

Juvenile Goliath Grouper
© Don DeMaria

□ _____ ★**Black Drum** (*Pogonias cromis*) Nicknames: drummer, sea drum / Status: FL=stable, IUCN=NE / Life span: to 43 years / Length: 14-66 in. (35-170 cm) / Weight: 4-35 lb (1.8-15.8 kg); Florida record: 96 lb IGFA: 113 lb 1 oz / Spawns: in the offshore waters / Found: SFP, CWFP, MZ, BB, REDP.

The black drum is a close cousin of the redfish and seatrout, all of which are members of the drum family. The major differences are size and feeding habits. The black drum grows to be enormous and is predominantly an inshore species, seldom found in water deeper than 35 feet. The redfish, on the other hand, migrates offshore as it approaches maturity and

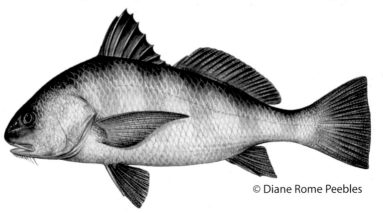

© Diane Rome Peebles

eventually leaves the estuaries altogether. The seatrout stays inshore but seldom grows much larger than 10 pounds.

The black drum, which is commonly found under the causeway, can readily top 50 pounds. It is a bottom feeder, dining largely on crabs, shrimp, and larger fish. The chin of the adult black drum is covered in small barbels. The juvenile shows a black and white convict pattern similar to the sheepshead, which it can easily be mistaken for during this phase of growth.

As a food fish, black drum is not a good choice. Its flesh is dark red and strongly flavored. As a sport fish, the black drum is incredibly boring. Once hooked it simply pulls straight down, has a short run, and never really puts up much of a fight. It is very much like pulling up a dozen pair of old boots at once. The young drum is taken by any number of fish, from snook to tarpon, while the mature drum is too big to be eaten by anything other than large sharks. It ranges from Nova Scotia to Argentina.

□ _____ ★**Tarpon** (*Megalops atlanticus*) Nicknames: silver king, silverfish / Status: FL=stable, IUCN=NE / Life span: to 55 years / Length: 45-90 in. (114-228 cm) / Weight: 50-150 lb (22.6-68 kg); Florida record: 243 lb IGFA: 283 lb 4 oz / Spawns: in the offshore waters / Found: SFP, CWFP, MZ, BB, REDP, GB, OFFSR.

The tarpon—along with the snook, redfish, and seatrout—is the most commonly sought-after fish in Southwest Florida. These four fish form the backbone of many of the area's fishing tournaments, and catching all four in one day is

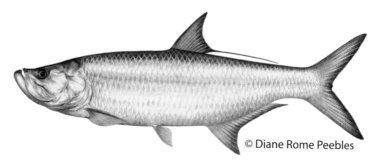

© Diane Rome Peebles

considered an inshore grand slam. Of the four, the most difficult to hang onto is the magnificent silver king—the tarpon.

Every spring, beginning in late March with the warming of the gulf waters, the first schools of tarpon arrive from the south, some from as far away as the west coast of Africa. Anglers, who have just recovered from last year's brawls, spool on fresh line, sharpen their circle hooks, and oil their reels in anticipation of fresh battles. Strictly a catch-and-release sport, tarpon fishing is a major draw for anglers the world over. From Boca Grande Pass to Bonita Springs, fishing guides and amateurs alike try their hands at catching one of these powerful adversaries.

The tarpon does not fight like any other fish. Once firmly hooked, it literally explodes with energy. Tales have been told of green fish (a term used by anglers to describe a fish that's freshly hooked) jumping into boats, breaking ankles and legs, then jumping back out. Lines part, leaders break, knots fail, rods snap, and guides wince as the gears in their reels start to make that crunching sound familiar to anyone who has tangled with a tireless silver king.

The tarpon loves to go airborne, and it is unusual not to have a big fish jump a half dozen times or more before it decides to sound. Some fish are never caught as the angler on the other end of the line gives up before the tarpon does. Fights can last for hours, testing the mettle of angler and fish. Hooking, then landing, then safely releasing a tarpon is an adventure you will never forget.

Anglers use heavy tackle, with a minimum of 80-pound monofilament leader, 5/0 to 7/0 circle hooks and a variety of baits to hook the tarpon. Pinfish or greenback tossed in front of a school with a stout spinning outfit is a favorite, while bottom fishing with boat rods and cut mullet or catfish tails is another. There are dozens of different techniques to get a silver king to bite, but it's when you finally touch the leader and release the fish that teaches you just how difficult catching one of these creatures can be.

By June the tarpon run starts to dissipate. By this time the fish can be found spawning in water 300 feet deep, due west of the passes it abandons. The larvae return to the estuaries on the incoming tides and hide in the safety of the gnarled roots of the red mangrove, waiting a year or more before venturing into deeper water. Two- to three-foot tarpon can sometimes be found along the spillways of the "Ding" Darling refuge.

The tarpon feeds on a wide variety of animals. In Boca Grande Pass it feasts on tiny pass crabs, each weighing less than an ounce, often consuming hundreds of crabs a day. Along the beaches the tarpon will crash into balled schools of glass minnows, charging through them with its mouth wide open, taking in 20 or 30 minnows at a time, and repeating this process for hours on end. Other favorite prey is striped mullet, catfish, stone and blue crabs, menhaden, greenbacks, threadfin herring, and shrimp. The tarpon is capable of surviving in the hot, oxygen-poor gulf waters because of a primitive lung that allows it to gulp air. This is the reason the tarpon can often be spotted rolling on the surface.

A host of predators take young tarpon: pelicans, herons, osprey, larger tarpon, and alligators. Only bigger sharks are capable of tackling a mature tarpon, weighing 50 pounds or more. Two sharks in particular are famous for following schools of tarpon; the great hammerhead and the bull shark. Many stories have been told about Old Hitler, the 12-foot-plus hammerhead that is rumored to haunt Boca Grande Pass. An equal measure of tall tales have been told about 10-foot-plus bull sharks biting hooked fish a few miles off of Tarpon Beach on Sanibel.

☐ _____ ★**Snook** (*Centropomus undecimalis*) Nicknames: linesiders, robalo, sergeant fish / Status: FL=stable, IUCN=NE / Life span: to 7 years / Length: 12-40 in. (30-101 cm) / Weight: 2-25 lb (.90-11.3 kg); Florida record: 44 lb 3 oz, IGFA: 53 lb 10 oz / Spawns: in the inshore waters / Found: SFP, CWFP, MZ, BB, REDP, GB, OFFSR.

A magnificent game fish, the snook is not only exciting to catch, but also beautiful in design. It has a long, thin body with a distinctive black stripe running along

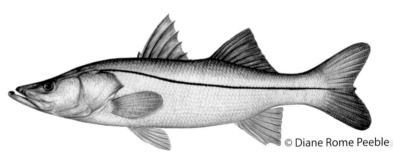

© Diane Rome Peeble

the lateral line the length of its body. This solitary line gives it the nicknames: sergeant fish and linesider. Its lower jaw has a clear underbite, allowing the snook to feed on surface minnows and lures.

In the late spring and summer, the large female snook moves into the passes to spawn. Some of these fish top 40 pounds and are all but impossible to land in the tangled root system of the tidal creeks. When hooked, the snook is just about as frenetic as the tarpon. It jumps, twists, and dives, but it is most famous for heading straight toward the oyster-covered roots of the mangroves, which can cut fishing line faster than a razor blade.

The snook ranges from Rio de Janeiro, Brazil, to North Carolina. A good time to spot a large snook is during a strong winter cold front. It is a tropical species and cannot tolerate cold water. When the water temperature drops below 56 degrees Fahrenheit, snook begin to expire. Severe cold snaps have been known to kill thousands of snook locally. During these cold snaps the snook seeks shelter in the warmer canal systems and under boats and docks in marinas, where it lies dormant. Before it became a game fish, islanders used to scoop snook up with large nets for dinner.

Snook   © Lorraine Sommer

The snook is predominantly an inshore fish, although very large specimens have been caught on the nearshore reefs located in less than 40 feet of water. It feeds on threadfin herrings, scaled sardines, pinfish, grunts, shrimp, and crabs. It readily takes surface lures such as Zaraspooks and slow-sinking Mirrorlures, as well as silver and gold spoons. There is possibly no more exciting strike than a 20-pound snook inhaling a surface lure on a calm summer evening in the back bay.

Bottlenose dolphins, sharks, and cobia prey upon the snook. Immature snook are taken by ospreys, herons, and egrets. Because of declining stocks of this much-desired game fish, strict regulations govern its harvesting, including a special snook stamp. Before targeting this exciting game fish, check for the latest updates at www.myfwc.com/RULESANDREGS/SaltwterRules.

❏ _____ ★**Red Drum** (*Sciaenops ocellatus*) Nicknames: redfish, channel bass / Status: FL=stable, IUCN=NE / Life span: to 50 years / Length: 12-40 in. (30-101 cm) / Weight: 2-25 lb (.90-11.3 kg); Florida record: 52 lb 5 oz, IGFA: 94 lb 2 oz / Spawns: in the nearshore waters / Found: SFP, CWFP, MZ, BB, REDP, GB, OFFSR.

The redfish is an easy fish to identify because of the characteristic single black spot at the base of its tail. Sometimes there is more than one spot, and a few local fishing tournaments have a category for bringing in the redfish with the most tail spots.

A popular game fish, the redfish is targeted in the winter months on the grass flats where it can often be seen tailing, a behavior typified by the redfish rooting about for crabs and crustaceans in shallow water, causing the large caudal fin to lift clear out of the water. For light spinning and fly fishermen, a tailing redfish is a dream come true.

The redfish caught in the mangroves and local passes are all juveniles. Once it reaches 30 inches (g e n e r a l l y around 4 years of age), it leaves the inshore

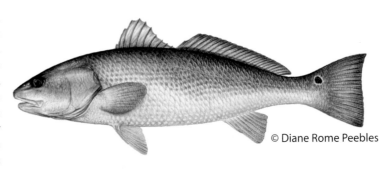

© Diane Rome Peebles

waters to join large schools of offshore fish commonly called ocean-running reds. In the late fall these ocean reds have been known to come close to Redfish Pass; they have also been caught at the Sanibel fishing pier. Because of the slot limits, keeping one of these monsters is illegal, but it is an exciting catch-and-release fish. One such redfish, weighing just shy of 100 pounds, set the world record in 1984 off of Avon, North Carolina.

The redfish is predominantly a bottom feeder but has been known to take surface lures as well. It feeds on shrimp, crabs, and a variety of minnows. The Spanish sardine cut into one-inch pieces is a favorite bait of fishing guides hunting redfish. As juveniles they are preyed upon by snook, ospreys, herons, egrets, and otters. As adults only porpoise, sharks, and goliath grouper are capable of taking them. Although a popular game fish, the redfish is more renowned for its long runs and steady fights; it seldom breaks the surface as do tarpon and snook.

❏ _____ ★**Spotted Seatrout** (*Cynoscion nebulosus*) Nicknames: seatrout, speckled seatrout, weakfish / Status: FL=stable, IUCN=NE / Life span: to 18 years / Length: 10-26 in. (25-66 cm) / Weight: 1-4 lb (.45-1.80 kg); Florida record: 17 lb 6 oz, IGFA: 17 lb 7 oz / Spawns: in the inshore waters / Found: SFP, CWFP, MZ, BB, REDP, GB.

Perhaps the most frequently caught sport fish in Lee County, the spotted seatrout is ubiquitous once you start drifting over three- to five-foot-deep grass flats. It is easiest to catch using a popping cork with light leader and a small #2 or #3 hook and a fresh, live shrimp. Once you discover a school, you can catch 50 of these fish in an afternoon.

The seatrout is not a strong fighting fish, but the larger s p e c i m e n s— those longer than 20 i n c h e s—w i l l put up quite a

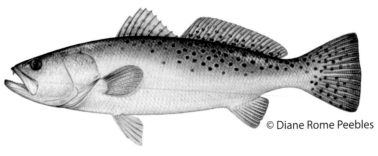

© Diane Rome Peebles

fight. It is a popular eating fish, although the flesh is fairly soft and does not freeze well.

The seatrout lives out its entire life in the estuaries. It feeds on shrimp, crabs, small fish, sea worms, and other crustaceans. It is eaten by snook, redfish, cobia, sharks, bottlenose dolphins, and grouper, as well as ospreys, herons, and cormorants. It can often be seen swimming along the beaches in the summer months and is easily recognized by its trout-like colors and numerous black dots across the back half of its body. The seatrout is a close relative of both redfish and black drum, although it does not really look like either of these other species.

Sharks and Rays

□ _____ **Southern Stingray** (*Dasyatis americana*) Nicknames: stingray, whip stingray / Status: FL=stable, IUCN=DD / Life span: to 15 years / Length: 3-5 ft across (.91-1.5 m) / Weight: 20-50 lb (9-22 kg); Florida record: n/a, IGFA: vacant, but known to grow to 214 lb / Found: SFP, CWFP, MZ, BB, REDP, GB, OFFSR.

Although fatalities are extremely rare, the poisonous barbs of stingrays have been known to kill people. The most famous incident was the untimely death of Australian crocodile hunter Steve Irwin, who was stabbed by a stingray while filming on the Great Barrier Reef. Irwin made the fatal mistake of pulling the barb out, leaving a hole where it had pierced his heart. A similar incident occurred in Florida in 2006 when an 81-year-old man was stung in the chest by a stingray. The medics left the barb in until it was later removed from his heart by surgeons. The victim survived.

The stingray is normally docile and will flee almost any disturbance. In the Cayman Islands, as well as Antigua, several dive sites are designated for swimming with stingrays. Exercise caution when encountering these cartilaginous relatives of the shark, as larger

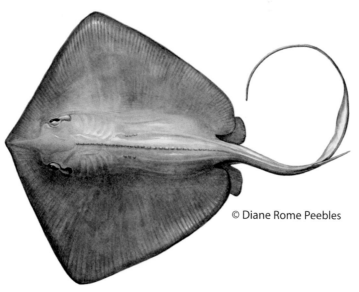

© Diane Rome Peebles

members of this species have been known to be aggressive, and the barbed tail is a formidable weapon. Although most stingrays found in and around Sanibel and Captiva are less than 50 pounds, the stingray can grow to be seven feet across and weigh more than 200 pounds.

Every spring and summer children and adults are "stung" by stingrays all along the gulf coast. The warm gulf waters bring mating rays into the shallows along the beaches where the unsuspecting victim may step on one. The best method of avoiding this painful mistake is by shuffling your feet as you enter and leave the water. Locally, this is known as the "Sanibel shuffle."

Getting stabbed by a stingray is extremely painful. It has been compared with having a hot andiron stuck into your foot or leg. Immediate treatment includes application of near-scalding water, which eases the pain by denaturing the complex venom protein covering the barb. Immediate medical attention should follow since the wound needs to be thoroughly cleaned to prevent infection. Further exploration of the injury is often needed to remove any embedded barb fragments. If you or someone you are with is injured by a stingray, get to a clinic or hospital immediately. Do not attempt to remove the barb, which generally breaks off at impact, as it may have penetrated a large vein or artery.

The stingray is a bottom feeder, consuming crustaceans, mollusks, and annelids such as tube worms. Young stingrays are born live and are heavily preyed upon by larger fish such as snook and tarpon. Adult stingrays are a favorite food for the larger sharks, including bulls, lemons, and hammerheads. Stingray meat is consumed in Singapore and Malaysia, where it is barbecued. It is also eaten in Iceland, where it is pickled. Although not authenticated, stingray wings are said to be an illegal substitute for scallops at some restaurants. The texture and flavor of the meat are very similar to shark meat.

☐ _____ **Cow-nose Ray** (*Rhinoptera bonasus*) Nicknames: cowfish, lotus of the sea / Status: FL=stable, IUCN=NT / Life span: to 15 years / Length: 25-36 in. across (63-89 cm) / Weight: 26-36 lb (11.7-16 kg); Florida record: n/a, IGFA: not listed but rays have been recorded up to 50 lb / Reproduces: live pups in the nearshore waters / Found: SFP, CWFP, BB, REDP, GB, OFFSR.

Courtesy Wikipedia Commons

This ray is a common sighting in the early spring from the causeway where schools appear to be flying through the clear aquamarine waters. When mating it sometimes congregates along the beaches where it is confused with its close cousin, the stingray. The easiest method of telling these two similar-size species apart is the squared front of the cow-nose ray and the much more angular, almost pyramid-shaped front of the stingray.

Although the cow-nose ray has a barb, its venom in nowhere near as poisonous as the stingray, and it seldom stings anyone. Because it is almost always swimming, the chances of stepping on one are slim. For people who have been barbed, the symptoms are reported to be similar to a bee sting.

Swimming as deep as 70 feet, schools of cow-nose rays numbering more than 10,000 have been verified. It ranges from the western tip of Africa, to the Chesapeake, down through northern Brazil.

The cow-nose ray gives birth to three to six live pups in the late summer. The young rays are preyed upon by cobia, snook, and larger grouper. Adult cow-nose rays are a favorite food for large sharks, including hammerheads, lemons, and bulls. It has no food value and is considered a nuisance fish in the Chesapeake Bay area where it feeds prolifically on oysters. It also feeds on clams, mussels, crustaceans, and crabs.

🗌 _____ **Spotted Eagle Ray** (*Aetobatus narinair*) Nicknames: eagle ray, leopard ray, white-spotted ray / Status: FL=stable, IUCN=NT / Life span: to 30 years / Length: 3-7 ft across (.91-2.13 m) / Weight: 25-80 lb (11.3-36 kg); Florida record: n/a, IGFA: vacant, but these rays can reach lengths of 8.2 feet and weigh in excess of 500 lb / Found: SFP, CWFP, BB, REDP, OFFSR.

The spotted eagle ray is sometimes seen launching six feet or more out of San Carlos Bay. No one understands why this species is so prone to jumping, but the speculation is that it has something to do with parasites. This jumping behavior was responsible for a freak accident in the Florida Keys in March 2008. A 55-year-old Michigan woman was riding on the bow of her boat off Marathon when a 75-pound eagle ray rocketed out of the water and hit her in the face and chest, resulting in a fatal blunt force trauma to the skull. Several other eagle ray collisions have been verified, but this is the only one that resulted in death.

Although not called a stingray, the spotted eagle ray nonetheless wields a venomous barb. It rarely comes close enough to shore to be stepped on. The tail of the spotted eagle ray can exceed the length of its body, at times making the tip-to-

© John Norton, Courtesy Wikipedia Commons

tip length more than 16 feet (5 meters). It is seldom eaten but is sometimes taken by trawlers and used as fishmeal. Its population worldwide is in serious decline, although the cause for this decline is unknown. The spotted eagle ray is listed as near threatened by the IUCN.

The eagle ray wanders most of the world's tropical and subtropical oceans but is seldom seen more than a few hundred miles from shore. It has a very unusual diet that includes clams, sea urchins, whelks, oysters, and other mollusks. Its mouth has two bony plates capable of crushing these animals and extracting the meat while removing and discarding the hard shell portion prior to ingestion. The eagle ray is similar to the stingray in that its only real predators are large sharks, including the great hammerhead, bull, and great white.

⬜ _____ ★**Nurse Shark** (*Ginglymostoma cirratum*) Nicknames: cat shark, carpet shark / Status: FL=stable, IUCN=NE / Life span: to 25 years / Length: 4-9 ft (1.2-2.7 m) / Weight: 60-200 lb (27-90 kg); Florida record: n/a, IGFA: 263 lb 8 oz / Reproduces: in the nearshore waters by laying egg cases / Found: SFP, CWFP, MZ, BB, REDP, GB, OFFSR.

Although the nurse shark looks formidable, it poses little danger to humans. It lacks large teeth, instead relying on rows of smaller teeth that crush its prey instead of biting through it. It is a beautiful fish, with a large head and attractive light brown skin. It is capable of sitting motionless on the bottom, which can sometimes startle local snorkelers. It generally swims away when approached but should be observed with caution since it can deliver a nasty, vice-grip like bite.

The nurse shark is rarely found along the beaches. It inhabits the back bay and is a fairly common by-catch of inshore and nearshore tarpon fisherman. It is never targeted for catch-and-release fishing

© Lorraine Sommer

because its fight is anything but dramatic. It basically comes up like an old boot, with short, slow runs, no aerial acrobatics whatsoever, and an end game that leaves the angler bored at best. No one harvests the nurse shark, not even for its fin. As a result the nurse shark is one of the least endangered of all the major sharks.

It is a nocturnal bottom feeder that dines on crabs, octopi, squid, and clams. It eats carrion and small finfish, but its mouth is too small to consume stingrays or larger fish such as grouper. Juvenile nurse sharks are preyed upon primarily by other more aggressive sharks such as tigers, bulls, lemons, and hammerheads. The adults, because of their size, are seldom targeted. It is common only to the western edge of Africa and the subtropical shores of North and South America, including the Mexican and California coastline.

◻ _____ ★**Bull Shark** (*Carcharhinus leucas*) Nicknames: cub shark, Zambezi shark, river whaler, tiburón / Status: FL=stable to slightly declining, IUCN=NT / Life span: to 32 years / Length: 3-11 ft (91-350 cm) / Weight: 50-350 lb (22.6-159 kg); Florida record: 517 lb, IGFA: 636 lb 14 oz / Reproduces: in the inshore waters / Found: SFP, CWFP, MZ, BB, REDP, GB, OFFSR.

In recent years the bull shark has replaced both the great white and the tiger shark as the most dangerous shark in the ocean. The reason is simple. The other two sharks prefer deeper, offshore waters while the bull shark spends most of its life in shallow, nearshore waters. It is the only saltwater species capable of living in both salt and freshwater environments. This adaptation has given it access to brackish and freshwater environments that would kill any of the other large shark species. It transitions from saltwater to freshwater through a complex osmotic system. The scientific term for this ability is euryhaline—the ability to tolerate wide ranges of salinity. The American and Indo-Pacific crocodiles have this same ability.

The bull shark inhabits all the tropical and subtropical oceans worldwide. It has also been reported some 2,200 miles up the Amazon River in Iquitos, Peru, and has been observed attacking juvenile hippos hundreds of miles up the Zambezi River in Africa.

Like all sharks, the bull shark seldom attacks people. There are confirmed fatalities in Florida attributed to bull sharks, but these are extremely rare. Your chances of getting hit by lightning are 1,000 times greater, and your chances of dying in an automobile accident are more than 10,000 times greater. When these rare attacks do occur, the bull shark bites but typically does not eat the victim. Only the tiger shark and oceanic white-tip have been verified to eat human flesh. The trouble is with the bull-shark bite itself, which is generally so devastating that without immediate medical attention, the victim bleeds to death.

Worldwide, 100 million sharks are killed every year, most for their fins. These make their way to China where they are the main ingredient in shark-fin soup. This single dish is responsible for one of the most ruthless slaughters of wildlife in the history of mankind. After the fins are removed with a finning knife, the live sharks are tossed back into the sea to drown. Annually, 10 people a year are killed by sharks. The ratio of mortality between people killing sharks and sharks killing people stands today at 10 million to one. This is not a sustainable or an honorable equation. Shark finning, like whale hunting, should be banned worldwide.

Sharks, whales, and dolphins are the ocean's top predators. They serve a vital role in the food chain by removing the sick, aged, and weak from the species they target. If a sick fish is allowed to survive in a school because there are no sharks available to remove it, the entire school can become sick and the loss is far graver than that of a single individual. Sharks cull the oceans of diseased or infirm animals helping to keep gene pools healthy. Without them the entire marine ecosystem is at risk.

The bull shark is a carnivore. It eats fish, other sharks, rays, and sea mammals including bottle-nosed and spotted dolphins, seabirds, mollusks, and crustaceans. It is sometimes killed by dolphins and killer whales, but a mature bull shark has few

Bull Shark   Courtesy Wikipedia Commons

wild predators willing to take it on. In the Zambezi River, the Nile crocodile has been known to attack and eat the bull shark.

In the waters around Sanibel and Captiva the bull shark is common. It can be found in the passes, off the Sanibel fishing pier, and in the back bay. It roams all the way up the Caloosahatchee River, and in all probability there are bull sharks living in Lake Okeechobee. After all, one was found living in Lake Michigan, having swum there via the Mississippi and the Chicago River.

Tarpon fishermen just a few miles off the beaches frequently encounter the bull shark, which is known to feed on exhausted, hooked tarpon. A large shark can generally eat a full-grown tarpon in three or four bites. If you happen to see one being caught off one of the island's fishing piers or from the beach, consider yourself blessed. This is a magnificent animal and nowhere near as dangerous as the person who reeled it in.

☐ _____ ★**Lemon Shark** (*Negaprion brevirostris*) Nicknames: requiem shark, lemons / Status: FL=stable, IUCN=NT (lower risk) / Life span: to 25 years / Length: 4-8 ft (121-242 cm) / Weight: 50-290 lb (22.6-132 kg); Florida record: 397 lb, IGFA: 385 lb / Reproduces: live pups in the nearshore waters / Found: SFP, CWFP, BB, REDP, GB, OFFSR.

Although the lemon shark can grow to 10 feet, it poses little threat to humans. The International Shark Attack files, located at the ichthyology department at the University of Florida, has recorded only 10 unprovoked attacks by lemon sharks (going back more than 100 years), and none of these attacks ever proved fatal.

The lemon shark is approaching near-threatened status chiefly as a result of commercial over-harvesting, with shark finning being the primary problem. Lemon shark meat is said to be excellent; its skin can be used for shark leather; and the liver pressed for vitamin oil. This combination of uses makes the lemon shark a highly prized target species and does not bode well for its future.

Around the islands catching a lemon shark is very common. Most are small, seldom measuring more than four or five feet long. The preferred bait for catching the lemon shark matches its diet: cut catfish, cut mullet, pinfish, and grunts. It also eats

© Terry Goss - Wikipedia Commons

porcupine fish, stingrays, crabs, pelicans, seabirds, and crayfish. Juvenile lemon sharks are targeted by bull sharks and larger finfish. Adult lemon sharks are rarely attacked by anything other than larger sharks.

☐ _____ ★**Blacktip Shark** (*Carcharhinus limbatus*) Nicknames: blacktip reef shark, black finned shark, guliman / Status: FL=stable, IUCN=NT / Life span: to 15 years / Length: 2.5-6 ft (76-182 cm) / Weight: 20-75 lb (9-34 kg); Florida record: 152 lb, IGFA: 270 lb 9 oz / Reproduces: live pups in the nearshore waters / Found: SFP, CWFP, BB, REDP, GB, OFFSR.

Pine Island Sound is one of Florida's major blacktip shark nurseries. This small, timid shark is a regular catch of inshore fishermen and considered to be one of the better eating sharks found in our local waters. There are 28 unprovoked blacktip shark attacks recorded in Florida, with no fatalities. The blacktip shark is not considered dangerous when compared with the bull, great white, and tiger sharks.

The blacktip is one of only a handful of animals known to be capable of parthenogenesis, allowing the female blacktip to give birth to pups without fertilization. The Nile monitor lizard, Komodo dragons, and bonnethead sharks are also capable of this highly unusual asexual reproduction. The reasons for this unusual ability are unclear.

The blacktip is considered a game fish by the IGFA. It makes long, quick runs, leaps out of the water frequently, and does not come to the boat easily. Wire is mandatory, as its sharp teeth will tear through monofilament leader in seconds. Unless taken for the dinner table, the blacktip, as well as all sharks, should never be lifted out of the water (especially vertically!). Its internal organs are not designed to withstand

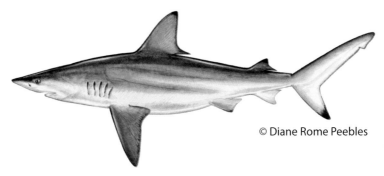

© Diane Rome Peebles

the forces of gravity for any length of time. Although holding one up high with a pair of Boca-grips might make for a great photo op, in all likelihood you are killing or seriously injuring the fish for a snapshot. If you are planning to release your fish, keep it in the water, take your picture, revive it if necessary by dragging it behind the boat, and set it free.

It is best to use nonstainless steel circle hooks (the kind that rust quickly) and either remove the hook (very carefully) or cut the wire as close to the hook as possible. The hook will rust away within a short time, and if the fish is never lifted out of the water, internal injuries will be avoided. Catch-and-release shark fishing can be a thrilling way to spend an evening to say the least.

The blacktip dines predominantly on fish. It takes menhaden, Spanish sardines, pinfish, grunts, catfish, mojarras, and triggerfish, as well as skates and rays. It is preyed upon, especially the pups, by finfish and most of the other sharks. The mortality rate for Pine Island Sound juvenile blacktips has been estimated to exceed 85 percent. Unlike most sharks, blacktips tend to stay close together, and once a school is located, the fishing can become quite frenetic.

☐ _____ ★**Bonnethead Shark** (*Sphyrna tiburo*) Nicknames: bonnet hammerhead, shovelhead, bonnetnose shark / Status: FL=stable, IUCN=LC / Life span: to 12 years / Length 1-3.5 ft (.45-1 m) / Weight: 3-14 lb (1.3-6.2 kg); Florida record: n/a, IGFA: 23 lb 12 oz / Reproduces: in the nearshore waters bearing five to nine live young / Found: SFP, CWFP, MZ, BB, REDP, GB, OFFSR.

The smallest shark found in the waters surrounding Sanibel and Captiva, the bonnethead seldom tops 15 pounds. It is the smallest member of the hammerhead family of sharks and is readily identified by its unusually shaped head.

It is too small to deliver a serious bite, and there is only one unprovoked bonnethead shark attack on record. Most bonnetheads are caught while anglers are targeting other species. It fights hard on light tackle but is not considered table fare.

Because of its small size the bonnethead has avoided the plague of finning. Throughout its range, which runs from northern South America to the Carolinas, as well as the southern California coast, the bonnethead population is not endangered.

The bonnethead feeds on clams, crustaceans, crabs, and some fish. It uses an electro-magnetic sensory mechanism, known as the ampullae of Lorenzini, to detect the minute electrical charges given off by living organisms. In essence, it is able to hunt by auras, which are the invisible e l e c t r i c a l fields radiated by all living things. When a bonnethead senses one of these fields buried in the

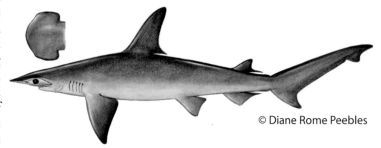

© Diane Rome Peebles

Bonnethead   © Lorraine Sommer

bottom, it bites down without knowing what creature lies below, be it a flounder or a scallop. This organ, which does not exist in humans, is effectively a sixth sense.

❑ _____ ★**Scalloped Hammerhead** (*Sphyrna lewini*) Nicknames: bronze hammerhead, kidney-headed shark, southern hammerhead / Status: FL=stable, IUCN=NT, lower risk / Life span: to 30 years / Length: 4-9 ft (1.2-2.75 m) / Weight: 60-350 lb (27-159 kg); Florida record: 991 lb, IGFA: n/a / Reproduces: in the inshore waters, giving birth to 12-38 live pups / Found: SFP, CWFP, BB, REDP, GB, OFFSR.

Very similar to the great hammerhead in size and appearance, the scalloped hammerhead differs only in the wave-like or scalloped pattern across the front of its large hammer-shaped head. Of the 10 species of hammerhead sharks worldwide, three are common to the waters around Sanibel and Captiva.

The range of both the scalloped and the great hammerhead covers all the major tropical and subtropical oceans and seas in the world. The exact function of the hammerhead's strangely shaped head is still being debated among marine biologists. With its eyes located at either end of the hammer, its stereoscopic vision is extraordinary, but other sharks do fine without this configuration, so that alone does not explain this adaptation.

The scalloped hammerhead sometimes schools in vast numbers. The seamounts located off Baja, Mexico, have recorded massive schools numbering in the thousands. While large enough to be a threat to man, hammerheads

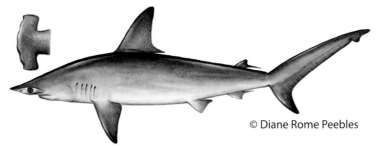

© Diane Rome Peebles

overall are not likely to attack. Worldwide there have been only 21 unprovoked attacks, resulting in two fatalities.

Locally the scalloped hammerhead is seldom found inshore. Like its larger cousin, the great hammerhead, it tends to stay well offshore where it is a fairly common by-catch of tarpon fishermen. Its flesh is edible, but it is not considered a good eating shark. Commercially it is killed for its fin, liver, and excellent hide. Most are taken by long-lining.

The hammerhead dines extensively on stingrays. One adult specimen that was killed for research had 50 stingray spines embedded in its stomach. It also eats barracuda, kingfish, dolphins, parrotfish, and blacktip sharks. Nothing preys on the adult scalloped hammerhead, but the pups are vulnerable to an array of predators, including other sharks.

> ☐_____ ⦿**Great Hammerhead** (*Sphyrna mokarran*) Nicknames: hammerhead shark, squat-headed hammerhead / Status: FL=stable, IUCN=E / Life span: to 30 years / Length: 5-12 ft (1.5-3.6 m) / Weight: 80-500 lb (36-226 kg); Florida record: 1,262 lb, IGFA: 1,262 lb (pending) / Reproduces: in the inshore waters bearing 6-42 live pups / Found: REDP, OFFSR.

The great hammerhead is the second-largest animal found in Southwest Florida, topped only by the docile manatee (which can weigh more than a ton). It could be argued that the great hammerhead is entitled to first place because this behemoth has been verified to grow to 20 feet. The world record great hammerhead was caught off of Boca Grande Pass in May 2006. The fish was 14 ft 6 inches in length and weighed 1,262 pounds (572 kg). A hammerhead shark measuring 20 feet could weigh twice as much since girth increases exponentially with length in sharks. The pending world-record Boca Grande hammerhead was three feet wide. It took Bucky Dennis of Port Charlotte five hours to land it. He was using a whole stingray for bait.

Courtesy Wikipedia Commons

Killing sharks this size is controversial, especially since the great hammerhead is listed as an endangered species by the IUCN. The Boca Grande hammerhead killed in 2006 was a female carrying 56 pups. Fortunately, most sharks anywhere near this size are released; unless an angler is prepared to do battle for hours on end with extremely rugged deep-sea tackle, a shark this size usually releases itself by either breaking the line or destroying the tackle.

There is little doubt that the appearance of this monster in late May coincided with the northern migration of the tarpon schools in Boca Grande. These massive great hammerheads have been seen swallowing 125-pound tarpon whole!

Since the great hammerhead is the largest predatory fish in the Gulf of Mexico, nothing attempts to kill the adults. The pups are preyed upon by goliath grouper, sharks and, cobia. The great hammerhead prefers deeper water and is seldom taken by hook and line off the beaches. It comes into Redfish Pass on occasion and is hooked quite frequently in the spring by tarpon fishermen two to five miles offshore from Sundial Beach Resort. Like the scalloped hammerhead, its range is circumglobal.

🐟 How to Catch and Release Saltwater Fish 🐟

- **Avoid using stainless steel hooks.** Use wire or other hooks that are quick to rust in the saltwater environment. The same applies to wire leaders.
- **Never try to pull out a hook that is lodged** in the fish gut or gills. It is better to cut the line as close as possible to the hook, then release the fish.
- **Use a hook-removing device** or long-handled pliers and try to remove the hook while the fish still in the water.
- **If you have to lift the fish out of the water, remove the hook quickly,** and immediately put the fish back into the water where it can breathe again.
- **Wet your hands before picking the fish up** to avoid removing the protective mucous coating many fish employ to fend off bacteria and parasites. Towels can be especially hard on fish as they tend to strip this mucous off much quicker than bare skin.
- **Avoid netting the fish if possible.** This can remove scales and damage fins, leaving the fish vulnerable to infection.
- **Don't let the fish flop around** on the boat or ground as it can injure itself or tire itself out to the point where it cannot be revived.
- **Bring the fish in quickly** and try not to "play them out," as this will tend to exhaust the fish and make it more vulnerable to predation when you do return it to the water.
- **Release the fish back into the water gently**; never toss it back in.
- **If necessary, revive the fish** after your hook has been removed by holding it gently and slowly idling the boat forward, or if you are on the beach, pulling the fish forward in a circle around you until enough water has passed through its gills to revive it.
- **If you are catching grouper** in deeper water and the fish is undersized, it is now mandatory to have a venting kit (a special, oversized hypodermic needle available at bait shops). Vent the fish properly before releasing it, as it more than likely has the bends and will not survive unless the gases built up in its swim bladder are released. Instructions for this procedure can be found online. Catch-and-release grouper or snapper fishing is not advisable since their mortality rate is too high to justify this kind of sport. Circle hooks are now mandatory for the catching of all reef fish.
- **When you do have to take a fish out of the water, do so quickly** and support the fish horizontally. Pulling large fish up and holding it vertically can dislodge its internal organs; though it might appear that the fish is fine when released, it often dies from these injuries a few days later. This is especially true for tarpon, permit, and large shark.

Freshwater Fish

☐ _____ **Mosquitofish** (*Gambusia holbooki*) Nicknames: gambusia, mosquito fish / Status: FL=stable, IUCN=LC / Life span: to 3 years / Length: 2-2.5 in. (5-6.35 cm) / Weight: n/a / Spawns: in all of the islands' lakes and ponds including brackish waters / Found: year-round, IW, MZ.

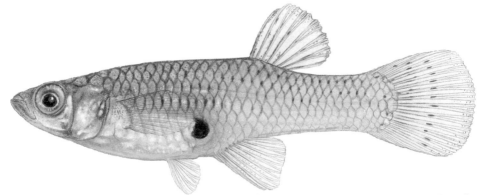

© Joe Tomelleri

Don't let its small size and quiet demeanor fool you: the mosquitofish is now believe to be the most common freshwater fish in the world. The reason for this lies in its preferred diet, which as its name implies, is the larval and pupal stages of mosquitoes. In an effort to control mosquito populations, this fish has been introduced into Australia, Southeast Asia, Asia, India, Europe, and Africa. Sadly it has done no better in these locations at eradicating mosquitoes than has the indigenous species it displaced. In Australia, for example, the introduction of the mosquitofish resulted in the extinction of the native rainbow fish, with no substantial change in the mosquito population.

The mosquitofish is a survivor. It can thrive in water twice as saline as ocean water, as well as in freshwater systems. It is able to survive for brief periods in stagnant waters as warm as 107 degrees Fahrenheit (42 C) with oxygen levels so low that most fish would expire within minutes. It has a tremendous reproduction rate, with isolated populations increasing from 7,000 to 120,000 fish in just five months.

On Sanibel and Captiva the mosquitofish has been introduced into every open body of water available. The best place to see mosquitofish is along the south side of Wildlife Drive in The "Ding" Darling refuge, where it is often found in large schools up against the shoreline. Native to this region, the mosquitofish has not caused the same problems here as it has in Australia, New Zealand, and Tasmania, where as an invasive species it has displaced or eradicated native frogs, insects, and other larval-eating fishes.

The mosquitofish is taken by snook, redfish, bass, bream, and a host of other fresh and saltwater fish. It is also heavily preyed upon by herons and egrets. It eats larva but will also dine on frog eggs, fish spawn, and aquatic insects.

☐ _____ **Longnose Gar** (*Lepisosteus osseus*) Nicknames: garfish, gar / Status: FL=stable, IUCN= NE / Life span: to 36 years / Length: 1.4-3 ft (45-91 cm) / Weight: 2-6 lb (.90-2.7 kg) / Spawns: in the freshwater lakes and ponds, as well as throughout the Sanibel River / Found: year-round, IW.

© Joe Tomelleri

The maximum published weight of this gar is more than 50 pounds, but on Sanibel a longnose gar larger than five or six pounds is rare. Its close cousin, the alligator gar, is one of the largest freshwater fish in North America, with some weighing more than 300 pounds. The gar is easy to identify and not all that difficult to locate. The hardest part about finding a freshwater gar on the islands is finding water clear enough to spot one.

Look for gar in the Sanibel River or in the larger ponds in the Bailey Tract. The gar is not considered a game fish in Florida and for good reason. There is some question about its meat being toxic, and gar roe is poisonous. It is a voracious predator, feeding on mosquitofish, bluegill, sunfish, and small bass. It also eats frogs, tadpoles, and aquatic insects, and will even take small birds and mammals when possible. The gar, along with the largemouth bass, is the top freshwater predator on the islands. Because of its toxicity it is seldom preyed upon by birds; only the alligator appears to be willing to eat one.

☐ _____ ★**Bluegill** (*Lepomis macrochirus*) Nicknames: sunfish, bream, panfish / Status: FL=stable, IUCN=LC / Life span: to 10 years / Length: 5-15 in. (12-36 cm) / Weight: .75-2 lb (340-907 g); Florida record: 2 lb 15 oz, IGFA: 4 lb 12 oz / Spawns: in the freshwater lakes and ponds, as well as the Sanibel River / Found: year-round, IW.

Bluegill and redbreast sunfish are sometimes referred to as bream (pronounced brim) in Florida. The term is a colloquial name for a variety of sunfish species throughout the South and is more of a general term than a reliable species identification. There are 22 species of sunfish in Florida waters, with several of them readily found on Sanibel. This family also includes the popular game fish, crappie, which is not known to exist on either island.

The bluegill is a popular game fish throughout the Sunshine State but is rarely fished for on Sanibel or Captiva. It can grow up to a pound or better on the islands, and the state record is close to three pounds. A good eating fish, it is best sautéed, hence, the nickname panfish. As a game fish it is subject to freshwater licensing and limits, but the current limit on Lake Okeechobee is 100 bluegills per person per day, so it is clearly not endangered.

The bluegill feeds on worms, aquatic insects, larvae, and small minnows. It is a favorite food for anhingas, great blue herons,

© Joe Tomelleri

turtles, alligators, otters, ospreys, and largemouth bass. Look for it hovering over nesting sites in the spring and summer where it congregates to spawn.

☐ _____ ★**Redbreast Sunfish** (*Lepomis auritus*) Nicknames: sunfish, bream, panfish / Status: Fl=stable, IUCN=LC / Life span: to 5 years / Length: 8-12 in. (20-30 cm) / Weight: .50-1 lb (226-452 g); Florida record: 2 lb 1 oz, IGFA: 2 lb 1oz / Spawns: in all the islands' lakes and ponds, as well as the Sanibel River / Found: year-round, IW.

Because it is smaller than the bluegill, the redbreast sunfish is not as targeted as the bluegill. Most redbreasts seldom exceed one pound, and it takes a considerable number of them to make a meal. Few people fish for this species on Sanibel. Because of its attractive coloration, the redbreast sunfish is a popular freshwater aquarium fish. The redbreast feeds on insects in both larval and adult stages. It eats mayflies, dragonflies, moths, and even butterflies. It takes readily to imitation flies and surface poppers. The redbreast is preyed upon by almost every aquatic mammal on the islands, including raccoons, otters, and even bobcats. It is also eaten by alligators, gars, largemouth bass, turtles, and snakes. The birds of the islands feast on immature redbreast, while ospreys can quite often be seen with an adult held firmly in their talons.

© Joe Tomelleri

□ _____ ★**Largemouth Bass** (*Micropterus salmoides*) Nicknames: black bass, green trout, bass / Status: FL=stable, IUCN=NE / Life span: to 23 years / Length: .50-2.5 ft (15-76 cm) / Weight: 1-5 lb (.90-2.2 kg); Florida record: 17 lb 4 oz, IGFA: 25 lb 1 oz / Spawns: in all the inshore lakes and ponds, as well as the Sanibel River / Found: year-round, IW, UA. (Man-made lakes)

© Joe Tomelleri

It is not uncommon to land a five-pound largemouth on the islands, and there have even been reports of bass in excess of 10 pounds being landed. This is especially true for some of the older, larger bodies of water such as Lake Murex and the ponds and freshwater canals surrounding both the East and West Rocks subdivisions. The Sanibel River also harbors some monster largemouths.

The largemouth bass is the most popular freshwater game fish in the U.S. While some northern states may focus on muskellunge, walleye, and northern pike, the rest of the nation, from California through the entire South, targets the largemouth bass. More money is spent on lures, minnows, and fishing tackle to catch bass than any other freshwater species. Professional bass fishermen enter contests with prizes into the six figures

The largemouth will readily take spinners, flies, and live baits, and is a handful once hooked. This prize fighter jumps as readily as any snook, tangles the line around deadfalls and underwater obstructions, runs long and hard, and has earned its solid reputation as America's premier freshwater game fish. It is also regarded as an excellent eating fish, though it can have an earthy taste when taken from muddy ponds.

The bass is a consummate predator. It eats crayfish, frogs, insects, and small fish. It is also cannibalistic and will prey upon its own offspring. Larger fish have been observed eating small turtles, baby ducks, and adult redwing blackbirds that aren't paying attention. In turn, the largemouth bass is taken by everything. Smaller fish are preyed upon by herons, bitterns, and kingfishers, while the larger fish fall victim to alligators, great blue herons, and ospreys.

To find bass on the islands look for the clear, circular sandy bedding areas it fans out for spawning season. If the water is clear, then the bass is not far away. A freshwater fishing license is required to fish bass on Sanibel and Captiva, and freshwater slot and take limits apply. Go to http://myfwc.com/RULESANDREGS/Freshwater_FishRules for additional information.

The Shells of Sanibel and Captiva

One of the most diverse groups of organisms on earth, mollusks rank second behind insects for the sheer number of distinct species worldwide. The number of identified species lies somewhere between 93,000 and 120,000. Unlike other phylum, the invertebrate mollusk group is growing rapidly, with improved technology and DNA analysis helping to identify dozens of new species weekly. As recently as the 1950s there were only 50,000 recognized species. Current estimates put the projected number of living species at more than 200,000 worldwide and at least twice that number of extinct species.

Mollusks have more variety of forms—snails (gastropods), bivalves, and squid and other cephalopods—than any other animal phylum. On land they inhabit every continent except Antarctica and thrive in every sea and ocean in the world, including the Antarctic Ocean where the colossal squid can be found. They inhabit lakes, streams, rivers, ponds, jungles, the abyssal zone of the deep oceans below 12,000 feet, shorelines, and mangroves—virtually every ecological niche on the planet has

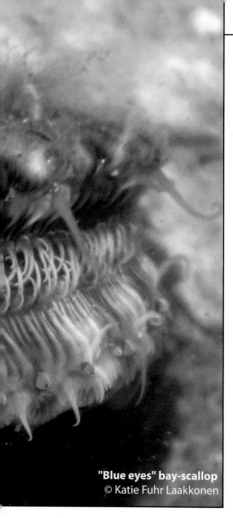

"Blue eyes" bay-scallop
© Katie Fuhr Laakkonen

an endemic snail, clam, or cephalopod living within.

For centuries, going back to when this stretch of Florida was called Costa de Caracol (Coast of Shells) by the Spanish, Sanibel and Captiva have been famous for their shells. José Leal, curator of the Bailey-Matthews Shell Museum, puts the number of different shells that wash up on our beaches somewhere between 250 and 275 species. Many of these are tiny specimens with subtle differences that only an experienced malacologist (malacology is the study of mollusca) would be able to identify. If you take to scuba diving, it is possible to add another 50 to 60 shells to that list. These numbers pale in comparison with the number of species believed to exist between our shoreline and the edge of the continental shelf 175 miles to the west. Recent estimates put that total at more than 2,000 species, many of which have yet to be identified.

Most of the shells we collect on our beaches are skeletons of the actual living organism. The word mollusk itself is derived from the Latin molluscus, which stems from mollis, meaning soft. All living mollusks are soft-flesh animals. The shells are their armor plating, hardened with calcium carbonate and designed to protect them from the elements and predation. The beaches and backwaters of Sanibel and Captiva contain millions of these exquisite but abandoned containers we call shells, but far, far fewer living organisms.

Only six living bivalves (clams, mussels, scallops, and oysters) and 11 living gastropods (terrestrial snails, marine snails, sea slugs, and limpets) are identified in this book. While this section is by no means extensive, it represents those shells that are the most likely to be identified by an average beachcomber while taking an early morning stroll down almost any section of beach on the islands. If you happen upon that stretch of beach shortly after a tropical storm or a strong winter cold front, there will undoubtedly be shells strewn about that are not included here. A great resource for identifying other local species is the official Web site of the Bailey-Matthews Shell Museum (www.shellmuseum.org).

Sanibel is named repeatedly as one of the top shelling beaches in the world—and more often than not as the top shelling beach in the world! So check your tide chart for the lowest tide possible, dig out your flashlight for that midnight search, and enjoy. Remember, the taking of live shells on either island is strictly prohibited, but there are more than enough empty shells around to stuff your suitcase to your heart's content.

The Bivalves/Clams and Oysters

☐ _____ **Eastern Oyster** (*Crassostrea virginica*) Nicknames: coon oyster, oyster / Status: FL=stable, IUCN=NE / Life span: to 10 years / Length: 3-8 in. (7-20 cm) / Weight: .15-.35 lb (90-158 g) / Spawns: in the nearshore waters / Found: BB, MZ / Very common.

In the 1930s, fishing guide Esperanza Woodring used to gather "coon oysters" from the mangroves of Tarpon Bay for oyster roasts on Woodring Point. The coon oyster is smaller than the commercially grown variety ordered at raw bars across Florida every day. It grows close enough to shore to make easy prey for raccoons—hence, its nickname.

This is an abundant shellfish. Look anywhere along the canals on either side of Wildlife Drive in the "Ding" Darling Refuge, especially at low tide, and you will see the long roots of red mangroves covered in oysters. Some of the local oysters you see may be *Ostreola equestris*, which is a similar but smaller species.

Courtesy The Bailey-Matthews Shell Museum

Worldwide, there are more than 40 species of oysters. They have been a food source for humans for tens of thousands of years, and Paleolithic oyster shell middens have been verified from Australia to the United Kingdom. There is little doubt that the indigenous Calusa Indians harvested and ate local oysters. The oysters we eat are not closely related to the pearl oysters. Although the eastern oyster can produce pearls, they are small and irregular with no commercial value.

The oyster is considered a keystone species. Oyster bars provide habitat for many marine species, including crabs, minnows, and barnacles, which in turn attract red drum, snook, and sea trout. The oyster is a filter feeder and plays an essential role in removing excess nutrients from the water. A single oyster can filter up to 1.3 gallons of water per hour. Think of oysters as the kidneys of our estuaries. The species is so important in maintaining a healthy estuary ecosystem that various environmental organizations across Southwest Florida will seed oyster beds to maintain stable populations.

While oysters are not farmed locally, there are large oyster farms in Florida, especially in Apalachicola Bay and along the Panhandle. The oyster is unusual in that it will change sex one or more times during its life. The biological reasons for this are unclear.

Live oysters on red mangroves © Charles Sobczak

In the wild the oyster is eaten by raccoons, a host of gastropods, the American oystercatcher, and fish such as the sheepshead, whose strong, forward-facing teeth have evolved to crack the oyster shell open.

☐ _____ **Coquina** (*Donax variabillis*) Nicknames: bean clam, wedge clams / Status: FL=stable, IUCN=NE / Life span: to 2 years / Length: .50-.75 in. (12-19 mm) / Weight: .1-.2 oz (3-6 g) / Spawns: along the beaches / Found: GB / Common.

© Blake Sobczak

This tiny bivalve, a member of the genus *Donax*, is a true delight to observe on a calm summer stroll along the gulf beaches. It lives in colonies along the littoral zone where the saltwater washes up and over them with almost every breaking wave. The coquina actually uses these waves, running west to east on Sanibel and Captiva, to move to new locations in search of the microscopic foods it filters from the breaking saltwater.

Because it is so small, the coquina can be difficult to spot, but fascinating to watch once you find a colony. As a wave washes over the colony, then retreats, each coquina tips itself vertically, with its small foot burrowing down into the soft sand. You can sometimes watch it extend its translucent siphon while feeding. The various colors and delicate, ray-like patterns of these shells appear to be infinite and can be compared with the uniqueness of snowflakes in that every shell is ever so slightly different from every other coquina.

Over time, deposits of these old shells, cemented by their own lime, compact together to form a limestone called coquina stone, so soft that it can be hand cut with a saw. The Calusa Indians and early settlers used coquina stone as a building material. The coquina is also used in shell art and for other decorative purposes.

The coquina is edible and was once commonly used to make a broth. Bear in mind that the taking of live shells, including coquinas, is prohibited on our beaches, so don't try making coquina broth while on the islands.

The coquina forms a major portion of the diet of many shorebirds, some of which have adapted their bills to feed almost exclusively on this delicacy. It is also eaten by a variety of beach-running fish, ghost crabs, and predatory mollusks and crustaceans.

☐ _____ **Giant Atlantic Cockle** (*Dinocardium robustum*) Nicknames: giant heart cockle, Van Hyning's cockle / Status: FL=stable, IUCN=NE / Life span: to 15 years / Length: 3-5 in. (7.5-12.7 cm) / Weight: n/a / Spawns: in the nearshore and inshore waters / Found: GB, GW / Fairly common.

The giant cockle is one of the largest bivalves living along the Southwest Florida coast. It is quite common, inhabiting the gulf waters from 6 to 60 feet in depth. Because of its strong shell and formidable size, the giant cockle is able to withstand the tumbling of the surf better than most shells, so it is fairly easy to find nice specimens along the Sanibel and Captiva beaches. This is the shell that is most commonly used as a soap dish and a variety of other decorative uses.

A closely related subspecies, the Van Hyning's cockle, ranges from Tampa to the Southeast Atlantic coast. All cockles are very active clams, with a long, powerful, sickle-shaped foot that enables the clam to leap several inches off the bottom. Finding a live giant cockle will take some luck but can be done during low tide when long tide pools are formed between the beach ridges. The cockle is collected in England where it is used to make chowder in lieu of clams or mussels.

© Blake Sobczak

Young cockles are heavily preyed upon by fish, while mature shells are taken by predatory gastropods, stingrays, and nurse sharks.

☐ _____ Pen Shell (Two species: *Atrina serrata, Atrina rigida*)

Nicknames: saw-toothed pen shell, rigid pen shell, fan shell / Status: FL=stable, IUCN=NE / Life span: n/a / Length: 5-8 in. (12.7-20 cm) / Spawns: in nearshore to offshore waters / Found: BB, GB, GW / Common.

Although difficult to find alive in less than 5 to 10 feet of water, the two species of pen shell do become dislodged after heavy storms and can sometimes be found in tidal pools at low tide. The difference between the two species is in the ribbing along the outside of the shells.

© Blake Sobczak

Atrina rigida
Courtesy The Bailey-Matthews Shell Museum

The saw-toothed pen shell has more than 30 fine ribs, whereas the rigid pen shell has 15 or fewer. The rigid pen shell tends to grow roughly an inch larger than the saw-toothed and displays a distinctive and beautiful mother of pearl iridescence at the pointed base of the shell.

The pen shell buries itself in the soft bottom in depths up to 20 feet and attaches to the limestone substrate or shell fragments though the use of byssus (pronounced "biss-

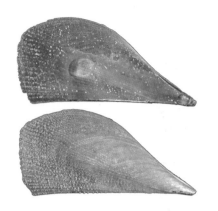

Atrina serrata
Courtesy The Bailey-Matthews Shell Museum

us") threads, which are commonly found on mussels and other sedentary bivalves. The pen shell has a symbiotic relationship with a tiny crab (*Pinnotheres maculatus*) that lives its entire life inside the filtering end of the pen shell. It is believed that these crabs help the pen shell feed, though the details of this unusual relationship are still being studied.

The pen shell is edible and is commonly made into a soup in New Zealand and Japan where it is sometimes combined with shiitake mushrooms. It is heavily preyed upon by gastropods, rays, and nurse sharks, which scour the bottom looking for colonies of these large bivalves.

☐ _____ **Atlantic Bay Scallop** (*Argopecten irradians*) Nicknames: bay scallop / Status: FL=declining, IUCN=NE / Life span: to 2 years / Length 2.5-3 in. (6-7.5 cm) / Weight: n/a / Spawns: inshore in the grass beds and turtle grasses / Found: BB, MZ / Uncommon.

A combination of over-harvesting and habitat loss has placed this once-common species in serious decline. In the early 1950s, up to 120,000 pounds of bay scallops were taken out of Pine Island Sound annually. Today it is difficult to find even a small bucketful during the summer scallop season. This same situation exists in Sarasota and Tampa; the only remaining viable populations are found north of the Crystal River and in St. Joseph Bay in the Florida Panhandle.

© Blake Sobczak

Most of the bay scallops purchased at the local fish market are commercially grown, while the wild populations throughout the U.S. have been steadily declining over the past 60 years. Efforts to reseed various populations have thus far been disappointing, though various organizations, including the Marine Lab at SCCF, remain committed to bringing this once-plentiful species back into our estuaries.

One of the only mobile bivalves, the bay scallop is capable of free-swimming behavior. It does so by rapidly opening and closing its shell, jetting out the water, and propelling itself through the sea grasses with surprising speed. This swimming ability helps it to escape predators such as stingrays and cow-nosed rays. The bay scallop also has dozens of tiny blue eyes that run along the entire outer edge of the shell when opened. These eyes cannot see objects per se but help the shellfish detect and flee potential predators.

Look for Atlantic bay scallops in the back bays, especially in the sea grass beds. The best method of finding a wild scallop is by snorkeling, though you might be able to spot one from a kayak or canoe if the water is clear.

The scallop is taken by wading birds, otters, and any number of sharks and rays, but its biggest threat comes from changes in its environment brought about by human activities. The building of the Sanibel Causeway in the early 1960s was reputed to change the salinity of San Carlos Bay, thereby destroying vast scallop beds in the tidal flats between Sanibel and Punta Rassa.

☐ _____ **Atlantic Calico Scallop** (*Argopecten gibbus*) Nicknames: calico scallop / Status: FL=stable, IUCN=NE / Life span: to 2 years / Length: 2-3 in. (5-7.3 cm) / Weight: n/a / Reproduces: to depths of 100 feet / Found: GB, GW / Very common.

© Blake Sobczak

One of the most commonly found shells on the beaches of Sanibel and Captiva, the calico scallop is also one of the most beautiful. It washes ashore in a vast array of colors and is fairly resistant to damage in the rough-and-tumble world of the surf zone. The calico scallop is widely used in shell art and for decorative purposes. It has the classic shell shape made popular by the Shell Oil Company, and it is the centerpiece of one of the world's most famous paintings, *The Birth of Venus* by Botticelli.

Although calico scallop shells are easy to find and identify on the beach, it presents a much more difficult challenge to find one alive. Because it is free swimming, it occasionally washes up alive on the beaches after a major storm. Under normal circumstances the best place to find a live calico scallop is in a tide pool, sitting on the bottom in ankle- to waist-deep water.

The calico is widespread and is not as commercially harvested as the bay scallop. It ranges from Delaware to Brazil. Like all scallops, the calico is a filter feeder, taking in vast amounts of seawater and removing microscopic particles of algae, diatoms, and other phytoplankton. It is eaten by rays, nurse sharks, and a number of other fish.

Other Island Shells/Clams and Oysters

☐ _____ **Turkey Wing** (*Arca zebra*) Length: 3 in. (7.5 cm) / Lives in gulf waters from 3 to 25 feet / Found: GB / Common.

© Blake Sobczak

❏ _____ **Florida Prickly Cockle**
(*Trachycardium egmontianum*) Length: 2.5 in.
(6.25 cm) / Lives in gulf waters from 1 to 25 feet /
Found: GB / Fairly common.

© Blake Sobczak

❏ _____ **Ponderous Ark** (*Noetia ponderosa*)
Length: 2 in. (5 cm) / Lives in gulf waters from 1 to 25
feet / Found: GB / Common.

© Blake Sobczak

❏ _____ **Angel Wing** (*Cyrtopleura costata*)
Length: 5 in. (12.7 cm) / Lives in the mudflats and
tidal flats in the back bay and gulf from 1 to 5 feet /
Found: BB / Rare.

© Blake Sobczak

❏ _____ **Buttercup Lucine** (*Anodontia alba*)
Length: 2 in. (5 cm) / Lives in gulf waters from 3 to 30
feet / Found: GB / Common.

© Blake Sobczak

❏ _____ **Common Jingle** (*Anomia simplex*)
Length: 1 in (2.5 cm) / Lives in gulf waters from low
tide line to 30 feet / Found: GB / Very common.

© Blake Sobczak

❏ _____ **Florida Spiny Jewelbox**
(*Arcinella cornuta*) Length: 1.5 in. (3.77 cm) /
Lives in gulf waters from 12 to 60 feet / Found: GB /
Fairly common.

© Blake Sobczak

☐_____**Northern Lion's Paw**

(*Nodipecten fragosus*) Length: 2.5-4 in. (6.3-10 cm) / Lives in gulf waters from 20 to 100 feet / Found: GB / Very rare.

© Blake Sobczak

☐_____**Pointed Venus**

(*Anamalocardia auberiana*) Length: 0.6 in. (1.5 cm) / Lives in gulf waters from 1 to 40 feet / Found: GB / Uncommon.

© Blake Sobczak

☐_____**Rose Petal Tellin**

(*Tellina lineata*) Length: 1 in. (2.5 cm) / Lives in gulf waters from 3 to 60 feet / Found: GB / Common.

© Blake Sobczak

☐_____**Southern Quahog**

(*Mercenaria campechiensis*) Length: 3.5-5 in. (8.9-12.7 cm) / Lives in gulf waters on sandy bottom from 3 to 50 feet / Found: GB / Uncommon.

© Blake Sobczak

☐_____**Sunray Venus**

(*Macrocallista maculata*) Length: 5 in. (12.7 cm) / Lives in gulf waters on sandy bottom from low tide mark to 12 feet / Found: GB / Common.

© Blake Sobczak

☐_____**Alternate Tellin**

(*Tellina alternata*) Length: 3 in. (7.5 cm) / Lives in gulf waters from 6 to 120 feet / Found: GB / Common.

© Blake Sobczak

❏ _____ **Yellow Egg Cockle**
(*Laevicardium mortoni*) Length: 0.8 in. (2 cm) / Lives in gulf waters on sandy bottom from low-tide mark to 20 feet / Found: GB / Common.

© Blake Sobczak

❏ _____ **Lightning Pitar** (*Pitar fulminatus*)
Length: 1.5 in. (3.75 cm) / Lives in gulf waters from 12 to 200 feet / Found: GB / Uncommon.

© Blake Sobczak

❏ _____ **Atlantic Pearl Oyster**
(*Pinctada imbricata*) Length: 3 in. (7.5 cm) / Lives in gulf waters from 6 to 60 feet / Found: GB / Uncommon.

© Blake Sobczak

❏ _____ **Calico Clam**
(*Macrocallista maculata*) Length: 2.5 in. (6.35 cm) / Lives in gulf waters from 6 to 60 feet / Found: GB / Uncommon.

© Blake Sobczak

❏ _____ **Broad-ribbed Cardita**
(*Carditamera floridana*) Length: 1 in. (2.5 cm) / Lives in gulf waters from 5 to 200 feet / Found: GB / Uncommon.

© Blake Sobczak

❏ _____ **Atlantic Kittenpaw**
(*Plicatula gibbosa*) Length: 1 in. (2.5 cm) / Lives in gulf waters from the low-tide line to 200 feet / Found: GB / Fairly common.

© Blake Sobczak

Living Gastropods

☐ _____ **Tulip Shell** (*Fasciolaria tulipa*) Nicknames: none / Status: FL=stable, IUCN=NE / Life span: n/a / Size: 4-6 in. (10-15 cm) / Weight: n/a / Spawns: inshore / Found: BB, MZ / Common.

© Blake Sobczak

Although more difficult to find than some other gastropods, living tulips can still be located in the tidal flats of the J.N. "Ding" Darling Wildlife Refuge, as well as Tarpon Bay, the back side of Captiva, and along the shallows of the out islands. Look for them in areas of soft, muddy, and weedy bottoms. It is generally covered in algae growth and small barnacles, looking nothing like it does on display in a showcase. When moving, the tulip tends to look much like an oversized underwater snail crawling slowly along the bottom.

The tulip is a predatory gastropod, related to the horse conch, and is a carnivore. It feeds on other gastropods, including its relative, the banded tulip, as well as any number of bivalves such as clams, oysters, and scallops. The tulip wraps itself around a bivalve and methodically pries it open to feed upon the soft tissue inside. When picked up the tulip will immediately start to dislodge whatever water it has inside and close its trap door (the operculum), sealing itself completely inside its protective shell.

The tulip is found in water from a few inches to 30 feet in depth. This species has been known to grow to more than nine inches long, though it rarely reaches that size. It is preyed upon by grouper, octopus, and squid, and when inshore it is sometimes taken by wading birds such as egrets and herons.

☐ _____ **Banded Tulip** (*Fasciolaria hunteria*) Nicknames: tulip / Status: FL=stable, IUCN=NE / Life span: n/a / Size: 2-5 in. (5-13 cm) / Weight: n/a / Spawns: inshore / Found: BB, MZ / Common.

Similar in many ways to its slightly larger cousin, the true tulip, the banded tulip is also found in the shallow mudflats and sandy bottoms of the back bay. It is a predatory gastropod, feeding on a variety of bivalves, as well as smaller tulips. All tulips are cannibalistic and will readily attack and eat members of their own species.

Unlike the oyster, the tulip is dioecious, meaning each is distinctly

© Blake Sobczak

Live Banded Tulip   © Charles Sobczak

male or female. The female tulip's egg capsules resemble flattened, V-shaped stemmed vases with frilly edges, clumped together in masses. They are generally attached to rocks or dead shells. The larvae emerge as crawling young.

Neither the banded nor true tulip population appears to be in trouble. Although both of these tulips are edible, their meat is tough and they have no real food value. The banded tulip is preyed upon by true tulips, wading birds, fish, and octopus.

Banded Tulip
Courtesy The Bailey-Matthews Shell Museum

☐ _____ **Florida Horse Conch** (*Triplofusus giganteus*) Nicknames: giant band shell / Status: FL=stable, IUCN=NE / Life span: n/a / Length: 14-18 in. (35-46 cm) / Weight: n/a / Reproduces: in the nearshore and inshore waters / Found: BB, MZ, GB / Common.

Officially declared the Florida state shell in 1969, the horse conch is an impressive shell. Known to be the largest gastropod living in the Atlantic Ocean, this predatory marine snail can grow to almost two feet in length and weigh more than 10 pounds. The world-record horse conch, at 23.8 inches, was taken by Sanibel resident Ed Hanley while scuba diving in 130 feet of water off the island. This specimen is on display at the Bailey-Matthews Shell Museum. Only a handful of shells in the world grow to be larger than the Florida

© Blake Sobczak

horse conch. The single largest shellfish is the giant clam, which inhabits the South Pacific and can weigh more than 500 pounds.

Although it is called a conch, the horse conch is not related to the queen conch and is not in the genus *Strombus*. Unlike the queen conch, which is popular food in the Caribbean, the horse conch is not considered good table fare today, though it was probably eaten by the Calusa and other Florida tribes. Its meat is reported to have a peppery flavor.

The Calusa Indians made extensive use of the horse conch. The sharp central axis of the shell, or columella, was attached to a wooden handle and used as a hammer or woodworking tool. The outer whorl was used as a drinking cup, and various parts of the conch's heavy shell were used as sinkers for fishing lines and trap nets.

When young, the shell is a bright orange but over time it fades to a salmon or grayish color. The soft, fleshy part of this shellfish is a bright orange. It can be found in waters from a foot to more than 100 feet in depth. It feeds upon a variety of bivalves, as well as other gastropods such as tulips, lightning and paper figs, and other horse conchs.

The horse conch is too large to be taken by wading birds and seldom by fish, but is preyed upon by octopus and cannibalized by other conchs. Large specimens have been known to damage boat props in shallow water.

❑ _____ **Lightning Whelk** (*Busycon sinistum*) Nicknames: left-handed whelk, perverse whelk / Status: FL=stable, IUCN=NE / Life span: to 10 years / Length: 2.5-16 in. (6-40 cm) / Weight: n/a / Reproduces: in the nearshore and inshore waters / Found: GW, BB, MZ / Very common.

Unusual in its left-handed, counterclockwise shell spiral, the lightning whelk and its distinctive egg casings are common finds along the beaches of Sanibel. Named for the beautiful "lightning" streaks that radiate from the axis, or top of the shell, this gastropod is a welcome addition to anyone's collection.

© Blake Sobczak

Like the tulips and the horse conch, the lightning whelk is a predatory carnivore. It feeds predominantly on clams, oysters, scallops, and other gastropods. Although it may seem as though the bivalve population could be decimated by so many carnivorous gastropods roaming the depths, it's important to point out that a large whelk eats little more than one shellfish a month. It accesses its bivalve prey by wrapping its soft body around the animal, then using the leading edge of its shell as a crowbar, pries its victim's shell open. Once opened, it inserts its radula (toothed tongue) into the animal to devour the soft, fleshy shellfish within.

Failing that, the whelk will sometimes grind the clam or oyster with its own shell until it opens up a hole large enough to insert its radula into the animal.

Both of these behaviors can take weeks to accomplish, but in the slow-motion world of mollusks nothing but the cephalopods (squid, octopus, and cuttlefish) moves quickly.

© Blake Sobczak

The lightning whelk's egg casings, commonly seen on the beach, are long, snakelike structures (a foot in length or longer) that appear to be made out of parchment paper. Inside of each compartment, if you take a moment to open one, are between 20 and 100 tiny whelks. As soon as the first whelk emerges from the case, it immediately turns around and feeds on the rest of the living shells inside the chamber. This is a process known as *adelphophagy*, which translates into "eating one's brother," in which the largest and strongest embryo consumes its lesser womb mates. Although a morally repugnant concept for humans, this kind of behavior has proven to be a successful adaptation for some shellfish, insects, and sharks.

The whelk is eaten by horse conchs, stingrays (whose bony plates are capable of crushing their shells), and nurse sharks. Although the whelk was commonly eaten by the Calusa, it is seldom if ever taken for table fare today.

☐ _____ **Crown Conch** (*Melongena corona*) Nicknames: king's crown / Status: FL=stable, IUCN=NE / Life span: n/a / Length: 1.5-2.5 in. (4-6 cm) / Weight: n/a / Reproduces: in the inshore waters / Found: BB, MZ / Common.

Next to the oyster, the crown conch, or king's crown as it is more commonly referred to, is probably the easiest live shellfish to find on Sanibel and Captiva, but it requires patience. Unlike the highly cleaned and polished shells you find in an island shell shop, a wild gastropod is often covered in growth or partially buried in the soft muddy bottom of the mangrove intertidal zone. It looks more like a slow-moving rock than a live animal.

© Blake Sobczak

In the J.N. "Ding" Darling Wildlife Refuge the best viewing areas are the mangrove overlook on Wildlife Drive, located just before milepost 1, or the freshwater side of the cross-dike path (in the brackish water on the western side), located 1.85 miles from the entrance. The best way to spot one is to lean over, preferably with polarized sunglasses on, and scan the bottom carefully for two to three minutes. If you don't see one at the first spot, walk down the cross-dike a bit farther and try another area. The crown conch tends to congregate in small colonies,

Live Kings Crown   © Blake Sobczak

so once you locate one living specimen you are likely to see more.

Just remember that you cannot take one home with you, as the taking of live shells on Sanibel and Captiva is strictly prohibited. With more than half a million visitors driving through "Ding" Darling a year, if everyone took just one shell each, how could they survive?

The crown conch is related to the lightning whelk, and like most of the gastropods, is predatory in nature. It is unusual in that it is able to adapt to a wide range of salinity and water temperatures, allowing it to thrive in low-oxygen and high-salinity conditions.

Some birds feed on the crown conch, as do any number of competing gastropods. It is sometimes odd to think of the shellfish world as a vicious, predatory bloodbath, because all of these creatures move at less than one mile per hour and eat only monthly. It is the sedentary nature of their primary prey—immobile (oysters and mussels) or barely mobile (scallops)—that allows for a very slow capture.

Courtesy The Bailey-Matthews Shell Museum

☐ _____ **Lettered Olive** (*Oliva sayana*) Nicknames: olive, golden olive / Status: FL=stable, IUCN=NE / Life span: n/a / Length: 2-2.5 in. (5-6.5 cm) / Weight: n/a / Reproduces: in the nearshore waters / Found: GB, GW / Uncommon.

The best location to find a living lettered or golden olive is along the beaches and near the sandy bottoms of the passes and shoals. Named for its dark surface markings that vaguely resemble blurry cuneiform writing, this shell is a highly prized find. Although the olives you find at a shell shop may appear to be mechanically polished, this process is done by the animal itself. When moving, it extends its fleshy mantle around the outside of the shell to protect it. This constant rubbing of the outer surface, coupled with the tiny fragments of sand

Courtesy The Bailey-Matthews Shell Museum

and grit between the shell and the living organism, polishes the shell over time. Because it is so attractive, the Calusa, as well as many Native American tribes, used the lettered olive to make jewelry and other decorative objects.

The far more uncommon golden olive, which is a color variant of the lettered olive, can also be found along the surf line. If the water is calm enough, you can track either of the olives by following its trail through the soft sand. It is in this surf zone where the olive feeds on coquinas, small clams, and other shellfish. The olive, like many gastropods, is a carnivore. A handful of birds eat the olive, as do stingrays, sharks, and other predatory gastropods.

© Blake Sobczak

☐ _____ **Fighting Conch** (*Strombus alatus*) Nicknames: Florida fighting conch / Status: FL=stable, IUCN=NE / Life span: to 10 years / Length: 3-4 in. (7.6-10 cm) / Weight: n/a / Reproduces: in the nearshore waters / Found: GB, GW / Common.

Oddly enough, the common name of this species might lead one to believe that it is the toughest, meanest carnivore of all the gastropods out there, but that's not the case. The fighting conch is an omnivore, dining in large colonies on algae growth along the sandy bottom in depths from 5 to 25 feet.

When Carl Linnaeus, the father of modern taxonomy, gave this shell its tough-sounding name in the 1700s, he thought the points on the top of the fighting conch resembled

© Blake Sobczak

the spikes worn by ancient gladiators. It turned out to be a good choice. Although it is not a predatory, carnivorous gastropod, the fighting conch will fight hard for survival, as anyone who picks one up will discover when the shell starts kicking about wildly in an attempt to escape.

Because it grazes in deeper water, most of the fighting conchs you find onshore have been damaged in the surf zone. Finding a live specimen is rare but more likely in the spring when the fighting conch migrates closer to shore to breed and lay eggs.

Related to the queen conch of the Bahamas, the fighting conch is edible but seldom taken as table fare because of its smaller size. It is heavily preyed upon by carnivorous gastropods such as lightning whelks and horse conchs, as well as sharks and rays. Young fighting conchs are eaten by various fish.

☐ _____ **Apple Murex** (*Chicoreus pomum*) Nicknames: none / Status: FL=stable, IUCN=NE / Life span: to 5 years / Length: 2-4.5 in. (5-11.5 cm) / Weight: n/a / Spawns: in the nearshore waters / Found: GB, GW / Common.

Ranging from North Carolina to Brazil, the apple murex is one of the most abundant murex shells found in Florida and the West Indies. It feeds predominantly on the common eastern oyster, boring almost perfectly round holes into its shell. This drilling may take the apple murex weeks to complete, but this pales in comparison with some species of small drills in the South Pacific, which, dining on much larger and thicker-shelled clams and oysters, may take up to eight months to drill into the soft, edible parts of the animal. Imagine waiting that long, without appetizers, for your dinner.

© Blake Sobczak

Although this is a fairly common shell to find washed up along the beach, it is not easy to find alive. Look for it beyond the surf zone, preferably with a mask and snorkel, in water from 3 to 10 feet. Finding one will probably depend more on water clarity than any other factor.

The apple murex is preyed upon by carnivorous gastropods, including other murex species. In is also eaten by rays and sharks.

☐ _____ **Garden Slug** (Family *Arionidae*) Nicknames: slug, small striped slug, black field slug / Status: FL=thriving, IUCN=NE / Life span: to 1 year / Length: 1-1.5 in. (2.5-3 cm) / Weight: n/a / Spawns: in dense, moist undergrowth throughout the islands / Found: UA, MZ, IW / Common.

The evolution of the garden slug from its marine environment to the development of a pallial lung and its ability to breathe air began 360 million years ago. Over time this terrestrial gastropod, related to the sea hare and other nudibranchs, has forsaken its shell and taken up permanent residence on land.

With several species on Sanibel, this gastropod is easy to find. Look for it after heavy summer rains crossing the bike path or crawling along shell roads around the island.

Its specially adapted rasp-like mouth can do considerable damage to domestic plants and gardens. Certain species of these slugs, such as the spotted garden slug of New England, can grow to seven inches in length.

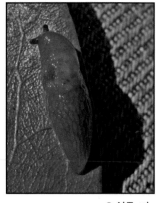

© Al Tuttle

The banana slug of the West Coast of the U.S. can grow up to 10 inches long, surpassed only by the *Limax cinereoniger*, or keelback slug of Europe, which grows to an amazing length of 12 inches.

Slugs are eaten by turtles, freshwater fish, birds, and small mammals such as mice and rats.

☐ _____ **Common Land Snail** *(Helix Pomatia)* Nicknames: snail / Status: FL=stable, IUCN=NE / Life span: to 3 years / Length: .5-1.5 in. (1.3-3.8 cm) / Weight: n/a / Spawns: along the edges of ponds and wetlands throughout the islands / Found: UA, IW, MZ / Common.

© Blake Sobczak

Well adapted to tropical regions, the land snail is a common sighting on both Sanibel and Captiva. Two specific adaptations allow this small mollusk to thrive under the hot Florida sun in times of both drought and deluge. The first is that unlike many land snails, the Sanibel snails have a shell "door," or operculum, which it closes during the dry season to preserve its internal moisture. The second amazing adaptation is the envy of every scuba diver: it has both gills and lungs to take in the oxygen every animal needs to survive.

The right side of this snail's body contains a system comparable to the gills of a fish, allowing it to survive and breathe underwater, while the left side has a primitive but effective lung allowing the snail to breathe air. When the food supply runs low in a nearby pond, the snail crawls out of the water and starts to forage on land. It eats algae, plants, brine shrimp, carrion, and even small insects. The snail is a freshwater gastropod and a true omnivore.

The land snail description itself applies to a wide array of species. Some aquarium varieties can be six inches in diameter. The snail is heavily preyed upon by birds such as the red-winged blackbird, as well as lizards, juvenile alligators, bass, rodents, and larger mammals such as raccoons and otters.

☐ _____ **Florida Tree Snail** *(Linguus fasciatus*- var. subspecies) Nicknames: tree snail / Status: FL=Species of special concern, populations declining statewide, IUCN=NE / Life span: n/a / Length: 0.25-1.5 in. (6.3-38 mm) / Reproduces: in the moist leaf litter at the base of various species of native trees / Found: UA, IW / Fairly common.

One of a handful of terrestrial snails found on Sanibel and Captiva, the tree snail was once far more common throughout Florida than it is today. The reasons

Florida Tree Snail   ©Charles Sobczak

for its decline are not understood but may be related in part to climate change and over-harvesting by shell collectors. In areas where the black iguana thrives, such as Gasparilla Island to the north, these aggressive predators have almost totally eradicated the tree snail.

Statewide the species ranges from Pinellas and Broward counties south, then continues into Cuba and some of the other Caribbean Islands. It comes in a variety of colors and somewhat resembles a miniature banded tulip. You must look closely to find one of these very small snails, as they can readily be mistaken for a clipped-off branch or an irregular growth.

The tree snail feeds on fungi growing on the bark of any number of trees, its favorites being smooth-barked species such as wild tamarind, gumbo limbo, poisonwood, mastic, and Jamaican dogwood. The tree snail is eaten by a host of predators including invasive tokay geckos, black rats, and some birds.

Other Island Shells/Univalves and Gastropods

☐ _____ **Junonia** (*Scaphella junonia*) / Length: 4-6 in. (10-15 cm) / Lives in the deep gulf waters from 60 to 200 feet / Found: GB / Extremely rare.

© Blake Sobczak

☐ _____ **Nutmeg** (*Cancellaria reticulata*) / Length: 1-1.5 in. (2.5-3.8 cm) / Lives in the gulf waters from 6 to 30 feet / Found: GB / Fairly common.

© Blake Sobczak

☐ _____ **Scotch Bonnet**
(*Semicassis granulata*) Length: 3 in. (7.8 cm) /
Lives in the gulf waters from 3 to 35 feet / Found: GB
/ Fairly rare.

© Blake Sobczak

☐ _____ **Rose Murex**
(*Haustellum rubidum*) Length: 1-1.5 in (2.5-
3.8 cm) / Lives in the gulf waters from 1 to 25 feet /
Found: GB / Uncommon.

© Blake Sobczak

☐ _____ **Pitted Murex**
(*Favartia cellulosa*) Length: 0.7 in. (1.77 cm) /
Lives in the gulf and back bay from the low-tide mark
to 20 feet / Found: GB, BB / Uncommon.

© Blake Sobczak

☐ _____ **Lace Murex** (*Chicoreus dilectus*)
Length: 1.5-2 in. (3.8-5 cm) / Lives in the gulf waters
from 10 to 60 feet / Found: GB / Fairly common.

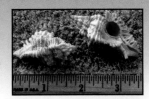

© Blake Sobczak

☐ _____**Chestnut Turban**
(*Turbo castanea*) Length: 1.5 in. (3.8 cm) / Lives
in the gulf waters from 5 to 40 feet / Found: BB, GB /
Fairly common.

© Blake Sobczak

☐ _____ **Mangrove Periwinkle**
(*Littoraria angulifera*) Length: 1 in. (2.5 cm) /
Lives in the mangrove waters from the tide line to 10
feet / Found: BB, MZ / Common.

© Blake Sobczak

☐ _____ **American Carrier Snail**
(*Xenophora conchyliophora*) Length: 3 in. (7.6 cm) / Lives in the gulf waters from 3-20 feet / Found: GB / Uncommon.

© Blake Sobczak

☐ _____ **Florida Worm Snail**
(*Vermicularia knorri*) Length: 3 in. (8 cm) / Lives in the gulf waters from 6 to 30 feet / Found: GB / Common.

© Blake Sobczak

☐ _____ **Fargo's Worm Shell**
(*Vermicularia fargoi*) Length: 5 in. (12.7 cm) / Lives in the gulf from the low-tide line to 60 feet / Found: GB / Uncommon.

© Blake Sobczak

☐ _____ **Colorful Moon Snail**
(*Naticarius canrena*) Length: 1 in. (2.5 cm) / Lives in the gulf waters from 3 to 50 feet / Found: GB / Uncommon.

© Blake Sobczak

☐ _____ **Shark Eye** (*Neverita duplicata*)
Nicknames: moon snail / Length: 2.5-3.5 in. (6.35-8.9 cm) / Lives in the gulf waters from 2-30 feet / Found: GB / Fairly common.

© Blake Sobczak

☐ _____ **Alphabet Cone**
(*Conus spurius*) / Length: 1.5-2 in. (3.8-5 cm) / Lives in the gulf waters from 1 to 50 feet / Found: GB / Uncommon.

© Blake Sobczak

☐ _____ Florida Cone

(*Conus anabathrum*) Length: 1 in. (2.5 cm) /
Lives in the gulf waters from 1 to 40 feet / Found:
GB / Uncommon.

© Blake Sobczak

☐ _____ Tampa Drill

(*Urosalpinx tampaensis*) Length: 1 in. (2.5 cm) /
Lives in the gulf waters from the surf zone to 25 feet /
Found: GB / Common.

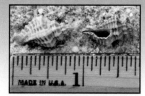

© Blake Sobczak

☐ _____ Gulf Oyster Drill

(*Urosalpinx perrugata*) Length: 0.7 in. (1.77 cm) /
Lives in the gulf and bay from low-tide line to 25 feet /
Found: BB, MZ, GB / Common.

© Blake Sobczak

☐ _____ Mauve-mouthed Drill

(*Callotrophon ostrearum*) Length: 0.8 in. (2 cm)
/ Lives in the gulf from the low-tide line to 20 feet /
Found: GB / Uncommon.

© Blake Sobczak

☐ _____ Sharp-ribbed Drill

(*Eupleura sulcidentata*) Length: 0.5 in. (1.25 cm)
/ Lives in the gulf from the low-tide line to 20 feet /
Found: GB / Uncommon.

© Blake Sobczak

☐ _____ **Pear Whelk** (*Busycotypus spiratus*) / Length: 4-5 in. (10-12.5 cm) / Lives in the gulf waters from 3 to 50 feet / Found: GB / Uncommon.

© Blake Sobczak

☐ _____ **Atlantic Fig Snail** (*Ficus communis*) Length: 3 in. (7.6 cm) / Lives in the gulf waters from 2 to 30 feet / Found: GB / Fairly common.

© Blake Sobczak

☐ _____ **Tinted Cantharus** (*Pollia tincta*) Length: 1 in. (2.5 cm) / Lives in the back bay and mangroves from 1 to 25 feet / Found: BB, MZ / Common.

© Blake Sobczak

☐ _____ **Ribbed Cantharus** (*Cantharus multangulus*) Length: 1 in. (2.5 cm) / Lives in the gulf from the low-tide line to 20 feet / Found: GB / Uncommon.

© Blake Sobczak

☐ _____ **Ladder Horn Snail** (*Cerithidea scalariformis*) Length: 1 in. (2.5 cm) / Lives in the intertidal zone of the bay and mangroves from the low-tide line to 10 feet / Found: BB, MZ / Common.

© Blake Sobczak

☐ _____ **Costate Horn Snail** (*Cerithidea costata*) Length: 0.4 in (1 cm) / Lives in the intertidal zone of the bay and mangroves from the low-tide line to 10 feet / Found: BB, MZ / Common.

© Blake Sobczak

☐ _____ **Boring Turret Snail**
(*Turritella acropora*) Length: 1 in. (2.5 cm) /
Lives in the gulf waters from 6 to 600 feet / Found:
GB / Common.

© Blake Sobczak

☐ _____ **Humphrey's Wentletrap**
(*Epitonium humpreysii*) Length: 0.6 in. (1.5 cm)
/ Lives in the gulf waters from the low-tide line to 300
feet / Found: GB / Uncommon.

© Blake Sobczak

☐ _____ **Angulate Wentletrap**
(*Epitonium angulatum*) Length: 0.9 in. (2.28 cm)
/ Lives in the gulf waters from the low-tide line to 90
feet / Found: GB / Common.

© Blake Sobczak

☐ _____ **Brown-band Wentletrap**
(*Epitonium rupicola*) Length: 0.5 in. (1.25 cm)
/ Lives in the gulf from the low-tide line to 60 feet /
Found: GB / Uncommon.

© Blake Sobczak

☐ _____ **Brown Baby Ear**
(*Sinum maculatum*) Length: 1 in. (2.5 cm) / Lives
in the gulf waters from 3 to 50 feet / Found: GB /
Common.

© Blake Sobczak

☐ _____ **One-tooth Simnia**
(*Simnialena uniplicata*) Length: 0.5 in. (1.25 cm)
/ Lives in the gulf waters from 6 to 50 feet / Found:
GB / Uncommon.

© Blake Sobczak

❐ _____ **Common Atlantic Slippersnail**
(*Crepidula fornicata*) Length: 1.5 in. (3.75 cm) /
Lives in the gulf waters from 1 to 40 feet / Found: GB
/ Common.

© Blake Sobczak

❐ _____ **Cayenne Keyhole Limpet**
(*Diodora cayenensis*) Length: 0.7 in. (1.8 cm) /
Lives in the gulf waters from 3 to 30 feet / Found: GB
/ Fairly common.

© Blake Sobczak

❐ _____ **Sculptured Top Snail**
(*Calliostoma euglyptum*) Length: 0.8 in. (2 cm)
/ Lives in the gulf waters from 3 to 200 feet / Found:
GB / Uncommon.

© Blake Sobczak

❐ _____ **Coffee Bean Trivia**
(*Niveria pediculus*) Length: 0.5 in. (1.25 cm) /
Lives in the gulf waters from 3 to 80 feet / Found:
GB / Uncommon.

© Blake Sobczak

Courtesy The Bailey-Matthews Shell Museum

The Arthropods of Sanibel and Captiva —
Insects, Spiders, Butterflies and Crustaceans

The Phylum Arthropoda, in the sheer number of known species, dwarfs all living creatures on earth. There are more than 1.2 million identified species, and estimates put the number of insects yet to be classified between 6 and 10 million. There are 40,000 recognized spider species and more than 52,000 crustacean species. More than 90 percent of all living organisms on earth are insects, spiders, or crustaceans.

In terms of discovering new species, the field of entomology (the study of insects) is in its infancy. By all accounts, a mere 10 to 15 percent of insects have been catalogued, and in some parts of the developing world, new insect species are lost to extinction before they can even be identified. They thrive on every continent, including Antarctica, where more than 67 tiny species of insects have been verified to date.

North America, including all of the continental United States and Canada but excluding Mexico and Central America, has some 90,000 species of insects. Florida, with its subtropical climate and scores of different habitats, is one of the top five states for species diversity, rivaled only by Texas, California, and North Carolina. Estimates put the number of species living in the Sunshine State at approximately 50,000. On Sanibel and Captiva, the number of species is estimated to be somewhere around 5,000. The best way to appreciate just how many bugs are out there is to take a bright, white light outside after dark and leave it on for an hour or two. Within minutes you will find dozens of different moths, beetles, midges, and flies drawn to the light. By midnight you will find hundreds.

With so many species to choose from, and each and every one having its unique set of adaptations and environmental niche, deciding which ones to include in this book wasn't easy. I decided to start with the ones that effectively "bug us." That's why this section starts with no-see-ums and remains true to that theme through the Florida ivory millipede. It naturally includes the most dangerous living organism found on Sanibel and Captiva—the ubiquitous mosquito. The bite of an alligator pales in comparison with the bite of a tiny insect vectoring yellow fever, though we are fortunate in that none of the eight species of mosquitoes found on Sanibel and Captiva is, at present, a carrier.

The section concludes with butterflies. While I have tried to squeeze in as many species as possible, there are still quite a few that are native to the islands, but there simply wasn't room to include them in this book. The same is true for some of the larger and stunningly beautiful moths found on Sanibel and Captiva, including the luna, sphinx, and imperial.

Several insects presented here are truly amazing and do not pose any threat or serious danger to us, such as the stick bug, the grampus bug, and many lovely dragonflies that flourish on these small barrier islands. The section ends with a handful of crustaceans, or what I commonly call sea bugs. These are the crabs, shrimp, and other crustaceans that help nurture the estuary; although they might appear to be better suited for the fish section, they are in fact more closely related to insects and are members of the Phylum Arthropoda.

Bugs have some of the strangest life cycles and adaptations of any living organism. They outnumber us by trillions and outweigh us by billions of tons. They range in size from microscopic to four inches long and can be found everywhere on the islands. Unfortunately, all too many of them make us itch, or sting, or run for cover, so make a quick note of your sighting, then head to the medicine chest for relief.

The Insects

_____ **No-See-Um** (Family *Ceratopogonidae*) Nicknames: sandflea, no-see-em, sand gnat, granny nipper, chitra, punkie, flying teeth, biting midge / Status: FL=thriving / Life span: 6 weeks or less / Length: 0.06 in. (1-2 mm) / Reproduces: around salt-marsh and mangrove swamps, as well as along the intertidal zone of the beach, the Sanibel River, ponds, and mud puddles. / Found: GB, MZ, IW, UA.

The no-see-um is the smallest blood-sucking insect on earth, and, like the mosquito, only the female bites. She requires the proteins from blood to make her eggs. There are more than 4,000 species of these biting midges worldwide. Florida alone has 47 different species. Since their behavior, size, and feeding habits are similar, knowing exactly which species is taking a bite out of you is all but impossible.

While the amount of blood a no-see-um takes is insignificant, many people have an allergic reaction to the anticoagulant this insect injects into its victim to prevent the blood from clotting and gumming up its microscopic beak. It's the reaction to these chemicals that causes the itchy, painful welts that can last for days. Over a prolonged period of time, which varies among individuals, the body's immune system builds up a tolerance to these bites and the welts stop forming. This offers little comfort, however, to a visitor who is staying on the islands for a week or less.

Because the no-see-um's life span is so short and its habitat so varied, Lee County Mosquito Control is unable to offer any kind of islandwide control for this biting midge. Such an effort would result in almost daily spraying, and the environmental harm that resulted would far outweigh the benefits.

There are several preventive measures you can take to avoid no-see-um bites. Long sleeves and pants help to a degree. The chemical DEET, which is also effective for mosquitoes, in a concentration of at least 30 percent, seems to help. Another topical preventative is the Avon beauty product, Skin So Soft (or any baby oil), which effectively traps the no-see-um in the oil on your skin before it can bite. Be careful not to use sunscreen and DEET together as the combination not only increases the absorption of the DEET into your bloodstream (which isn't good), but also breaks down the protective ingredients in sunscreen.

For people who want to avoid the use of chemicals, the Centers for Disease Control recommends the oil of lemon eucalyptus, which is almost as effective as DEET. *Consumer Reports* recommends a product called Repel Lemon Eucalyptus, which contains a minute amount of a pesticide that is far less toxic than DEET. A breeze is one of the best ways avoid no-see-um attacks. A ceiling fan, small house fan, or an afternoon breeze will keep the tiny no-see-um from flying.

The remedies for dealing with the ensuing welts of no-see-um bites are varied, ranging from dipping a cotton Q-tip in boiling water and applying it to the welt as soon as possible (the cure might well be worse than the bite!) to the use of various patches, sprays, and ointments, including hydrocortisone cream and ibruprofen and Xylocaine gels.

Fortunately, many other insects feed on the tiny no-see-um and its larvae. Although troublesome, the local no-see-um does not carry the diseases found in flying midges in other tropical regions.

___

☐ _____ **Saltmarsh Mosquito** (*Aedes taeniorhynchus*) Nicknames: skeeter, Jersey bird / Status: FL=all too stable / Life span: to 2 months / Length: 0.15 in. (4 mm) / Reproduces: in the tidal flats of the "Ding" Darling Wildlife Refuge, as well as the bay side of Captiva / Found: UA, IW, MZ, GB.

One of eight species that inhabit Sanibel and Captiva, the saltmarsh mosquito was once so numerous on Sanibel Island that it set a world record: 365,000 collected in a single night on the east end of the island in September 1950. The mosquito ditches that can still be found throughout the islands were dredged by the Sanibel-Captiva Mosquito Control District in the early 1950s to provide native fish access to mosquito breeding habitat, thereby allowing them to consume more mosquito larvae.

In January 1958 several local mosquito control districts were combined to create the Lee County Mosquito Control District (LCMCD). Today the LCMCD uses an array of chemical and biological controls to

keep Sanibel and Captiva habitable. Every property owner on the islands pays a special tax to help fund the ongoing pest control, whose annual budget exceeds $16 million dollars. (To learn more about LCMCD go to www.lcmcd.org.)

Worldwide, mosquito-borne diseases are a significant threat. This year, more than 1 million people will die from malaria. When we add deaths from dengue fever, yellow fever, and a wide array of various equine and other forms of encephalitis, the number exceeds 2 million, with hundreds of thousands of cases in the Third World going unreported.

Fortunately, the saltmarsh mosquito is not a major vector in the transmission of diseases. Although capable of transmitting St. Louis encephalitis and eastern equine encephalitis in the laboratory, in the wild it does not fare as well with these two diseases. It is a known vector for dog heartworm and Venezuelan equine encephalitis.

This isn't the case for some of the other species that inhabit Sanibel and Captiva. In fact, of all the creatures described in this book, from bull sharks to 400-pound alligators, the single most deadly of them is the mosquito. The most deadly of all the species on the islands is *Aedes aegypti,* an invasive species that originated in Africa and has now spread via the various industries of *Homo sapiens* to every tropical and subtropical region in the world. This is the insect responsible for the spread of yellow fever, dengue fever, chikungunya, and other diseases. Although it exists in fair numbers on the islands, we are all blessed that there is no yellow or dengue fever present in the human population to serve as a reservoir for the disease.

Another potentially dangerous species that lives on the islands is *Anopheles quadrimaculatus,* a well-known vector for malaria, but once again, lacking a host with a case of active malaria to transmit, this tiny mosquito is no more deadly than its bite. The other two species of concern are *Culex nigripalpus,* which carries West Nile virus and Saint Louis encephalitis, and the Asian tiger mosquito (*Aedes albopictus*), which carries dengue fever. The other species found on the islands are not known to carry any human diseases, but all are capable of transmitting dog heartworm.

Although the mosquito is eaten by small birds and bats and its larvae is taken by mosquitofish, frogs, and turtles, these natural controls cannot rival its amazing ability to reproduce. Before the cross dike (aka Wildlife Drive) was built in "Ding" Darling, entomologists estimated that there were 2 billion saltmarsh mosquito eggs per acre on the surrounding tidal flats. Even though the chemicals used by LCMCD have been environmentally controversial at times, the fact is that Sanibel and Captiva would probably be uninhabitable were it not for our sustained program of mosquito control. Although they are unwitting hosts of the diseases they can carry, the islands' mosquitoes are the most frightening creatures in LIVING SANIBEL.

☐ _____ **Fire Ant** (Family *Formicidae*) Nicknames: zombie ant, biting ant, RIFA (red imported fire ant) / Status: FL=thriving / Life span: the queen can live for 6 to 7 years / Length: 0.12-0.24 in. (2-6 mm) / Reproduces: in upland areas including lawns, fields, and woodlands / Found: UA, IW, MZ.

The ant, along with the termite, is one of the most successful species in the insect world. There are 11,000 known ant species to date (more are added yearly)—700 in North America, including, in Florida, 207 natives, 53 exotics, and two imported

fire ant species. The most notorious is *Solenopsis invicta Buren*, which is the imported Brazilian fire ant most southerners are all too familiar with.

The *invicta* (which means unconquered) fire ant originated in the grasslands of Brazil, where its mounds of dirt helped to keep it out of danger during the annual floods of the rainy season. It first arrived in Florida, via the port of Mobile, Alabama, between 1933 and 1945. From there it has spread to every state in the South, as far north as Virginia and west to California. The sheer scope of its range makes eradication of this invasive and notorious insect impossible. The fire ant has few natural predators in its newfound range, where it is eaten by only a handful of birds. It displaces native ants and is very damaging to a host of native flora and fauna. It has recently spread to Taiwan, China, and Australia where it is wreaking havoc on natural insect populations and environments.

When accidentally stepped upon, fire ants react in defense of their nest, crawling up the legs of the intruder, and, through the release of pheromones by the lead ant, the entire colony is signaled to sting at once. The result can be not only excruciatingly painful, but sometimes even deadly. For smaller animals, such as alligator hatchlings, baby sea turtles, fledgling birds, and small mammals, this *en masse* sting can cause paralysis and death. Some humans are allergic to the fire ant toxins and can go into anaphylactic shock, requiring immediate medical attention. Worldwide, dozens of people succumb to fire ant stings annually. In fact, more people are killed by fire ant attacks than shark attacks annually. In the United States, more than $5 billion is spent annually on medical treatment, damage, and control in *invicta*-infested areas.

The sting of a fire ant is very painful, like holding a lit match against your skin. It originates from the abdomen of the ant, which injects into its victim a toxic alkaloid venom called solenopsin. The welts that result can last for weeks.

Treating the bites properly is essential to avoid infection. Do not squeeze or pick at the pustule as that will greatly increase the chances of infection. Wash the bite with antibacterial soap for two minutes or longer. Disinfect the site using Betadine, rubbing alcohol, or hydrogen peroxide. If it continues to itch, apply a dab of hydrocortisone cream. Cover with a bandage and repeat the process three times a day until it is healed.

The best way to rid your yard of fire ant mounds is through the use of various chemical applications available at most hardware stores. Pouring boiling hot water on the mound can sometimes work, but the queen, who can lay up to 1,500 eggs per day, is sometimes hidden below ground as deep as seven feet, so boiling water is not always effective. People have been known to soak the nests in gasoline, then light the ground on fire. Aside from being exceedingly dangerous, this approach has been proven to be ineffective.

◻ _____ **Sugar Ant** (Family *Formicidae*) Nicknames: house ant, crazy ant, Pharos ant / Status: FL=thriving / Life span: varies with each individual species / Reproduces: in the walls and attics of homes and condominiums throughout the islands / Found: UA, IW, GB, MZ.

There are at least a dozen species of the tiny intrusive sugar ant. Most of the small sugar and food-scrap-loving species are all but impossible to identify without the aid of an entomologist. The crazy ant (*Paratrechina longicornis*), which scurries around so frantically that it appears to be out of its mind, is easier to identify because of its ridiculous behavior.

Getting rid of any of these ants in your house or condo could be the subject of an entire book. Various treatments include fumigation, whole cloves, caulking up everything, boric acid, various ant poisons, red pepper powder, diatomaceous earth, or simply burning your house down and walking away smiling. In more than 25 years on Sanibel, I have tried just about everything to stop the minuscule ant's tireless invasion of my kitchen, all to no avail. Like the fire ant, the sugar ant is unconquerable. I have come around to a more Buddhist philosophy toward this little pest and have learned to live with it. It doesn't bite and it doesn't harbor any diseases, and let's face it, it just wants some measly crumbs and a place to call home.

❏ _____ **Carpenter Ant** (Genus: *Camponotus*) Nicknames; none / Status: FL=thriving / Length: 0.25 to 1 in. (6-25 mm) / Life span: to 60 days / Reproduces: in damp wood within trees, homes, or wood piles / Found: UA, IW, MZ.

© Wikipedia Commons

Once again the sheer number of species prevents easy identification of any particular type of carpenter ant on the islands. In the United States there are more than 20 different species that are commonly called carpenter ants. The most common of these is *Camponotus pennsylvanicus*.

In the wild, the carpenter ant plays an important role in the breaking down of decaying wood. It carves extensive tunnels and chambers into rotting trees and may take as long as six years to establish a mature colony. Some species, especially when disturbed, can deliver a powerful bite. It is heavily preyed upon by pileated woodpeckers, rats, mice, lizards, juvenile alligators, opossums, armadillos, and scores of other insects. In the interior of Florida, it is a favorite food for black bears. The larvae are especially sought after.

The carpenter ant can cause considerable damage to home, though generally it poses nowhere near the risk of the termite. Preventing moisture from collecting in the home and caulking cracks in the walls of the house will help keep carpenter ants away.

❏ _____ **Antlion** (Family *Myrmeleontidae*) Nicknames: doodlebug / Status: FL=thriving / Life span: varies by species, from 20-25 days to up to 3 years / Length: 0.78-5.9 in. (20-150 mm as adults) / Reproduces: in larval form in cone-shaped sand pits throughout the islands / Found: UA, IW, MZ.

Worldwide there are about 2,000 species of antlion. Florida is the antlion capital of the eastern United States with a total of 22 different species. It reproduces in small cone-shaped sand pits and exhibits the greatest disparity in size between larva and adult of any of the metamorphic insects. The adult resembles a large damselfly.

One of the most common places to find antlion larvae is in areas of soft sand where its distinctive concave ant trap resembles an upside-down volcano.

© Scott Robinson, Wikipedia

Some antlions live exclusively in gopher tortoise burrows, while others do not make the familiar ant traps at all.

As the name implies, the antlion's favorite food is ants, which fall into the trap and start sliding down the steep slope toward the bottom. Once the waiting antlion detects a victim, it throws sand up above the ant, creating a small avalanche that brings the ant into reach. The antlion then grabs the ant with its formidable jaws and injects it with a digestive venom that consumes all but the hard-shelled exoskeleton of the insect.

Oddly enough, the larval antlion does not have an anus. All the metabolic waste that is generated during its brief larval stage is stored and eventually emitted as meconium when the adult antlion emerges from its pupal cocoon a month later. Although the larval antlions are seldom preyed upon while in their traps, the adults are taken by nighthawks, bats, and rodents.

❒ _____ **Subterranean Termite** (Order: *Isoptera*) Nicknames: termite / Status: FL=thriving / Life span: varies with species, from 2 to 4 years for the workers and up to 15 years for a queen / Length: 0.15-0.45 in. (4-11 mm) / Reproduces: in large, complex colonies that thrive on stumps, buried wood scraps, and other wood products / Found: UA, IW, MZ.

Though it looks similar to an ant, the termite is more closely related to the cockroach with which it shares a common ancestor that scuttled about the

earth 300 million years ago. Colonies of termites form what is called a "superorganism," reducing the role of the individual termite to being completely dependent on the survival of the entire colony. The queen, through a complex system of pheromones, completely controls the colony, from producing backup queens, to the number of workers and the number of fertile kings she might have.

The subterranean termite requires moisture and contact with the soil or another water source to survive. When it first emerges from the egg, a termite is unable to digest wood, which is its primary food. A young termite starts out by eating the feces of older termites to ingest symbiotic microorganisms that allow it to break down the cellulose it feeds on. The scientific name for this strange behavior is called "proctodeal trophallaxis."

There are more than 4,000 species of termites on earth, and combined, they equal three times the mass of the 6.7 billion people on the planet. In Africa and India, people eat termites, which are a highly nutritious source of protein. The U.S. Department of Energy is studying the termite as a source of hydrogen production. The 200 species of microbes in its stomach makes it one of the most efficient bioreactors on earth. A single sheet of 8½ x 11 paper, when consumed by termites, can produce two liters of hydrogen. With the development of fuel cells that burn hydrogen, we may all be driving cars on termite-produced gas in the not-too-distant future.

When termites invade a home and decide that it is their personal buffet of cellulose, the outcome can be catastrophic. Some homes in Southwest Florida have been so riddled with termite damage that the only effective treatment was to tear them down and start over. In Key West and New Orleans almost every home has some degree of infestation. The cost of termite damage in North America runs into the tens of billions of dollars. If subterranean termites are discovered in or around your house, the best advice is to call a certified termite inspector and take whatever action is recommended as soon as possible.

Green and brown anoles, opossums, armadillos, rodents, insects, and birds all feast on termites. Ironically, termites have yet to make it to the table in the U.S., even though our homes are regularly eaten by them.

☐ _____ **Dry wood Termite** (Family: *Kalotermitidae*) Nicknames: termite / Status: FL=thriving / Life span: varies with species, from 2 to 4 years for the workers and up to 7 years for the queen / Length: 0.15-0.45 in. (4-11 mm) / Reproduces: in colonies that thrive on wood scraps and other wood products / Found: UA, IW, MZ.

There are more than 400 species of the dry wood termite worldwide. It is not cold tolerant so its range is limited in the United States to the extreme southern perimeter from North Carolina to Southern California. Unlike its cousin, the subterranean termite, the dry wood termite does not need a source of water or contact with the soil to survive.

Because of this ability, it can sometimes be found in attics, rafters, and other locations where other termites would fail to thrive.

It differs in other ways as well. The dry wood termite is not as well organized as the subterranean termite and does not form complex tunnel systems or build large, above-ground mounds. A mature colony will contain no more than a few thousand individuals, which, compared with the tens of millions in some colonies of subterranean termites, makes them much easier to control. As a result, infestations tend to be much smaller, though over time, the damage to structures can be just as bad.

One way of identifying a possible infestation is the presence of fecal pellets, which resemble a pile of tiny, six-sided grains of sand, one-sixteenth of an inch across and either black- or cream-colored.

Colonies can sometimes be found swarming, especially in the spring, when scores of them may land on porches or woodpiles looking for a new place to call home. The dry wood termite is eaten by bats, birds, other insects, lizards, rodents, and spiders.

❒ _____ **American Cockroach** (*Periplaneta americana*)
Nicknames: palmetto bug, waterbug / Status: FL=thriving, IUCN=LC / Life span: to 1 year / Length: 1.2-1.6 in. (30-40 mm) / Reproduces: in the damp understory, sabal palms, and the crawl spaces of homes, condominiums, and businesses / Found: UA, IW, MZ.

While this common insect has an American name, its origins are believed to be in western Africa. It arrived in North America as a stowaway as early as 1625, probably crossing the Atlantic during the era of slave ships, where the wretched conditions provided ample food for an insect whose dining preferences include carrion and raw sewage.

The cockroach is a survivor. Ancestors of today's cockroach date back to the Carboniferous period, originating some 360 million years ago. Its ability to withstand lethal doses of radiation, toxic levels of chemicals, and a host of other conditions that would kill most other living things makes the future secure for this enduring insect.

In Florida the American cockroach is kindly referred to as a "palmetto bug." In New York, where it is common inside of buildings, it is referred to as a "waterbug."

The adage, "a rose by any other name is still a rose," applies equally well to roaches—it's easier to say your house has a palmetto bug infestation than to admit it is full of roaches.

The cockroach is common in the wild where it feeds in rotting woodpiles and the thick understory of the wetlands, as well as in garbage bins. The American cockroach is not cold tolerant and will retreat into homes during excessive cold snaps. In the north it survives the cold by living in sewers, basements, and wall cavities. A female cockroach will produce an average of 150 offspring during her one-year life cycle.

The cockroach is a favorite food of many birds, mammals, and lizards. Fire ants prey on the cockroach, stinging it en masse, killing it, then devouring all but the exoskeleton. Although it may appear to run at 20 miles per hour when you are chasing one with a newspaper, this is only an illusion. Researchers at the University of California at Berkeley registered a record speed of a mere 3.4 mph. The illusion is created because that equates to 50 body lengths per second. An Olympic athlete who could match that number would be running at 205 mph.

☐ ____ **Florida Stinking Roach** (*Eurycotis floridana*) Nicknames: Florida woods cockroach, palmetto bug / Status: FL=thriving / Life span: 1 to 2 years / Length: 1-2 in. (25-50 mm) / Reproduces: in palmetto thickets and cabbage palms / Found: UA, IW, MZ.

A native of Florida, the stinking roach is easy to mistake for its African cousin, the American cockroach. Upon closer inspection, however, the differences between the two are quite dramatic. For one, behind its head the stinking roach has a tiny set of wings that are useless for flying. The American cockroach, though awkward, does fly. The other major difference is the segmented section of the body, which, unlike the American cockroach, is exposed and considerably darker. Its name comes from the foul odor it emits when approached that some say smells like rotten amaretto.

This native Florida roach is more truly a palmetto bug and seldom enters homes except during periods of drought or extreme cold spells when it tends to move much slower and is easy to catch. It feeds in leaf litter or under old boards

and is often seen in bushes and wooded areas. Never kill a roach that is outdoors because by doing so you are inadvertently participating in reverse natural selection. It is better to strengthen the outdoor population so its gene pool will eventually triumph over the roaches that seek human habitat.

The Florida woods cockroach is preyed upon by birds, raptors, small mammals, lizards, and other

© Charles Sobczak   insects.

☐ _____ **Firefly** (Family *Lampyridae*) Nicknames; lightning bug / Status: FL=thriving / Life span: varies among species, but generally between 2-4 months / Reproduces: in the soil throughout the islands, but prefers upland habitat / Found: UA, IW.

More than 2,000 species of fireflies are found in the world, mostly in temperate and tropical climates. Sanibel and Captiva have several different species. The firefly is one of the few land creatures capable of bioluminescence, which is more common in plants and animals living in the ocean, especially at depths of 3,000 to 16,000 feet. The ability of sea creatures to light themselves up allows them to find their prey, and each other for mating, in total darkness.

The firefly, which feeds at night, uses its pale green or yellowish lamp the same way as these deep-sea creatures. In one species of firefly, *Photuris*, the female mimics the mating flashes of other fireflies, then devours the males when they come courting. Because of this behavior, this species is often referred to as the "femme fatale firefly." During the early months of the summer, you will see one species on Sanibel and Captiva that does not flash at all, but whose lower abdomen glows continuously throughout the evening.

Larval fireflies prey on other insects, slugs, and snails, but what the adult firefly eats, if anything, is unclear. It is eaten by bats, birds, other insects, and night-roving mammals such as rats.

☐ _____ **Love Bug** (*Plecia neactica*) Nicknames: honeymoon fly, telephonebug, kissybug, double-headed bug, March fly / Status: FL=thriving / Life span: up to 1 year, including the larval stage / Length: 0.33-0.45 in. (8-11.5 mm) / Reproduces: in grassy and wooded areas around the entire Gulf of Mexico / Found: UA, IW.

In its larval stage, the love bug is a beneficial insect that feeds in grassy areas on the dead vegetation found within the thatch. It lives for up to nine months in this stage, but once it becomes a flying adult it seldom lasts longer than a week. The male is the first to perish, generally within the first 48 hours after breeding, whereupon the female drags the male's body around until she lays her eggs. As adults, they are almost always seen in pairs, flying stuck together in a prolonged mating arrangement that can last up to 12 hours.

It is the massive love bug swarms that have made them such a nemesis in Florida, especially on the highway where they can completely cover the front of a car. The swarms, which can number in the hundreds of thousands, occur in Florida in the late spring, late summer, and sometimes in mid-December. Although the love bug does not bite or sting, its body contains an acidic yellow blood that has been known to take the paint off of cars. Swarms have also been known to clog up radiators to the point of overheating.

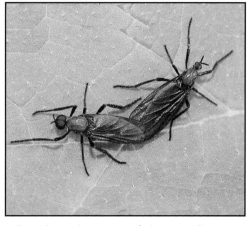

Very few insects, birds, or lizards eat love bugs because of their acidic taste. A handful of spiders eat them, but most of the predation comes during the larval stage when they are far more palatable.

☐ _____ **European Honey Bee** (*Apis mellifera*) Nicknames: western honey bee, Italian bee / Status: FL=stable but suffering from a disease called colony collapse disorder / Life span: the queen can live 3 to 4 years; the drone lives for a month or two / Length: 0.50-0.66 in. (13-17 mm) / Reproduces: in hives and natural cavities throughout the islands / Found: IW, MZ, UA.

There are 20,000 species of bees in the world, but only seven of these are recognized as honey bees. In the United States, the honey bee is at the center of a multi-billion-dollar industry and is vital to the pollination of fruit trees and flowering plants that we rely on for food. Sadly, in many parts of China, the environment has become so degraded that the honey bee is no longer present, and most flowering plants must now be pollinated by hand.

Of course, the honey bee produces honey, made up of fructose and glucose derived from the nectar of the flowers that bees are known to frequent. It has 97 percent of the sweetness of granulated sugar. One impressive aspect of honey is that it does not spoil. The honey bee also produces a wax, used for making candles, as well as for a host of industrial applications.

Spotting a honey bee on Sanibel and Captiva is not difficult. The best way to find bees is to find flowers, and there are literally hundreds of flowering plants on the island that attracts the honey bee. Beehives are still being brought to the islands by Elliot Curtis and Sons, Beekeepers, and can sometimes be spotted in vacant fields. Mangrove honey is considered a delicacy.

Every hive contains three types of bees: the queen; a small number of male drones, who stay in the hive to fertilize the queen; and 20,000 to 40,000 worker bees. These worker bees are the only ones you will see unless you are with a beekeeper, as they are responsible for gathering the nectar, which in turn feeds the hive during winter hibernation. Upon returning to the hive, worker bees perform

Honey Bee © ThroughTheLensGallery.com

a complicated bee dance that conveys directions to both nearby and sometimes very distant flowering plants. Like ants and termites, the hives are living social organisms that cannot survive without these complex relationships, many of which remain a mystery.

You can sometimes find wild nests on the islands, though always exercise caution around any beehive for fear of an attack, which can produce dozens of stings and in some cases put the intruder into anaphylactic shock. The recently introduced African honey bee, which is far more aggressive than the European variety, has already been responsible for two to three deaths annually in the U.S., making it more deadly than venomous snakes.

☐ _____ **Mud Dauber Wasp** (*Sceliphron caementarium*)
Nicknames: dirt dauber, dirt diver, mud wasp / Status: FL=thriving / Life span: 2 to 5 years / Length: 0.75-1.25 in. (19-32 mm) / Reproduces: in small, mud-based nests under piling homes, in crevices, and on natural rock formations / Found: UA, IW, MZ.

There are actually three species of the mud dauber wasp on Sanibel and Captiva. The most prevalent of these is the black and yellow mud dauber (*Sceliphron caementarium*), but the other two, the solid black organ pipe mud dauber (*Trypoxylon politum*) and the iridescent blue mud dauber (*Chalybion californicum*), are also fairly common.

Although the mud dauber looks threatening enough, it seldom stings and is not at all aggressive. The biggest danger it poses comes not from the nasty sting it is

© Wikipedia Commons © Wikipedia Commons

capable of delivering but from where it builds its nest. A mud dauber wasp nest built in the air speed indicator of a passenger plane was the primary reason for the crash of Birgenair Flight 301 on Feb. 6, 1996, killing all 189 people on board.

The mud dauber can also cause electrical shorts in outdoor ceiling fans, which may sit for months without rotating and thereby allow the mud dauber to build multiple nests that can jam the mechanism. The mud dauber can be a real nuisance under piling homes where it is prone to building its little mud huts just about everywhere.

The mud dauber is beneficial in that it is a good pollinator and is a predator of the venomous black widow spider, which is found on the islands.

☐ _____ **Paper Wasp** (Family *Vespidae*) Nicknames: umbrella wasp / Status: FL=thriving / Life span: to 1 year / Length: 0.75-1 in. (19-25 mm) / Reproduces: in paper-like nests under porches, palm leaves, and numerous other locations throughout the islands / Found: UA, IW, MZ.

Closely related to the yellow jacket, the paper wasp is found throughout Sanibel and Captiva, most commonly nesting under wooden railings, under porches, in carports, and under the large fronds of cabbage and ornamental palms. It builds its combed nest by mixing fibers from dead wood with its saliva, anchoring them to the structure with a petiole, a fibrous stalk that is amazingly strong.

The paper wasp is not nearly as aggressive as the yellow jacket, but if its nest is directly disturbed, it will attack the intruder and is capable of delivering a very painful sting. Such an attack can be dangerous in that it could consist of a dozen or more wasps delivering stings.

The paper wasp feeds on spiders, caterpillars, and nectar. It is a beneficial species whose nest should not be

© Charles Sobczak

© Al Tuttle

disturbed unless located where it poses an imminent threat to humans. It is preyed upon by parasitic wasps, birds, and lizards.

Of the more than 1,100 species of paper wasp worldwide, 22 reside in North America and several are found on the islands. Identifying each and every one of these is beyond the scope of this book.

❑ _____ **Velvet Ant** (Family *Mutillidae*) Nicknames: cow killer, cow ant, red velvet ant / Status: FL=stable / Life span: 50 to 60 days, varies with different species / Length: 0.5-0.75 in. (12-19 mm) / Reproduces: by means of parasitic behavior on bee and wasp larvae / Found: UA, IW.

The velvet ant is not an ant at all; it is a wasp. The female is wingless, but the male velvet ant looks far more like a traditional wasp. In fact, the two sexes can vary so much in appearance, that unless caught in the act of mating, they do not look like the same species. The scientific term for this is sexual dimorphism.

The female velvet ant is covered in a heavily textured hair-like material that grows out of an extremely tough exoskeleton. This insect version of armor plating protects the parasitic female velvet ant from stings when she lays her eggs on the mature larvae in the nests of other bees and wasps. When her eggs hatch the larvae kill and eat the host.

© Lorraine Sommer

There are more than 5,000 species of this flightless wasp worldwide, with more than 400 in North America. It is not common on the islands but can be spotted crossing shell roads or along the bike paths where they look like oversized red and black ants. The velvet ant is not aggressive but will deliver a nasty sting if provoked. It is taken by birds, lizards, and snakes, but because its sting is quite nasty, it is not as popular a prey as more defenseless insects.

☐ _____ **Grandpus Bug** (Family *Thelyphonidae*) Nicknames: giant whipscorpion, vinegaroon, grampa bug, whip scorpion / Status: FL=stable / Life span: to 7 years / Length: 1 to 3.3 in. (25-85 mm) / Reproduces: under logs, rocks and woodpiles / Found: UA, IW.

Upon your first encounter with this formidable-looking insect, your reaction might be to run. The grandpus bug looks altogether too similar to the scorpion, and the long whip appears ready to strike at any moment, but the whip is harmless and the grandpus bug is nonvenomous.

The grandpus is a type of spider, though more closely related

© Wikipedia Commons

to true scorpions than your typical spider. It has a unique defensive mechanism that sprays a foul odor when attacked. The smell comes from acetic acid, the main ingredient in vinegar—hence, the nickname vinegaroon. The best place to find one of these bugs is under rocks, rotting logs, or inside water-meter boxes.

It feeds on millipedes, caterpillars, cockroaches, and crickets. It is preyed upon by armadillos, opossums, rats, mice, and snakes. It is considered a beneficial species in that it helps to keep the cockroach and millipede population in balance.

❒ _____ **Florida Ivory Millipede** (*Chicobolus spinigerus*)
Nicknames: millipede / Status: FL=thriving / Life span: 1.5-2.5 years / Length: 1-4 in. (25-100 mm) / Reproduces: in the moist understory of wetlands and uplands habitat / Found: UA, IW, MZ.

© Charles Sobczak

There are more than 10,000 species of millipedes worldwide. The largest of these, the giant African millipede, can grow to 11 inches. Almost all millipedes are detritivores, eating almost exclusively decaying leaves and other dead plant matter. Fossil records indicate that the first known land creature was a one-centimeter-long (0.39 in.) millipede that ate mosses and decaying plants some 428 million years ago during the Silurian geologic period. The basic shape and diet of this species has changed little since then.

In the past decade the Florida ivory millipede has become increasingly populous on Sanibel and Captiva. It can be found in the Bailey Tract, as well as the Sanibel Gardens Preserve, from Wulfert to the Sanibel Lighthouse. The juveniles are roughly an inch long, while the mature millipedes can grow to four inches. It has the unwelcome tendency to get into garages, workrooms, and houses where, lacking the detritus it needs to survive, it soon curls up and dies. Sweeping up dead ivory millipedes has become a common chore for many islanders.

It is completely harmless to people, but some millipedes do contain defensive chemicals that can cause minor skin irritation. Its only real defense against predation is to curl up into a ball, exposing its hardened outer shell and protecting its soft underside.

The millipede plays a vital role in the cycle of life. It turns decaying wood and plant life back into soil and rids the understory of excess thatch. It is heavily preyed upon by snakes, birds, and reptiles. Fire ants will also overwhelm this slow-crawling bug, stinging it into shock, then consuming it.

☐ ___ Two-striped Walking Stick (*Anisomorpha buprestoides*)

Nicknames: stick bug, palmetto walking stick, devil rider, musk mare, prairie alligator, devil's darning needle / Status: FL=stable / Life span: 1 to 3 years / Length: 2-3 in. (50-76 mm) / Reproduces: in the uplands region in palmetto thickets and dense foliage / Found: UA, IW.

Note the male on the female's back © Blake Sobczak

The walking stick is one of the most fascinating bugs found on the islands. Its extensive list of nicknames clearly indicates its uniqueness. The first thing to point out about the two-striped walking stick is to keep your distance. When in danger it will squirt, with accuracy up to a distance of one foot, a strong-smelling and caustic spray that is painfully irritating to the eyes and mucous membranes. Victims have reported that the pain is so excruciating that it is as though someone has poured hot, molten lead into your eye, impairing vision for a week or longer. If sprayed, you should flush the eye immediately.

Another bizarre aspect of the walking stick is that the male spends almost its entire adult life riding on the back of the female. The male is roughly one-third the size of the female and generally is positioned near the rear of the female. Forcefully separating the two will sometimes result in death. The two-striped walking stick is similar to the millipede in that it is a detritivore, as well as a herbivore, feeding on both living and decaying plant life. It uses its chemical spray to deter would-be predators such as birds, rats, snakes, and lizards.

Some rodents have learned to keep their distance and wait until the large female has sprayed five or six times, leaving her reservoir depleted, then pounce upon her to dine. The walking stick is closely related to the family of insects known as preying mantises, and many species are parthenogenetic (capable of asexual reproduction).

❐ _____ **Lubber Grasshopper** (*Romalea guttata*) Nicknames: eastern lubber / Status: FL=thriving / Life span: n/a / Length: 1.5-4 in. (38-101 mm) / Reproduces: in the understory of uplands habitat / Found: UA, IW.

© Hung V. Do

This large, unmistakable grasshopper is brightly colored, for good reason. Like many other toxic animals, the lubber grasshopper proudly displays its bright colors as a warning to birds, snakes, and other predators that it is inedible. When threatened, it quickly raises its wings defiantly and bubbles out a poisonous froth. It can also shunt poisons from the toxic plants it eats, making it anything but a tasty snack.

One Florida predator, the loggerhead shrike, has learned to impale the lubber on a barbed wire fence or other spike and wait until its poisons dry out before dining on one. The primary cause of lubber mortality, however, comes from within: it is especially vulnerable to parasites that consume the grasshopper from the inside out.

The lubber is a herbivore, dining on various leaves, berries, and grasses. The immature lubber is black with yellow markings and looks a bit like an oversized cricket. Look for large lubbers in the late summer and fall in dry inland habitats.

There are more than a dozen species of other grasshoppers on Sanibel and Captiva, scores of species in Florida, and more than 11,000 species worldwide. They are commonly eaten by humans in Mexico, Africa, and China.

The Spiders

> ☐ ____ **Housekeeper Spider** (*Heteropoda venatoria*) Nicknames: giant crab spider, "Banana" spider, huntsman spider, cane spider / Status: FL=invasive, thriving / Life span: to 2 years / Length: 3-5 in. (76-127 mm) / Reproduces: in crevices and heavily wooded areas / Found: UA, IW.

Of the dozens of spiders that live on Sanibel and Captiva, the housekeeper is probably the one you are most likely to see. Originally from Asia, this spider arrived in the New World during the time of whaling ships and trading ships that frequented the Far East. The housekeeper can deliver a formidable bite that may take two or three days to heal, but it is not considered a venomous spider. A small housekeepers can sometimes be mistaken for a large brown recluse spider, which is venomous but extremely rare on the islands.

Because of its intolerance to cold weather, the housekeeper prefers living and breeding indoors. It is able to hide and slip through incredibly tiny cracks and crevices. It is exceedingly quick and agile, and feeds on cockroaches, silverfish, and smaller, potentially more dangerous spiders, including the black widow. This is the primary reason for its common name: housekeeper. In most parts of the world, having a housekeeper spider in your home is considered good fortune, and it is seldom killed.

Look for the spider dashing across the ceiling of your home or in the rafters of any piling home. It has recently gone completely feral, living in cabbage palms, avocado trees, and other plants. It does not build webs or nests, but carries its young around with it in a special egg sac. It is eaten by snakes, small rodents, and birds.

☐ _____ **Crevice Spider** (Family *Filistatidae*) Nicknames: southern house spider, crevice weaver / Status: FL=common / Life span: to 8 years / Length: 1.2-2 in. (30-50 mm) / Reproduces: in finely woven webs that all have a narrow tunnel where the spiders hide and raise their brood / Found: UA, IW.

© Charles Sobczak

The crevice spider is probably the second most common spider found on the islands, after the housekeeper. It is especially fond of older wooden structures where it builds its unmistakable nest under floor joists, next to light fixtures, or in the corner of windows where it can prey upon insects that are attracted to the house lights at night.

The crevice spider uses its sheetlike web to trap and entangle its prey. When a moth or fly becomes caught in this wooly (cribellate) silk, the large, dark brown spider rushes out and subdues its victim with its fangs, quickly injecting a venom. Bites to humans, though very rare, are not life threatening, and the swelling seldom lasts for more than a few days.

© Charles Sobczak

The crevice spider, because of its unsightly nest, is not as welcome in homes as is the housekeeper. After time, its silken web becomes host to dead flies, wasps, moths, and other insects, and the spider itself is dark and foreboding. By and large, however, the crevice spider does more good than harm, killing stinging hornets, black widows, and cockroaches. It is eaten by geckos, anoles, small rodents, and a handful of birds.

☐ _____ **Black Widow** (*Latrodectus mactans*) WARNING: VENOMOUS SPIDER / Nicknames: none / Status: FL=stable / Life span: to 1 (male); to 5 years (female) / Length: 0.5-1.5 in. (12-37 mm) / Reproduces: under logs, in low shrubs, and in places such as water-meter holes / Found: UA, IW, MZ.

This is one spider you probably do not want to look for. The black widow is easy to recognize by its shiny black body and distinctive red hourglass marking on the rounded abdomen. The female is aggressive and will inject a potentially

With her egg sac   © Lorraine Sommer

lethal neurotoxic venom into her bite. Sixty-three deaths from black widows were confirmed in the United States between 1950 and 1959. Improvements in antivenin have significantly reduced this mortality rate, but the black widow is still considered one of the most dangerous spiders on earth.

The female black widow is aptly named. The local species, *Latrodectus mactans*, is the only known black widow that practices sexual cannibalism. Shortly after the male mates with the female, she kills him with her powerful venom, then consumes him. Not all pairings result in this bizarre ending, and males that manage to escape can go on to fertilize other black widows, if they dare!

The female is very fertile, laying four to nine egg sacs per year, each containing up to 400 eggs. In keeping with the temperament of their mother, the juvenile spiders practice cannibalism, and only a few make it to maturity. The black widow feeds on woodlice, other spiders, and a variety of insects. It is preyed upon by preying mantis, spider wasps, and a number of specialized flies. If you happen across a black widow, do not attempt to pick it up or get too near it. It is fast and aggressive, and if you are bitten by one, seek medical attention immediately!

☐ _____ **Spinybacked Orb Weaver** (*Gasteracantha cancriformis*) Nicknames: star spider, jewel box spider, crab spider / Status: FL=common / Life span: less than 1 year / Length: 0.25-0.50 in. (9-13 mm) / Reproduces: in woodland edges and shrubby garden areas, building typical spider webs / Found: UA, IW, MZ.

Several species of spiny orb weavers are found on Sanibel and Captiva. The spinybacked orb weaver is the most common, but several other closely related spiders are also plentiful here. It is easy to identify because of its unique six-pointed

body. Its unusual shape is thought to be a defense mechanism against bird attacks. It does not look very easy to swallow, though anoles and larger spiders take their toll on this unusual arachnid.

The spinybacked orb weaver likes to build its nest under stairwells, near pools, and in heavy shrubs. It weaves into its nest a small silk flag that is thought to keep birds and larger insects from accidentally flying into the nest, destroying a hard day's work. After spinning a web, which can be more than two feet in diameter, the spinyback returns to the center of the web to wait for a misguided moth or other flying insect to become entrapped in the fine silk. The spider then rushes out and subdues the hapless bug with its mild venom. Its bite is not harmful to humans.

☐ _____ **Golden Orb Weaver** (*Nephila clavipes*) Nicknames: banana spider, golden orb silk weaver, golden silk spider, writing spider / Status: FL=common / Life span: 1 to 2 years / Length: 0.5 (male) to 3 in. (female) (12-75 mm) / Reproduces: in taller trees, telephone lines, and eaves, making large webs that can stretch for more than six feet / Found: UA, IW, MZ.

An impressive-looking spider, the golden orb weaver is arguably the largest spider on the islands. Prior to the arrival of Hurricane Charley in 2004, followed by Wilma in 2005, it was always possible to find multiple golden orb weaver webs in the power lines running north along Dixie Beach Blvd. After the hurricanes blew through, most of these massive webs were destroyed, and the golden orb weaver has yet to recover.

While it is a venomous spider, the golden orb weaver seldom bites humans and will do so only if pinched. The ensuing sting is relatively harmless and leads to a slight redness and localized pain. Its web, which can exceed a meter in diameter, is woven with beautiful golden threads that have six times the tensile strength of steel.

Golden Orb Weaver
© Wikipedia Commons

Recently the silk of this spider has been used to help in neuronal regeneration, connecting neurons in the human body from where they were severed. Further research is being done on other uses for the golden orb weaver's amazingly strong silk.

This large spider is preyed upon by a handful of mammals, snakes, and reptiles, but seldom by birds. It catches any number of flying insects, including dragonflies, in its large web and quickly subdues them with its toxin.

❒ _____ **Daddy Longlegs** (Family *Leiobunidae*) Nicknames: harvestman, granddaddy longlegs / Status: FL=common / Life span: 2 to 3 years / Length: 0.25-0.35 (body only) (6.3-9 mm) / Reproduces: in thickets and around homes and condominiums / Found: UA, IW, MZ.

Although it belongs to the class of arachnids, the daddy longlegs is not a true spider. Recent DNA evidence indicates it is more closely related to ticks and mites than to spiders. It belongs to the larger order *Opiliones*, which is divided into four suborders.

Worldwide there are more than 6,400 identified species of this spider; most scientists are convinced the actual number will exceed 10,000 species, since hundreds are being discovered and added to the order every year. Many of them do not have the typical long, threadlike legs of the daddy longlegs, but have short legs and are brightly colored with sharp spines on their backs. These spiders are primarily tropical, found in the rainforests of Africa, South America, and Southeast Asia.

The daddy longlegs is often identified as venomous but it is a myth. They are not. In the wild it is an omnivore, feeding on small insects, plants, fungi, and carrion. Like a handful of reptiles and fish species, some daddy longlegs are parthenogenetic, meaning they are capable of asexual reproduction. This attribute is more common in the phylum Arthropoda than in any other phylum.

A number of insects, birds, and reptiles, including toads, feed on the daddy longlegs. It also suffers high mortality at the hands of internal parasites, which they ingest when feeding on dead organisms, bird droppings, and other fecal matter. Several cave-dwelling species are considered endangered or threatened.

Dragonfly   © Hung V. Do

Dragonflies and Butterflies

☐ _____ **Dragonflies** (Family *Aeschnidae*) Nicknames: mosquito hawk, darner, devil's darning needle / Status: FL=common / Life span: 7 months to 1 year, depending on the species / Length: 2-4 in. (50-101 mm) / Reproduces: in standing water such as small ponds, the Sanibel River, and larger residential lakes / Found: UA, IW, MZ.

At certain times of the year, especially in the spring and early summer, massive swarms of this aerial insect appear in upland areas such as the Bailey Tract. Literally thousands of dragonflies can be seen at once, dashing about feeding on a mass emergence of prey (commonly called "a hatch") well into twilight.

The color and pattern variations of this beautiful insect are nothing short of astounding, in many ways rivaling the beauty of butterflies. They range from iridescent blue, to a deep scarlet, to pink, to gold

© Hung V. Do

Dragonflies mating   © Hung V. Do

and jet black. The names are equally diverse: emperor, keeled skimmer, azure hawker, roseate skimmer, and green darner. The jeweler Louis Comfort Tiffany was so inspired by the dragonfly that he used it as a motif for his stained-glass creations.

Watching one pursue and capture its prey—mosquitoes, moths, bees, and flies—is enthralling. It is one of the most adroit flying insects in the world, capable of sharp turns, instant ascents and descents, and stunning agility. The adult dragonfly can propel itself in six directions: upward, downward, forward, backward, and side to side. Only the hummingbird rivals the dragonfly in flying prowess. The dragonfly is revered for its swiftness and agility by the Native Americans.

Worldwide there are more than 6,500 species of dragonflies. Most live in tropical and subtropical regions; some 425 species reside in North America. While no one has an accurate number of how many dragonfly species are found on Sanibel and Captiva, the number is probably in the dozens.

The dragonfly is considered beneficial for its ability to feast on mosquitoes and biting flies. Birds of prey, including the swallowtail kite, are known to feed on the dragonfly, and the nymphs are heavily preyed upon by frogs, fish, and even immature alligators. Look for them on Island Inn Road, in the Pick Preserve, near the Indigo trail in the "Ding" Darling Wildlife Refuge, and the cemetery on Captiva. The photographs herein are of several species you might find on Sanibel and Captiva.

☐ _____ **Butterflies** (Order *Lepidoptera*) Nicknames: none / Status: FL=stable, except for the endangered Miami Blue Butterfly / Life span: two weeks to 9 months, depending on the species / Length: 3-5 in. (wingspan) (76-127 mm) / Reproduces: in four stages—egg, larva (caterpillar), pupa, and adult (imago)—generally in dry, upland habitats / Found: UA, IW, MZ.

The butterfly is the subject of literally hundreds of books and thousands of scientific papers. One member of the species, the monarch butterfly, is famous for its annual 3,000-mile migration from the fields and forests of North America to the trans-volcanic mountains of central Mexico, settling in the Oyamel fir forests at altitudes over 10,000 feet. The most amazing aspect of this migration is that four to five generations separate the populations that make the voyage, yet they are able to fly these vast distances, know where to go without ever having been there before, and then pass that information on to future generations. The mechanisms that allow this remain a mystery.

Monarchs on their way to Mexico will often stop, dine, and gather their energy on Sanibel and Captiva before flying nonstop across the Gulf of Mexico to the mountains of Mexico. The monarch is also

Queen butterfly   ©ThroughTheLensGallery.com

fascinating because it is poisonous, and it dines on milkweed sap, which is toxic. Several other species of nonpoisonous butterflies mimic the wing patterns and coloration of the monarch to ward off potential predators. Locally these include the viceroy, queen, and to a lesser extent, the gulf fritillary.

The zebra longwing (*Heliconius charithonia*) is Florida's official state butterfly. The hurricanes of 2004 and 2005 severely impacted the local butterfly populations, and finding a zebra longwing on Sanibel or Captiva today can be quite challenging.

Zebra Longwing butterfly   ©ThroughTheLensGallery.com

Of course, the easiest way to find local butterflies is by going to the Lolly Cohen Memorial Butterfly House at the Sanibel-Captiva Conservation Foundation, which is open daily. If you want to learn more about these amazing insects, the SCCF gives regularly scheduled guided tours. Any number of other native plants are known to attract butterflies. Blue porterweed is among the more popular butterfly plants. The staff of the Native Plant Nursery at SCCF will advise you on how to create a butterfly garden.

In its caterpillar form, this insect is often called an "eating machine" because it consumes vast amounts of vegetation. As an adult, the butterfly dines primarily on nectar from flowers. Large dragonflies, anoles, small rodents, and many different species of birds prey on the butterfly. It is also taken in caterpillar and pupa form.

Following are some photographs of the species you are most likely to find on Sanibel and Captiva.

Buckeye ©ThroughTheLensGallery.com

Yellow Sulfur ©ThroughTheLensGallery.com

White Peacock
© Charles Sobczak

Giant Swallowtail
Courtesy Wikipedia Commons

The Crustaceans: Crabs and Shrimps

❒ _____ **Blue Crab** (*Callinectes sapidus*) Nicknames: Maryland blue crab / Status: FL=stable, IUCN=NE / Life span: to 3 years / Length: 3-7 in. across the carapace (76-177 mm) / Weight: 8-14 oz (0.22-0.39 kg) / Reproduces: in the estuary of the back bay / Found: MZ.

The official state crustacean of Maryland, the blue crab was once very abundant in the waters and inlets of the Chesapeake Bay. In recent years these crabs, along with horseshoe crabs and Chesapeake oysters, have decreased dramatically as a result of coastal pollution. Locally the blue crab can still be found around the seven spillways that run beneath Wildlife Drive in the "Ding" Darling Wildlife Refuge, though nowhere near the numbers of 20 years ago.

This prized commercial shellfish can be purchased fresh at several fish markets in Lee County. During the harvest season the deeper waters of Pine Island Sound and San Carlos Bay are riddled with the floating Styrofoam crab-trap markers, making every boat captain concerned about "catching a trap or wrapping a trap-line." It's interesting to note that although it's a popular food from the Atlantic coast to Argentina, the blue crab is considered too small to bother with along the Pacific Coast of Central and South America and is left un-harvested.

© Wikipedia - wpopp

Hitch-hiking across the ocean in the ballast of commercial shipping vessels, the blue crab is considered an invasive species in the Baltic Sea, North Sea, Mediterranean, and the Black Sea where, when discovered, it is immediately eradicated. The blue crab is fed upon by humans, cownose rays, tarpon, permit, and sharks; immature crabs are speared by great blue herons and anhingas.

❑ _____ **Stone Crab** (*Menippe mercenaria*) Nicknames: mud crab, Florida stone crab / Status: FL=stable, IUCN=LC / Life span: 7 to 8 years / Length: 3.5-4 in. (91-101 mm) / Weight: 1-1.5 lb (0.45-0.70 kg) / Reproduces: in the estuaries and nearshore waters of the gulf / Found: BB, GW.

Long considered a Florida delicacy, the stone crab is highly sought after by seafood lovers. Literally tens of thousands of stone crab traps are put into the nearshore gulf waters from the Panhandle to the Florida Keys every season, which runs from October 15 to May 15. The annual harvest of claws in 2008 was estimated to be more than 3.1 million pounds. Stone crab, per pound, is the most expensive seafood served in the U.S.

The stone crab harvest is different from the blue crab in that the whole crab is never taken, only its claws, which constitute 50 percent of its body weight. The living animal is tossed back into the ocean, allowed to regenerate its lost claws over the next two to three years. The mortality rate of the de-clawed stone crabs is quite high, however, with studies indicating that as many as 47 percent of the crabs die when both claws are taken and 28 percent die after a single amputation. As high as these numbers are, they are still more sustainable than the blue crab fishery where the whole crab is taken.

The stone crab is fairly commonly observed inshore, often found clinging to the edge of the concrete spillways under Wildlife Drive in "Ding" Darling. The crabs seen in these areas are juveniles, seldom larger than an inch or two across. They are a popular food for night herons, bonnethead sharks, stingrays, and cownosed rays, as well as octopus. The stone crab feeds on detritus, carrion, algae, and marine mollusks, including oysters and scallops.

❑ _____ **Mole Crab** (*Emerita talpoida*) Nicknames: sand flea, sand crab, sea pig, beach hopper, lookie cookie / Status: FL=stable, IUCN=NE / Life span: 2 to 3 years / Length: 0.75-1.37 in. (20-35 mm) / Weight: n/a / Reproduces: in the swash zone of the beaches / Found: GB, GW.

Locally the mole crab is commonly called the sand flea. Most people are probably unaware that this crab exists in staggering numbers right along the edge of the beach where the water laps up against the shoreline. Ranging in size from the quarter-inch-long juvenile to the 1.5-inch female, this small crab is easily overlooked because its camouflaged coloration is almost identical to the color of the surrounding sand. It is sometimes found in groups of thousands.

Along the shoreline it uses specialized antennae to filter out and feed on plankton and organic debris. The breaking waves constantly churn the water in the swash zone, allowing the crab to feed easily on the detritus carried in by the tides.

The mole crab is a popular bait for

© Blake Sobczak

anglers. It lacks any kind of pincers or claws and can be dug up by hand or by using either a shell net or a small metal scooping device. It is especially productive as bait for pompano, seatrout, and whiting, all fish that feed on this bait naturally along the surf line. The mole crab is a favorite food of the larger shorebirds such as willets and dowitchers, whose long beaks are capable of prodding deep into the soft sand where the mole crab thrives.

☐ _____ **Ghost Crab** (*Ocypode quadrata*) Nicknames: sand crab / Status: FL=stable, IUCN=NE / Life span: 2 to 3 years / Length: 2.5-4 in. (63-101 mm) / Weight: n/a / Reproduces: in deep burrows located between the surf line and the vegetation line along the beaches / Found: GB.

© Charles Sobczak

The ghost crab is aptly named. Capable of running across the sand at speeds in excess of 10 miles per hour and making abrupt, sharp twists and turns, this small semi-terrestrial crab appears and disappears like a ghost. Its coloration blends in well with the surrounding sand, making it all but impossible to keep an eye on one, even in broad daylight. When threatened it dives into its burrow, which can descend four to five feet. With stalked eyes capable of 360-degree vision, the ghost crab is exceedingly difficult to approach without being noticed.

The ghost crab is an example of a species transitioning from an aquatic to a terrestrial environment. It is still capable of taking in oxygen from the water, and to survive on land must wet its gills in saltwater at least twice daily. Predominantly a night predator, the ghost crab feeds on fish carcasses, detritus, leftover picnic foods such as potato chips and bread crumbs, as well as sea turtle hatchlings. In fact, the ghost crab is one of the largest natural threats to sea turtle egg clutches, in part because it is capable of burrowing into a turtle nest and feeding on the hatchlings before they emerge from the nest.

Finding a ghost crab is nowhere near as easy as finding where it lives. Look up the beach in the area approximately 20 feet from the surf to the vegetation line, where it digs two- to three-inch-diameter holes into the sand at a 45-degree angle. The best time to find the crab itself is at dusk or dawn when it is the most active. It is heavily fed upon by gulls, crows, and larger shorebirds.

☐ _____ **Mangrove Tree Crab** (*Artus pisonii*) Nicknames: red mangrove crab / Status: FL=stable, IUCN=NE / Life span: 3 to 5 years / Length: 1.25-2.3 in. (2.5-6 cm) / Weight: n/a / Reproduces: in the roots and detritus found in the red mangrove forest / Found: MZ.

© Charles Sobczak

The mangrove crab is an important food source for several specialized species of birds, as well as a number of fish species that frequent the labyrinth-like root systems of the red mangrove during periods of high tide. Both the black- and yellow-crowned night herons feed extensively on the mangrove tree crab, earning these birds the nickname "crab-eaters." From the water, both the redfish and the mangrove snapper are partial to the mangrove tree crab, which they sometimes snatch off of low-hanging branches at high tide. It is also preyed upon by the much larger blue crab.

The mangrove tree crab is a vertical feeder, ascending into the red mangrove canopy during high tide then descending into the roots and exposed mud flats during low tide. It shares this mangrove environment with the similar-looking mangrove root crab (*Goniopsis cruentata*). Distinguishing one from the other is problematic in the field, but the primary difference is that the root crab has distinctive reddish-colored legs and lacks the spots generally present on the mangrove tree crab.

The mangrove tree crab lays between 5,000 and 35,000 eggs after mating. Less than 1 percent survive into adulthood. Most of the predation occurs during the larval stage of the crab's life when the animal is small enough to be considered zooplankton. This tiny creature is eaten by barnacles, oysters, minnows, and filter feeders as they drift through the water column.

Although the mangrove tree crab population experienced a decline after the hurricane seasons of 2004 and 2005, it appears to be rebounding on the islands. One of the best locations to spot one is the red mangrove overlook located just before mile marker one on Wildlife Drive. It takes some time to spot this small crab because it disappears into the bark patterns found on the red mangrove and seldom moves. The best method is to scour a single tree and its roots. It takes a while, but on average you can find 30-50 of them between the road and the end of the overlook.

☐ _____ **Fiddler Crab** (*Uca rapax*) Nicknames: mudflat fiddler / Status: FL=stable, IUCN=NE / Life span: 1 to 1.4 years / Length: 0.73-2 in. (1.9-5 cm) / Weight: n/a / Reproduces: in the mudflats and sandbars of the back bay / Found: MZ.

There are 97 species of fiddler crabs in the world, and 65 of them are very similar in appearance and design. The fiddler crab often seen in "Ding" Darling and on the back side of Captiva could be one of any number of regional species, including the Atlantic sand, the saltpan, or the red-jointed fiddler. They are all very similar in habitat choice and behavior. The mudflat fiddler is well known for its herding behavior and is the one described here.

The fiddler crab was hit particularly hard after the hurricane and algae events of 2004 and 2005. The local population crashed, and for several years it was all but impossible to find any of these once-plentiful crabs on either island. Since then it has rebounded, though still nowhere near the astronomical numbers of the past. In the 1940s this crab frequented the gulf beaches with numbers sometimes in the tens of thousands in a single herd. Today it is fairly easy to spot on the cross-dike path located just before the tower overlook on Wildlife Drive, as well as along most of the back bay coastline on Sanibel and Captiva.

The fiddler crab feeds on detritus and microscopic nutrients found along the water's edge. The male sports a large claw that it holds up during courtship and territorial displays. It gets its name from this larger claw, which vaguely resembles a fiddle. When disturbed a fiddler crab scrambles into its small burrow found along the edge of the water.

The fiddler crab is a popular food source for many wading birds including egrets and black-crowned night herons. It is also eaten by raccoons and otters. The blue crab will prey upon the fiddler crab, and it is an excellent bait for redfish and sea trout. Its egg production and survival rate are very similar to that of the mangrove crab.

☐ _____ **Spider Crab** (*Libinia emarginata* and *Libinia dubia*)
Nicknames: portly spider crab, decorator crab / Status: FL=stable, IUCN=NE
/ Life span: n/a / Length: 2.5-4 in. (6-10 cm) / Weight: n/a / Reproduces: in
the back bay and estuaries / Found: MZ, BB.

The most common place to observe the homely spider crab is clinging to the flood-control gates on the spillways running under Wildlife Drive in "Ding" Darling, where it often hangs onto the barnacle- and oyster-encrusted edges of the concrete culverts and feeds on the nutrient-rich waters pouring through the spillways. It is often found near the far more desirable blue crab.

© Wikipedia Commons

The spider crab is found throughout the world. The largest crab in the world, the Japanese spider crab (*Macrocheira kaempferi*), is related to the local spider crab. An adult Japanese spider crab can reach a leg span of almost 13 feet and weigh more than 44 pounds. The local spider crab seldom has a leg span that exceeds a foot and weighs mere ounces. It is a filter feeder, dining on macro algae, as well as plant and animal tissue. It is heavily preyed upon by pinfish, gag grouper, and oyster toadfish. To avoid being detected, its shell is "decorated" with unpalatable algal and sponge growth. This is what makes it so unattractive, since it tends to be a dull brownish-gray as a result.

The islands are home to two common species and telling them apart without the aid of an experienced marine biologist is nearly impossible. Both species range from the shallows of the back bay all the way out to 160 feet of water. There is no commercial use for the spider crab, and it is seldom, if ever used for bait.

☐ _____ **Horseshoe Crab** (*Limulus polyphemus*) Nicknames:
Atlantic horseshoe crab, king crab, horsefoot, saucepan crab, helmet crab /
Status: FL=species of special status, IUCN=NT / Life span: 20 to 40 years /
Length: 18-24 in. (46-61 cm) / Weight: n/a / Reproduces: in the estuary and
back bay / Found: GB, MZ, BB.

A living fossil, the horseshoe crab has remained essentially unchanged for the past 250 million years. The present-day species is little changed from an earlier relative that dates back to the Silurian period, more than 400 million years ago. It is the closest living relative to one of the oldest known fossil finds on earth, the trilobite.

Horseshoe crabs

© Blake Sobczak

The horseshoe crab is actually far more closely related to spiders, ticks, and scorpions than to any other species. It is sometimes called a "living museum" because of the wide array of species it carries, including algae, flatworms, mollusks, barnacles, and byozoa. As adults they are heavily preyed upon by raccoons and otters, and as juveniles they are taken by birds, fish, and larger crabs.

The horseshoe crab is unique in that it has blue blood, based on copper rather than iron, making it valuable to scientists. The pharmaceutical industry, for example, uses horseshoe crab blood derivatives to detect bacterial endotoxins in drugs. A single horseshoe crab can be worth $2,500 over its lifetime in blood extractions alone.

Horseshoe crab at Blind Pass   © Maggie May Rogers

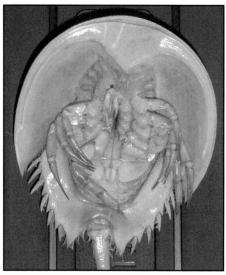

Horseshoe molt   © Maggie May Rogers

The animal is also studied for its unusual vision. It has four eyes and a complex method of sight that is still not fully understood. Lacking jaws, it grinds its food—bits of fish, mollusks, annelid worms, and other invertebrates—with bristles on its legs and a primitive gizzard containing sand and gravel.

The horseshoe is a very important part of the estuary system, and because of its recent declining numbers, scientists are concerned about its future. A decade ago thousands of these living fossils were found along either side of Wildlife Drive in "Ding" Darling. Today finding a single living horseshoe crab is rare.

☐ _____ **Bay Shrimp** (*Panaeus dourarum*) Nicknames: pink shrimp, gulf shrimp / Status: FL=stable, IUCN=NE / Life span: 1 to 2 years / Length: 6-11 in. (17-28 cm including antennae) / Weight: n/a / Reproduces: in the back bay and estuaries / Found: MZ, BB, GW.

The bay shrimp is actually the juvenile stage of the familiar pink gulf shrimp commonly sold in shrimp houses throughout the gulf coast. The spawn of these shrimp drift into the estuaries where they find safe harbor amidst the sea grasses and mangrove roots of the back bay. Upon maturity, generally in the fall, the shrimp begins its offshore migration, leaving the back bay for the deeper waters of the Gulf of Mexico.

While in the back bay and the tidal flats of Pine Island Sound, the bay shrimp is heavily preyed upon by cormorants, anhingas, pinfish, herons, redfish, snook, and a host of other predators. There is almost no bird, fish, or crab that does not make shrimp a part of its diet.

Shrimp and Cormorant   ©ThroughTheLensGallery.com

The bay shrimp tends to become active after dark and seldom moves in the water column during a full moon. At this time it tends to burrow into the mud or sand to avoid predation. It eats copepods, benthic diatoms, blue-green and filamentous green algae, as well as slim molds, yeast, and detritus. Ironically, the bay shrimp thrives on nutrient-laden and polluted waters, as these yield high amounts of the algae growth and yeast that the shrimp is fond of feeding on. When the algae growth exceeds the capacity of the water to sustain dissolved oxygen, however, in periods of hypoxia, the shrimp, along with all other sea life, is unable to survive.

Most shrimp are buried in the sand and mud during daylight hours. The easiest place to find them are the bait tanks at the local tackle shops where they are purchased for fishing.

The bay shrimp is the center of an important Florida industry, though the recent aquaculture industry, especially in the Far East, has flooded the market with inexpensive, farm-raised shrimp and seriously impacted the shrimp fleets of Ft. Myers Beach and other locales. The days of "wild caught" shrimp are probably drawing to a close.

Sea oats at sunset

The Plants of Sanibel and Captiva

Everything begins with the soil. After studying the hundreds of different species that thrive on Sanibel and Captiva, I have discovered that this book, and all wildlife books, should be reversed. Plants should come first. Without plants, not a single living creature in this book could survive. The warblers and passerines that rely on the drupes, figs, seeds, and fruits would perish, as would the kestrels and merlins that feed upon the warblers and passerines. The insects, which rely on plants for pollen, leaves, detritus, and fruit, would soon perish. Even the panther, which dines on the meat of the browsing deer and wild boar, would go hungry and die. Take away the tons of detritus falling into the intertidal zone from the red mangrove, and the estuary would collapse. All healthy ecosystems start with a healthy biosphere filled with a diversity of plants. Plants are the essence of life on earth.

There are more than 350,000 extant species of plants identified on earth to date. The true number of plants is probably more than twice that, and botanists are still discovering new species at an unprecedented rate. These include new varieties of the familiar organisms we know as trees, herbs, bushes, grasses, vines, ferns, mosses, and green algae. In North America, excluding Mexico and Central America, there are an estimated 21,000 species of plants. Florida ranks third in the number of plant species, behind California and Texas. There are more than 4,200 species of endemic or naturalized plants in the Sunshine State and twice that number when we include the vast array of imported ornamental and landscape plants that thrive here.

Estimates of the number of indigenous plants on Sanibel and Captiva, from tiny flowering grasses to towering strangler figs, put the number between 1,000 and 1,200 species. When you include all of the imports and exotics, it more than doubles, putting the total number of plant species found on these 18 square miles somewhere near 2,500 species, second only to insects in diversity and by far the heaviest mass of living organisms on the island.

Choosing from this incredible array of life was not easy. I wish there were room in this book for three or four times the number of plants covered. Excluding such amazing and beautiful species as beautyberry (*Callicarpa americana*), coontie (*Zamia pumila*), and lignum vitae (*Guaiacum sanctum*) was a difficult but necessary decision.

The plants chosen represent a good cross-section, and many of them form the breadbasket of life on Sanibel. This is especially true of the gumbo limbo, strangler fig, cabbage palm, and poison ivy.

If there is just one thing to take away from this section, it is that while we cannot go out and purchase the threatened Sanibel rice rat or order another mangrove cuckoo, we all have the ability to purchase the plants these birds and animals require for shelter and sustenance. Plants are the only living things available to us as useful tools to create a better environment. Native plants require no fertilizers, herbicides, or other chemicals that produce runoff and wreak havoc on our ponds and estuaries. They need little to no watering, since they have adapted to the feast-or-famine monsoonal rain patterns of South Florida, and they are every bit as beautiful as anything we import into this ecosystem to replace them.

For most wildlife, a lawn is a monoculture desert. A yard filled with spartina grasses, cocoplum hedges, leather ferns, and cabbage palms is a yard filled with wildlife. Not only does planting natives help every living organism on the island, but it also avoids future disasters such as the Brazilian pepper or melaleuca fiascos that have cost the state of Florida billions of dollars in eradication programs.

Of course, planting a mahogany in your back yard in northern Ohio won't work. In that case, plant a native species that will. Plant an oak or a red maple, a poplar or a birch, but make certain that whatever your choice of species, it belongs in the environment where evolution has made it well adapted and able to thrive. Plant native and plant often. Native plants and shrubs not only help wildlife, but they also aid in the reduction of greenhouse gases, converting carbon dioxide to oxygen and ridding the air of other harmful pollutants. Large trees, through transpiration, help to cool a house in the summer and break the wind in the winter.

Last but not least, I should mention the strangler fig (*Ficus aurea*). If you read about only one plant in this section, make it the story of the strangler fig. Considered by many botanists as one of the 10 most fascinating plants on earth, this member of the Ficus family is astonishing. From its symbiotic relationship with the tiny gall wasp to its amazing ability to survive devastating hurricanes, the strangler fig has one of the most fascinating backstories of any living organism in this entire book. Here then are a handful of the thousands of plants of Sanibel and Captiva.

The Trees

☐ ____ **Red Mangrove** ★ (*Rhizophora mangle*) Nicknames: mangrove, mangle, walking tree / Status: FL=stable, but Florida has lost approximately 50 percent of its original mangrove forests to development, IUCN=LC / Life span: to 150 years or more / Height: 15-33 ft (4.5-10 m) / Reproduces: by propagules; thrives along the back bay / Found: IW, MZ.

It is impossible to underestimate the value of the red mangrove forests on Sanibel and Captiva. Without them there might not be a Sanibel or Captiva. The formation of both islands was in part dependent on these trees catching and trapping the sand and sediments in their extensive root systems.

Beyond its island- and land-building capabilities, the red mangrove offers an extensive list of other benefits to the estuarine and marine ecosystems. To begin with, every acre of mangroves produces 3.6 tons of leaf litter per year. This litter falls into the tidal waters and helps to feed a host of living organisms, from the microorganisms that break down this detritus to oysters, barnacles, crabs, shrimp, and the fish that feed on them. An estimated 75 percent of all of Southwest Florida's game fish and 90 percent of all commercial species depend on the mangrove system for reproduction, nursery habitat, cover, and as an endless source of nutrients.

Its lush canopy serves as roosting and nesting sites for dozens of birds, including almost all of the herons and egrets, pelicans, cormorants, mangrove cuckoos, roseate spoonbills, and ibises. Its trunk and tangled root system harbors fiddler

Leaves, left to right: red mangrove, black mangrove, white mangrove and buttonwood. Red mangrove propagule and buttonwood seeds also pictured.

© Charles Sobczak

Red mangroves at the bay
© Maggie May Rogers

crabs, mangrove crabs, periwinkles, apple snails, and scores of spiders and insects. Its flowers feed butterflies, moths, hummingbirds, and honey bees. In short, the red mangrove is the cornerstone of our estuaries. Without it, most, if not all, of the back-bay food chain would collapse.

Under ideal conditions the red mangrove can grow to a height of 80 feet, though locally it seldom exceeds 30 feet. It has the unique ability to survive and thrive in water that is so salty that 99 percent of the plants on earth would die within weeks if exposed to the same level of salinity. It grows in soil that is anaerobic (holding little to no oxygen). To compensate for its harsh environment, the gnarled, exposed root system of the red mangrove is covered in tiny holes, allowing the tree to take in oxygen directly from the air.

Its seeds, called propagules, are fully matured when they drop from the tree and may last as long as a year floating in saltwater until they find a shallow mudflat or tide pool where they can take root. The red mangrove is a hermaphrodite, capable of self-pollinating. Another unique adaptation is that as older leaves accumulate excess salt, they drop, adding to the detritus below and ridding the tree of unneeded sodium. The mangrove also varies the orientation of its leaves throughout the day to reduce evaporation from the tropical midday sun.

The saddest part of the story is our disregard and abuse of the mangrove ecosystem. Studies indicate that more than half of the mangrove forests have been uprooted and destroyed by coastal development in the past 100 years. Where mangrove forests once dominated the environment we now find only barren seawalls and development. In some coastal regions, such as in Louisiana and Mississippi, vast tracts of mangrove forests have been lost to agriculture and development, which allowed Hurricane Katrina's massive storm surge to penetrate much farther inland than it would have if these wave-reducing plants had been left in place.

Efforts are under way to replant and re-propagate the red mangrove all across South Florida. Special permits are required to trim red mangrove, and uprooting or killing it is strictly prohibited. It is available at the SCCF Native Plant Nursery, as are all the plants in this section marked with a star (★).

The red mangrove lines both sides of Wildlife Drive and inhabits almost all the back bay of Captiva, including Roosevelt Channel and the bay side of South Seas Island Resort. Worldwide there are more than 110 recognized mangrove species, with the largest diversity found in Indonesia and Malaysia. In Hawaii, where it is not a native species, the red mangrove is considered an invasive plant and is eradicated accordingly.

☐ _____ **Black Mangrove** ★ (*Avicennia germinans*) Nicknames: mangrove / Status: FL=stable, though it is being impacted by the invasive Brazilian pepper plant, IUCN=LC / Life span: more than 200 years / Height: 25-50 ft (7.6-15.2 m) / Reproduces: in the tidal zone just up from the red mangrove forests along the back sides of both islands / Found: UA, MZ.

The black mangrove is a communal species that plays a vital role in the mangrove ecosystem. Unable to survive while submerged in saltwater as does the red mangrove, the black mangrove thrives a few meters inland at the high-tide water mark. It lacks the tangled root system and has developed a different adaptation to deal with the anaerobic soil in which it grows. The base of the black mangrove trunk is surrounded by pneumatophores, which are pencil-like breathing tubes that allow it to gather the oxygen it needs directly from the air, as well as stabilize the tree in the wet, soggy soil.

The black mangrove rids itself of excess salt by exuding it from special cells located on the underside of its leaves. It does this at night and on cloudy days. You can generally find salt crystals on the underside of most black mangrove leaves. Like the red mangrove, the black mangrove's roots, detritus, and canopy all provide food and habitat for a host of avian, marine, and land animals. The tree helps stabilize coastal erosion and mitigates the effect of storm surges.

The wood of the black mangrove

Typical black mangrove pneumatophores
© Charles Sobczak

Black mangrove leaves and flowers   © Maggie May Rogers

is dark brown to black and has been used for fence posts, fuel, and marine construction. The tannin from the tree has been used to prepare leather products, and its flowers produce an excellent honey. Unlike the red mangrove, the black mangrove reaches its full height locally; several trees located along the bay side of "Ding" Darling are more than 50 feet tall. The black mangrove can be seen growing in Tarpon Bay and along the Indigo Trail as well as the Shell Mound Trail in the "Ding" Darling Wildlife Refuge.

☐ _____ **White Mangrove** ★ (*Laguncularia racemosa*) Nicknames: mangrove, mangle blanco (Spanish) / Status: FL=stable, IUCN=LC / Life span: more than 200 years / Height: 39-59 ft (12-18 m) / Reproduces: near the tidal zone inland from both red and black mangroves / Found: UA, MZ.

Although only distantly related, the white, red, black, and buttonwood mangroves are grouped together based more on their ecological function than their genetic ties. Like the other species, the white mangrove is important in its multifunctional role of stabilizing soil, providing wildlife habitat, and adding leaf litter and detritus to the estuary ecosystem. The white mangrove is generally mingled in with the black mangrove, growing farther inland than the red mangrove.

The white mangrove is easily differentiated from the other mangrove species by both its leaves and its root system. The leaves are more rounded at the base and tip and are smooth underneath. Some, but not all of the leaves, have a distinctive notch located at the very tip of the leaf. The tree excretes salt through its leaves, though not to the same extent as the black mangrove. It possesses a second gland, called nectaries, located at the base of its leaf, which excretes sugar. Many insects, including ants and wasps, feed on this excreted sugar.

The white mangrove produces prop roots, as does the red mangrove, or, depending on its habitat, pneumatophores, similar to those grown by the black mangrove. The white mangrove is bisexual and produces a reddish-brown drupe, which is a fruit-like seed roughly one-half to three-quarters of an inch long. The drupe resembles a leathery nut with a deep rib running through the middle section and is sometimes eaten by certain mammals. White mangrove wood is strong and in South and Central America is used for sailing masts, roof beams, and fence posts.

White mangrove leaves © Charles Sobczak

Look for the white mangrove along Wildlife Drive, near Tarpon Bay, and all along the bay side of Captiva. There are a few trees located on the west side of the Mangrove Overlook boardwalk located just before mile marker 1 on Wildlife Drive.

☐ _____ **Buttonwood** ★ (*Conocarpus erectus*) Nicknames: buttonbush, button mangrove, button tree, false mangrove, green buttonwood / Status: FL=stable, IUCN=NE / Height: 10-35 ft (3-10.6 m) / Life span: more than 100 years / Reproduces: throughout the island / Found: UA, IW, MZ.

Often more of a shrub than a true tree, the buttonwood grows much farther inland than the other three species of mangroves. The trunk of the buttonwood can look very similar to that of a mature Brazilian pepper tree. Easy to identify by its distinctive, cone-like seeds that ripen in the fall, the buttonwood is an important fourth element in Florida's mangrove forest ecosystem. It does not grow north of Cedar Key on the west coast or Cape Canaveral on the east coast.

Buttonwood's distinctive seeds © Charles Sobczak

Unlike the other mangroves, which can prove difficult to grow, the buttonwood is a hardy tree that is well suited for use as a landscape ornamental. It is tolerant of full sun, sandy and salty soil conditions, and moist, saturated hammocks.

The buttonwood is renowned for its use in smoking fish and meats because it burns slowly and generates ample heat. It is also used for firewood, cabinetmaking, and charcoal.

Look for the buttonwood in lowland areas around the Bailey Tract, Sanibel Gardens Preserve, the Pick Preserve, and along Captiva Drive.

⬜ _____ **Silver Buttonwood** ★ (*Conocarpus erectus* var. *sericeus*) Nicknames: buttonwood, mombo tree / Status: FL=stable, naturalized species, IUCN=NE / Life span: more than 100 years / Height: 15-20 ft (4.5-6 m) / Reproduces: by sapling and plantings but does not appear to be able to reproduce naturally on the island / Found: as an ornamental in UA, IW, MZ.

The silver buttonwood is native to Florida's east coast and the Florida Keys; it was not on the islands 100 years ago, but like the royal palm and periwinkle, this small tree is considered a naturalized plant. It is able to thrive here and is not considered invasive since it does not have any substantial negative impact on native species.

The leaves are covered with a dense mat of silky hairs, which impart the beautiful silver-gray color to the tree. Because of its attractive coloration and ability to thrive in a range of soil conditions—acidic, alkaline, clay-to-sandy, wet-to-dry, salty—the silver buttonwood is a popular ornamental tree on Sanibel and Captiva. The only thing it doesn't like is frost. It makes an excellent informal or clipped **Note the leaves' fuzzy texture on the silver buttonwood**

© Charles Sobczak

hedge or a nice specimen tree. In ideal growing conditions the silver buttonwood can reach a height of more than 30 feet.

Like the green buttonwood, the silver produces tiny button-like seed pods that burst when ripe, providing food for birds, insects, and wildlife. Common along the west coast of Africa, it is thought that the tree originated there, with the small seed clusters floating across the Atlantic and taking root in the New World millennia ago.

In Central and South America the silver buttonwood is used for making charcoal and is a favorite choice for smoking meat and fish. There are numerous specimen silver buttonwoods planted along either side of Island Inn Road. The silver buttonwood is also a favorite tree for bonsai gardeners.

☐ _____ Strangler Fig ★ (*Ficus aurea*) Nicknames: Florida strangler fig, golden fig / Status: FL=stable, IUCN=NE / Life span: more than 200 years / Height: 30-60 ft (9-19 m) / Reproduces: via a complex relationship with the fig wasp / Found: MZ, IW, UA, GB.

Strangler fig surrounding a cabbage palm
© Charles Sobczak

Considered by many botanists to be one of the most fascinating plants on earth, the strangler fig is also one of the most important plants on the islands. Worldwide there are more than 900 species of the fig tree, with most occurring in the Australasian region. One species (*Ficus bengalensis*), native to India, has a trunk that measures more than 100 feet in circumference. The century-old banyan fig planted at the Edison and Ford Winter Estates in Fort Myers covers a half-acre and is well worth visiting (see www.efwefla.org for hours, information, and directions).

On Sanibel and Captiva, the strangler fig is one of a handful of plants that form the islands' breadbasket for wildlife. The small, good-tasting figs produced by this tree are eaten by almost everything, be it a flying, crawling, or climbing creature. The fruit of the strangler fig was used for food by the early Floridians as well.

This is a favorite shelter tree for birds, from warblers to pileated woodpeckers. Its niches, twisted trunks, and nooks and crannies of the strangler fig also provides habitat for insects, lizards, raccoons, rodents, and snakes.

The reproductive cycle of the strangler fig is so bizarre that it demands telling. It has a relationship, scientifically referred to as obligate mutualism, with a single wasp species known as the gall wasp. This wasp is only slightly larger than a no-see-um, and each fig has a tiny hole, just large enough for a female gall wasp, full of eggs, to squeeze into. Its delicate wings are torn off in the process, and the wasp is unable to leave. It unknowingly deposits the pollen that it has carried from another tree and lays its eggs in the stigma of the flowers located within the fig seed.

The female then dies, and the entrance it came through seals shut as the fig walls close. After a while, the larval wasps are born. After mating, the males chew a hole in the wall of the fig, crawl out, and die. The females remain inside the fig, collecting pollen in preparation for their own escape. The females are born with delicate wings capable of making a single flight. If the female gall wasp fails to find a tree before its fragile wings fail, it dies. If she finds another tree, her life cycle is completed, and the strangler fig's flowers are pollinated. It's believed that this evolutionary codependency has been going strong for 60 million years and that there are hundreds of different species of fig wasps matched to hundreds of specific fig species.

Strangler fig detail after a controlled burn
© Charles Sobczak

As if this unbelievable symbiotic relationship weren't enough, the story of the strangler fig continues. Once pollinated, these figs ripen and are fed upon by a host of hungry wildlife. The fruit is packed with tiny seeds, passed in the dung of various animals. On Sanibel and Captiva, birds are responsible for most of the seed dispersal.

After feeding, a bird might land in a cabbage palm and dispose of its waste. That waste is often trapped in the upturned bases of the palm fronds, where detritus and standing water allow the tiny seeds to germinate. At this stage in its development the strangler fig survives as an epiphyte. As this epiphyte matures it sends down long, thin tendrils that eventually reach the soil near the base of the host tree. With the newfound nutrients in the soil now feeding it, the strangler fig grows rapidly. Its tendrils twist and turn, eventually wrapping themselves around the trunk of the host tree, which is generally a cabbage palm. Over time the fig grows so large that the cabbage palm no longer receives enough sun to survive. Eventually, the host tree and its root ball decay into nutrients that help to make the mature strangler fig the largest native plant on Sanibel and Captiva.

In one last amazing feat of adaptation, the strangler fig's limbs are designed with a breakaway system that allows it to survive hurricanes. The leaves are the first to let go, with the branches quick to follow. This system allows the base of the tree to survive and flourish soon after the storm has passed. If the storm is so strong that it takes down the trunk, the root suckers left buried in the soil will generate a new sapling. The strangler fig is salt tolerant, which makes it resistant to storm surges as well. All said, the strangler fig is a true survivor.

☐ _____ **Gumbo Limbo** ★ (*Bursera simaruba*) Nicknames: tourist tree, cork tree / Status: FL=stable, IUCN=NE / Life span: more than 40 years / Height: 35-60 ft (10.6-18 m) / Reproduces: through a single seed encased in a fatty aril (seed coat) / Found: UA, IW, MZ, GB.

Gumbo limbo bark   © Charles Sobczak

The nickname "tourist tree" is given to the gumbo limbo because its bark is red and peeling, just like the tourists who come down every winter and go home with a sunburn. The wood of the tree is extremely light and is the primary material used in the manufacture of carousel horses in the United States. Early settlers used it for making the cork floats found on their gill nets.

The gumbo limbo is an important food source for birds, including many of the winter migrants to the islands. Its arils, rich in fatty lipids, are like eating an energy bar for the migrating birds. The seed within the aril passes through the bird's digestive system intact, helping to spread the gumbo limbo throughout the islands. This tree is salt tolerant and is very fast growing. It does not like soggy soil and will often be found growing on top of ancient Calusa shell mounds such as those found on the Shell Mound Trail near the exit of Wildlife Drive. Some gumbo limbo trees grow to be enormous, with bases up to three feet in diameter.

The gumbo limbo tree has the interesting ability to create a sapling from a living branch. Anyone can break off a branch and stick it in the soil, where it will take root and grow. For this reason, the gumbo limbo is often used in making living fences throughout South and Central America.

An excellent specimen gumbo limbo can be seen at the entrance to the subdivision that carries its name. The tree is located just behind the subdivision sign, two blocks up Dixie Beach Blvd. from Periwinkle Way, on the west side.

© Charles Sobczak

☐ _____ **Sea Grape** ★ (*Coccoloba uvifera*) Nicknames: coccoloba tree / Status: FL=stable, IUCN=NE / Life span: more than 60 years / Height: 15-35 ft (4.5-10.6 m) / Reproduces: by a grape-like fruit that is spread by wildlife / Found: UA, IW, GB, MZ.

The clusters of sea grapes from this tree were once commonly harvested by the early settlers of Sanibel and Captiva. They ripen in the fall and can be eaten directly from the tree or squeezed into jellies, jams, juices, and wine. The sweet taste of this fruit makes the sea grape a favorite for the island's raccoons, opossums, and other rodents. The seed inside of the fruit is capable of surviving the digestive tract and is spread across the island via the droppings of several mammals and birds.

Grape stems are still present on this sea grape tree
© Charles Sobczak

Only the female sea grape bears fruit, and its flowers are pollinated predominantly by honey bees. The sea grape is extremely salt tolerant and, therefore, well adapted to surviving on the islands. One of its favored habitats is right along the beach dunes, where it tends to grow more as a shrub than a tree. It is hurricane resistant but vulnerable to freezes and cold weather.

The sea grape is an evergreen but does shed its leaves mid-winter on the islands. The coloration of these large, round leaves bears a striking resemblance to the fall foliage found in northern, deciduous forests. Sea grape wood is used in cabinetmaking; early settlers used its dried leaves to write on; and the Calusa used the sap of the sea grape for healing purposes.

The sea grape can be found throughout the islands; a particularly large stand is located in the cemetery on Captiva Island.

Sea grape colors   © Maggie May Rogers

◻ _____ **Live Oak** ★ (*Quercus virginiana*) Nicknames: southern live oak, oak tree, bay live oak, scrub live oak, plateau oak / Status: FL=thriving, IUCN=NE / Life span: more than 300 years / Height: 25-50 ft (7.6-15 m) / Reproduces: by the acorn, which appears in the late fall and early winter / Found: IW, UA.

The live oak thrives from the Florida Keys north to Virginia and west to Texas. Although it appears to be an evergreen, the live oak is a semi-deciduous tree, shedding its leaves and growing new ones over a period of two weeks in the early spring. In its more northern range, it is a true deciduous oak, becoming leafless throughout most of the winter.

Young live oak   © Charles Sobczak

Live oak wood is one of the heaviest in North America, drying to a weight of 55 pounds per cubic foot. The *U.S.S. Constitution*, built in the early 1800s, was constructed completely out of live oak. When fired upon in the War of 1812 with England, cannonballs would literally bounce off of the ship, earning it the nickname, "Old Ironsides." Live oak is excellent for cooking because it burns hot and long. It was a favorite cooking wood for the islands' early settlers.

In the wild the live oak is an extremely important tree. It serves as a host tree for dozens of epiphytes, including Spanish moss, numerous bromeliads, and resurrection fern. The acorns it produces are a favorite for birds and mammals such as the gray squirrel and white-tailed deer. Its thick foliage is a favorite shelter for warblers and catbirds and is a common nesting site for doves, mockingbirds, and cardinals. The trunk of the live oak is generally peppered with holes drilled by red-bellied and pileated woodpeckers.

A wonderful shade tree, the live oak has one of the most sprawling canopies of any tree in North America. A mature live oak with a height of 50 feet can produce a canopy that measures 165 feet across. Found mostly as an ornamental tree on Sanibel, there is a large native stand located in an inaccessible section of the "Ding" Darling National Wildlife Refuge on the north side of San-Cap Road. One of these trees lies at mile marker 3.17 (west from Tarpon Bay Road) where one of its sprawling branches once draped over the bike path. Look for it near the cupola shelter that was erected beside it. A number of young live oaks are located along Island Inn Road.

Live oak with epiphytes
© Maggie May Rogers

☐_____ **Wild Tamarind** ★ (*Lysiloma latisiliquum*) Nicknames:
false tamarind / Status: FL=stable, IUCN=LC / Life span: more than 30 years / Height: 30-50 ft (9-15 m) / Reproduces: from a legume seed pod that arrives in the winter / Found: UA, IW.

Because the wild tamarind does not produce an edible fruit, fig, or acorn, it is not as popular with birds as are some of the other trees on the islands. It does provide one of the primary habitats for native tree snails, and its fragrant white, puff-ball flowers, which bloom in the early spring, are a favorite for sulpher and mangrove skipper butterflies. The wild tamarind is a host plant for the cassius blue butterfly.

Wild tamarind detail of leaves   © Charles Sobczak

The tamarind is a distinctive tree with numerous small leaves that grow in zigzag clusters off of its numerous branches. This tree is easily confused with the invasive lead tree, whose delicate leaf structure resembles the wild tamarind. Lead trees are considered a nuisance species on Sanibel.

The wild tamarind is fast-growing but is not as salt tolerant as many island trees. It prefers well-drained soil in upland locations. It can be planted by opening up a ripe seed pod, spreading the seeds across an area of cleared soil, then covering with a thin layer of topsoil. The seeds germinate within a few weeks.

Dozens of young wild tamarinds are planted along Island Inn Road. If you search the trunks and branches, you will likely find numerous tree snails.

☐_____ **South Florida Slash Pine** ★ (*Pinus elliottii* var. *densa*)
Nicknames: slash pine, yellow slash pine, swamp pine / Status: FL=stable, IUCN=LC / Life span: more than 200 years / Height: 59-98 ft (18-30 m) / Reproduces: by pinecone in upland areas / Found: UA, IW.

The slash pine is not a common tree on Sanibel but is abundant throughout rural areas of Lee County and on Pine Island just across Pine Island Sound, where it commonly towers above unbroken stands of saw palmetto. This beautiful tree can grow to 100 feet and live more than 200 years under ideal conditions. Perhaps the biggest reason for the lack of large specimens on the barrier islands is that it is

South Florida slash pine   © Charles Sobczak

intolerant of salt intrusion and tends to die off after hurricane storm surges or when its deep taproot hits a high-saline water table.

The slash pine was heavily cut for its lumber across most of Florida during the early years of settlement. It is still commonly planted in large pine plantations in parts of the state where its excellent wood is harvested for construction, railroad ties, pilings, and the production of turpentine and rosin. The seeds within the pinecones are fed upon by both birds and small mammals. Deer, wild boar, and cattle graze on the saplings.

A few slash pines can be found on Sanibel on San-Cap Road across from the Shell Museum; some young pines are newly planted along Island Inn Road.

☐ _____ **Mahogany** ★ (*Swietenia mahagoni*) Nicknames: West Indian mahogany / Status: FL=declining, IUCN=EN / Life span: more than 50 years / Height: 35-50 ft (10.6-15 m) / Reproduces: by seed in upland, drier habitats / Found: UA, IW.

This semi-evergreen tree is commonly planted as an ornamental in both residential and commercial landscape designs. A number of mahogany trees can be found in the parking lot of SCCF and along the northern side of Palm Ridge Road near where it merges with Periwinkle Way.

The mahogany casts a light shadow and consequently does not discourage grass and other plantings from growing beneath it. It sheds its leaves annually near the end of winter, but new growth quickly replaces these fallen leaves so the tree is leafless for only a week or two. The seeds develop in a fairly large capsule roughly the same size as a baseball. The pod bursts open in the spring to release its seeds, and the tree can be cultivated from these seeds with proper care.

In the wild the mahogany is in serious trouble. While the mahogany's range once extended much farther north in Florida, over the years it has been cut to extinction, with most of the wood shipped to England and Europe in the 1800s. The fine, straight-grained wood of this species is considered to be the finest cabinet- and furniture-making wood in the world. Early American Chippendale and Hepplewhite cabinetmakers used *Swietenia mahagoni* in the construction of pieces that over the

Mahogany tree at Sanibel-Captiva Conservation Foundation
© Charles Sobczak

centuries have become worth a small fortune. Because of continued demand for this excellent wood, large trees are still poached out of hardwood hammocks in Everglades National Park and other South Florida locations. These and other factors have led the IUCN to place the species in the endangered category of the official Red List.

A number of young mahogany trees are planted on either side of Island Inn Road, and the tree can be found throughout the island as an ornamental. The mahogany is fairly salt tolerant, and because of its hard, dark red wood, it stands up well to hurricane-force winds.

Mahogany seed pod and leaf detail
© Charles Sobczak

☐ _____ **Bald Cypress** ★ (*Taxodium distichum*) Nicknames: cypress, wood eternal, pecky cypress / Status: FL=stable, IUCN=LC / Life span: more than 1,000 years / Height: 60-150 ft (18-40 m) / Reproduces: by a golf-ball-sized pinecone / Found: IW, UA.

Bald cypress needles close-up

© Charles Sobczak

Cypress tree among palms at SCCF

© Charles Sobczak

A naturalized native, the bald cypress was probably not found on Sanibel when it was first settled in the 1800s. Today it is quite commonly planted in low-lying locations by residents who enjoy the unusual nature of this magnificent tree. There are several larger cypress trees growing near the boardwalk of SCCF's nature trails, but the true marvels can be found at Audubon's Corkscrew Swamp Sanctuary in Collier County (go to www.Corkscrew.audubon.org for information and directions).

The bald cypress is the tallest tree in Florida, once approaching 200 feet. In the ancient swamps at Corkscrew are cypress trees that are more than 10 feet in diameter and towering 140 feet high. At Corkscrew, these tall trees are used by the endangered wood stork for nesting sites. The smaller trees on Sanibel are used by perching birds, insects, and snakes. The seeds are eaten by squirrels.

Corkscrew's 2.25-mile raised boardwalk takes you past some of the last virgin stands of bald cypress remaining in South Florida. Throughout its original range the bald cypress has been mercilessly harvested, with clear-cutting in the early 1900s completely decimating huge tracts of these trees for construction lumber, railroad ties, barrels, bridges, and shingles. The fine-grained wood is rot and termite resistant and was highly prized by the early lumber barons.

The bald cypress is unusual in that it is a deciduous conifer. It sheds its needle-like foliage in the late fall, leaving the tree leafless throughout the winter (this is how the tree received its common name "bald" cypress). In the spring the leaves re-sprout.

The bald cypress is renowned for its cypress knees, which grow around the base of the tree and are thought to provide stability in the swamp substrate, as well as assist in the intake of oxygen, similar to the pneumatophores of the black mangrove. These knees are often used to make lamps and other decorative furnishings. Some trees, when cut, reveal wood that has been damaged by fungi. These irregularly shaped boards are commonly referred to as "pecky cypress."

Palms of Sanibel and Captiva

☐ _____ **Cabbage Palm** ★ (*Sabal palmetto*) Nicknames: palmetto palm, palmetto, swamp cabbage palm, sabal palm / Status: FL=stable, IUCN=NE / Life span: more than 100 years / Height: 25-90 ft (7.6-27 m) / Reproduces: by an edible date that is widely eaten by wildlife / Found: IW, UA, GB, MZ, CW.

The cabbage palm is the official state palm of both Florida and South Carolina. The early settlers of these two states found many uses for this prolific palm. Perhaps the most important is the consumption of its edible heart, a delicacy known as heart of palm. Although harvesting the heart kills the tree, this was of little concern to the inhabitants of Florida 100 years ago. These settlers used the pure white heart in salads and stews. It tastes much like the water chestnut and is generally available today at most grocery stores in the canned vegetable section. The city of LaBelle, located along the Caloosahatchee River in Lee County, hosts the Swamp Cabbage Festival every winter. (To learn more about this unique festival go to www. Swampcabbagefestival.org)

Cabbage Palms   © Charles Sobczak

Native Americans used cabbage palm fronds for thatching chickee huts; the trunks were used for building log cabins; and in the modern era, this hearty palm is

Cabbage Frond   © Maggie May Rogers

Cabbage palm boots   © Maggie May Rogers

used as a highway and landscaping ornamental. In fact, this palm is probably planted more widely and used more often across the Sunshine State than all other palms put together.

Wildlife loves the cabbage palm. The dead fronds provide the primary roosting habitat for the yellow bat, and the deep crevices left on the tree after its fronds fall make ideal nesting sites for small birds, rats, mice, and other insects and animals. The fruit and seeds, along with the strangler fig, form the backbone of the natural food staple for many of the island's native inhabitants, from raccoons and squirrels to dozens of bird species.

The cabbage palm is exceptionally easy to transplant and will thrive in sun or shade. It adapts well to brackish water or salty soils and is drought tolerant. It is well adapted to surviving hurricane winds and winter grass fires. Its large, showy canopy provides good shade. It is by far the favored host tree for the strangler fig.

To locate a cabbage palm, all you really have to do is go outside and look around—it is literally everywhere on Sanibel and Captiva. Note that despite appearances, the pruned cabbage palm is not a different species. In the wild the old fronds simply hang down until they eventually fall off. In a condominium complex all of these dead fronds are removed, and the tree has a completely different, thinner look.

🔲 _____ **Royal Palm** (*Roystonea elata*) Nicknames: none / Status: FL=stable, IUCN=NE / Life span: more than 100 years / Height: 50-90 ft (15-27.4 m) / Reproduces: by producing a drupe and can propagate naturally on the islands / Found: UA, IW.

The name of this palm fits it perfectly. With its tall, stately trunk and canopy that displays long, dark green palm fronds that rustle in the slightest breeze, this palm symbolizes the tropical nature of South Florida. Miami's Biscayne Boulevard and McGregor Boulevard in Fort Myers are both beautifully lined with these towering palms.

The royal palm in Florida, *Roysonea regia*, was long considered a separate species, but recently botanists reclassified it as a subspecies of the Cuban royal, so it is no longer considered a different species.

On Sanibel and Captiva the royal palm is a naturalized tree. It did not grow in this environment originally but has adapted well to both islands and is not invasive. It is salt tolerant and well adapted to living with hurricanes. In major storms the royal uses its break-away palm fronds, releasing all of its foliage long before a storm's powerful winds can topple the tree. The living bud remains safe inside the dark green cap of the royal, called the crownshaft, and new fronds begin appearing within weeks after a storm has passed.

Finding royal palm specimens on the islands is much easier than it used to be. After the destruction of all the large Australian pines down Periwinkle Way by Hurricane Charley in 2004, the city of Sanibel replanted with both Sanibel and Florida native species, including the royal palm. Look for them scattered along Periwinkle Way on either side of the road. These royal palms will grow quickly and within a decade will tower over almost every other tree planted. Hundreds of fully mature landscape royals are planted throughout both islands as well.

The royal palm produces a drupe—a seed covered in an edible exterior—which is eaten by birds and other wildlife. The internal seed passes unscathed through the digestive tracts of these animals and is dispersed accordingly. This method of propagation came onto being only after the arrival of land animals some 400 million

Royal Palms towering above   © Charles Sobczak

years ago during the Devonian period. Today, this relationship is so entwined that most trees, palms, shrubs, and plants, lacking birds, mammals, and insects to pollinate and disseminate their seeds, would perish.

☐ _____ **Coconut Palm** (*Cocos nucifera*) Nicknames: Jamaican tall, Malayan dwarf / Status: FL=stable, IUCN=LC / Life span: more than 90 years / Height: 50-80 ft (15.2-24.4 m) / Reproduces: fairly easily by its large, husked seed, or coconut / Found: IW, UA, GB.

© Charles Sobczak

Nothing says you are sitting on a beach better than that long, sprawling coconut palm growing behind you. Although the image of the coconut palm swaying in the Caribbean trade winds is familiar to everyone, this tree is not native to Sanibel and Captiva. The consensus is that the coconut palm originated in Melanesia or Southeast Asia, crossing the Pacific and Atlantic during prehistoric times. There is still some debate over whether these migrations were natural or had the assistance of humans. The coconut seed (it is a seed, not a nut) is capable of remaining fertile after exceedingly long periods drifting in the ocean, so it could have arrived unassisted, but it has also been noted that the coconut tree appears to follow human migrations. One theory is that the coconut tree was brought to the Americas by prehistoric Polynesian mariners.

However the coconut palm got here, it is here to stay. The uses of the coconut, especially the edible seed, are extensive. In fact, the coconut tree is the most utilized palm in the world, rivaled only by the monoculture plantations of the oil palm, *Elaeis guineensis*. The extensive cultivation of the oil palm for its oil (used primarily in soaps and, more recently, biofuels) is threatening tropical rain forests.

The Philippines alone produces 1.7 million tons of coconuts, followed by Indonesia, India, and Brazil. Uses include copra, coconut water, coconut meat, coconut milk, coconut cake, toddy, and candy, as well as shell-based products such as cups and folk art, and coconut wood-based products including coconut charcoal. The leaves are used for thatching, hats, and floor mats, and the husk is used to produce coir, which is then made into rope and twine. There is virtually no part of the coconut tree that has not been found useful in one capacity or another, including reading a good novel beneath its cooling shade.

On Sanibel and Captiva the coconut palm is still recovering from a disease called lethal yellowing. The initial onslaught of this contagion began in 1956 in Key West. Spread by a leaf-hopping insect (*Myndus crudus*), the disease is caused by phytoplasma, which are organisms larger than viruses but smaller than bacteria. As the phytoplasma attack the healthy palm, all of its fronds begin to turn yellow, then eventually fall to the ground, killing the tree within 18 to 30 months. The disease has swept through Lee and Collier counties several times over the past three decades, resulting in the loss of thousands of these beautiful palms.

Coconut cluster hanging in a tree top
© Charles Sobczak

More recently nurseries have developed disease-resistant trees, and the lovely coconut palm is once again flourishing across Southwest Florida. One species, the Malayan dwarf, is resistant to lethal yellowing but does not grow nearly as tall as some of the other species; it produces a yellow coconut.

Because the coconut palm is almost as salt tolerant as the red mangrove, it grows readily along the salt-saturated sandy soil of the back bay and beaches. Finding one is not really any harder than taking a stroll along the beach. Look for dozens of them scattered across South Seas Island Resort, Sundial Beach and Golf Resort, and Casa Ybel Resort. Be careful not to plant yourself directly underneath a mature tree holding large pods of ripe coconuts, however, as falling coconuts can really hurt.

Planting a coconut is quite easy. Place one horizontally in a large (five- to ten-gallon) planting container or a five-gallon bucket with a hole cut in the bottom for drainage. In the summer, you can simply leave it alone and let the summer rains germinate it. When it is still less than three feet tall, transplant it to the desired location. A coconut can also be mailed through the U.S. Post Office anywhere in the world—it makes for one very interesting postcard from paradise.

Small Trees, Shrubs and Plants of Sanibel and Captiva

☐ _____ Coastal Plain Willow ★ (*Salix caroliniana*) Nicknames: Carolina willow / Status: FL=stable, IUCN=LC / Life span: more than 50 years / Height: 12-18 ft (3.6-5.4 m) / Reproduces: naturally from a seed / Found: IW.

On Sanibel and Captiva the coastal plain willow seldom exceeds 20 feet in height, though in other parts of the state this tree can grow to 30 feet and, at this height, more closely resembles other willows, with its long, slender leaves drooping downward. The coastal plain willow ranges from the eastern and central U.S. to South Florida and Texas. It is the most widely distributed willow in Florida.

The coastal plain willow likes moist, freshwater locations. It grows well next to ponds and flowing rivers. It provides dense cover for small birds, insects, and other wildlife. The fruit is a small capsule 4-6 **Coastal Plain Willow**   © Charles Sobczak

mm long and is eaten by birds and mammals. It is the native larval host plant for the viceroy butterfly and io moth.

Excellent examples of this shrub-like tree can be found in the Bailey Tract, as well as throughout the Sanibel Gardens Preserve and the walking trails of SCCF. It is a good ornamental tree, sprouting multiple stocks when planted in the low-lying areas it prefers.

🔲 _____**White Indigo Berry** ★ (*Randia aculeata*) Nicknames: indigoberry / Status: FL=stable, IUCN=NE / Life span: n/a / Height: 6-15 ft (2-4.8 m) / Reproduces: by a small, white berry that is a favorite for birds / Found: IW, UA.

An excellent but underutilized shrub in landscaping, the white indigo berry is a favorite for birds and small mammals. It is salt and drought tolerant and will thrive in full sun or partial to full shade. Though it is not as popular an ornamental as cocoplum and some of the other natives, its clusters of lovely white berries make it an attractive addition to any landscape.

The white indigo berry is an evergreen, with small white flowers that can bloom year round. It does well in pots, along driveways, and in other locations where the soil is fairly well drained. Its

© Wikipedia Commons

range extends from the Florida Keys to north Florida and all of Texas. It is also common throughout the Caribbean basin.

There are marked indigo berry trees on the hiking trails of SCCF, and the plant can be found in most upland locations, including the Bailey Tract, Sanibel Gardens Preserve, and the Pick Preserve. There is a large stand of it located next to the bike path just before the entrance to J.N. "Ding" Darling Wildlife Refuge.

Wild coffee ★ (*Psychotria nervosa*) Nicknames: shinyleaf wild coffee / Status: FL=stable, IUCN=NE / Life span: n/a / Height: 4-10 ft (1.2-3 m) / Reproduces: by a bright red berry that is a favorite for birds / Found: IW, UA.

© Charles Sobczak

The rich, dark green color of the leaves of the wild coffee make this an attractive plant to use in understory or ornamental planting, especially when several are grouped together. Its glossy leaves are puckered with impressed veins on the upper surface, and it produces a bright, showy display of red berries in the fall. It is a native of both islands and it is related to the coffee that we drink. Although the wild coffee is not known to be poisonous, no human uses for this plant are known.

The plant is propagated by birds and other wildlife eating its berries, which then pass through the digestive system and sprout in other locations. Look for wild coffee just about anywhere in the interior wetlands and uplands of Sanibel and Captiva. It grows well as a hedge and is generally pest free. The wild coffee is fairly drought tolerant but will wilt during the late winter months for lack of rain. Generally it recovers well from these episodes, but sometimes, if water does not arrive in time, it will turn brown and perish.

Cat's Claw ★ (*Pithecellobium unguis-cati*) Nicknames: blackbeard cat's claw, catclaw blackbeard, Uña de gato (Sp) / Status: FL=stable, IUCN=NE / Life span: n/a / Height: 6-15 ft (2-4.5 m) / Reproduces: from a hard, black seed / Found: IW, UA.

Anyone who has brushed against one of these bushes in the wild will quickly understand why it's called cat's claw. The aptly named bush has razor-sharp inverted thorns that scratch with ease. For this reason it is not very popular as an ornamental.

The mature seeds of this plant have been used to make necklaces in the Caribbean. It is being investigated by the pharmaceutical industry for use in treating arthritis, bursitis, allergies, and intestinal disorders. It has been proven to have anti-tumor and anti-inflammatory properties and holds promise in relieving some of the side effects of chemotherapy.

The cat's claw can be readily found in the understory of many upland habitats where it looks more like a thorny vine than a tree, but it will sometimes find you before you find it.

Leaves and thorns of the cat's claw bush   © Charles Sobczak

❑ _____ **Pond Apple** ★ (*Annona glabra*) Nicknames: alligator-apple, corkwood, bobwood, monkey-apple / Status: FL=stable / Life span: n/a / Height: 25-35 ft (7.6-10.6 m) / Reproduces: by a large, edible fruit roughly the same size as a small apple / Found: IW.

Considered an invasive species in Australia, the pond apple growing Down Under has choked out mangrove swamps, where its seedlings carpet the banks of coastal rivers and estuaries preventing native species from taking root. The pond apple was once extremely common in parts of the Everglades where huge forests of it grew south of Lake Okeechobee. Those forests have been uprooted and replaced with sugar cane fields.

The pond apple prefers growing in damp, swampy soil and is very salt tolerant. The fruit is oblong or spherical and falls when it is still green or slightly yellow. Many mammals and birds eat the fruit. The early settlers used it to make pond apple jam. The flesh is sweetly scented and agreeable but is now believed to be strongly narcotic so it is seldom consumed today.

The best place to find this unusual tree on Sanibel is along the city's Pond Apple Park Trail that starts at the Chamber of Commerce

Pond Apple   Courtesy Wikipedia

building on Causeway Road. The trees are located in the low-lying areas shortly after you cross Bailey Road heading west on the trail. Look for signs of the large, rounded fruit that have fallen along the path.

☐ _____ **Wax Myrtle** ★ (*Myrica cerifera*) Nicknames: bayberry, candleberry, tallow shrub / Status: FL=stable / Life span: n/a / Height: 15-25 ft (4.5-7.6 m) / Reproduces: by a waxy berry that is a favorite of warblers and other birds / Found: IW, UA.

Wax Myrtle berries and leaves
© Charles Sobczak

The early settlers of Sanibel and Captiva processed the seeds of the wax myrtle to make candles for lighting their homes. The wax myrtle is a close relative of the northern bayberry tree (*Myrica pensylvanica*), which is used as the commercial source of wax for the bayberry candles we burn at Christmas. In addition to supplying candle wax, the aromatic compounds present in the wax myrtle foliage repel insects. It was a tradition in many southern homes to plant wax myrtle around the house to keep fleas and cockroaches out. The wax myrtle also has a long history of medicinal properties that go back to Native Americans who used the plant to reduce fever and control diarrhea.

The most important role of the wax myrtle today is its use as a high-energy food source for winter birds. It is a particular favorite of the Carolina wren, tree sparrow, and the entire family of warblers that migrate to and from Central America by way of Sanibel and Captiva. These warblers dine extensively on the high-octane waxy berries. In yet another example of the many symbiotic relationships found in nature, it is only by going through the digestive tract of these birds that the wax myrtle's fruit is able to rid itself of its waxy coating, thereby allowing it to germinate.

One drawback of this plant is that its branches, leaves, and stems contain flammable aromatic compounds that make it burn easily. The roots survive the fires and will re-sprout when conditions allow.

The wax myrtle is an evergreen and makes an excellent yard ornamental that will attract birds for decades to come. Examples can be found throughout the hiking trails of SCCF, as well as in the Bailey Tract of "Ding" Darling and the Sanibel Gardens Preserve.

☐ _____ **Cocoplum** ★ (*Chrysobalanus icaco*) Nicknames: redtip cocoplum / Status: FL=stable / Life span: n/a / Height 5-12 ft (1.5-3.6 m) / Reproduces: by a purple fruit that is eaten by mammals and birds / Found: IW, UA.

The cocoplum is one of the easiest and most commonly used native bushes found on Sanibel and Captiva. There are three varieties: the redtip is the far more common and cultivated one on the islands; occurring far less frequently is the horizontal, or beach, cocoplum, which seldom grows above three or four feet and has a peach-colored fruit. The third variety is the greentip cocoplum which is most commonly found in nature in interior wetland areas.

Red-leaf cocoplum

© Charles Sobczak

One of the nicest features of the cocoplum is that it responds well to pruning. It fills in nicely and can be trimmed into just about any shape or size imaginable. It is therefore a favorite choice for hedgerows, groundcover, and border plantings.

In addition to having attractive waxy leaves, the cocoplum produces a Ping Pong-sized edible fruit that resembles a small plum. When ripe the fruit can be plucked directly from the shrub and eaten like a grape. It is slightly sweet and the flesh is pure white, while the texture is reminiscent of eating a dryish grape. The early settlers harvested cocoplum fruit for jellies and jams.

The cocoplum fruit is eaten by insects, raccoons, and small mammals, and is picked open by birds. The seeds are then dispersed through the animal's waste,

The peach colored fruit of the horizontal cocoplum © Charles Sobczak

The purple fruit of the red-leaf cocoplum © Blake Sobczak

allowing the cocoplum to spread naturally in the wild. The plant has become a thriving invasive in the South Pacific where it is out-competing native plants in the coastal regions. Large-scale eradication programs, similar to our local attempts to control Brazilian pepper, are under way to rid the South Pacific islands of this species.

❒ _____ **Saltbush** (*Baccharis halimifolia*) Nicknames: cotton-seed tree, consumption weed, silverling, sea myrtle, salt marsh elder / Status: FL=stable, IUCN=NE / Life span: n/a / Height: 5-12 ft (1.5-3.6 m) / Reproduces: by a dandelion-like seed that blooms and spreads in the early winter or late fall / Found: UA, IW.

The saltbush is, without question, the most prolific bushy plant found throughout the interior wetlands of Sanibel. The plant is not showy, except when it flowers in the fall, and because of that it is easily overlooked and not commonly used in landscaping. One of the easiest methods of identifying saltbush is by its leaves,

© Charles Sobczak

which are one to three inches long with a coarsely toothed edge.

In the late fall and early winter the saltbush tree blooms in a wild display of light, fluffy seed pods that resemble cotton and can sometimes blow so thick in the wind that it seems as though it might be snowing on Sanibel. Do not attempt to use or eat these seeds, however, as they are poisonous.

This plant thrives because it is extremely salt and soil tolerant. It is also resistant to drought, heat, and salt spray. Finding a saltbush plant is as easy as walking the trails of SCCF, the Bailey Tract, or the Sanibel Gardens Preserve, where it is abundant along the trails.

❒ _____ **Sea Oxeye Daisy** ★ (*Borrichia frutescens*) Nicknames: seaside daisy, bushy seaside tansy / Status: FL=stable, IUCN=NE / Life span: n/a perennial / Height: 2-4 ft (0.60-1.2 m) / Reproduces: from seed and spreads naturally / Found: IW, UA, GB, MZ.

Commonly seen throughout the islands, this groundcover flower is used widely in residential and commercial landscaping. The sea oxeye daisy is very salt tolerant, sometimes growing within a few feet of red mangroves. It can flourish in direct sun or partial shade and thrives in Sanibel and Captiva's sometimes poor

Sea Oxeye Daisy   Courtesy NOAA

sandy soil conditions. It is a good alternative groundcover for grass, requiring almost no fertilizer or pest control.

A popular flowering plant for bees, wasps, and butterflies, this member of the aster family is also a favorite seed food for birds. It flowers in the late spring and summer, and its range extends from the Yucatan in Mexico to the Rio Grande in Texas all the way east to North Carolina. Although it is possible to grow from seed, most of the sea oxeye daisies on the islands are purchased from nurseries and allowed to spread naturally.

Look for this plant on either side of Wildlife Drive, as well as in numerous yards throughout the islands. There are also large, native stands of this plant along the beach-side trails at Bowman's Beach.

❑ _____ **Railroad Vine** ★ (*Ipomoea pes-caprae* / subspecies: *brasiliensis*) Nicknames: beach morning glory, goat's foot / Status: FL=stable, IUCN=NE / Life span: n/a / Height: 0.5-1 ft (0.15-0.30 m) / Reproduces: by seed, which can float unscathed for months in saltwater / Found: GB.

The railroad vine is a native flowering plant that occurs almost exclusively along the beaches. It roots on the upper part of the beach, beneath the sea oats and sea grape trees, sending long runners down the beach toward the water's edge. It has large showy purplish flowers that open in the morning. The vine is extremely salt tolerant. Its most important role on barrier islands is as a

© Charles Sobczak

beach stabilizing plant, helping to prevent both wind and water erosion during storm events.

The railroad vine ranges from Brazil to Georgia and westward to Texas and Mexico. In Brazil it is called salsa-da-praia and is used as a local folk medicine to treat inflammation and gastrointestinal disorders.

Unusual in that its small seeds are impervious to saltwater, the plant spreads through these floating seeds. They can wash ashore and sprout hundreds of miles from the host plant. Varieties of railroad vine can be found as far away as Australia and the South Pacific. Look for railroad vine almost anywhere along the upper sections of the beaches of both Sanibel and Captiva.

⬜ _____ **Sea Oats** ★ (*Uniola paniculata*) Nicknames: dune grass / Status: FL=protected species, IUCN=NE / Life span: n/a / Height: 4-7 ft (1.2-2 m) / Reproduces: by seed along the upper sections of the beach dune / Found: GB.

Wild sea oats, although not formally endangered or threatened, is a protected species in Florida. It once flourished along almost every stretch of beach statewide, but because of coastal development, vast tracts of this important member of the grass gamily have been uprooted and lost. Although its eradication was considered standard operating procedure through the 1970s, today's developers are often forced through the permitting process not only to mitigate any sea oats loss but also to plant additional stands to help secure the beach dune system.

During hurricanes and winter storms the extensive root system of sea oats is vital in protecting the beach dunes from extensive erosion. Sea oats, along with a host of other dune plants, help diffuse tidal surges and lessen subsequent property damage during major storms. It is extremely salt tolerant and spreads predominantly by its extensive system of underground roots (rhizomes).

© Charles Sobczak

The mature seed heads are large and decorative and are sometimes used in dried floral arrangements. The early settlers used to dry and cook these seeds to make a flavorful cereal similar to oatmeal.

The sea oats plant can also flourish inland, where it is often used as a landscaping ornamental. To prevent it from spreading via its root system, a plastic barrier located below ground has to encircle the planted area. It can be found almost anywhere along the beaches of Sanibel and Captiva.

☐ _____ **Spartina Grass** ★ (*Spartina bakeri*) Nicknames: sand cordgrass, cord-grass, Baker's cord grass / Status: FL=stable, IUCN=NE / Life span: more than 25 years / Height: 4-6 ft (1.2-1.8 m) / Reproduces: naturally in the wetland regions of both islands / Found: IW, UA.

© Charlie Sobczak

Worldwide there are 14 different species of cordgrass, growing from Europe, Africa, and North and South America. The largest number of species occurs in the Americas, with the majority in Florida. *Spartina bakeri* is the most common cordgrass found on Sanibel and Captiva; other Floridian species include *Spartina alternifora*, *Spartina patens*, and *Spartina cynosuroides*.

The name *cordgrass* derives from the nature of the leaves, which are long, rounded, and have a sandpapery feel. The plant grows in large clusters, with the height of each cluster matched by the circumference of the plant. In a natural marsh setting, spartina grass grows in a great number of these clusters, providing cover and habitat for marsh rabbits, rodents, and wrens. The seeds are a popular food source for birds.

In the late spring when controlled burns are often conducted by SCCF or the city of Sanibel, the parched stands of spartina grass are the first to burn and the first to reshoot when the summer rains return. Farther north and throughout coastal Georgia and the Carolinas several species of cordgrass form the basis of vast salt marshes, where fish and wildlife thrive on the rising and falling of the tides.

Spartina grass is one of the most underutilized native plants in Florida. It is salt tolerant, thrives in difficult soil conditions, and forms an attractive border. It has become increasingly popular for use in golf courses and can readily be seen at the Sanctuary Golf Club, the Dunes Golf and Tennis Club, Beachview Golf and Tennis Club, and South Seas Island Resort. It stabilizes pond and river banks and is a favorite for wildlife. Look for vast stands of spartina grass in the Bailey Tract and the Sanibel Gardens Preserve.

☐ _____ **Leather Fern** ★ (*Acrostichum danaeifolium*) Nicknames: giant leather fern / Status: FL=stable, IUCN=LC / Life span: more than 25 years / Height: 6-8 ft (1.8-2.4 m) / Reproduces: through spores located on the underside of the large leaves / Found: IW, UA.

In *The Nature of Things on Sanibel*, George Campbell writes that the young fiddleheads of the leather fern are edible. Generally harvested in the spring, the six- to nine-inch-long budding shoots are cooked and eaten in much the same fashion as asparagus. He adds that they taste better than asparagus but should never be harvested from preserved lands.

A number of ferns thrive on Sanibel, but the most conspicuous and largest is the leather fern. Named for its tough, leathery-like leaves, this plant is fairly common throughout wetland habitats and along the Sanibel River. Other island ferns include the Boston fern (*Nephrolepis exaltata*), the golden polypody (*Phlebodium aureum*), and the swamp fern (*Blechnum serrulatum*). All of these species do well on the islands and are available at SCCF's Native Plant Nursery.

The leather fern grows quite tall, and each plant, consisting of multiple shoots, can cover an area more than 10 feet in diameter. It is an unusual fern in that it can grow in direct sunlight. Look for this massive fern throughout the islands, especially near wetlands. A large stand of leather ferns can be found roughly two-tenths of a mile down on the north side of San-Cap Road. The leather fern makes an excellent landscape plant, provided it is in a fairly low and preferably shaded area.

Leather ferns © Charles Sobczak

☐ _____ **Poison Ivy** (*Toxicodendron radicans*) WARNING: TOXIC PLANT! Nicknames: kudzu of the north, eastern poison ivy / Status: FL=thriving, IUCN=NE / Life span: n/a / Height: can reach 50 ft or higher but is generally under 8 ft (2.4-15 m) / Reproduces: by a grayish-white drupe that is consumed and spread by birds / Found: everywhere.

Although it would not look as good on the Chamber of Commerce's tourist brochures, Sanibel could well be nicknamed "Poison Ivy Island." This familiar,

© Charles Sobczak

three-leafed vine grows just about everywhere. The only place it does not seem to thrive is in the red mangrove forests, but a few steps back from the water's edge, poison ivy can be found climbing the trunks of black mangroves.

Numerous rhymes describe the appearance and danger of this highly toxic plant: "Leaves of three, let it be." "Hairy vine, no friend of mine." "Longer middle stem, stay away from them." These refer to different identifying characteristics of this plant. Everyone is familiar with the three-leaf clusters of poison ivy. The "hairy vine" refers to the reddish hairs that can be found on most poison ivy plants, and the "longer middle stem" distinguishes the poison ivy plant from similar-looking vines such as the Virginia creeper, which is also quite common on the islands. In the fall and winter, the three-leaf clusters of poison ivy turn an attractive reddish-orange, similar in color to an autumnal maple leaf.

The biggest reason poison ivy is so prolific lies in its drupes. More than 60 species of birds feed on this grayish-white fruit and the seed hidden inside, which passes through the bird's digestive system intact, creating a dynamic dispersal system that is unrivaled by any other vine. For this reason alone, it is unwise to stray far from the marked and cleared trails that are identified in the map section of this book. Once off of these paths, poison ivy lies in an endless field of leafy land mines, and getting brushed by one of these plants is almost a certainty.

The physical reaction to the plant's oil, called urushiol, varies widely among individuals. Around 15-30 percent of people have no allergic reaction at all. The remaining 70 percent can develop anything from a mild rash that vanishes in a few days to severe dermatitis, requiring hospitalization. There are recorded cases of people going into anaphylactic shock and dying from contact with this toxic plant. Eating poison ivy, which would be an incredibly stupid thing to do, can damage the digestive tract, airways, lungs, and kidneys of the victim. Even the smoke from burning poison ivy has been known to make people extremely ill. People who are allergic to poison ivy should also avoid contact with the mango tree and the outside skin of the mango fruit, as it is from the same family and produce a chemical compound similar to urushiol. The Brazilian pepper and cashew are in this same family.

With seeds   © Charles Sobczak

Once contact is made with poison ivy, a blistering rash soon develops. This is followed by oozing or weeping, wherein the toxins are excreted from the initial point of contact, making a single incident last as long as four weeks. Remedies include Calamine lotion or Burow's solution during the early stages of the dermatitis. Do *not* wash the rash with soap and water as this will only serve to spread the toxins; use rubbing alcohol instead. As the rash develops into blisters, oatmeal baths and baking soda solutions are recommended. To relieve the itching, soaking or showering in the hottest water possible gives some relief. In severe cases, injections of corticosteroids are one of the best weapons.

There are more than 350,000 cases of poison ivy dermatitis reported annually in the United States alone. Worldwide these cases number in the millions. Recent studies have shown that one of the many negative impacts of climate change, especially an increase in carbon dioxide in the atmosphere, is that poison ivy will flourish in this environment. We are inadvertently building a perfect greenhouse for a toxic plant.

In its natural setting poison ivy is an important plant. Birds love the drupes, and its leaves provide a safe haven for butterflies, since nothing will attack them when they are resting on its toxic surface. Look for poison ivy along the bike path that runs from West Gulf Drive to Bailey's General Store along Tarpon Bay Road. There are stands of it on the west side of the bike path that are nothing short of amazing. Just don't fall into one of them!

☐ _____ **Southern Sandspur** (*Cenchrus echinatus* and *Cenchrus spinfex*)
Nicknames: none / Status: FL=thriving, IUCN=NE / Life span: less than 1 year / Height: 2-2.8 ft (0.60-0.85 m) / Reproduces: through a hard, thorny seed called a sandspur / Found: IW, UA, GB, MZ.

Though nowhere near as dangerous as poison ivy, this vexatious grass plant also deserves special mention here. There are eight different species of sandspur found in Florida. The two most common are the southern sandspur and the coastal or field sandspur. Both of these species are summer annuals, taking a single season to grow, flower, and produce seeds for the next generation.

It is these clusters of seeds, which form in the fall and hang on until the following spring, that cause problems. Adapted to cling to the fur of mammals, the feathers of birds, and more recently the skin, shoes, bike tires, and clothing of people, these razor-sharp hitch-hikers have found a successful if not devious method for dissemination. There is nothing more painful than walking barefoot down a beach-access path to take in a sunset and stepping on an unseen batch of sandspurs.

The trouble with the plant is, unless you are familiar with the seeds, it looks harmless enough. The spurs lie at the tips of the tallest grassy shoots, similar in appearance to a tiny patch of wheat. As the plant dries out, the spurs, which are spiked seeds roughly an eighth of an inch across, fall from the plant and lie hidden in the surrounding grass or sand. If you step on one, don't move because there are probably more of them very close to where you are standing. Pull out the spur, even though it has microscopic barbs on it that make its removal very painful. Treat the puncture wound with an antibiotic ointment such as Neosporin to prevent infection, and keep your sandals on the next time you walk to the beach.

The sandspur can also puncture bicycle tires. Standard inner tubes offer little resistance to a sandspur's sharp points, and there are probably hundreds of bikes on Sanibel and Captiva today

© Charles Sobczak

that have a slow leak caused by one of these nasty little seeds. The best solution is to purchase sandspur-resistant inner tubes, which are twice as thick as regular tubes and cut way down on the number of punctures.

Herbicides are available to target sandspurs in your yard. Go to www.okeechobee. ifas.ufl.edu/News/sandspur to learn more about what to use to get rid of these irritating plants. It is a native plant, just as poison ivy, but that doesn't mean we have to like it.

☐ _____ **Periwinkle Flowers** (Family: *Vinca* and *Catharanthus*)
Nicknames: pervinka (Russian meaning first flowers), Madagascar periwinkle, rosy periwinkle, old maid / Status: FL=stable, naturalized species, IUCN=NE / Life span: 1 year or less / Height: 1-2 ft (0.30-0.60 m) / Reproduces: naturally on the islands by seed / Found: IW, UA.

There is some question as to exactly where the nonnative periwinkle that graces our islands originally came from. Some believe the species originated in Europe or Asia, making its way to the Americas hundreds of years ago. Others contend that the island's periwinkle came from the island of Madagascar, located off the eastern coast of Africa. Two families claim the common name, *periwinkle*,

© Charles Sobczak

making the origins that much more difficult to determine.

Although the plant known as *Vinca minor* does somewhat resemble the periwinkle found on the islands, the more likely plant is one of the many species of *Catharanthus*, specifically, *Catharanthus roseus*, which more closely resembles those found in many yards and along roadsides throughout the islands. There is an ongoing debate as to whether it's this flowering plant or the mollusk of the same name that is the namesake of Sanibel's main street—Periwinkle Way.

In Madagascar, extracts from the periwinkle flower have been used for hundreds of years in the treatment of diabetes and in disinfectants and tranquilizers. The sap is poisonous if ingested, but the alkaloids found in this flowering plant are being studied by pharmaceutical companies for the treatment of leukemia and lymphoma. Compounds found in the flowers are already used for the treatment of cancer and in immune-suppressive drugs.

The periwinkle is considered a naturalized species. It propagates by both seeds and cuttings.

❒ _____ **Brazilian Pepper** (*Schinus terebinthifolius*) Nicknames: Florida holly, Florida folly, rose pepper / Status: FL=invasive species, thriving, IUCN=NE / Life span: more than 30 years / Height: 15-30 ft (4.5-9 m) / Reproduces: through a bright red seed that is a favorite food of dozens of species of birds / Found: IW, MZ, UA, GB.

Introduced in Florida around 1891, the Brazilian pepper represents a classic and costly example of the tremendous amount of damage a single species can do to an environment. Sanibel and Captiva have spent well over $1 million in an endless battle to rid the islands of this troublesome shrub. Because the bright red berries are a prized food for robins, starlings, mockingbirds, and a host of passerines, the seeds contained within are relentlessly spread across the landscape.

The city of Sanibel has been working since 1998 to eradicate all Brazilian pepper from the island. This task is tantamount to the myth of Sisyphus, wherein the Greek king is punished by being cursed to roll a huge boulder up a hill only to watch it roll back down again. Like this Sisyphean myth, removing all the pepper from Sanibel and Captiva is an endless task. To help manage the problem, the city has divided the island into six zones and is working its way through each one. As of this writing it is on the fourth zone, with the final two zones to be completed within the next few years. All of the preserved lands on the island have been cleared of pepper,

Bright pink pepper berries © Charles Sobczak

and annual maintenance is conducted in all of these preserves. This is an enormous task. The Sanibel Garden Preserve covers 265 acres alone.

A mature Brazilian pepper forest is an ecological nightmare. The plants form a continuous monoculture of growth, shading out almost every living thing in its understory. The trunks and branches twist and tangle, making the forest useless for most wildlife. In Brazil where the plant originated, there are ample natural controls for the plant, but in Florida none exists, so controlling its rampant spread is left to us. There are sections of Lee County where Brazilian pepper covers tens of thousands of acres, but there is no financially viable method of eradicating these massive forests.

In South America the berries of this plant are dried and sold as pink peppercorns for cooking. If you crush a pepper tree leaf in your hand and smell it, the scent is distinctively pepper-like. Some people are allergic to Brazilian pepper and have a reaction similar to poison ivy. The treatment for pepper dermatitis is virtually identical to treating poison ivy.

Sadly, it is still all too easy to find Brazilian pepper on the island. Look for it on vacant lots, near beach accesses, or just about anywhere. The bright red berries, which are most obvious in December, make the tree easy to identify. The species is legally prohibited from sale, transport, or planting anywhere in Florida, and it is not available in any nursery in the state.

❐ _____ **Australian Pine** (*Casuarina* two species: *C. cunninghamiana* and *C. equisetifolia*) Nicknames: Botany oak, she oak, ironwood, beefwood / Status: FL=thriving, IUCN=NE / Life span: more than 100 years / Height: 70-90 ft (21-27 m) / Reproduces: by means of a small, rounded seed about the size of a marble / Found: IW, UA, GB, MZ.

In a classic case of misnaming, the Australian pine is not a pine. It is a hardwood member of the Casuarinaceae family that has evolved to survive in arid and semi-arid environments. The misnomer comes from the apparent "pine needles," which are actually multijointed branchlets covered with minuscule leaves that resemble scales. These adaptations help reduce water loss in the dry continent where this tree originated: Australia.

Australian pine at the beach   © Charles Sobczak

The species was brought into Florida to serve as a windbreak for agricultural purposes. Sanibel's Bailey brothers, Sam and Francis, can recall the days before the Australian pine was planted on the islands. The Australian pine is an exceptionally dense and heavy wood, ideal for fireplaces because it lacks pitch, but it is dangerous to remove because of its weight.

The Australian pine is not currently found on the city of Sanibel's invasive plant list, but it should be. Many island residents admire this tree, and that admiration is understandable if ill conceived. The tall tree has an attractive wispy look, and the ancient giants that formed a cathedral-like corridor down Periwinkle Way pre-Hurricane Charley were indeed spectacular. Recent studies, however, indicate that this tree has allelopathic properties that make it far more sinister than its appearance.

The study of allelopathy is relatively new to biological science. It is a phenomenon characteristic of certain plants, algae, bacteria, fungi, and coral reefs in which the species, invasive or native, produces biochemicals that inhibit the growth of competing plants in its immediate vicinity. This phenomenon is apparent when you walk beneath a large stand of mature Australian pines. Although there is ample sunlight and water, virtually nothing grows beneath the trees, and the ground is covered in a thick mat of fallen branchlets. Recent studies indicate that the root system of the tree itself is chemically altering the soil around it to prevent other plants from sprouting. Like the punk tree (*Melaleuca quinquenervia*), the Australian pine is deceptively charming but harmful to other living organisms.

The Australian pine's allelopathy, coupled with the devastation it can deliver during tropical storms and hurricanes, makes it a prime candidate for complete removal. The Australian pine does not have a deep taproot like the slash pine. Instead, the roots of this massive tree spread out in a shallow, pancake-like formation that allows the tree to topple over in storms. More than 20,000 Australian pines were taken down by Hurricane Charley, and although the city attempted to eradicate them after Charley, there was still too much opposition by misguided tree huggers to approve the necessary policy changes. While there is nothing wrong with being a tree hugger, you should always be sure you are hugging the right tree. The casuarina is not that tree. In many other parts of Florida this species has been removed and banned.

☐ _____ **Lead Tree** (*Leucaena leucocephala*) Nicknames: white leadtree, jumbay, white popinac / Status: FL=invasive, thriving IUCN=one of the world's top 100 invasive species / Life span: more than 30 years / Height: 4-16 ft (1.2-5 m) / Reproduces: by an edible seed disseminated by mammals and birds / Found: UA, IW.

© Charles Sobczak

The lead tree is native to the Americas, from Peru through Texas. There are roughly 24 different species of the *Leucaena* genus, but only one (*Leucaena leucocephala*) is present on Sanibel. In its native environment the lead tree does not pose any environmental problems. The tree is used for charcoal, livestock fodder, green manure, and, because of its rapid growth rate, soil conservation. It is also being tested, with promising results, for biofuel in electrical generating plants.

It is the "green manure" aspect of this tree that makes it such a problem on the islands. The term refers to an agricultural process in which a farmer plants a rapid-growing cover crop in a fallow field in the spring for the sole purpose of plowing it under in the fall. This practice increases nutrients, fixes nitrogen, and adds organic matter to the soil. In the Midwest, clover and vetch are used as green manure but in the poorer soil conditions of Central and South America, the lead tree serves much the same function.

This ability to grow quickly and shade out all other living organisms makes the lead tree especially troublesome. In areas of disturbed soil the lead tree can spread like wildfire. A single mature tree will send up root shoots and produce abundant, edible seeds. It can overtake a vacant lot in months.

Sanibel and Captiva are not alone in their battle against this plant. The same species of lead tree has invaded Taiwan, Hawaii, Fiji, and northern Australia. Care should be taken when removing the lead tree from your property, however, as it is commonly mistaken for the native tamarind. The trunks and canopies of the two trees closely resemble each other, though the leaves of the tamarind are half the size of those of the lead tree.

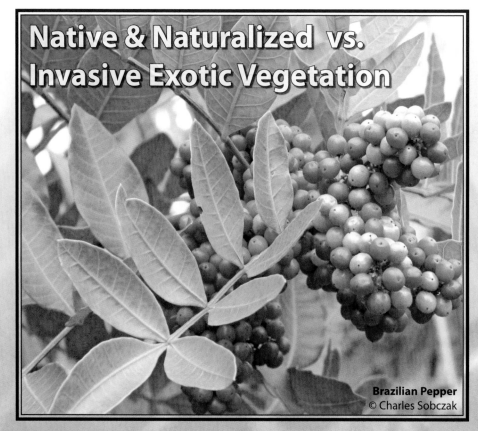

Native & Naturalized vs. Invasive Exotic Vegetation

Brazilian Pepper
© Charles Sobczak

The City of Sanibel has posted the following plants and trees on its Web site (www.mysanibel.com/Departments/Natural-Resources/Vegetation-information) as invasive, exotic vegetation:

1. **Brazilian pepper**
   (*Schinus terebinthefolius*)
2. **Melaleuca / Punk tree**
   (*Melaleuca quinquenervia*)
3. **Earleaf acacia**
   (*Acacia auriculiformis*)
4. **Java plum**
   (*Syzgium cumini*)
5. **Scaevola/Exotic inkberry**
   (*Scaevola taccada, S. fruescens, S. sericea*)
6. **Lead tree**
   (*Leucaena leucocephala*)
7. **Mother-in-law's tongue / Bowstring hemp** (*Sanservieria hyacinthoides*)
8. **Air potato**
   (*Dioscorea bulbifera*)

The Web site has a downloadable PDF file that provides detailed information about each of these invasive plants, as well as useful information about how to remove and control them. The Department of Natural Resources (239-472-3700) will also assist you in identifying these plants and advise you on how best to properly eradicate them.

For a complete list of native or naturalized species available for purchase at SCCF's Native Plant Nursery go to and click on the Native Plant Nursery tab. Scroll down to the native plant price list and download a complete, eight-page PDF of available plants and prices, or visit the native plant nursery located next to the nature center and education facility at 3333 Sanibel-Captiva Road (239-472-1932).

Museums and Eco-Attractions

Sanibel and Captiva are unique among barrier islands in that they host several museums and numerous eco-attractions within an easy bike ride from most of the resorts, inns and rental condominiums. The majority of these are located on Sanibel along Sanibel-Captiva Road not further than 2.4 miles from the intersection of Tarpon Bay Road.

Two of these are genuine museums—the Sanibel Historical Museum and Village and the Bailey-Matthews Shell Museum. Both offer fascinating displays, interesting historical or archaeological artifacts and are great places to learn more about the Native American history and development of these barrier islands.

The other five facilities, Tarpon Bay Explorers, Sanibel-Captiva Conservation Foundation (SCCF), CROW, "Ding" Darling Educational Center and the Sanibel Recreational Center, while having some museum-like displays, are more eco-attractions. Places such as Tarpon Bay Explorers offer bicycle, canoe and kayak rentals, guided tours, fishing guides, tram tours and other environmental and educational programs. SCCF as well offers a host of educational programs and tours as well as having more than four miles of well-maintained hiking trails located on their property behind the Nature Center. These are the only trails on Sanibel reserved exclusively for hiking.

CROW has just completed a brand new, state of the art, educational and information facility called the *Healing Winds Visitor Educational Center*, where visitors and residents can learn more about CROW and their commitment to treating, healing and rehabilitating injured wildlife. The spacious facility located at the entrance of J.N. "Ding" Darling National Wildlife Refuge is a multi-faceted space that offers lectures, a bookstore, interactive displays, museum-like displays as well as extensive information about the different refuge habitats and wildlife you might expect to find there. Since each and every one of these facilities are dedicated to teaching us about everything from water quality to the safety of wildlife, calling them attractions alone is incorrect. They are eco-attractions, dedicated to informing people about their role in the natural world and what each and every one of us can do to make these islands, and the world, a better place for all living things.

Finally the Sanibel Recreational Center is a place to go to stay healthy. They offer pools, gyms, lit tennis courts and training rooms as well as any number of classes including yoga, dance and swimming lessons. Whether you live on Sanibel or Captiva or are here visiting, seeing one or all of these places is a "must do" to better understand and appreciate everything these islands have to offer. Please support all of them generously.

Sanibel Historical Museum and Village

Location: 950 Dunlop Road (directly west of city hall on the north side of Dunlop approx. .2 miles from Palm Ridge Road)/ Telephone: 239-472-4648 / Fax: 239-472-2277 / E-mail: calusa1513@embarqmail.com/ Website: www.sanibelmuseum.org

The Rutland House   © Blake Sobczak

The seeds of the current historical museum were planted in 1975 when island historian and author of *The Sea Shell Islands,* Elinor Dormer, formed the Historical Preservation Committee. Shortly thereafter, the City of Sanibel set aside approximately four acres for the future museum, and the committee raised the $3,500 to move the Clarence Rutland House to its present site. Nine years later that single house became a museum. It was open one day a week, eight months a year, and staffed by committee members and a handful of volunteer docents.

Today the Historical Museum and Village consists of eight buildings, staffed by more than 100 volunteers, and is open four days a week, 10 months of the year. The hours of operation are Wednesday through Saturday, 10 a.m. to 4 p.m. November through April, and 10 a.m. to 1 p.m. May through August. Admission is $5. (Note: hours of operation and admission fees are subject to change.)

The real treasures of the village are the former homes and businesses of the pioneer islanders. The Rutland House, built in 1913, represents a typical "cracker"-style home. It has 11-foot ceilings and ample cross-ventilation, standard features during the days before air conditioning. Inside you will find walls covered in old island maps, authentic period furnishings, and the petrified mastodon humus bone featured earlier in this book.

The Burnap Cottage is the oldest building in the village. It was constructed around 1890 on the old Woodring homestead on Woodring Point. The Morning

Inside Morning Glories House   © Blake Sobczak

Glories House dates back to 1925 and was originally ordered out of a Sears and Roebuck catalog. It originally cost $2,211 and arrived on Sanibel on a barge in 30,000 pieces. A group of early islanders assembled the cottage, which originally overlooked San Carlos Bay.

The Historical Village also houses five commercial buildings. The old Bailey's Store was formerly located not far from the Mornings

The Old Schoolhouse   © Blake Sobczak

Glories House on San Carlos Bay just north of where the causeway enters the island. The store, then known as the Sanibel Packing Company, was built shortly after the deadly Miami hurricane of 1926. Inside you will find shelves stocked with old canned goods, dry goods, and all the supplies needed to survive on the islands during the Great Depression. The ridiculously low prices on the goods in the store show you just how much things have changed since 1926.

Miss Charlotta's Tearoom was built in 1926 as a gas station but was never used as such. Between 1928 and 1935 it was the island's tearoom, hosted by Charlotta Matthews, a member of the same family whose name is given to the Bailey-Matthews Shell Museum and whose relatives owned the Matthews Hotel, which became the Island Inn.

The Old Post Office is the smallest building in the village. Built from the debris left on the island after the 1926 hurricane, the post office was in operation until 1943.

The Old Schoolhouse was built in 1898 and is a classic one-room schoolhouse where children in grades one through eight took turns taking lessons from a single teacher. It was moved to the village in 2004 and restored by a group of volunteers called the Hammerheads. Finally, the Sanibel Packing House, which is the only replica building in the village, serves as a storehouse for the museum's collections, including an old wagon and an antique Model-T delivery truck dating back to 1926.

The Sanibel Historical Museum and Village is one of the best-kept secrets on the island. It is a welcome change of pace from bird-watching and beachcombing. The various displays provide an excellent idea about what life was like in the early years of Sanibel when there were seldom more than 100 people on the island at any given time and the pace of life was far slower than today's frantic world. The docents are courteous and always willing to answer your questions about this important window into Sanibel's fascinating history.

Tarpon Bay Explorers

Location: 900 Tarpon Bay Road, Sanibel (at the northern end of Tarpon Bay Road approximately .27 miles past the stop sign on Sanibel-Captiva Road)/Telephone number: 239-472-8900 / Fax: 239-395-2772 / e-mail: n/a / Website: www.tarponbayexplorers.com.

Courtesy Tarpon Bay Explorers

Offering a wide array of tours and services to the eco-tourist, Tarpon Bay Explorers is one of the top destinations to take in while on Sanibel and Captiva. It is open seven days a week, 8:00 a.m. to 5:00 p.m. October 1 through February 14, and 8:00 a.m. to 6:00 p.m. February 15 through September 30. Unlike the main section of the J. N. "Ding" Darling Wildlife Refuge, Tarpon Bay Explorers is always open on Friday. There is no admission charge to visit the expansive grounds and unique gift shop, and ample free parking is available.

Famous for its canoe and kayak trails, Canoe & Kayak Magazine recently named Tarpon Bay "one of the top 10 places to paddle in the nation." The most popular of these trails is Commodore Creek, which winds through a labyrinth of overhanging red mangroves and open, saltwater ponds. You can opt to explore on your own or sign up with one of Tarpon Bay's experienced naturalists on a guided tour. They will introduce you to the various birds, fish, crabs, and sea grasses and enlighten you about the fascinating details of the mangrove forest ecosystem. The rates are affordable but are subject to change, so go to the Website or call for reservations before visiting. In addition to canoes and kayaks, Tarpon Bay Explorers rents bicycles, motorized canoes, and pontoon boats. If you have your own canoe or kayak, there is a nominal launch charge for putting in at the Tarpon Bay boat ramp.

Another popular activity run by Tarpon Bay Explorers is the refuge tram tour (230-472-1351 for reservations), which begins in the parking lot in front of the refuge headquarters. The 90-minute tour takes you down Wildlife Drive in a bus that operates on low emissions and reduces noise and air pollution. The wheelchair-accessible vehicle has wide-open viewing. Experienced naturalists guide you through the expansive mudflats and mangrove forests, pointing out roseate spoonbills, ibis, herons, and egrets, as well as the more difficult to spot mangrove crabs, fiddler crabs, and American alligators.

Touch Tank   Courtesy Tarpon Bay Explorers

Tarpon Bay Explorers also offers Nature

Sunset at Tarpon Bay   Courtesy Tarpon Bay Explorers

and Sea Life Cruises three times daily (up to five times daily during season) out of Tarpon Bay. The breakfast, daytime, and evening cruises each lasts approximately 90 minutes and offers slightly different experiences that might include dolphin and manatee sightings, bird rookery observations, and any number of different fish and bird species. These boats are wheelchair accessible. If fishing is your passion, Tarpon Bay Explorers has several experienced fishing guides available, including fly-fishing specialists. Common catches include snook, redfish, and spotted seatrout.

Deck talks, given Monday through Friday around noon, are free lunchtime presentations by qualified naturalists on the deck at Tarpon Bay Explorers. Sample topics include manatee and shark biology, dolphin behavior, sea turtle and alligator information, and Calusa Indians. These talks are an enjoyable way to discover more about Sanibel and Captiva.

For the young naturalist, Tarpon Bay Explorers offers a large touch tank, teeming with live shells, including lightning whelks, hermit crabs, oysters, and more. The aquarium display introduces visitors to seahorses, puffers, and pipefish, as well as a number of local baitfish. A visit to the touch tank is included with every Nature and Sea Life Cruise.

Whereas the greater "Ding" Darling National Wildlife Refuge is more of an individual experience, Tarpon Bay Explorers offers visitors an in-depth look at island flora and fauna. The guides are trained professionals whose extensive knowledge of the region and its environment make for an intimate look at the intricacies of the mangrove ecosystem. Any visit to Sanibel and Captiva can hardly be called complete without stopping to investigate the numerous activities to be discovered at Tarpon Bay Explorers.

The Bailey-Matthews Shell Museum

Location: 3075 Sanibel-Captiva Road (on the south side of the road .8 of a mile west of the stop sign at Tarpon Bay Road) / Telephone: 239-395-2233 / Fax: 239-395-6706 / Toll-free: 888-679-6450 / E-mail: jleal@shellmuseum.org / Website: www.shellmuseum.org

© Charles Sobczak

The idea for building a shell museum on Sanibel, one of the world's renowned shelling locations, more than likely dates back to the first Sanibel Shell Fair in 1927. The dream started to become a reality in 1984 when Charlene McMurphy, a local shell collector, bequeathed $10,000 toward that goal, while her husband, Rolland McMurphy, selected a committee consisting of Sanibel-Captiva Shell Club members to explore the formation of a museum.

In early 1990 pioneer residents Francis, Sam, and John Bailey deeded more than eight acres of land on San-Cap Road for the museum. At about the same time, the Shell Museum and Educational Foundation Inc., a not-for-profit corporation, was established. The group soon kicked off a capital fund drive and hired renowned malacologist R. Tucker Abbott, Ph.D., as a consultant. After four years of fund raising, ground was broken in May 1994. The grand opening was November 18, 1995, sadly, two weeks after Dr. Abbott had passed away.

The Bailey-Matthews Shell Museum is open daily from 10 a.m. until 5 p.m. Admission for children 4 and under is free, $4 for children ages 5-16, and $7 for adults. (Note: hours of operation and admission fees are subject to change.)

The museum contains more than 30 different displays, ranging from a life-size model of a giant squid (*Achiteuthis dux*) to the largest horse conch (*Tripofusus giganteus*) in the world. Other exhibits include a display of the most common species of shells found on Sanibel and Captiva, as well as an extensive collection of fossil shells and a life-size diorama of the Calusa Indians using local shells for

Calusa exhibit   © Blake Sobczak

© Blake Sobczak

tools and utensils. The learning lab features a hands-on play area for children and a tank filled with living indigenous mollusks.

Beyond the museum itself, the foundation is involved with outreach and educational programs that extend far beyond the islands. Dr. José Leal, the current museum director, is the editor of *The Nautilus*, an international journal of malacology, published since 1886. Other programs include producing school kits that are sent to interested educators worldwide, the sale and distribution of videos such as *Mollusks in Action* and *Shells of the Sea,* as well as extensive summer programs for children and young adults. The museum has one of the world's most extensive library collections of books, scientific journals, and newsletters pertaining to shells and mollusks. Access to this collection is through the Sanibel Public Library (239-472-2483).

The museum store offers a variety of shell-related items. Memberships, which include free admission to the museum for one year, start as low as $40 annually. The museum also sponsors a weekly article that appears in *The Islander* called "The Shell Seeker." To view past articles about local and regional shells, go to the museum's Website.

Any visit to Sanibel and Captiva, islands made world famous for their shelling, should include a trip to the Bailey-Matthews Shell Museum. The information gathered there will help both young and adult naturalists better understand the critical role shells have played in the history of Southwest Florida, from the days of the Calusa Indians to the present. New exhibits are under way, including a special display detailing the role of shellfish as food throughout mankind's history. Access to the museum, with its central location, is an easy bike ride from anywhere on the island.

Sanibel-Captiva Conservation Foundation (SCCF)

Location: 3333 Sanibel-Captiva Road (located one mile west of the stop sign at Tarpon Bay Road) / Telephone number: 239-472-2329 / Fax: 239-472-6421 / E-mail: sccf@sccf.org / Website: www. sccf.org.

Courtesy Sanibel-Captiva Conservation Foundation

One of the first things you notice as you drive around Sanibel is all of the open, green, undeveloped space: more than 65 percent of Sanibel is held in conservation land. The Sanibel-Captiva Conservation Foundation (SCCF) owns and manages 1,200 acres on Sanibel plus 600 acres on Captiva and other islands in the area—all of it acquired over the past 40 years through the support and generosity of islanders.

You can explore Sanibel's unique interior freshwater wetlands on trails in SCCF preserves that are open to the public. Four miles of trails at the SCCF nature center meander through its 250-acre center tract, where SCCF has an observation tower. The nature center features a butterfly house, touch tank, information on the marine lab, island habitat exhibits, plus a small interactive museum and a gift shop. Hours of operation are 8:30 a.m. until 4:00 p.m. from October to May and 8:30 until 3:00 p.m. from June through September. There is a small admission charge to visit the trails; members are free.

Touch Tank   Courtesy SCCF

SCCF also has trails at the Periwinkle Preserve on Periwinkle Way across from Sanibel Community Church; the Bob Wigley Preserve on Casa Ybel Road, and Sanibel Gardens off Island Inn Road. Note that Periwinkle Preserve and Bob Wigley Preserve are accessible only by bicycle or on foot; there is no vehicle parking.

SCCF was established in 1967 to preserve the islands and the health of the surrounding waters. Land acquisition has always been a priority, but SCCF's long-standing commitment to water quality was formalized with the establishment in 2002 of a marine laboratory and the addition of a natural resource policy director in 2006. Other key mission areas include educational outreach and the native plant nursery, which works to promote diverse ecosystems and quality wildlife habitat through the sale of native plants.

Classes and cruises (many are seasonal) explore the wildlife, sea life, and plant

Preserved Land Trail   Courtesy SCCF/ Maggie May Rogers

life of the islands: topics include sea turtles, alligators, bobcats, the fishing history of Pine Island Sound, the history of the Caloosahatchee River, how to landscape your yard for wildlife, and introductory programs for new residents. SCCF's educational programs and wildlife cruises (in partnership with Captiva Cruises) reach more than 44,000 people each year.

SCCF's sea turtle research and monitoring program coordinates more than 100 volunteers who keep track of nests daily during the summer nesting season. Sanibel and Captiva beaches are also important nesting and wintering habitat for shorebirds. SCCF staff and volunteers help protect nesting areas and conduct research on habitat quality and human disturbance. SCCF also educates people about living safely with alligators and other predators that are a natural part of the local environment.

The SCCF Marine Lab conducts research, monitoring, and restoration projects in local waters. The lab's RECON (River, Estuary, and Coastal Observing Network) consists of six water-quality sensors spanning almost 90 miles, from Moore Haven by Lake Okeechobee to Redfish Pass, monitoring key water-quality parameters including salinity, temperature, and chlorophyll a (an indicator of the presence of algae). Near real-time data is available at www.recon.sccf.org.

SCCF's policy staff develops policies, provides outreach, and advocates for the protection and restoration of important habitats, land management issues, marine and wildlife conservation, and water resources. After the active hurricane seasons of 2004 and 2005 led to the dumping of billions of gallons of polluted water from Lake Okeechobee down the Caloosahatchee, water quality became a major focus. The work of the Marine Lab helps provide a scientific grounding for SCCF's policy efforts.

Marine Research
Courtesy SCCF

Karen Nelson, Communications Coordinator, SCCF

The J.N. "Ding" Darling Educational Center

Location: 1 Wildlife Drive, (the main entrance is located two miles west of Tarpon Bay Road on Sanibel-Captiva Road)/Telephone number: 239-472-1100 / Fax: 239-472-4061 / E-mail: dingdarling @ fws.gov / Website: www. fws.gov/dingdarling/.

© Blake Sobczak

Completed in 2001 at a cost of $3.3 million, the "Ding" Darling Environmental Education Center was funded by monies raised by the "Ding" Darling Wildlife Society (DDWS). Founded in 1982 by Bud Ryckman, DDWS is a 501(c)3, not-for-profit organization whose mission is to support environmental education and services at the J.N. "Ding" Darling National Wildlife Refuge. This partnership has proven to be an integral part of the refuge experience. Not only has the DDWS built the center, but it also supports the various educational and biology intern programs, operates the bookstore in the center, and much more. DDWS has more than 1,400 members. To learn more about becoming a member or a volunteer for DDWS, go to www. dingdarlingsociety.org.

The "Ding" Darling Environmental Education Center has no admission charge and is open daily from 9:00 a.m. to 4:00 p.m. May 1 through December 31, and from 9:00 a.m. until 5:00 p.m. January 1 through April 30. Wildlife Drive, which has a small admission fee that remains with the refuge, is open every day except Fridays, from sunrise to sunset. (Admission is free for an entire year with the purchase of a Federal Duck Stamp, currently $15.) For the complete schedule, go to www.fws. gov/dingdarling/. (Note: hours of operation and admission fees to Wildlife Drive are subject to change, so call the museum prior to visiting.)

Though it is possible to take in "Ding" Darling without visiting the education center, its numerous displays help tremendously in understanding the history, the

Touch table   © Blake Sobczak

future, and the complex ecological systems of the refuge. The dioramas include an inside look at J.N. "Ding" Darling's studio, with displays of all the beautifully designed Duck Stamps, starting with "Mallards" (1934-1935) by "Ding" himself. There are several exquisitely carved pieces by world-renowned wood sculptor Jim Sprankle, as well as numerous mounts of some of the more familiar birds found in the

An informative display   © Blake Sobczak

refuge, from brown pelicans to great blue herons.

A large interactive area for children includes a touch tank of various objects relating to life in the refuge and on the islands in general, such as a sea turtle shell, otter fur, horseshoe crabs, skulls, and an assortment of shells and feathers. There is an interactive video display of the many birds found in the refuge and a number of other educational videos well suited for holding the attention of younger conservationists.

Other displays include "The Changing Estuary," "Behaviors and Adaptations," and a photography collection by Dick Fortune and Sara Lopez, who are the primary photographers for this book. The gallery section has several more art and photography displays, including the finalists in the annual Federal Junior Duck Stamp Program. The bookstore offers a fine selection of field guides, birding guides, and natural history books, as well as postcards, magnets, and souvenirs of your visit to the refuge.

The refuge encompasses 5,223 acres and is home to more than 238 bird species and 51 reptile and amphibian species. The seven culverts that run beneath Wildlife Drive present some of the best locations on the island to view various fish species, including mangrove snapper, mullet, and snook.

The refuge has more than 800,000 visitors annually, making it one of the most popular wildlife refuges in the United States. While it isn't mandatory for any visitor to Sanibel and Captiva to take in the Environmental Educational Center and go for a leisurely bike ride through the J.N. "Ding" Darling National Wildlife Refuge, it should be. The "Ding" Darling Refuge is at the very core of what Sanibel and Captiva have stood for over the past 100 years and represents a lifelong dream come true for the man who helped create the National Wildlife Refuge system.

C.R.O.W. Clinic for the Rehabilitation of Wildlife, Inc.

Location: 3883 Sanibel-Captiva Road (on the south side of the Road 2.3 miles west of the stop sign at Tarpon Bay Road) / Telephone number: 239-472-3644 / Fax: 239-472-8544 / e-mail: crowclinic@aol.com / Website: www. crowclinic. org / Volunteer information: 239-395-0031.

© Blake Sobczak

Established in 1968, CROW is one of the leading wildlife rehabilitation centers in the United States. Under the direction of two full-time staff veterinarians—Dr. P.J. Deitschel, clinic director, and Dr. Amber McNamara, staff veterinarian—CROW treats 4,000 patients annually, representing 160 different wildlife species. Its primary mission is the rescue, care, rehabilitation, and eventual release back into the wild of sick, injured, and orphaned native wildlife. Inherent in this mission is the education of adults and children to ensure a peaceful coexistence with their wild neighbors.

After a multiyear capital fund-raising drive of $3.2 million with a substantial contribution from the Lee County Visitor and Convention Bureau, CROW completed a new visitor center and wildlife hospital in 2009. Whereas the hospital itself is not open to the general public, the Healing Winds Visitor Education Center is one of the most interesting interactive facilities of its type in the nation. The center is open from 10:00 a.m. until 4:00 p.m. Tuesday through Sunday (summer hours may vary). A $5 donation is recommended and a family rate is available. Members are admitted free of charge. (Note: hours of operation and admission fees are subject to change so please call the museum prior to visiting.)

Designed by Malone Design Fabrication, a firm that has worked with the Smithsonian Institution and the Statue of Liberty National Monument, the visitor center lets you "be the vet" and try your hand at diagnosing wildlife injuries, as well as identifying the appropriate treatments for the injured animals.

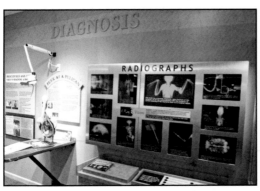

Diagnosis Center   © Blake Sobczak

Other educational displays include case studies that walk visitors through the rescue, treatment, rehabilitation, and release of CROW's numerous patients, many of which are on the endangered or threatened species lists. The visitor center also has a unique gift shop

CROW's Interactive Visitor Center   © Blake Sobczak

and a televised link to the sea turtle and otter rehabilitation pens where you can watch these wonderful animals get well.

The leading causes of injuries for CROW's patients are automobile collisions, followed by entanglements with improperly discarded fishing line. Other frequent causes include red tide poisoning of pelicans and shorebirds, boat collisions with sea turtles, and orphaned or abandoned immature animals.

From its humble beginnings operating out of the home of co-founder Shirley Walter to the current state-of-the-art hospital and visitor center, CROW has been an integral part of Sanibel's commitment to living with wildlife. If you chance upon an injured animal, call CROW at 239-472-3644, or go to its Website for information about how to capture and transport the animal to the hospital. Be careful, as many birds can inflict painful pecks and scratches, and animals such as raccoons and turtles are capable of vicious bites.

As Dr. Deitschel put it in a 2002 interview in *Times of the Islands*, "It's their home, too. Accept personal responsibility for their care and safety. This responsibility is a lesson for all life but certainly on this island, where living with wildlife is a way of life."

Be certain to include a visit to the Healing Winds Visitor Education Center while you are visiting Sanibel and Captiva, and remember to drive the speed limit and watch for wildlife crossing San-Cap Road, especially at dawn and dusk. The signs along the road say it best: "Please slow down for us!"

City of Sanibel Recreation Center

Location: 3880 Sanibel-Captiva Road (directly west of The Sanibel School on the north side of the road 2.4 miles from the stop sign at Tarpon Bay Road) / Telephone number: 239-472-0345 / Fax: 239-472-0804 / e-mail: reccenter@ mysanibel.com / Website: www. mysanibel.com (look on the right-hand side under Quick Links, and click on the third arrow down: Register for Activities... etc.

© Blake Sobczak

The grand opening of the $14 million Sanibel Recreation Center was held December 1, 2007. Paid for largely by a special bond issue that was approved by an island-wide vote by the citizens of Sanibel (the Lee County School District contributed approximately 13 percent and Lee County approximately 25 percent), the state-of-the-art building and pool replaced an aging facility that was originally constructed in 1974 and built without the benefit of air conditioning.

The new rec center has 186,000 square feet of air-conditioned space. Shortly after completion, it won an architectural award for incorporating numerous green features such as a state-of-the-art air conditioning system, solar thermal systems, environmentally sensitive building materials, and a monitoring system for indoor air quality, as well as specialized electricity demand systems to keep power usage at a minimum. The facility includes two full-size gymnasiums, a weight room, dance/fitness room, locker rooms, meeting rooms, four lighted tennis courts, a six-lane competition swimming pool (75 feet x 45 feet), plunge pool (24 feet x 22 feet), exercise pool, and a shallow splash pool and wading area. A waterslide is open from noon until 5:00 p.m. every Saturday and Sunday.

Fees vary, depending on whether you are a resident, on-island employee, member guest, or visitor. Visitor rates at the time of publication (January 2010) were: individual: $12 daily, $50 weekly, $235 for six months, and $395 annually; family: $20 daily, $105 weekly, $395 for six months, and $495 annually. Hours of operation are 6:30 a.m to 8:00 p.m. Monday-Thursday; 6:30 a.m to 6:30 p.m. Friday; 8:00 a.m. to 5:00 p.m. Saturday; and noon to 5:00 p.m. Sunday. (Note: hours of operation and admission fees are subject to change so please call prior to visiting.)

Weight Room　　　　© Blake Sobczak

Lap Pool　　　　　　　　　　　　　　　　　　　　　　© Blake Sobczak

The rec center offers numerous fitness programs free to all members. These programs, tailored to every age group, include after-school programs for children and teens, stability ball strength training, karate, yoga, volleyball, basketball, tennis, swimming lessons, shallow- and deep-water aerobics, water Pilates, aqua jogging, and salsa dance aerobics. New fitness and wellness programs are added and changed weekly, so the best resource for all of the programs and their schedules is the recreation center's Website.

The Sanibel Recreation Center is within a short bicycle ride of most of the island's motels and rental condominiums and offers visitors an opportunity to keep fit while enjoying the many outdoor activities available here. It is always important to remember that we are large mammals (*Homo sapiens*) who need both calories and exercise to stay fit enough to walk the trails and beaches,

Splash Pool　　　　　　　　　　　　　　　© Blake Sobczak

bike, kayak, canoe, and enjoy the beautiful nature that surrounds us. From a game of tennis to swimming laps in the largest pool on the islands, a day at the Sanibel Recreation Center is a welcome change of pace from shell collecting or bird watching and a good thing for your health, mind, and heart as well.

© Blake Sobczak

Getting Around Naturally

The best way to observe nature is by slowing down. Finding a two-striped walking stick or spotting a tiny, flitting warbler from the front seat of an automobile is impossible. If you want to see the natural world as it is, then become part of it. Leave the car keys at home and hop on a bicycle, rent a canoe or kayak, or better still, head out for a leisurely walk on the beach or along one of the dozens of hiking trails throughout Sanibel and Captiva.

The benefits are twofold. Not only do you reduce greenhouse gases by burning fewer fossil fuels, you receive the added value of healthy exercise. Biking, hiking, canoeing, and kayaking are good for your cardiovascular system and your waistline. If you are concerned about "bugs" or "rain," then bring along some bug spray and rain gear. Going green is good.

The most important thing to do is to slow down and become aware. Find a tamarind tree and search the trunk for the elusive Florida tree snail. Look for the hidden mangrove and fiddler crabs in the J.N. "Ding" Darling Wildlife Refuge. Walk the beach at sunset and watch the shorebirds work the edge of the sea; and then stop, remain silent, and listen to the sounds of the natural world. You will hear the surf, the ospreys above, and the gulls and terns surrounding you; and then you just might remember what the world sounded like before we invented cars and the ceaseless noise they add to our lives.

Following are several Sanibel and Captiva businesses where you can rent bikes, bike trailers (for toddlers), canoes, and kayaks. Many hotels, motels, and resorts offer their own bike and boat rentals, usually to guests only. The following five businesses are all open to the general public and have a good reputation for renting quality products. They will help you get on your way to discovering the real *Living Sanibel*.

Billy's Bikes and Rentals

Location: 1470 Periwinkle Way (on the north side of Periwinkle Way approximately one mile west of Causeway Road) / Phone: 239-472-5248; toll free: 800-575-8717 / E-mail: info@billysrentals.com / Website: www.billysrentals.com.

© Charles Sobczak

Owned and operated by island residents Billy and Salli Kirkland, Billy's Bike Rentals is a well-established bike rental business that has always been very supportive of the community. It is open 8:30 a.m. to 5:00 p.m., 365 days a year. Its rates are fair and competitive and vary depending on what kind of equipment you are renting and the length of time you are renting it (half-day, full day, weekly, or monthly). Rates are posted on the website.

Not only does Billy's rent single- and multi-speed bikes, but it also has bike trailers, hybrids, specialty bikes such as recumbent bikes, surreys, joggers, add-ons, and beach rentals. It is the only operation on either island to offer electric Segway tours. It also rents beach wheelchairs and specialized bicycles designed for the physically challenged.

Directly across the street at 1509 Periwinkle Way, Billy's offers bike repair and maintenance, as well as bike and Segway sales.

Billy's provides helmets, locks, and bike-path maps, and the experience staff is ready to find the bike that fits your biking skills, adjust your seat, and send you on your way.

Finnimore's Cycle Shop

Location: 2353 Periwinkle Way (on the south side of Periwinkle Way approximately 2.3 miles west of Causeway Road, behind the Winds beach store) / Phone: 239-472-5577 / E-mail: finnimores @aol.com / Website: www. finnimores.com.

© Charles Sobczak

Owned by long-time island resident Barbara Craig and operated by her son, Joe Craig, and assistant manager Bill Pindle, Finnimore's has been renting bikes and beach equipment for more than a decade. It is open 9:00 a.m. to 4:00 p.m., 364 days a year (closed on Christmas). Its rates are fair and competitive and vary depending on what kind of equipment you are renting and the length of time you are renting it (half-day, full day, weekly, or monthly). Rates are posted on Finnimore's website.

Finnimore's offers single-speed, six-speed, and 21-speed hybrids. It also rents adult trikes, recumbent bikes, trail-a-bikes, bikes with child seats, single and double joggers, as well as four-passenger surreys and a custom roadster. Its beach rentals include beach chairs, umbrellas, and Boogie and skimboards, as well as fishing rods and reels.

Its spacious facility is a little difficult to find because it is hidden behind the Winds beach store on Periwinkle Way. The experienced staff will match you up with a bike that suits your skills, adjust your seat, then supply you with a safety helmet and trail map, and send you off to explore the natural beauty of Sanibel and Captiva.

'Tween Waters Inn

© Blake Sobczak

Location: 11951 Captiva Drive (1.95 miles north of the bridge at Blind Pass on the east side of the road) / Phone numbers: 239-472-5161, ext #3; toll-free: 800-223-5865 / E-mail: n/a / Website: www. tween-waters.com.

Established in 1931 and frequented shortly thereafter by J.N. "Ding" Darling and his wife, Penny, in the mid-1930s, 'Tween Waters Inn has been an integral part of Sanibel and Captiva's conservation movement for more than 75 years. It offers a host of accommodations and services, including bike rentals, though these are generally limited to 'Tween Waters guests.

Two kayak rental businesses operate out of 'Tween Waters, and there is a kayak launching area to put in your own craft (no trailers and off-season only) for a small fee. Situated on Roosevelt Channel and within an easy paddle to Buck and Patterson keys, the location offers well-protected waters and a seven-mile journey around the island. Excellent fishing and wildlife sightings, including manatee and dolphin, abound in this stretch of water, especially near the recently reopened Blind Pass.

The kayak and canoe rental operated by the inn is open 7:30 a.m. to 5:00 p.m. (5:30 p.m. on Fridays and Saturdays), 365 days a year, depending on weather. The other kayak operation, Adventure Sea Kayak, is an independent contractor that specializes in high-end sea kayak rentals, as well as guided nature and wildlife tours and instruction in advanced, intermediate, and beginning kayaking skills. It is owned and operated by the father/son team of John and Brian Houston, who have been in the kayak business for more than 30 years (phone: 239-822-3337; website: www. kayak-captiva.com; e-mail: kayakadventures @aol.com).

© Blake Sobczak

Captiva Kayak Co. and Wildside Adventures

Location: McCarthy's Marina, 11401 Andy Rosse Lane (2.83 miles from the bridge at Blind Pass, then east (right) at the stop sign at Andy Rosse Lane) / Phone: 239-395-2925 / E-mail: ckc.wsa @gmail.com / Website: www. captivakayaks.com.

© Blake Sobczak

Owned and operated by Greg LeBlanc and Barb Renneke, the business was originally known as Wildside Adventures. It began without a home marina in the mid-1980s and found a permanent home at McCarthy's Marina 15 years ago. It is open 9:00 a.m. to 5:00 p.m., 364 days a year (closed for Christmas).

Captiva Kayak Co. specializes in quality kayak rentals, both on- and off-site, as well as guided wildlife, historical, and archaeological tours. Suggested self-guided tours include the Buck Key Trail loop, Buck Key Island circumnavigation, Chadwick's Bayou paddle adventure, and the Blind Pass Beach excursion. Captiva Kayak Co. provides take-away rentals for longer periods (three-day minimum) for individuals who want to explore other area waterways. In addition,

Greg LeBlanc © Blake Sobczak

it offers nonmotorized sailboats including WindRider trimarans, Hobie Cats, and Hobie Kayaks, which are pedal, sail, or paddlecraft in any number of unique designs.

The experienced staff offers kayak instruction and takes special care not to put people out in bad weather. Life jackets, paddles, and dry bags are available at no additional charge with every rental. Captiva Kayak Co.'s years of experience make it an excellent choice when considering an island kayaking adventure.

YOLO ("You Only Live Once") Watersports

Location: 11534 Andy Rosse Lane, Captiva (2.83 miles from the bridge at Blind Pass, then west (left) at the stop sign at Andy Rosse Lane and roughly one block down on the right) / Phone: 239-472-9656 and 239-472-1296 / Fax: 239-472-1162 / E-mail: info@yolowatersports.com / Website: www.yolowatersports.com.

© Blake Sobczak

Owned and operated by Sanibel Island resident Marcel Ventura, YOLO Watersports has been renting bikes and water equipment since 1986. It is open 9:00 a.m. to 5:00 p.m., 364 days a year (closed on Christmas). Its rates are fair and competitive and vary depending on what kind of equipment you are renting and length of time you are renting it (half-day, full day, weekly, or monthly). Rates are posted on the YOLO website. The website also has a real-time Captiva weather link that makes it easy to find out the current wind and weather conditions on the island.

In the early 1990s, YOLO Watersports took over Jim's Rentals, and the combined businesses rent a combination of beach bikes, tag-alongs, bike trailers for kids, baby joggers, baby seats, and little red wagons. YOLO offers a unique watercraft called a stand-up paddle board (SUP) that operates like a cross between a surfboard and a kayak. You can also find Hobie Cat sailboats, skateboards, and beach chairs and umbrellas at the well-equipped facility. Free bike locks, helmets, and bike-path maps come with every rental.

Located just a few hundred feet from the pristine beaches of Captiva Island, YOLO Watersports can get you on the water or on a bike journey within minutes. The staff is friendly and experienced. This is the only commercial bike rental facility on Captiva that is open to the general public.

© Blake Sobczak

Bike Safety

With more than 65 miles of bike and hiking trails to explore, it is important to know the rules of the road. Because some of the more traveled shared-use paths can get very busy during peak season, not only with bicyclists, but also with Rollerbladers, walkers, and joggers, please observe the following protocols while enjoying your day.

© Blake Sobczak

Ride on the right: Remember, you are sharing the path with others. Maintain a safe interval between riders.

Pass on the left after an audible warning: Ring your bell or call out "Passing on your left!" to ensure the person in front of you doesn't cut you off.

Signal your moves: Use hand signals to let others know you are slowing, stopping or turning. When stopped, please clear the path to allow others to get by.

Always wear a helmet: Your head will thank you. (Helmets are required by state law for those under 16.)

Don't wear earphones: Stay alert and make sure you can hear what's going on around you.

Be visible at night: Use front and rear lights and wear light-colored or reflective clothing.

Give right-of-way to pedestrians: That includes walkers, skateboarders, and Rollerbladers.

Be cautious at driveways: Motorists may not see you and are prone to pulling out directly in front of you, especially along the busy commercial sections on Periwinkle Way.

Report all crashes and accidents: If the accident is not an emergency, call the Sanibel Police Department at 239-472-3111 while on Sanibel and the Lee County Sheriff Department at 239-477-1000 while on Captiva. For all medical emergencies, dial 911.

Bike safety rules courtesy of the Sanibel Bike Club.

Sanibel Beach Access & Parking

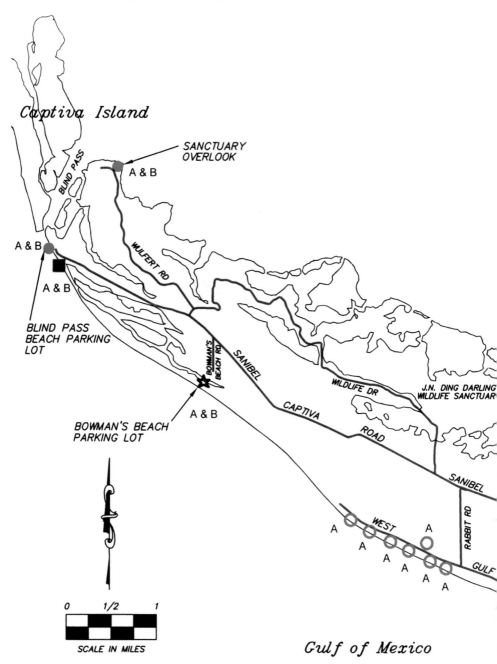

Pine Island Sound

Captiva Island

SANCTUARY
OVERLOOK

A & B

BLIND PASS

WULFERT RD

A & B

A & B

BLIND PASS
BEACH PARKING
LOT

BOWMAN'S BEACH RD

SANIBEL

CAPTIVA

ROAD

WILDLIFE DR

J.N. DING DARLING
WILDLIFE SANCTUAR

A & B

BOWMAN'S BEACH
PARKING LOT

SANIBEL

RABBIT RD

WEST

GULF

A

A

A

A

A

A

A

A

A

A

0   1/2   1

SCALE IN MILES

Gulf of Mexico

LEGEND

■ GENERAL PUBLIC BEACH ACCESS PARKING
GENERAL PERMIT (HOURLY FEE).
CITY RESIDENTIAL ("A") OR RESTRICTED ("B") PERMITS REQUIRED

☐ GENERAL PUBLIC BEACH ACCESS PARKING
GULFSIDE CITY PARK, CAUSEWAY PARKING LOT, BOAT RAMP
HOURLY FEE - "C" PERMIT REQUIRED

☆ GENERAL PUBLIC BEACH ACCESS PARKING
GENERAL PERMIT (HOURLY FEE), CITY RESIDENTIAL ("A"), RESTRICTED ("B"),
OR LEE COUNTY REGIONAL PARKS PASS REQUIRED

● RESTRICTED BEACH ACCESS PARKING
CITY RESIDENTIAL ("A") OR RESTRICTED ("B") PERMITS REQUIRED

○ RESIDENTIAL BEACH ACCESS PARKING
CITY RESIDENTIAL ("A") PERMITS ONLY REQUIRED

+ GENERAL PARKING - FREE

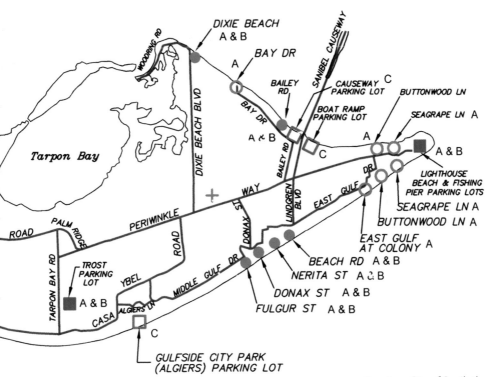

Courtesy City of Sanibel

City of Sanibel Public Facilities

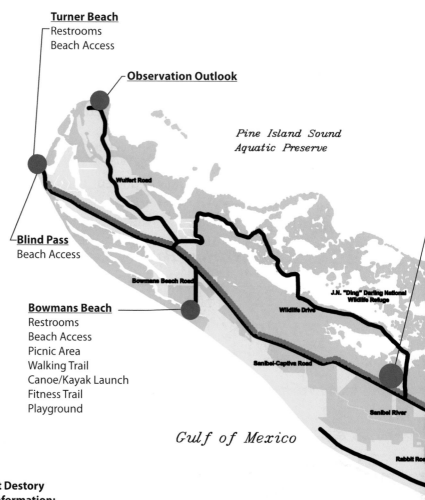

Turner Beach
Restrooms
Beach Access

Observation Outlook

Pine Island Sound
Aquatic Preserve

Wulfert Road

Blind Pass
Beach Access

Bowmans Beach Road

Bowmans Beach
Restrooms
Beach Access
Picnic Area
Walking Trail
Canoe/Kayak Launch
Fitness Trail
Playground

Wildlife Drive

J.N. "Ding" Darling National
Wildlife Refuge

Sanibel-Captiva Road

Sanibel River

Gulf of Mexico

Rabbit Road

Sanibel Ga...
Hiking Trail...
Picnic Area

Enjoy - Don't Destory
Important information:
- Public parking is permitted in designated areas only.
- Sanibel residents and property owners can obtain "A" & "B" parking stickers from
  the Sanibel Police Department, 8000 Dunlop Road, (239) 472-3111.
- Keep our wildlife wild, please don't feed.
- Our beach vegetation is fragile, please help us preserve it.
- Know and abide by Florida's fishing regulations.
- The taking of live shells including starfish and sandollars is prohibited on Sanibel. It's the law.
- Feeding alligators is dangerous and illegal, and violators are subject to fines and imprisonment.
- Dogs must be on leash.
- For more information visit City website, www.mysanibel.com.
- Report suspicious activity to the Sanibel Police Department, (239)472-3111.
- Report maintenance issues to the Sanibel Public Works Department, (239)472-8397.
- In case of emergency, call 911.

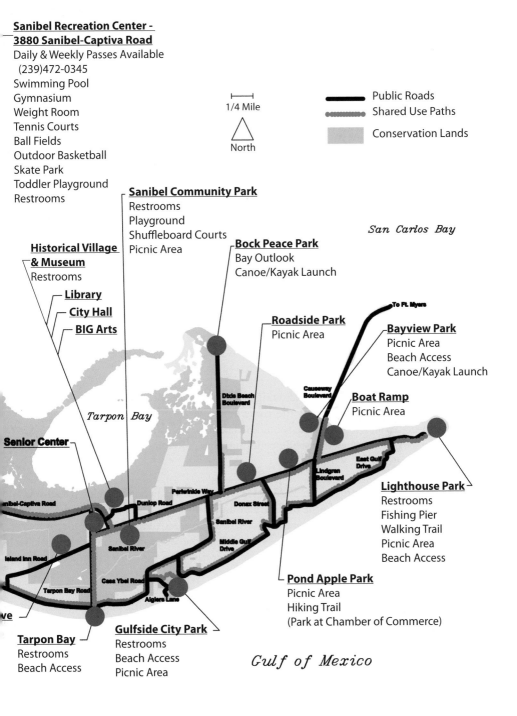

**Sanibel Recreation Center -
3880 Sanibel-Captiva Road**
Daily & Weekly Passes Available
 (239)472-0345
Swimming Pool
Gymnasium
Weight Room
Tennis Courts
Ball Fields
Outdoor Basketball
Skate Park
Toddler Playground
Restrooms

1/4 Mile

North

Public Roads
Shared Use Paths
Conservation Lands

San Carlos Bay

Sanibel Community Park
Restrooms
Playground
Shuffleboard Courts
Picnic Area

**Historical Village
& Museum**
Restrooms

Bock Peace Park
Bay Outlook
Canoe/Kayak Launch

Library

City Hall

BIG Arts

To Ft. Myers

Roadside Park
Picnic Area

Bayview Park
Picnic Area
Beach Access
Canoe/Kayak Launch

Causeway
Boulevard

Boat Ramp
Picnic Area

Dixie Beach
Boulevard

Tarpon Bay

East Gulf
Drive

Senior Center

Periwinkle Way

Sanibel-Captiva Road

Dunlop Road

Donax Street

Sanibel River

Lindgren
Boulevard

Lighthouse Park
Restrooms
Fishing Pier
Walking Trail
Picnic Area
Beach Access

Island Inn Road

Sanibel River

Middle Gulf
Drive

Casa Ybel Road

Tarpon Bay Road

Algiers Lane

Pond Apple Park
Picnic Area
Hiking Trail
(Park at Chamber of Commerce)

ve

Tarpon Bay
Restrooms
Beach Access

Gulfside City Park
Restrooms
Beach Access
Picnic Area

Gulf of Mexico

Courtesy City of Sanibel

LEGEND

AMENITIES

👫 Restrooms

🏠 Shelter

🥤 Drinking Water

🚴 Bike Rental

All distances in miles.

⟮ .5 ⟯

ACTIVITIES

🛶 Canoe Launch Access

🗼 Observation Tower

🥾 Hiking Trail

━━━━ Yellow lines are for shared use paths

━━━━ Green lines are for unpaved paths or roads

━━━━ Blue lines are paved roads shared with automobile traffic

Map #1—The Causeway

Overview: The new Sanibel Causeway opened September 8, 2007. The updated design included two eight-foot-wide shoulders on both sides of the traffic lanes, allowing ample room for bicyclists to travel the three spans safely. The new bridges have lower guardrails for better viewing, but care should be taken, particularly with younger cyclists, to remain safely away from the edge while peddling, especially on the high span, which rises approximately 75 feet.

Notes on distances: Starting from Periwinkle Way and heading north down Causeway Road the distance is .45 mile to the first turnaround, under the "C" span. From the start of the "C" span it is 2.31 miles to the second turnaround, under the "A" span, a good spot to turn back if you do not want to climb the steep hill of the "A" span. Both underpasses also offer safe haven from storms. The round trip between the stop sign at Periwinkle Way and the toll booth is 7.1 miles.

Wildlife viewing: The Sanibel Causeway presents an excellent viewing platform for spotting bottle-nosed dolphins, an occasional manatee, shorebirds, gulls, terns, eagles, ospreys, fish crows, and numerous fish species including Spanish mackerel, jack crevalle, tarpon, cow-nosed ray, and snook.

A—The first spoil island is a good launching area for canoes and kayaks. It is also commonly used by windsurfing and kite-surfing enthusiasts. Take care to paddle clear of the strong tides located at the mouth of the Caloosahatchee River, as well as the wakes of large boats that frequent the Intracoastal Waterway when passing under the high span of the bridge.

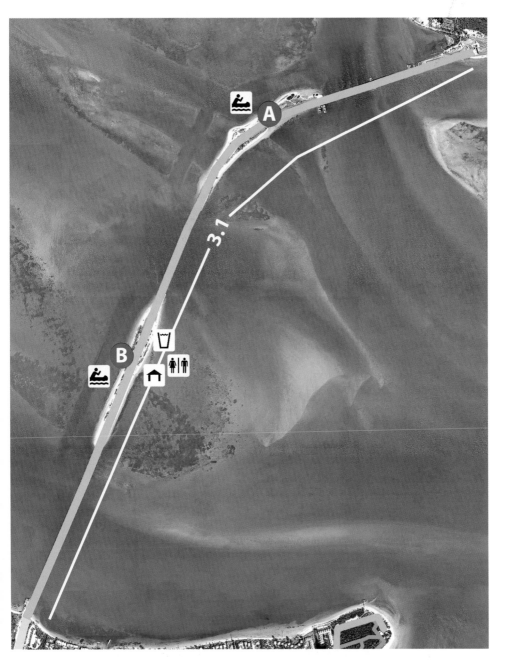

B—The second spoil island is another good launching area for canoes and kayaks, and it does not have as strong a tidal flow, nor anywhere near the boat traffic of the "A" span. Depending on the prevailing wind, either side of this island presents some interesting paddling opportunities. Fisherman's Key, located approximately 1.8 miles to the north, offers a good destination point from the second spoil island.

Map #2—East End (Lindgren Blvd. to the Sanibel Lighthouse)

Overview: The 38-acre Lighthouse Park located at the tip of the island has almost one mile of trails, crisscrossing the park in several directions. The entire east-end loop, from the stop sign at Lindgren Blvd. and Periwinkle Way to the East Gulf Drive intersection and back around East Gulf Drive is 2.56 miles. If you continue east on Periwinkle all the way to the Sanibel Lighthouse and head back, the trip is approximately 4.13 miles, provided you make the entire .57-mile loop around Lighthouse Park.

Wildlife viewing: Most of this section of shared-use path runs through residential and condominium developments with a small retail section including several restaurants, a deli, and an ice cream parlor located just past the East Gulf Drive intersection. The best nature viewing is found at Lighthouse Park. The Sanibel Fishing Pier affords great sightings of snapper, snook, sheepshead, mackerel, redfish, and shark, among others, and the beaches offer shorebirds, gulls, terns, ospreys, and magnificent frigatebirds. The vegetation is mostly buttonwood, with several other native species interspersed.

A—The Sanibel boat ramp (fee for car and boat-trailer parking). Ideal put-in for canoes, kayaks, and trailered watercraft such as small sailboats or larger canoes. Annual stickers (A/C) are available for residents and property owners; a pay station for the general public is on-site for day use.

Area of map detail

B—Sanibel Fishing Pier (fee for parking). Early mornings and evenings are the best times to wet a line at the pier. Annual stickers (A/B) are available for resident or property owners; a pay station is on-site for day use.

C—Kiosk and trails (fee for car parking). A kiosk displaying many of the island's most common shells is located just west of the lighthouse on a sandy trail. Restrooms, water, and shelter are available near the lighthouse.

Map #3—Mid-Island North
(Bailey Road to Dixie Beach Blvd.)

Overview: From Periwinkle Way west of Causeway Road, the shared-use path heads north 1.3 mile along Dixie Beach Blvd., then ends at Albatross Road. The Dunes loop is 2.58 miles through a residential subdivision with no designated bike path, but traffic moves slowly and the residents respect bikers and joggers. Traveling from Periwinkle Way up Dixie Beach Blvd. to the end of Woodring Point and back is a 4.9-mile journey.

Wildlife viewing: Dense forests of red, black, and white mangroves line either side of Dixie Beach Blvd., then continue along much of Woodring Road. Look for spiders, wading birds, and raccoons along the way. Two culverts flow beneath Dixie Beach Blvd., where you can see mullet, snapper, snook, and redfish. Views to the bay at the end of Bailey Road and along Woodring Road offer sightings of dolphins, manatees, herons, and black skimmers.

A—The Sanibel and Captiva Islands Chamber of Commerce, 1159 Causeway Road. Phone: 239-472-1080; fax: 239-472-1070; e-mail: island@sanibel-captiva.org; Website: www.sanibel-captiva.org. Open 9:00 a.m. to 5:00 p.m. 365 days a year (note: on major holidays closing time is 2:00 p.m.). Drinking water, restrooms, and shelter are available at the chamber building. The Chamber of Commerce offers an array of services for the general public, including island accommodations, where to dine, shopping tips, wedding information, and more. A visit to the Chamber of Commerce is highly recommended.

B—Pond Apple Park Trail. The trailhead for this medium-length loop trail (1.6 miles) begins just off the Chamber of Commerce parking lot. The trail crosses Bailey Road, then continues through a mixed forest of uplands and wetlands vegetation. The island's largest stand of pond apple trees can be found along this section, as can several immense strangler figs. The trail opens up at two large water-retention ponds frequented by numerous wading birds, ducks, eagles, and ospreys. The trail can become muddy during the rainy season, making travel difficult for bicyclists.

C—Billy's Bike Rentals, 1470 Periwinkle Way; phone: 239-472-5248 or 800-575-8717 (see "Getting Around Naturally" for additional information). A long-established bicycle rental operation that specializes in daily, weekly, and monthly bike rentals.

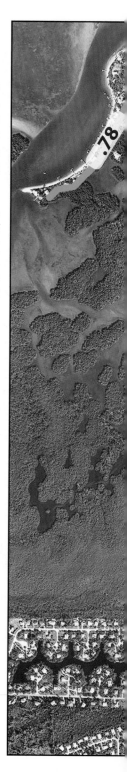

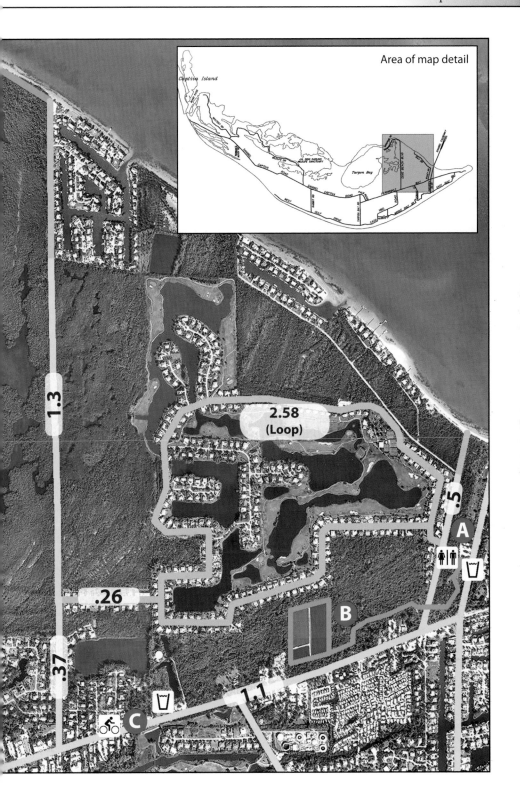

Map #4—Mid-Island East
(Lindgren Blvd. to Tarpon Bay Road)

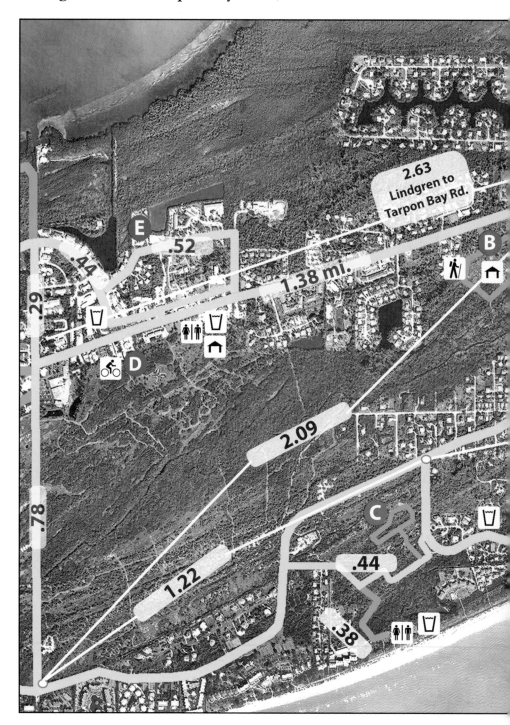

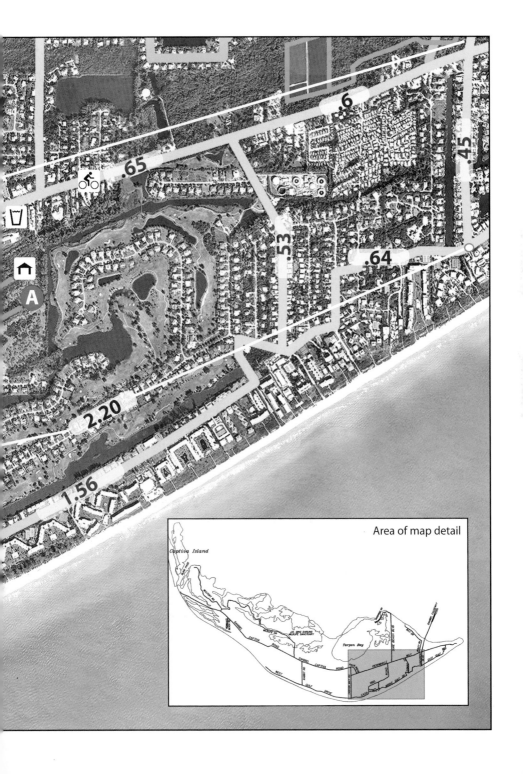

Area of map detail

Captiva Island

Tarpon Bay

Map #4 — Mid-Island East pg. 472-473

(Lindgren Blvd. to Tarpon Bay Road)

Overview: Numerous shared-use paths crisscross this section of the island. From the intersection at Causeway Road to the stop sign at Tarpon Bay Road, the well-traveled and extra-wide shared-use path is 2.65 miles long. The complete loop starting at the intersection of Causeway Road and Lindgren Blvd. and returning there via Middle Gulf Drive, Casa Ybel Road, up Tarpon Bay Road, then back down Periwinkle Way is 7.3 miles.

Wildlife viewing: Most of the bike paths along this section pass through the commercially developed Periwinkle Way or residential areas. Several species of birds and numerous anoles that have adapted to this urban environment are frequently seen here.

    A—Wigley/Boler/Allen/Carlton Preserve. A short trail (0.06 mile) takes you to a small pond with a shelter. A second short path (0.07 mile) takes you to the intersection of two freshwater canals. Look for passerines and wading birds in this area.

    B—Periwinkle Preserve. This short loop trail (0.6 mile) is for hiking only. The trail has several native plant species clearly marked and takes the hiker through an easy stretch of uplands habitat. Look for passerines, mourning doves, and gopher tortoises on this trail. A kiosk and a shelter area are located a few yards off of the shared-use path.

    C—Gulfside Park Preserve. Yet another short loop trail (0.44 miles), this one is open to both bikers and hikers, but can become quite muddy and difficult for biking during the rainy season. The habitat is a mixture of uplands and wetlands. Look for red-winged blackbirds, warblers, cardinals, and marsh rabbits. A kiosk marks the trailhead, and a fascinating old graveyard located 100 yards south of the trailhead is worth investigating.

    D—Finnimore's Bike Rental, 2353 Periwinkle Way; phone: 239-472-5577 (see "Getting Around Naturally" for additional information). A long-established bicycle rental operation that specializes in daily, weekly, and monthly bike rentals.

    E—Sanibel Historical Village and Museum, 950 Dunlop Road (admission fee); phone: 239-472-4648. A collection of historical buildings and artifacts from the Calusa through the days of the early island settlers (see the "Museum and Eco-Attractions" section).

Map #5—Mid-island West pg. 476-477

(Tarpon Bay Road to Rabbit Road)

Overview: The complete loop, starting at the "T" at the end of Periwinkle Way where it runs into Tarpon Bay Road, via Sanibel-Captiva Road, down the shared-use path running parallel to Rabbit Road, then east on West Gulf Drive to the point of beginning, is 5.37 miles. There are an additional seven miles of unpaved biking and hiking trails to be discovered in this area.

Wildlife viewing: This section has some of the best uplands habitat on Sanibel. The 160-acre Bailey Tract, with its numerous ponds, is one of the best places to find alligators, herons, egrets, ducks, passerines, black-necked stilts, red-shouldered hawks, river otters, bobcats, marsh rabbits, and the rare Sanibel rice rat. The trails behind SCCF offer more of the same great viewing, as do all the spurs and trails located in the 265-acre Sanibel Gardens Preserve.

A—Tarpon Bay Explorers, 900 Tarpon Bay Road (no admission fee); phone: 239-472-8900. One of the only sections of the J.N. "Ding" Darling Refuge that is open on Fridays, Tarpon Bay Explorers offers bicycle, canoe, and kayak rentals and a host of other tours and activities (see the "Museums and Eco-Attractions" section).

B—Sanibel Gardens Preserve. The trailhead for the 1.06-mile loop can be reached by biking west on Island Inn Road for a half-mile. The entrance is on the north with picnic tables and a water fountain beside it. A second spur trail (.30 mile), located farther down Island Inn Road, takes you to a pond overlook.

C—Freshwater kayak and canoe launch. Although not an official launch site, it is fairly easy to put a canoe or kayak into this branch of the Sanibel River where it flows under Island Inn Road. The best paddling is to the north where the river winds through uplands and wetlands habitat. With several portages it is possible to paddle some three miles to the underpass at Rabbit Road. Be cautious of alligators throughout this section. This trail is unnavigable during periods of low water.

D—The Bailey Tract of J.N. "Ding" Darling National Wildlife Refuge (no admission fee and open on Fridays). The entire outside loop is 1.25 miles starting at either the parking lot west of Tarpon Bay Road (the official entrance) or at the fence located .65 mile down Island Inn Road from Bailey's General Store. Several offshoots crisscross this tract, creating a little more than two miles of hiking and biking trails. These trails tend to stay dry and are suitable for bicyclists most of the year.

E—The Shell Museum, 3075 Sanibel-Captiva Road (admission fee); phone: 239-395-2233. Located 0.8 mile west from the start of Sanibel-Captiva Road at Tarpon Bay Road, this museum is an excellent place to learn more about these seashell islands (see the "Museum and Eco-Attractions" section).

F—Sanibel-Captiva Conservation Foundation (SCCF), 3333 Sanibel-Captiva Road (admission fee for access to trails only); phone: 239-472-2329. Located one mile west of Tarpon Bay Road on Sanibel-Captiva Road, this facility offers a variety of learning and viewing opportunities (see the "Museum and Eco-Attractions" section).

G—SCCF Nature Trails (note: **no bicycles allowed**). Directly behind the Nature Center are a series of trails (East River, West River, Upper Ridge, and Sabal Palm Trail) that crisscross hundreds of acres of uplands and wetlands. A tall wooden observation tower overlooks more than 1,000 acres of preserve. These trails are designated for hiking only and are an excellent opportunity to view alligators, warblers, wading birds, marsh rabbits, bobcats, otters, and various turtle species. SCCF members are admitted free; there is a nominal entrance fee for non-members.

H—The Lake Murex Loop. The 1.6-mile loop through the Lake Murex subdivision starts 1.34 miles west of the intersection of Tarpon Bay Road and West Gulf Drive. The loop is bordered by wildlife preserves along the entire outside edge. Bicyclists share the road with automobiles, but this is a pleasant ride and local motorists are used to watching for bikers and joggers.

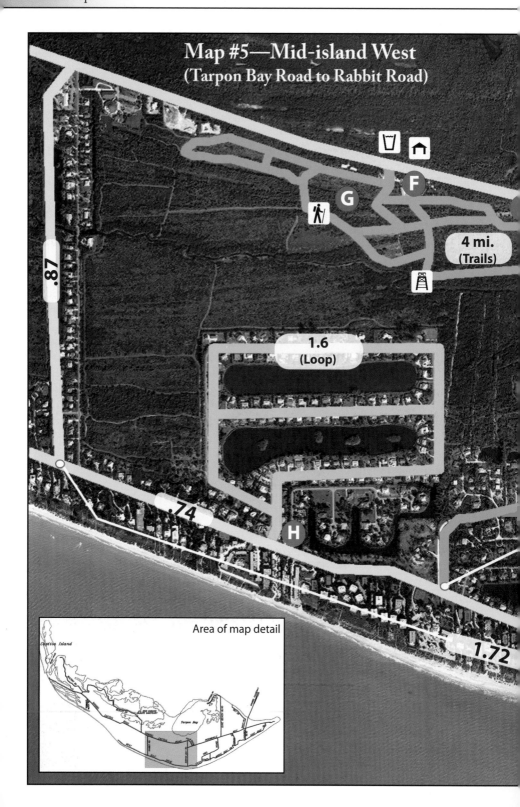

Map #5—Mid-island West
(Tarpon Bay Road to Rabbit Road)

.87

4 mi.
(Trails)

1.6
(Loop)

.74

G

F

H

1.72

Area of map detail

Captiva Island

Tarpon Bay

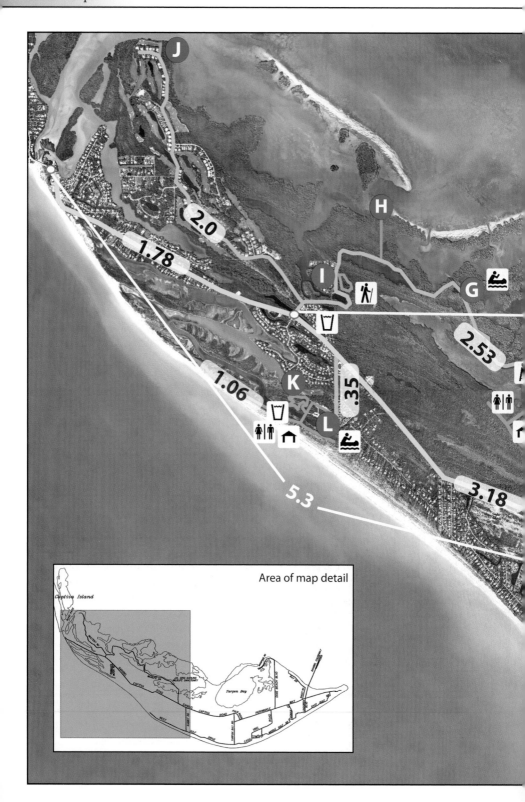

Area of map detail

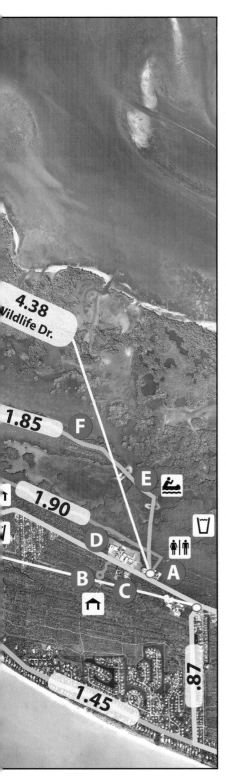

Map #6—West End
(Rabbit Road to Captiva)

Overview: This section of the island includes some 5,000 acres of the J.N. "Ding" Darling National Wildlife Refuge and affords some of the best wildlife viewing in all of Florida. A number of different trails are located off of Wildlife Drive, and the beach-side trails of Bowman's Beach Park offer additional biking and hiking opportunities. The loop starting from the parking lot of the "Ding" Darling Educational Center at 1 Wildlife Drive and returning via the Indigo Trail is 3.75 miles long. Biking the entire length of Wildlife Drive and returning to 1 Wildlife Drive (the refuge parking lot) is 7.56 miles.

Wildlife viewing: Without question the 4.38-mile-long Wildlife Drive affords some of the best bird watching in the world. At times as many as 2,000 white pelicans, shorebirds, egrets, herons, ospreys, roseate spoonbills, and mergansers can be observed in one morning or afternoon. It is very important to check the tides for the best viewing times. Because the refuge includes vast tracts of tidal flats, the best times to make the drive are during periods of low tide when the flats are exposed and offer birds the best feeding opportunities. The Bait Box, owned by long-time Islander Ralph Woodring, has an excellent Website for tide information (www.thebaitbox.com/tides).

A—J.N. "Ding" Darling Environmental Education Center, 1 Wildlife Drive (no admission except for entering Wildlife Drive); phone: 239-472-1100. Located two miles west of Tarpon Bay Road on Sanibel-Captiva Road, the education center, along with the Indigo Trail, are open seven days a week; Wildlife Drive is closed on Fridays (see the "Museum and Eco-Attractions" section).

B—The Pick Preserve. This short loop (0.48 mile) starts just across the street from the Sanibel School on the south side of Sanibel-Captiva Road. There is no parking area for this trail. Because of firebreaks it is easy to get lost, so remember to veer to the right when you enter the trailhead. You will come to a boardwalk and a shelter within a few hundred feet. The trail continues south and forms a small loop through uplands habitat. Look for marsh rabbits, gopher tortoises, wrens, and other passerines in this area.

C—CROW, 3883 Sanibel-Captiva Road (admission fee); phone: 239-472-3644. Located on the south side of Sanibel-Captiva Road 2.3 miles west of the stop sign at Tarpon Bay Road (see the "Museums and Eco-Attractions" section).

D—Sanibel Recreation Center, 3880 Sanibel-Captiva Road (admission fee); phone: 239-472-0345. Located directly west of the Sanibel School on the north side of the road 2.4 miles from the stop sign at Tarpon Bay Road. A multipurpose facility with pools, gyms, tennis courts, and a fitness room (see their piece in the "Museums and Eco-Attractions" section).

E—Canoe and kayak launch. Located just past the second culvert, this is an excellent place to put in and enjoy the backwaters of the refuge. No motorized craft allowed in this area.

F—Mangrove overlook (just before mile marker 1) This short boardwalk looks north over a vast tidal flat that is seldom exposed, even during low tide. An excellent place to see mangrove, horseshoe, and fiddler crabs; mullet; red, black, white, and buttonwood mangroves; and the elusive mangrove cuckoo.

G—Canoe and kayak launch. A symbol at mile 2.8 marks the location of a second canoe and kayak launch area. Paddling west, you will find yourself in Hardworking Bayou where you can take in sightings of ospreys, mullet, and bald eagles. Excellent fishing can be found in the three tidal cuts flowing through the mangroves.

H—Wulfert Keys overlook and trail (0.22 mi.). Located at mile 3.44 along Wildlife Drive, this short trail is well worth the stop. It takes you down power-line maintenance path beside a tidal creek to a large, open viewing area at the end. Sightings of blue crabs, oysters, wading birds, and various fish species are common.

I—Shell Mound Trail (0.33 mi.). Located on the east side of Wildlife Drive near the exit at mile 3.76, this short boardwalk takes you through ancient Calusa shell mounds. This is an excellent place to see large, mature gumbo limbo trees growing on the mounds. Also look for warblers, wrens, and cardinals in this area.

J—Sanctuary Overlook (0.09 mi). This very short trail is located 1.86 miles from the beginning of Wulfert Road. It takes you through a small buttonwood forest to a bench and viewing area overlooking the back bay.

K—World Fitness Trail (0.56 mile). This fascinating trail winds through upland beach ridges. The trail includes various fitness devices such as horizontal bars, sit-up boards, strength and stretch bars, and more. Two additional trails are located closer to the beach. One heads west .84 mile until it turns toward the beach and continues to Blind Pass; the other trail goes east .22 mile where it intersects with another beach trail.

L—Canoe and kayak launch (fee area for parking). Located within the parking area of Bowman's Beach Park, this launch provides access to the protected waters of Clam Bayou. There are several bays to explore, and the waters are ideal for inexperienced canoeists and kayakers because they are protected from winds and rough seas. You can find blue crabs, snook, redfish, trout, ospreys, and eagles in this area.

Map #7—Captiva Island

Overview: Although not an official bike path, the shoulder placed on either side of Captiva Road is sufficient for most experienced bicyclists to handle, though exercise caution with young children and inexperienced bikers. The path ends at the public beach access 3.5 miles from the Blind Pass bridge. The round trip to the beach and back to Blind Pass bridge is 7 miles. The total distance from the Sanibel Lighthouse at Point Ybel to the end of the bike path on Captiva is 15.11 miles, and the distance from the Causeway tollbooth is 17 miles.

<u>Wildlife viewing:</u> Most of the Captiva shoulder path a residential estate area until the first turn located at mile 1.58. The road then follows the beach, where numerous terns, gulls, pelicans, and various minnows and fish can be observed. This stretch runs about a mile, then heads inland again through residential and commercial areas. There is some excellent shorebird and gull viewing at the public beach at the very end of the bike path, just beyond the entrance (private) to South Seas Island Resort.

A—'Tween Waters Inn, 15951 Captiva Drive; phone: 239-472-5161. Two canoe and kayak rental operations run out of this historic inn, where "Ding" Darling first stayed in 1935. There is also a public launch with a small fee (see "Getting Around Naturally" for additional information).

B—McCarthy's Marina, 11401 Andy Rosse Lane, Captiva; phone: 239-472-5200. A nature tour on the 40-foot *Adventure* catamaran sailboat is available, and Captiva Kayaks (239-395-2925) rents sea kayaks and canoes by the hour, day, or week (see "Getting Around Naturally" for additional information).

C—YOLO Watersports, 11534 Andy Rosse Lane; phone: 239-472-9656. The only location to rent bicycles on Captiva, YOLO also rents a small sailing catamaran and skateboards (see "Getting Around Naturally" for additional information).

Contributors

Through the Lens Gallery

Dick Fortune and Sara Lopez share a deep understanding and love of nature that is reflected in their exquisite wildlife images. Both artistically unique and technically astounding, their photography truly honors the wildlife they represent. Their work has been displayed at the J.N. "Ding" Darling Educational Center. To view and/or purchase their photographs, visit www.throughthelensgallery.com.

Diane Rome Peebles

Diane Rome Peebles' artwork has appeared on the covers of sport-fishing and scientific periodicals, as well as on marine conservation stamps and many governmental educational publications. In both her oil paintings and scientific illustrations, her priorities remain with projects that enhance environmental conservation. Website: www.dianepeebles.com.

Sara Yunsoo Kim

Sara Yunsoo Kim is a nature photographer with a special focus on birds and plants. A photo aficionado all her life, Sara discovered her deep interest in wildlife in 2006. Since then her goal has been to peruse the beauty of nature through her camera and her fine-tuned aesthetic instincts. Her work and contact info can be found at www.flickr.com/photos/kphoto.

Blake Sobczak

Blake Sobczak is a freelance photographer and student photojournalist at Northwestern University's Medill School of Journalism. He is the staff photographer for Shop Evanston magazine and is assistant photo editor for North by Northwestern magazine. Contact: blakesobczak2012@u.northwestern.edu or via cell at 239-222-3792.

Eric B. Holt

Eric B. Holt has a B.S. in biology from the University of Central Florida and has been involved in turtle-keeping and breeding for more than 35 years. He is active in turtle conservation through the Turtle Survival Alliance and a project of his own, where eggs from road-killed turtles are incubated and the offspring released. If you are looking for a speaker, a writer, or more information about turtles, go to his Website: www.empireoftheturtle.com.

Rob Pailes, Santiva Images

Rob Pailes discovered nature photography soon after purchasing his first camera in the summer of 1997. A trip to the J.N. "Ding" Darling National Wildlife Refuge on Sanibel, simply to learn how to use the camera, quickly turned into a love affair that has changed his life forever. His works have appeared in Birder's World and on various wildlife calendars. Go to www. santivaimages.com to see more of his work.

Clair Postmus

A photographer for more than 40 years, Clair Postmus's work appears in many books, including the Stokes Beginner's Guide to Shorebirds and Dennis Paulson's Shorebirds of North America. His photos also appear regularly in the Sanibel-Captiva Nature Calendar. The J.N. "Ding" Darling Educational Center displays many of his bird images.

Maggie May Rogers

An award-winning book designer as well as an experienced nature and wildlife photographer, Maggie has always had a passion for the graphic arts. Her first book design was in 2005, when she collaborated with the SCCF staff in putting together A Natural Course, celebrating the 35th anniversary of the Sanibel-Captiva Conservation Foundation. Maggie lives in central Kentucky, and can be contacted at Maggs505@hotmail.com.

Judd Patterson

Judd Patterson has always been captivated by nature and strives to share his fascination through inspiring photographs. His time is spent exploring waist-high prairie, tannin-stained swamps, and snowcapped mountains. For inspiration, please visit www.juddpatterson.com and www.birdsinfocus. com. He can be contacted at judd@juddpatterson.com.

Alan S. Maltz

Alan S. Maltz is a renowned fine-art photographer whose distinctive style is both impressionistic and intuitive. Named Official Fine Art Photographer for the State of Florida by VISIT FLORIDA and the Official Wildlife Photographer of Florida by the Wildlife Foundation of Florida, Maltz is gracious and generous in sharing his passion with appreciative collectors throughout the world. Visit his gallery and studio in Old Town in Key West, Florida, or his Website: www.AlanMaltz.com

Joseph Blanda, M.D.

When not practicing orthopedics in Akron, Ohio, Joe Blanda enjoys visiting Sanibel and sharpening his bird photography skills. He has donated work to many charity auctions and has won several photography contests.

Lorraine Sommer

Lorraine Sommer is a nature and underwater photographer who splits her passion for photographing the wonders of nature between the waters of the Gulf of Mexico and the mountains of Tennessee. Her work has been seen in the Sanibel-Captiva Nature Calendar and local papers since 2000 and can be seen online at www.flickr.com/photos/ lsommer/. She can be contacted at lorrainesommer@yahoo.com.

Mark Kenderdine

Mark Kenderdine is a lifelong resident observer of much of Florida's wildlife who recently began photographing as a way to document the flora and fauna he sees. He is an avid outdoorsman and herpetoculturist who has kept and bred snakes and other reptiles since 1968. Contact him at markk15@msn.com.

Jennifer Smith

Jennifer Smith is the assistant director for the Florida Bat Conservancy in Bay Pines, Florida, where she focuses on education programs, surveys, and rehabilitation of Florida bat species. For more information on Florida bats, visit the Florida Bat Conservancy's Website: www.floridabats.org.

Sabrina Lartz

Sabrina Lartz was a wildlife biologist working as an intern at the J.N. "Ding" Darling National Wildlife Refuge in 2009, then took a position with the SCCF Marine Lab. Her background is in wildlife management with a degree from the University of Wisconsin at Stevens Point.

Hung V. Do

Hung V. Do is a graduate of the Ringling College of Art and Design with a degree in illustration. He took up photography in 2006 to aid his graphic design work. Some of his work can be seen throughout Miami Metrozoo and various other institutions. You can view more of his work at www.Flickr.Com/photos/roninstudio, and contact him at roninrtist@aol.com.

Michael Hughes

Michael Hughes has had a passion for photography for more than 20 years. His friends and family appreciate his ability to capture, organize, and share life's greatest moments. His motto is, "Review, relive, and revive life with photos!"

Susie Holly

Susie Holly is a book and magazine editor, as well as owner of MacIntosh Books, one of the longest-running businesses on Sanibel. Contact her at macintoshbooks@gmail.com; www.macintoshbooks.com.

<u>Additional contributors include:</u>

Rusty Farst — www. jawsproductions.com
James Anderson—www.imagesforsuccess.com
Joe Tomelleri — www.americanfishes.com
Sandy Ramseth — www.realteamsells.com
Mary Harper — www.accesspointsindexing.com
Don DeMaria
Chris Huh
Katie Fuhr Laakkonen
Chris Lechowicz

Daniel Parker
Al Tuttle
City of Sanibel
Sanibel Historical Museum
Sanibel-Captiva Conservation Foundation
Tarpon Bay Explorers
Karen Nelson
Kevin Filiowich
Bette Roberts

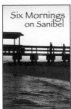

About the Author

Charles Sobczak is an award-winning author and real estate agent who lives and writes on Sanibel Island. He has two sons, Logan and Blake, and is happily married to Molly Heuer. They live very close to the Sanibel Gardens Preserve and the Bailey Tract of J.N. "Ding" Darling National Wildlife Refuge, where they enjoy their evening walks observing wildlife.

His first book, published in 1999, was a short novel called *Six Mornings on Sanibel.* Currently in its sixth printing, it is one of the best-selling books on Sanibel and Captiva. His second novel, *Way Under Contract, a Florida Story,* won the Patrick D. Smith Award in 2001 for the best work of Florida fiction that year. It is presently out of print.

Following his second novel, Sobczak published *Rhythm of the Tides,* a collection of his most popular poetry, short stories, and essays. His third novel, *A Choice of Angels,* was a departure from his previous books. Set in Atlanta, Georgia, and Istanbul, Turkey, it told the story of a forbidden romance between the son of a Baptist minister and the daughter of an Islamic family from Turkey.

Sobczak then turned to nonfiction with *Alligators, Sharks and Panthers: Deadly Encounters with Florida's Top Predator—Man.* It won several awards and is still in print. His most recent novel was *Chain of Fools,* set in northern Minnesota and based on his father's dysfunctional family. To read excerpts from any of his works, go to www.indigopress.net.

In addition to his writing, Sobczak is past president of the Sanibel Island Fishing Club, current president of Lee Reefs (Lee County's artificial reef organization), a lifetime member of SCCF (Sanibel-Captiva Conservation Foundation), and an avid offshore fisherman. To contact Sobczak via e-mail regarding this book, use livingsanibel@ earthlink.net.

A portion of the proceeds of the sale of *Living Sanibel* will go toward his continued support of organizations such as NRDC (Natural Resources Defense Council), Sierra Club, Audubon Society, WWW (World Wildlife Fund), and other groups dedicated to regional and worldwide conservation projects. Additional monies will be used to assist in the planting of more native trees on Sanibel and Captiva Islands.

Bibliography

To save paper and make it easier to link to the numerous research Websites used in this book, the bibliography is online. Go to www. indigopress.net and look for the link on the *Living Sanibel* Web page to access the bibliography.

INDEX

F

G